# The
# PARIS COMMUNE
# of 1871

# The
# PARIS COMMUNE
# of 1871

*by*

FRANK JELLINEK

*The Universal Library*

GROSSET & DUNLAP

NEW YORK

UNIVERSAL LIBRARY EDITION 1965
BY ARRANGEMENT WITH THE AUTHOR

First published 1937 by Victor Gollancz Ltd.
London, England

Introduction © 1965 by Frank Jellinek

For ELIZABETH BAILLIE

PRINTED IN THE UNITED STATES OF AMERICA

# CONTENTS

# CONTENTS

# Introduction to the
## Universal Library Edition

THE PARIS COMMUNE of 1871 was not merely the successor to the Commune of 1793, with its Committee of Public Safety and its guillotine; it was the culmination of the continuous struggle waged by the people of Paris against their various rulers which had found physical expression in the barricades of 1830, 1832 and 1848. It was hailed by Marx, and Lenin called it the first modern revolution, the first stage in a revolutionary process of which the Russian Revolution was the second.

Despite the spate of contemporary propaganda and the difficulties of accurately describing certain details, the outline of the actual events is clear. While the Prussians were closely besieging Paris, a fortified city of about 1,825,000 inhabitants, the Second Empire collapsed at Sedan; its successors seemed more interested in destroying domestic socialism than in resisting the foreign invader; after an armistice had been negotiated with Bismarck, the provinces, many unscathed by war, elected a majority that quite openly wished to reverse all French history since 1793; the Government made a clumsy attempt to disarm Paris, but it failed and, under Adolphe Thiers, withdrew to Versailles with the evident intention of collecting fresh troops and re-entering Paris by force. The more militant Parisians resisted, formed the Commune of Paris, held the cultural capital of Europe for ten weeks, and were massacred on an unprecedented scale in a military operation during which half the city was burned down. When Thiers had evacuated the political and administrative apparatus of government, the representatives of the people of Paris were compelled more by force of circumstance than by design to administer the city themselves. It was not an insurrection —certainly it was not planned—but it did, technically, amount to a seizure of power. In any case, revolutionaries have always been more interested in how the Communards of 1871 used their power than how they achieved it. For what they did in their brief ten weeks was truly revolutionary.

In 1871 "democracy" as practical politics was still not wholly accepted by the political leaders of most countries; in England, for instance, references to "the Great Unwashed" and "the Plebs" were current coin; not so long before, Tennyson had written of "the red fool-fury of the Seine"; and, outside Paris, socialism was a word that inspired fear. For those who had the guns, the troops, and the will—even the wish—to use extreme violence, the argument that socialism would mean disaster was more of a threat than a prediction, though it did show some foresight. The First International, as an organization, had very little influence on the Commune, but the political police, which may perhaps be said to embody a society's guilty conscience, were as emphatic as Karl Marx himself in stressing the essentially subversive nature of the Commune. Yet Marx, who had warned the Parisians against undertaking a hopeless struggle but had later praised them for "storming heaven," could not persuade the General Council to endorse his classic account, *The Civil War in France*. There is a straight line from the First to the Third International, through Lenin's gloss, *The State and Revolution*, on Marx's pamphlet on the Commune.

Hence, for many years the historical approach to the Commune was mainly political and partisan (as, indeed, was that to the Great Revolution, until the methods of Georges Lefebvre began to replace those of the pioneer Albert Mathiez). Access has at last been granted to the *dossiers* of the courts-martial, with their wealth of detail on the social origins, profession, and even motivations of many of the accused; investigation of the provincial archives, closer attention to social rather than political details in the abundant narratives of both Communards and anti-Communards, and better-organized studies of the social life of Paris in the nineteenth century as a whole may soon make it possible to obtain a much clearer view of the composition of what has loosely been called "the people of Paris." Naturally, the whole of Paris did not rise as one man against Thiers's attempt to disarm the Paris National Guard on 18 March 1871. On the other hand, the absence of any single dominant group, or even of any single set of ideas, has always complicated the understanding of this body which was effectively in control of the capital of Europe for nearly ten weeks.

While most of the things the Commune did and most of the decisions it took were without doubt revolutionary —some of them did not actually pass into French law until 1947—they were generally dictated by circumstances and by half a century of discussion and revolt. In retrospect, Bakunin's "spontaneous socialism of the masses" makes no more sense, politically, than it did at the time. Paris in 1871 was still mainly pre-industrial and so pre-proletarian, but almost everything the Commune did implied a shift in property relationships, the transfer of control from one class to another. "Class," in this context, certainly needs closer definition, but there was one inescapable distinction: that between the rich and the poor, enhanced by the cold and the hunger of the siege and the emigration after the armistice of those "bourgeois" who could hope to find better heating, more food, and less claustrophobia, physical or social.

Since 1848 France had been the only country in Europe, and Paris one of the few places in France, where the new political theories had been eagerly, if not always intelligently, discussed. In these discussions, carried on more or less illegally by large groups composed chiefly of young men who knew each other personally and engaged in the same conspiracies, two main lines of thought had emerged: on the one hand, the idea that the Republic One and Indivisible should be led by revolutionary Paris, on the other, that a federation of autonomous local units, usually called "communes," should be established and that Paris would merely be the largest of them and act as their guide. In both cases, however, Paris would be more or less socialist. To some extent, this clash of ideas reflected the struggle between centralism, federalism and confederation that plagued Spain and all the Americas throughout the century. Thus, former attempts to classify the groups within the Commune almost as if they had been Bolsheviks and Mensheviks may be less useful than it once seemed. The Commune, like most revolutionary assemblies, spent much valuable time on theoretical debates, but the immediate needs of the city's defence necessarily prevailed over theoretical solutions.

From a practical point of view, it is still hard to see what the Communards could have hoped to gain. It is just possible that if they had immediately marched on Versailles and dispersed the National Assembly—military action that might have been feasible even with no more than adequate leadership—or had seized the Bank of France, they might have negotiated with Thiers on some of their basic demands: municipal autonomy for Paris, matters of rents and due bills, even some sort of guarantee that the republican form of government would be maintained against the monarchist majority in the Assembly. They might have gained time for the industrial towns, at least, to come to their support. But it was extremely doubtful that Thiers could be brought to negotiate or could be trusted if he did so. In any case, the Commune's failure to attempt to rally support outside Paris is remarkable.

How long Paris could have administered itself in isolation, even if it had been left in peace, is of course impossible to tell. What was striking, however, was the comparatively efficient way in which quite untrained men succeeded in keeping the essential services running after Thiers had withdrawn almost all the higher administrative officials to Versailles in the expectation of causing hopeless chaos in Paris. Under the Second Empire the notion had been fostered that the Administration was virtually synonymous with Society.

The Communards' carelessness, their almost casual attitude toward the outcome of the crisis can be explained only by a general, and perhaps not quite conscious, feeling that matters had reached a point where it was really possible that "tomorrow would not be the same as today." Many of the fires set in the final days of the Commune were for tactical purposes; but quite sane and responsible members of the Commune deliberately burned such buildings as the Tuileries Palace, which to them were monuments to a past that should not return. The Communards, as is clear from the memoirs of the survivors, deeply felt not only that their ideas of social justice would "regenerate France," but also that the "backwoodsmen" of the Versailles Assembly must be eliminated from politics. And it is true enough that the Versaillese on the whole represented the same forces that were to emerge in the Dreyfus Case, in the fascist Leagues of 1934, at Vichy, as collaborators with the Nazis, and in parts of the OAS.

If it was indirectly the inspiration of the Russian Revolution, the Commune, or rather the extreme violence of its defeat, enabled France to join Britain and Germany in colonial expansion. The domestic problem had to be solved before the new class of industrial workers could be persuaded to live off the profits of cheap tropical labour. This was the work mainly of the "moderates," who did nothing to check the massacre of the Bloody Week, but did at least rally on the issue of the amnesty for the surviving Communards, an issue that eventually relegated the "backwoodsmen" to political obscurity and prevented them from obstructing the more progressive forces of French finance capitalism. To that extent, there might even be something to be said for Adolphe Thiers.

Such broader issues could not be dealt with in this book. To establish the course of events in Paris between 18 March and Whit Sunday 1871 was task enough. It has become yet more evident that the revolutions of 1848 may be regarded as the last eddies of the French revolutions of 1789 and 1792, whereas the Paris Commune was the beginning—confused, complex, and half-conscious—of a new period in French and European history. It started in hope, not in desperation; and it occurred to very few of the Communards even to consider negotiation, let alone surrender. This is hard, perhaps, to appreciate; but no harder than to understand why Republican Madrid held out for three years.

FRANK JELLINEK

*Whit Sunday, 1965*

# PART I

# CHAPTER I

# THE END OF AN EMPIRE

" The working-class movement itself is never independent, never of an exclusively proletarian character until all the different factions of the middle class . . . have conquered political power, and remodelled the State according to their wants. It is then that the inevitable conflict between the employer and the employed becomes imminent, and cannot be adjourned any longer. . . ."

FRIEDERICH ENGELS : *Revolution and Counter-Revolution in Germany.*

" Do you not feel that, in France, the extremities are chilly ? "

M. ERNOUL

I

IN THE LATE SUMMER OF 1868, Paris knew again the political ferment that it had not seen for seventeen years.

Louis Napoléon Bonaparte, the debt-ridden, fate-driven adventurer who had seized the power on that bitter December 2, 1851, was " crowning the edifice of the Second Empire " with the grant of more liberal institutions.

Seventeen years of absolute power had left its mark on his policy, his character and even upon his face. From year to year Appert's pitiless photographs revealed the ravages of the strain. Pressure from the masses, now becoming organised and conscious of their position, pressure from the professional classes, cheated of their success in 1848, pressure from the new class of financial magnates, pressure from his wife, the beautiful, obstinate, bigoted Eugènie, pressure from his closest advisers, who realised that an autocracy can break but cannot bend—all these bore so heavily upon the Emperor that he had been forced to revive the demagogy which had won him his presidentship in the confused, far-off days of 1849.

Voltaire of the coming revolution, the diabolic Marquis

Henri-Victor de Rochefort-Luçay, known to all Paris as plain Henri Rochefort, was selling his famous *Lanterne* in thousands. The vendors raced the police all down the Boulevards; for, although a modified freedom of the Press had been restored, Rochefort's shafts went in under the skin, especially the thin skins of the Imperial pair, and they rankled.

Watching the sport from the Café de Madrid, on the north side of the Boulevard Montmartre (a café which judicious Herr Baedeker deprecated as " not to be recommended to those escorting females since the company is too mixed"), were the leaders of the anti-Imperial movement: the veterans of the Forty-Eight and the rising men of the coming Republic.

There sat Rochefort himself, neither drinking nor smoking, always in motion, with his lean Mephistophelean jaw and jet beard, his wildly tufted black hair, his high lean cheek-bones, curiously veined flashing eyes, fine hands and slight body which had the graceful tautness of the trained duellist. There was Gambetta, the rising young Left-wing advocate, slim and black-bearded, waving his hands in Mediterranean gesture. Old Delescluze, angular, emaciated from his sufferings in the jails of Mazas, Belle-Isle, Corte, Ajaccio, Marseilles, Toulon and the hell of Cayenne, whither he had been transported after the Forty-Eight. He had been out on the barricades in the July Days of 1830, had been Ledru-Rollin's Commissioner for the North in 1848; had returned, broken in health but indomitable, from Cayenne after the 1859 amnesty to throw into the struggle against tyranny and obscurantism his inflexible determination, his chilly, cutting pen and his irreconcilable attachment to the Jacobin principles of 1793.

To the Madrid, too, came sometimes Delescluze's despised enemy, Félix Pyat, another Grand Old Man of revolution, but with a grandeur somewhat bogus. Superbly tall, with a romantic mane and beard, proud leonine gaze and a voice that could carry incredible distances, Pyat seemed to the young men, who respected, admired, but did not love

Delescluze, the old lion of revolt. His pen, in his *Vengeur*, rivalled Delescluze's in his *Reveil*. He used his experience in writing pseudo-Hugonic melodramas in the Thirties to clothe some perfectly vulgar notion in such emotional and even memorable phrase that it brought reminiscent tears to the eyes of his fellow-Forty-Eighters and called the young men to their feet in rapturous applause. A diamond edition of Mignet's *Abstract of the Revolution*, annotated, underlined, was the breviary he carried in his cloak-pocket. Pyat was the man of plots and evasions, the purest romantic terrorist that ever flung a paper bomb. Always he was on the spot with exactly the right revolutionary phrase: always he shirked responsibility for its consequences. In 1848, he had signed the call to arms on June 10, which led to the disastrous barricades of June 25—then vanished. He appeared again among the London exiles, where his Revolutionary Commune group involved them in all sorts of scandals, including the notorious Barthélemy-Cournet duel, until he got them expelled to Guernsey for an article in which he suggested that Queen Victoria had compromised her female modesty by visiting Napoléon III. It was inevitable that where opponents of absolutism were gathered together there should be this typical representative of romantic revolution; it was equally inevitable that he would, with the best possible excuse, betray his trust should the revolution he sincerely desired ever invest him with responsibility.

Jules Vallès, the fourth of the Big Four of the new republican journalism, sometimes came over from the Left Bank to talk with Rochefort. Editor of the *Cri du Peuple*, self-appointed and popularly confirmed spokesman of the Refractories, the Bohemians of the Second Empire, he had demolished once and for all the Bohemia of Murger in his autobiographical *Jacques Vingtras* trilogy. A permanently unhappy man, of whom Alphonse Daudet once remarked that he had the rasping laugh and bilious eye of one whose childhood had been miserable and who bore a grudge against all mankind because he had been obliged to wear absurd garments made from his father's old clothes. The

true cause of Vallès' misery was sheer hunger and the impossibility of showing his hatred of the smug inequalities
of Second-Empire society under the censorship. Again and
again he had been dismissed from papers which valued his
very real talents simply because he could not refrain from
" showing the tip of the red flag " between the lines of even
the most innocuous society notes.

With Vallès came the jest and admiration of them all, the
darling, even more than Rochefort, of the revolutionary
workers of Belleville: Gustave Flourens. If Pyat was a
romantic of the Forty-Eight, Flourens was the very quint-
essence of the revolutionary romanticism of all times. Son of
a noted professor of science at the Collège de France, and
no mean scientist himself—he took his father's courses
during his absence—Gustave Flourens had suddenly
renounced all dealings with a rotten society and sailed away
to fight under the Death or Glory banner of Cretan liberty.
Vain, childish, dashing, utterly genuine in his intense love
of liberty and his candid belief in his fellow-men, provided
they were good Republicans, he was ready to rally to the
help of his worst enemy at any threat to his freedom.
Prematurely bald, with flowing red mustachios and beard,
and command, some fantastic and magnificent command,
in his bright blue eyes, Flourens impressed the police as
having about him something of Tony Johannot's Don
Quixote. For once, the political police made no mistake.

Over on the Left Bank, in this year 1868, the Refractories
swarmed in the little cafés, talking rank treason, rank
nonsense, art, politics, wine and women in a ferment of
ideas from which something was to come. At neighbouring
tables the spies of Piétri, the hated chief of the political
police, took rapid, puzzled notes. Every now and then
there would be a round-up of political suspects, and a cart-
load of rowdy, cheerful students would disappear into
Sainte-Pélagie jail for a couple of months. And in jail there
was always the chance of meeting the veterans, even the
Old One himself, Auguste Blanqui, aged master of conspiracy, familiar of a hundred cells.

In these cafés and in the jails the younger revolutionaries met and debated the aims and means of sedition. Raoul Rigault was ubiquitous with his " revolutionary counter-police," suggested to him by Ranc, the mysterious Grey Eminence of the Third Republic. Urchins would hang about the doors of the Prefecture, noting the detectives and stool-pigeons passing in and out, then report to Rigault. Any morning you might meet him on the Quais, focusing his thick eyeglass, over a bookseller's box, upon police headquarters across the river.

A notable " character," this Rigault was a passionate upholder of the French Revolution, " the real revolution " of the Terrorists Hébert, Marat, Chaumette. He divided his leisure between the musty pages of Hébert's *Père Duchesne* pamphlets in the Bibliothèque Imperiale and Eugène Sue's romances of the Paris underworld. A perfervid Jacobin, he decapitated ecclesiastically named streets, so that the rue St. Hyacinthe-St. Michel became in his cockney the " rue Hya-Miche." " Nothing but a guttersnipe," said old Blanqui, a good judge of revolutionaries, " but a policeman of genius."

Theophile Ferré was his complement: the icy terrorist, utterly without fear or humour. Yet he envied and tried to ape Rigault's careless and brutal wit. Blanqui had his eye on him too. Very short, with tiptoe skip and nervous shrug of shoulder; shrill-voiced, with icy smile and snap, long brooding silences suddenly breaking into outrageous shrill shoutings framed in a fine rain of spittle. Bird-of-prey face, the great hooked nose with its deep wide nostrils jutting from between huge spectacles, the dead pallor of the cheeks accentuated by very long and very black hair and beard. Behind the spectacles, the eyes had the surprising mildness of the myopic.

A childhood tormented by poverty and the consciousness of physical inferiority had nurtured in him an implacable vengefulness. He had early realised that only a Jacobin terror would give him this personal revenge. At a conspiracy trial in 1870, where he was acquitted for lack of evidence, he astounded the Court by shrilling out: " You have the power now: use it ! But when I have it, beware ! "

There were hundreds of others of these young revolutionary intellectuals. There was Vermesch, Rigault's rival in the study of Hébert, who lived in Baudelaire's old rooms and emulated his poetry, which still seemed satanic to respectable bourgeois society, since, with the imposition of literary censorship, all that offends against morality is automatically sedition, as Baudelaire himself had discovered to his cost.

Here was Eugène Vermorel, a strange, masochistic young man rather like a renegade priest. Indeed, Rochefort, inspired by his smooth, felinely handsome face framed in sleek auburn " sideboards," had nicknamed him " the whiskered choirboy." Tall, stooping, bespectacled, a pile of books ever clutched under one arm, this law student walked in abstraction over the Latin Quarter. Forced to earn his living by indecent literary hack-work which revolted him, he was torn by a perpetual struggle between a somewhat sentimental sensuality and a clear metaphysical intelligence; a conflict resolved in him, as in so many others, by projecting his personal struggle into the struggle against the society which had produced it. He was one of the first and one of the most constant propagandists of the International, and one of the few young revolutionaries who could influence the icy, unscrupulous bourgeois opposition editor, Emile Girardin, one of the founders of modern journalism.

At the Union in the rue Monsieur-le-Prince, the disgruntled Royalist Barbey d'Aurevilly, who liked Socialists only because they exposed the abuses of unworthy monarchs, consorted with drunken old Courbet, who expounded to him the Socialism he had picked up from his friend the anarchist theorist Charles Proudhon, his " realist " theories of painting and his revolutionary system of absinthe-drinking, which he called " wringing the Customs-officer's neck ": " the first one bowls you over, but the second picks you up again."

With them was Georges Cavalier, nicknamed " Pipe-en-Bois "—no one quite knew why—or " the anthropophagous rabbit," less from  his habits than from his face.

Here, too, was the fiery little Corsican, Paschal Grousset, exquisitely dressed—Rochefort called him the " ladies' hairdresser," and English newspapermen noted that " his hair was as a rule nicely waved." He could, however, fight like a devil, either in duel or on barricade. After escaping from New Caledonia, whither he was transported after the Commune, he settled in London, translated *Treasure Island*, and, impressed by the physical excellencies of English boys, was largely responsible for introducing *le sporting Anglais* into France.

In Sainte-Pélagie jail, old Blanqui had already built up the nucleus of a disciplined conspiracy. Nearly all the leaders of the Opposition had met him there between 1861 and 1864, when he escaped in a wig. Consumptive, wealthy young Tridon, the rising Left-wing barrister Protot, a mild democrat, Vacherot, a brilliant young physicist, politically educated by Ranc, named Georges Clémenceau (he had not yet dropped the accent), the poet Catulle Mendès, the journalist Eugène Pelletan, Charles Longuet, editor of the *Rive Gauche*, in which Rogeard's "Propos de Labiénus" brilliantly analysed the abuses of the Empire, and Sully Prudhomme and Anatole France made their literary débuts, all met there. To Brussels, after Blanqui's escape, came Tridon, Regnard, the future translator of Buchner, Rogeard, Longuet and Lafargue. Longuet and Lafargue were to marry Marx's daughters. Longuet was even then translating Marx's famous *Inaugural Address to the International Working-Men's Association*.

All these young men were gaining conspiratorial experience. Their discussions, their abortive little newspapers, often of considerable literary and political merit, their comradeship in face of perpetual petty persecution were preparing them to take a leading part in the coming revolt. Even more importantly, the fact that this agitation existed and grew stronger as the Empire tried to bend before the

storm brought a new, exciting, dangerous element into the
political and social life of Paris during the autumn of 1868.
Republicanism, or at least anti-Imperialism of some kind or
other, had ceased to be eccentric.

There was really only one political choice open to the
young French intellectual or professional in the later
Sixties: Republicanism, either under the tricolour flag or
the red. But the tricolour held, in the past, present and
future, the possibility of unfortunate associations, personal
and political.

Many of these young men came from respectable small-
town families made by the Louis-Philippe bourgeois
monarchy, and consequently Royalist by tradition; but
they had been disgusted by the stupidity of the Orleanist
branch of the Royal Family. As Royalists, they could not
accept the usurping Bonaparte; as Orleanists, they had
compromised themselves with the Legitimist Bourbon
branch by their approval of their expulsion in 1830, for
" Bourbons forget nothing," if they learn nothing. Therefore, Republicanism was the only alternative, the " Left "
complexion depending largely upon the material success
they won in the fierce competition of Paris life under the
Second Empire.

Almost all the sons of respectable provincial families
began their career by studying *droit* in Paris. Gentleman's
privilege, social and economic, was determined, no longer
by birth, but by the possession of a degree. This class of
possessors of degrees, the *Mandarinat*, was even distinguished
by dress. The top-hat and whiskers had right of entry to
places utterly forbidden to the overall and moustache of the
artisan. To abandon the top-hat was to betray one's class;
and the traitor was condemned to a poverty more humili-
ating by the contrast with the glittering prizes won by those
who were willing or able to fit themselves into the well-
policed *Mandarinat*.

Taine is perhaps incorrect when he asserts, in a famous
passage, that budding Marats and Robespierres are to be
found in deserted consulting-rooms and attorneys' offices.

This is true only when overproduction of professionals is combined with a shrinking demand for their services. It was not so under the Second Empire. There was no large intellectual proletariat. The reason why men of talent, such as Jules Vallès, were condemned to the chill modern Bohemia was that the autocracy was necessarily so rigid that it could not afford to allow even the " tip of the red flag between the lines." The " declassed Mandarins " were created, not by direct economic pressure, but by the artificial restraints of police censorship.

The contradiction was inherent in the autocrat's position. Louis Napoléon, the President, had thought to represent the interests of the Napoleonic settlement, or, ultimately, of the Revolution: the middle farmers and provincial merchants. The enormous increase in industrialisation gave birth to a new class to cope with its expansive and distributive organisation: an elaborately organised, ambitious and grasping financial oligarchy.

The young intellectuals, therefore, were faced by a disgusting contradiction. They had been taught by a strongly nationalistic regime to love their country: they found it the paradise of financial sharks. They had been offered the rewards of industrial prosperity: they found them ugly shams in the hands of vulgar Philistines, so that the very word bourgeois came to have a hated significance no less æsthetic than political. They found all initiative in art, literature, science and philosophy crushed beneath the flat, heavy boot of the ubiquitous policeman.

They naturally reacted to an idealistic or tactical alliance with what seemed the one uncontaminated, the one strong and regenerative force, suffering injustice and exploitation more unjust than their own—the working masses. If they could, they adopted the people's own promise of more justice—Socialism. If their heredity and environment were too strong, they took their salvation into their own hands and dreamed of the revival of the one political enthusiasm which had long ago brought them their hour of glory, and which still might unite all that was best in Paris—the spirit

and creed of Seventeen Ninety-Three, of the " Spontaneous " Revolutionary Commune; with the prizes it
could offer to the pure and upright Saint-Justs among them.

Neo-Jacobinism became the creed not only of old
revolutionary die-hards like Delescluze and Pyat, but of
many militant bourgeois republicans, and even of some of
the workers who looked upon themselves as Parisians rather
than proletarians. In the neo-Jacobin legend—for legend it
was—the Great Spontaneous Commune of 1793, the
Commune of Marat, Pache, Hébert, Chaumette, was
supposed to have arisen under the leadership of the Jacobin
Club, annihilated kings and aristos, abolished God, swept,
by the irresistible surge of volunteer armies animated by
uncontrollable revolutionary enthusiasm, the foreign invader from the sacred soil of Republican France; the
Revolution carried its arms and its message of freedom
over Europe; despots trembled, tyranny, corruption and
privilege were dispersed, and Liberty, Equality and Fraternity triumphed to the blare of the " Marseillaise," the
challenge of the tricolour on the breeze, the clang of the
guillotine and the roar of Republican guns amid the gorges
of the Ardennes; and Paris, purged of traitors at home and
victorious in arms abroad, was the centre and directing force
of the whole Great Revolution.

The neo-Jacobins of the Sixties were thus republican,
anticlerical, terrorist and patriotic, seeing in 1848 a stifled
and ineffective continuation of 1793. They had little conception of a radical social revolution, confining themselves
to a hatred of the existing order, expressed by a romantic
harking-back to symbols which had little basis in historical
fact and less in actual reality.

This tendency was clearly shown in the revaluation of the
Revolution by historians of the Sixties. The preparation of
the nationalistic Napoleonic legend between 1823 and 1830
had begun this in Thiers's rehabilitation of Danton as a
great French patriot and in Mignet's, Lamartine's and
Michelet's studies published during the reign of Louis
Philippe. All these, however, had roundly condemned the

Terror, had been fascinated by Robespierre, but had condemned him; and had drawn little more distinction between his party and that of Hébert than that between fratricidal gangs.

In the Sixties, propagandists, looking for material to counteract the Napoleonic conception of the Revolution, began to search for other heroes, and were thereby actually led to analyse the stages of the Revolution more correctly. Serious historians such as Bougeart, Robinet and Avenel published studies of Marat and the Terrorists which were vigorously reproved by the censorship, but have been confirmed by modern scholarship.

Soon, mere propagandists began to draw upon their work. Tridon, a young follower of Blanqui, published, in 1864, a work on the Hébertists. An introductory paragraph is typical: " Hail, Hébert and Pache, pure and noble citizens; Chaumette, whom the people loved as a father; Momoro [sic], ardent of pen and generous of spirit; Ronsin, intrepid general; and thou, sweet and melancholy figure, through whom German Pantheism extended its hand to French Naturalism, Anarcharsis Klootz ! "

This apotheosis of men whom the average Frenchman had been taught to regard as unmitigated blackguards roused immense applause in the Latin Quarter. So much so that when quiet, democratic Professor Edgar Quinet " in an admirable book, *The Revolution*, protested in the name of the human conscience against the stupid ferocities of the Terror, condemned its authors and drove those sanguinary blackguards from the ranks of liberal democracy, a huge clamour of savage anger was raised against this eloquent cry of an indignant soul."

To the neo-Jacobins Robespierre, whom even Taine classed with Marat and Chaumette as a bloodthirsty monster, was a moderate, even a reactionary. " Robespierre," said Blanqui, " wished in reality to turn the guillotine against the revolutionaries and to rally round him the party of the past by the immolation of the Mountain. . . . His triumph in Thermidor would have been the triumph

of the counter-revolution." " Robespierre," said Tridon,
" died, crucified, on the 9th Thermidor and was resurrected
after 1830 [by Mignet, etc.]. At heart he was an ambitious
vulgarian, a man who wished to dominate at any price, a
dandy who paraded his puritan morality between a pair of
mistresses and three racehorses. His soul was hateful and
jealous, his spirit malignant and low."

Those of the bourgeois intellectuals who could not quite
assimilate working-class Socialism but demanded a more
concrete form of anti-governmental activity than mere
neo-Jacobin spouting enrolled themselves in the Blanquist
Party.

Auguste Blanqui's name, activities and doctrines dominated nearly half a century of illegal work in Paris, although
he himself had, by 1870, spent twenty-eight of his sixty-five
years in jail and many more in exile. He never left Paris save
under compulsion, was never voluntarily far from the scene
of Paris conspiracy. Even from jail he issued his instructions
to his devoted circle of lieutenants.

Blanqui, although recognised by Marx in his less irritated
moments as a true revolutionary, was not a Socialist. It is
true that he originated the phrase " the dictatorship of the
proletariat " as early as 1837, as he also invented the expression " the Industrial Revolution." But his conception of
proletarian dictatorship was not that of a stage in the
progress towards the classless Socialist society, but merely
that of the most effective method of smashing the present
capitalist structure.

Himself a pupil of the aged Buonarotti, that descendant of
Michelangelo who was the last survivor of Gracchus
Babeuf's conspiracy against the Directorate in 1797,
Blanqui, despite a very large body of economic and
theoretic writing, most of which has remained unpub-
lished, was primarily a master of insurrectionary technique.

Babeuf's plan had been to seize and massacre the Directors, transfer all property to the State, repudiate all public
and private debts, regulate the market and the particular
kind of production each individual was to undertake—a

crude form of revolutionary Communism. Blanqui adopted much of this programme, but was never really interested in more than the first part of it—the seizure of power. One of his followers has summed up his doctrine: " Nihilism first, then at the mercy of evolution." At the end of his long life Blanqui actually contributed to the Russian Nihilist Press, chiefly to Tkatchev's *Nabat*, organ of the Narodnaia Volya.

Blanqui continued the Babouvist system of " invisible manœuvres " employed by Buonarotti in 1814. Grouped in groups of ten, *decuries*, only the leader of which was in touch with the central organisation, they would meet and march together in the midst of a holiday crowd, their disciplined formation passing unnoticed in the crush.

His doctrines sprang from his life. A Parisian of Parisians, he could not avoid a strong tincture of Jacobinism. It is perhaps a mere verbal coincidence that his first appearance on the barricades coincided with the first reappearance in politics of the word *commune*.

This was in 1827, when Godefroy Cavaignac, Raspail and other Republicans organised secret "municipalities" to counter any attempt at an autocratic *coup d'état* by Charles X during the riots following the triumph of democratic Paris at the elections of that year. But it was none the less symbolic of Blanqui's role.

It was only occasionally that Blanqui was able to walk the streets of his beloved Paris, disguised as the complete bourgeois, in frock-coat and top-hat, a copy of the *Constitutionel* newspaper—which he called his Bible—ostentatiously sticking out of his pocket.

His appearance in the Chamber in May 1848 shocked de Tocqueville: " His cheeks were haggard and emaciate, his lips livid, his appearance sickly, sinister and unclean; a dirty pallor, the aspect of a rotting corpse, no visible linen, an old black frock-coat tightly draping ravaged and fleshless limbs, he seemed to have spent his life in a sewer, from which he had just emerged." Flaubert, on the other hand, describes his character Senecal as trying to look like Blanqui, " who imitated Robespierre: his black gloves and cropped hair gave him an air of formality which was extremely respectable."

Blanqui's predilection for Paris and his long sojourn in prison prevented his coming into contact with the masses, so that he formed a very low opinion of their political capacity. His chief associates were necessarily the young revolutionary intellectuals; and his organisation was formed chiefly in jail, rather in the way that Babeuf had formed his conspiracy in the prisons of Thermidor.

This circumstance led to the Blanquist revolutionary thesis, which may be stated in syllogistic form: the revolutionary proletariat, having neither theoretic nor practical experience, must be led by the revolutionarily educated *déclassé* bourgeois; these bourgeois can be so educated only in revolutionary Paris; therefore revolutionary Paris must lead the proletariat in the coming revolution, which must logically lead to the " Parisification " of France. " In the new era, with the acceptance of the life of reason by the entire country and with the ' Parisification ' of the whole of France, we shall see the voluntary abdication of Paris in favour of her children on attaining their majority, her maternal joy in the virility of her sons." This was barely removed from the Jacobin conception of " the Republic One and Indivisible " with the Commune of Paris at its head.

The membership of the Blanquist Party was necessarily limited by the conditions of conspiratorial work. By 1870 the armed section numbered between 2,500 and 3,000 men; while a larger group, under Eudes and Regnard, had the work of distributing propaganda.

Blanqui's undisguised contempt of Socialism would have alienated many of his best followers had not his personal magnetism been so strong. He had quarrelled with Marx in 1848, as he had abandoned Barbès, " the Bayard of Democracy," at a critical moment in 1836; and personal feelings as much as dogmatic disagreement were at the root of Blanqui's orders to his followers to boycott the International's congresses.

A group under Edouard Vaillant, a very accomplished scholar and later an intimate friend of Marx, dared to disobey this prohibition, in 1868. The consequent quarrels caused a definite split in the Blanquist ranks, although for fighting purposes the whole organisation still acted together. The importance of this split is that it does show, as too many writers, including Engels, have failed to emphasise, that there was a strong tendency towards effective Socialism within the Blanquist Party after 1868, which, persuasively explained by Vaillant, did something to soften the objections of the Old One himself.

The cardinal defect of Blanquism was its failure to distinguish between insurrection and revolution, its deliberate rejection of a mass basis. It suited the natural tendency of the *déclassé* bourgeois towards an impatient nihilism; and even so late as 1917 Lenin was forced to define the objection of the true revolutionist to Blanquism: " Insurrection must be based, not on a plot, not on a party, but on the advanced class. That is the first point. Insurrection must be based upon the revolutionary drive of the whole people. That is the second point. Insurrection must break out at the peak of the ascending revolution. That is the third point. It is by these three conditions that Marxism is distinguished from Blanquism."

By 1868, the workers' clubs and pubs out in the Red suburbs of Ménilmontant, La Villette, Belleville and Montmartre, the last two hills incorporated in the city only in 1859, came to life once more.

Although industrialisation had increased enormously during the third quarter of the nineteenth century, the Paris workers were still largely artisans. No proletarian class, organised by large-scale factory conditions, had yet arisen. In 1866, at the apogee of Parisian expansion in this period, the total population was 1,825,274. There were 570,280 workshops (as against 64,816 in 1847 and 101,171 in 1860), owned by 65,987 masters, employing only 442,310 workers (besides 34,846 clerks and 23,251 servants). This meant that the average number of workers per shop was only 7·7, sinking from 13 in the building and metal trades to 1.4 in the food industry. By far the largest numbers were employed in the garment industry: 306,567 (208,383 women); building, owing to Baron Haussmann's reconstruction of the capital, employed most men, 125,371 (63,675 women); and the various luxury industries, upon which the repute and prosperity of Paris mainly depended, employed 63,617 workers. In all, workers (468,337) and their dependants (286,670) made up about 40 per cent of the population of Paris.

Between 1857 and 1867, wages remained fairly steady in Paris around an average of 4 francs 98 per day. But real wages fell, so that Paris metal-workers' daily wage, which would buy the equivalent of 82 eggs or 2,310 grammes of butter in the Fifties, would, in the Sixties, purchase only 60 eggs or 2,030 grammes of butter. Similarly, a woman employed in the food industry would receive the equivalent of 29 eggs or 765 grammes of butter in the Sixties, whereas in the Fifties she had been able to earn 34 eggs or 925 grammes of butter.

These figures show that the workers of Paris might be expected to be politically undeveloped. The rapid worsening of conditions, however, which coincided with, because it had caused, the Emperor's grant of liberal institutions, made them the more ready to listen to the propaganda of hope and the more able to receive the message.

Socialism had been driven underground after the fiasco of 1848. The workers did not welcome Louis Napoléon, but they did not oppose him. They regarded him as the nemesis of that Second Republic which had mounted to power over the barricades erected by them in February, and had then massacred, in the June Days, those to whom they owed the command of the bayonets they used against them.

It was a period of consolidation and reflection. A new Socialism arose, primitive still, but far removed from the Utopianism of Saint-Simon and Fourier in the Thirties and the aimless militancy of Louis Blanc in the Forties.

Its chief exponent was Charles Proudhon, by far the most influential figure among the masses in the period.

No one ever doubted the passionate honesty of this man of the people. His books were translated into English, German, Russian. Courbet loved him and painted his portrait. Baudelaire, Barbey d'Aurévilly courted and respected him. Tolstoy, Morris and a whole generation of foreign Socialists and humanitarians were deeply influenced by his thought. Marx thought his ideas sufficiently typical of a stage in Socialist theory to devote a whole book, *The Poverty of Philosophy*, to demolishing Proudhon's *Philosophy of Poverty*.

Proudhon's ideas were the natural outcome of the economic standing of the French workers among whom he spent his life. His theory was fitted to an artisan society, still struggling under recent defeat and faced with a new form of exploitation—that of finance-capital. He therefore found the origin of poverty not in the maldistribution of the means of production, but in the maladministration of exchange. His remedy was an early form of Distributism. He suggested the organisation of a society composed of a federation of co-operative mutual-credit associations. Hence the name often applied to Proudhon's socialism— *Mutualism*.

Private property was not to be abolished, but property concentrated in a few hands was to be redistributed. The ideal society would be set up as it were on the margin of capitalism, and would be a community of small federated self-governing groups of producers. In French administration, then, a federation of self-governing local units— *communes*.

This Socialism must come from below: by the conviction and self-improvement of each neighbour-loving individual; the government of each by all—democracy; the government of each by each—self-government, or " an-archy."

As a militant creed, Proudhonism was not promising. As a means of restoring the workers' confidence in themselves, of bringing them to a realisation of their position, it was unrivalled. His book *On the Capacity of the Working Class* taught them once more that they were capable of taking their destinies in their own hands. They saw in Proudhon a reflection of their own capabilities. " The masses," he said, " do not read me, but, without reading me, they understand me."

The Emperor, something of an amateur economist himself—as he had shown in a sensible little pamphlet, *On the Extinction of Poverty*—was even more a student of modern methods of statecraft. He recognised that the new workers' movement must be conciliated and diverted. It would, if tamed and directed, act as a barrier against the Republican middle classes. He coquetted with what he considered the more harmless side of Proudhonism, making concessions which were in fact no concessions at all. His error lay in the fact that he did not observe that the workers themselves regarded these concessions as a weakening on the part of the autocracy, and " ungratefully " pressed for more.

The Government lent its aid to the formation of co-operatives, but it was careful to keep the financing of them in the hands of banks whose policy it was able to control. By 1866, there were twelve workers' mutual credit societies, seven co-operatives in Paris and more than fifty in the provinces.

The workers, however, took advantage of this policy to form co-operatives and unions of their own. Camélinat, an efficient organiser, founded the metal-workers' union, and led them in the victorious strike of 1867 which gained much sympathy for the new movement. The bookbinders, formed by Eugène Varlin, busy, quiet, self-educated, polite and enormously popular, gained better conditions by a strike as early as 1864.

Pursuing this policy, the Emperor yielded to pressure, and in 1864 repealed the Chapelier law forbidding strikes. In the next six years the unions called out their members in ten major strikes, all of them for better living conditions and wages. The Government, true to policy, legalised the strikes, but put troops at the owners' disposal to suppress them.

By far the most important result of this " police Social-ism " was the foundation of the International Working-Men's Association in London, on September 28th, 1864. This was the direct outcome of a move by the Emperor, who, against the advice of most of his Ministers, sent a delegation of 200 French workers to the London Exhibition of 1862.

The idea was that they should be impressed by the tame attitude of the English " intelligent mechanic "; and a Festival of International Brotherhood was duly addressed by the aged Chartist, Charles Murray, who recommended co-operation with the employers to study methods of coping with the unemployment which would be caused by the development of steam, gas and electricity.

But, as Bénoît Malon, one of the leaders of the French delegation, puts it, " quite naturally, the workers' delegates from the big Republican towns spent their time otherwise than in Bonapartist propaganda." Probably through the agency of the French exile colony, they got in touch with English trade-union leaders, and this connection was maintained, leading to the foundation of the International two years later.

Struck, possibly, by the advice of the English leaders, and Karl Marx, a militant section of the delegation split from the rest on their return. In the 1863 elections, they put up their own candidates. But the workers had not yet learnt that they should have any aim further than that of merely opposing the Empire, and allied themselves with the bourgeois Liberals, despite a " Manifesto of the Sixty," signed by the most prominent workers' leaders, and urging that the workers' interests were incompatible with those of bourgeois Republicans. At the 1864 by-elections, Tolain, the leader of the dissidents, received only 424 votes.

The same error led to the French workers' cold reception of Marx's draft of the International's theses, which de-clared that the emancipation of the working class must be won by the working class itself, and that the economic emancipation of the working class is therefore the great end to which every political movement ought to be subordinated as a means. Blanqui denounced the International as a Bonapartist attempt to mislead the workers. The Jacobins of the London exile, headed by Sue's rancorous ex-secretary, Vésinier, were outraged by Tolain's Proudhonism.

Vermorel, however, quick to perceive the historic and tactical importance of the new organisation, opened a column of his *Courrier Français* to Tolain. Vallès, Lafargue, Guesde and Guyot helped to popularise it. When Camélinat led his metal-workers' union to victory in the strike of 1867, the active participation of the International gained it a share in the general approval. But the French section, in these early years, was very weak. It had no more than 600 members. Marx complained bitterly that unions (themselves vague enough bodies) and whole districts would drift in and out of the organisation with the utmost levity. Its income was drawn from a subscription of 10 centimes per member per week; and the French treasurer, Héligion, declared that at no time between 1865 and 1868 had he more than 50 francs in his possession at one time. In 1867, the whole receipts of the General Council were only £67.

The Imperial police, however, were quick to scent dangerous conspiracy. The *Manifesto of the Sixty* and the International's statutes seemed to be diverting the association from its original purpose as a harmless toy for the masses. They swooped. The association was savagely prosecuted in March 1868, the sentences upheld and increased at an appeal heard in May. The association in Paris seemed dead; and Tolain, at the Brussels Congress later in the year, could hold out no hope of its revival.

Tolain's Proudhonist International was certainly dead. The beginning of the crisis which was to end the Empire in the blood and muck of Sédan had killed the Proudhonism as a mass-creed. The doctrine of the Paris section, influenced

by the exposition of Marxist Communism at the Lausanne
Congress in 1867, had broadened sufficiently to attract
an influx of militants as soon as a revolutionary situation
should arise.

The leadership had passed into the hands of a remarkable
band of self-taught, thoughtful, determined leaders, such as
Varlin, Malon, Camélinat, Combault. Richard, in Lyons,
and Aubry, in Rouen, imported Bakunin's Social-Democratic Alliance with its " democratic anarchism," a creed,
very different from that preached by Proudhon.

The crash of the Proudhonist labour-credit bank in 1868
brought home to the workers the insufficiency of Proudhonist credit theories. As the petty-bourgeois were increasingly " driven wild " by the pressure of the crisis,
as artisans were dragged from the petty-bourgeois class
to feed the factories, and were shot down when they
claimed decent conditions, the new temper of the International, its militant form of mutualism, exercised great
attraction.

The theoretic and tactical errors of the Paris branch
simply infuriated Marx; but the branch recruited adherents.
Malon and Varlin re-established it; and by 1870 it had
70,000 members in Paris alone—nearly one-seventh of all
the Parisian workers. Its headquarters were fixed in a
little dingy back room, furnished with three tables and a
defective stove, at Number 6 Place de la Corderie in the
Temple ward. Above it were the headquarters of the
Federation of Syndicated Workers' Chambers, a sort of
primitive T.U.C.

The Paris in which this ferment was brewing had become
a place very different from the city into which the
Prince-President had ridden nearly twenty years before.
Modern Paris was the Second Empire's one important
creation.

The centre of finance, luxury, amusement, railways, the
workshop where wages were high (in the provinces they
had risen, but only from 1 franc 89 to 2 francs 65 per day
between 1857 and 1867), the only town in France which was

readily in touch with the great new international Industrial Era, it exercised an irresistible fascination upon the younger generation. The population which had been 800,000 in 1793, and had reached the million only about 1840, suddenly increased from 1,277,064 to 1,825,274 between 1851 and 1866. By 1870, it was about 1,845,000. At least three-fourths of this increase was due to immigration.

Napoléon III was sufficiently skilled in statecraft to kill two or more birds with one stone. He had obtained seven and a half million votes from the provinces for the plebiscite to confirm his *coup d'état* by the claim that he alone, " the Man of Order," could save them from the ruinous folly of " Red Paris." It was necessary to maintain his lion-tamer role while simultaneously amusing Paris.

Here were advantages for those who could see them. Napoléon was one of the first modern rulers to realise the political power of advertisement. It was necessary for a parvenu ruler, regarded as little better than a usurper, to raise himself to the consideration of Europe's hereditary monarchs. Napoléon I had done this by war. Napoléon III, the modern man, did so by the arts of peace ; and succeeded so far as to gain the rapturous underlinings of Victoria herself. He set out to make Paris the " Mecca of Civilisation."

It was an idea of genius. The " improvements " of his prefect, Baron Haussmann, transformed the old, dirty, criminal, revolutionary city into the world's capital. Wide boulevards broke up the old conglomerations of mean hovels, breeding-places of crime and sedition. They attracted and facilitated a vast increase of traffic, and, simultaneously, their width and their macadam surface rendered impossible the raising of the old " spontaneous " paving-stone barricades. They opened a magnificent field of vision ; they opened an equally magnificent field for artillery fire and cavalry charges.

Yet Paris had less municipal liberty than the smallest rural community. Local administration had been given, by the laws of 1831 and 1835, at least some appearance of self-government: the prefect was to be advised by a council elected from those who could offer " guarantees of aptitude "—that is, wealth and rank—although he was not obliged to take the advice. Paris demanded more and received less. Napoléon I incorporated the city in the Seine Department, administered by the Prefect of the Seine, responsible only to the Minister for the Interior, who appointed him. Napoléon III rearranged the internal administration, dividing the city into twenty *arrondissements*, each subdivided into four *quartiers*. Each *quartier* elected a member to the local municipal council, composed of a mayor and three assistants (*adjoints*).

There was, however, no elective Mayor of Paris. The president of the Council of Mayors, appointed by his colleagues, merely acted as chairman at their meetings, which discussed and voted the city budget.

The executive was in the hands solely of the Prefects of the Seine and of the Police, to whom the Municipal Council could not refuse any vote of credit they demanded. In case of refusal, the Minister of the Interior simply inserted the credit in the budget. Any decision by the council could be overruled by the Government. Since the police budget came to about 20 millions annually, and since the Second Empire appropriated a very large proportion for the political police, whose function was to suppress the opinions held by a large majority of those who paid for their upkeep, Parisians were not unnaturally resentful. One of the first demands made by all Paris in time of revolution would be that for municipal liberties, an autonomous Commune of Paris.

The Emperor was well aware that he owed his success to the provinces. He was no less aware of the danger of coquetting with Paris, since his rise was due in the first instance to the Paris revolution which had expelled Louis Philippe. The eight different forms of government which had ruled France since 1791 had all been at the mercy of a Paris incident. It was doubtful whether the provinces would come to the rescue of a ruler deposed by Paris, although they might veto the further progress of the revolution. This had been their attitude in 1830 and 1848.

The ruler of France had, historically, been a hostage in Paris. The Tuileries Palace was built outside the city wall and connected to the old palace of the Louvre by a covered gallery mainly in order that the King might escape Paris revolts. Henri III had been trapped in the Louvre on the Day of Barricades in 1588; and Henri IV could only re-enter Paris after a three-year siege in which some 13,000 Parisians died of hunger. Mayor Etienne Marcel, some two and a half centuries before this, had expelled the King and set up an autonomous Commune of Paris (1357). This was a lesson which few rulers could wisely forget.

Although Napoléon III had strengthened his strategic position in Paris by Haussmann's improvements, and his political authority by the support of the new class of finance-capitalists into whose hands he had been forced to play, he was still careful to maintain an equilibrium by exploiting the traditional hostility of the provinces to Paris.

In 1870, more than three-fifths of the French were still engaged on the land. Of about 10,000,000 electors no less than 5,383,000 were engaged in agriculture, 3,552,000 being owners of their land. Only 3,102,000 were employed in industry, and of these 1,393,000, or nearly one-half, owned their workshops, generally employing no subordinate labour. Outside Paris, therefore, and a few large towns such as Lyons and Marseilles, where the increase of industry and railways had practically doubled the population, France was a country of small-holding farmers and artisans. Their interests were completely opposed to those of the more concentrated and developed Parisians.

Despite some effort to fulfil the promises he had made to them in 1851, Napoléon III did not entirely meet with the provinces' approval. Although he was still regarded as an evil less than the domination of Red Paris, and although he could always bring them to heel by Red Terror propaganda carefully disseminated by the provincial prefects, almost the only source of information from the capital besides the Government-controlled newspapers, Napoléon was accused of favouring Paris too highly. In the village cafés they spoke of him as " the Parisian."

The economically backward but stable provinces, and progressive but over-rapidly developed Paris despised one another as uncivilised. Paris blamed the provinces as a drag upon the country's expansion. The provinces blamed Paris for betraying French civilisation by whoring after ephemeral foreign gods. They disliked Paris levity and ostentation (which the Parisians called wit and magnificence), feeling that it could not be *solide*, not *sérieux*. They resented Paris's attraction for their sons. The civilisation of rural French went deeper, was more tenaciously held: *Il connaît les antiquités gallo-romaines de son pays*. In Paris " the only thing they produce is revolutions."

Politically, the provinces were conservative; and as the Second Empire became less able to fulfil its early promises, as it appeared to make ever greater concessions to Red Paris, as its guarantee of order weakened, the big landowners, the squires and the peasants they controlled returned to their earlier loyalties.

On the whole, the larger landowners and the villagers on their estates favoured the Legitimist branch of the Bourbons, the supporters of the Restoration regime of Louis XVIII, while the squires and yeomen created by the Napoleonic settlement of the Revolution preferred the constitutional monarchism of the Orleanist descendants of Louis Philippe. The Orleanists numbered among their supporters a great many merchants and professional men in the small towns; and thus were closer to the moderate Republicans than were the Legitimists. But both Orleanists and Legitimists hated Red Paris more than they hated the Usurper. They would not destroy the Empire to restore the throne; but, should Paris overthrow Bonapartism, they would advance their monarchist claims in the interests of order.

The Orleanists who tended towards a tactical alliance with the conservative Republicans possessed an important representative in Paris in the person of Adolphe Thiers.

This dangerous and intelligent politician, the last surviving pupil of Talleyrand, the opportunist who had put
Louis Philippe on the throne in 1830 and had been perhaps
his most unsuccessful Minister, the old rival of Guizot,
the brilliant but inaccurate historian of the Consulate
and the Empire, the indefatigable, brisk, eloquent, superbly
informed Opposition deputy for Paris since 1863, had,
in the closing years of the Second Empire, constructed for
himself an admirable disguise. At his famous and beloved
mansion in the Place Saint-Georges, with its notable
collections and library, he sat, waited upon by two aged
women, his wife and his sister-in-law, Mademoiselle Dosne,
studying the more liberal sciences, of which he erroneously
supposed himself master.

By the elections of 1869, the first which granted at least
a show of parliamentary liberties, the aged historian—
he was seventy-one—the mediocre Minister of a former
generation—it was thirty years since he had held office—
had " suddenly become the Parisians' idol," as the dying
Sainte-Beuve, who hated all that Thiers represented, was
forced to admit; with the malicious comparison, however,
" as M. Necker once was."

The explanation of this popularity is provided by a little
fable of Guizot's. Three workmen visit Theirs. The first:
" We belong to the *vile multitude* you have abused; yet we
are going to vote for you." The second: " We detest the
Pope; you are in favour of Temporal Power, yet we are
going to vote for you." The third: " We are Socialists;
you hate Socialists, yet we are going to vote for you."
Thiers, astonished, asks for an explanation. " Oh ! "
chorus the three workers, " it's because there's no one
like you, M. Thiers, for smashing Governments ! "

The pupil of Talleyrand, Thiers nicely adapted eigh-
teenth-century scepticism to nineteenth-century opportunist
realism. A superb casuist, he advocated the Republic
because it was " the form of government which divides
us least." At a meeting of thirty opponents of the Govern-

ment, of every shade of opinion, before the 1863 elections, Thiers expounded his political creed: he was for " the necessary liberties," the need, not for absolute individual freedom, but for the liberties necessary to the moral existence and development of man. No creed could have better fitted him for the Presidency of the Third Republic; and Thiers well knew this nearly a decade before he attained that position.

At seventy, Thiers was only at the beginning of his career. A brisk little man, with twinkling spectacles set on enormous head, a twinkling gait, a gesture almost effeminate, a voice shrill, harsh, unpleasing, which yet commanded the attention of the most hostile assembly. An eloquence fluent, sarcastic, persuasive, emotional; with a ready gift of tears. A dominating vanity, perhaps the effect of his small stature, which served him so well that he purposely exaggerated it into a set policy; for it left him impervious to ridicule and gave him the supreme gift of the professional politician—the faculty of so identifying his small person with the national cause that any opposition to him came to seem the most dastardly lack of patriotism.

As he sat in the Place Saint-Georges, Thiers, the Minister who had, thirty years ago, alienated the aristocrat by his parvenu pretensions, the industrialist by a blindness revealed by his ridicule of railways, the financier by his exaggeratedly nationalistic tariff policy, the workers by his hatred of their misery and demands, had at last achieved the disguise of the civilised gentleman typical of his time and place, the distinguished scholar, the eminent, but retired, statesman. Few realised that beneath this show there worked a formidable and incessant activity, chafing at enforced retirement from that leadership in political life which alone could satiate his vanity; ready to show itself in uncompromising, brutal, unscrupulous action whenever his almost feminine intuition should decide that the time was ripe for Adolphe Thiers once more to determine the course of French political history.

It is curious to note that, while Thiers's name is ubiquitous in French nineteenth-century history, no name is less
dominating. His most passionate apologists have been able
to confer upon him no legend. Even his street in Paris
(for they could hardly deny that honour to the first President
of the Third Republic) is a little alley off the magnificent
Avenue of Victor-Hugo. But in the wealthy suburbs, in
Saint-Germain and Versailles, Thiers has his boulevards
and his statues.

Thiers worked in close contact with the older members
of the Republican parliamentary Opposition. They were
a survival rather than a revival of the National Assembly
of 1849—Republicans, but in favour of a very mildly
liberal Republic, which should do nothing to change the
economic and social structure. Granted some liberty in
1863, more in 1869, when Rochefort also entered the
Chamber, they remained in platonic, if sincere, opposition
to the Empire, because it seemed to them rather obviously
undemocratic. Their former leader, Emile Ollivier, was so
far misled by the " crowning of the edifice " that he
accepted the Premiership in 1869, hoping to influence the
Emperor towards still greater latitude.

Lawyers, doctors, professors, detesting tyranny but detesting the class struggle still more, strongly attached to democracy and universal suffrage, ignorant or contemptuous of the
rising workers' movement, the rest remained in mild opposition under Thiers and " the three Jules," Simon, Favre and
Grévy. They had been able to formulate no more definite
programme than one of mere opposition to the autocracy;
and, as their numbers grew, the habit of parliamentarism,
the placid opportunism of political life weakened or diverted
what little constructive ability they had possessed.

Upon this solution at least those who used the Empire
could count: the official leaders of the Opposition would
slide into the easy-chairs of Republican Ministries without
prejudice to the social order.

" The Republic was never so splendid as it was under
the Empire."

II

" This is the way the world ends,
Not with a bang but a whimper."

T. S. ELIOT

The tempo of industrial expansion slowed. The hammers faltered and were silent on Haussmann's palaces. The forces which the Second Empire had released, which had made possible its long survival, had lost their initial impetus and were already being thrust back by the new forces implicit in their forward drive. The Second Empire was rotting within; and even those closest to the Emperor openly wondered how long it all could last.

The autocracy must be rigid or break: it could not now bend. It was the height of political unwisdom, as it was the deepest of dialectic necessities, to recall, after eighteen years, the demagogic promises which had carried the bankrupt prince to the presidency and the throne.

Significantly, in 1868, Ténot's books on the *Coup d'État* became enormously popular, the censorship dared not move and all that the Government could do was to hire a renegade Republican hack to split the Opposition by a pamphlet exposing the massacres of June 1848. Vermorel, for the Extreme Left, counter-attacked in his *Men of 1848 and the Opposition*, Tridon with his *Gironde and Girondins*. As Marx wrote gleefully, " the witches' cauldron of history " was bubbling.

In attacking the Liberals the Empire was in reality attacking its best friends. They alone stood in the way of an attempt at social revolution. As the decomposition of the Empire became more manifest the divergences between the Opposition factions grew wider. The political breakdown brought to a climax the struggle between those who wanted *Marianne*, the Democratic Republic, and those who were hoping for *La Sociale*, the Socialist Revolution.

It was now too late to exploit this cleavage. The political police merely covered itself with ridicule when it dressed its men in workmen's overalls and set them to riot, that the

Emperor might once more appear in the role of the Man of Order. It was necessary to exaggerate and even encourage the Left in order to retain provincial support against the mythical " hooligan Red Paris."

For the autocracy, seeking some means to unite the country behind it once more, there could be only one way out: an appeal to patriotism in defence of France. *La Gloire* of foreign conquest if possible; but, at all events, the common determination to defend the " sacred soil." The autocracy had been installed upon a few simple metaphorical platitudes: it was just possible that it might yet be saved by them.

By the beginning of 1869 war was inevitable, even if Bismarck had not been seeking this opportunity for his own purposes. The Franco-Prussian War was not the " clash of hereditary enemies," but a gigantic diversion undertaken to unite the German States and the French factions.

In the atmosphere of approaching calamity events which might have passed off with a couple of days' excitement began to assume a disproportionate significance. The executive, as represented by the police, had passed to the offensive, violating its own legality. Consequently, any failure in its true function, that of assuring the life and property of every citizen, aroused fiercer resentment.

The mass murders of the maniac Troppmann, arrested at last by what was clearly a series of flukes, demonstrated at the end of 1869 the inefficiency of the expensive and hated police. Vast crowds displayed a morbid interest in the ghastly hole in the Pantin plain where Troppmann had buried a whole hacked family. There was a sensation of blood and hatred in the air, and at Troppmann's trial, on December 28, the public almost applauded his Alsatian rants against *le pon Tieu*. All that winter, cartoons depicting " the Imperial Troppmann " were sold openly on the Paris streets.

When Troppmann was guillotined, on January 8, Rochefort's *Marseillaise* concluded a sensational (but astonishingly inaccurate) account of the execution with the query: " And the other ? "

The " other " was the Emperor's own cousin, Prince Pierre Napoléon Bonaparte, adventurer, duellist, poet, Carbonaro conspirator—the " Wild Boar of Corsica " they called him. He had shot and killed, under peculiarly dastardly circumstances, a popular young Left-wing journalist, Victor Noir.

This scandal in the Emperor's own family caused an explosion of anger not unlike that which followed the Choiseul-Praslins murder in 1847. Raspail, the aged and universally respected scholar and democrat, rose from his sick-bed to tell an applauding Chamber that not even Troppmann's crimes had produced so deep an impression of horror. Rochefort expressed the public disgust: " *Il faut en finir !* "—" This can't go on ! "

" This Pierre Bonaparte scandal," Engels wrote to Marx a week later, " is a splendid initiation to the new era in Paris. Louis is decidedly done for. For the bourgeois a most unpleasant awakening from their illusions, as if the whole foundation of corruption and vileness, built up so slowly and carefully for eighteen years, were about to collapse."

The previous year, the Opposition had demonstrated at the tomb of Baudin, a deputy killed during the *Coup d'État*, and Gambetta had made his reputation by a bold attack upon the Government. But the funeral of Victor Noir, on January 11, completely eclipsed that demonstration. Two hundred thousand Parisians, united in hatred of the autocracy, met in the driving rain, and only the persuasions of Rochefort and Delescluze prevented them from marching upon Paris, despite the certainty of massacre. A parade of 2,000 armed Blanquists, led by Rigault, showed the approving public that it had resolute fighters in the vanguard. The Opposition became aware, with some surprise, of its own strength.

The same evening, the Federation of Syndicated Workers' Chambers, the beginnings of a trades-union council, was founded at Number 6, Place de la Corderie, soon to become famous as the headquarters of the Paris branch of the International.

After the funeral, Paris would no longer be quiet. Sporadic rioting continued into February. Pyat, ever ready with the right word, sent a " Toast to a Bullet " to a Republican dinner at Saint-Mandé on January 21. He hinted very plainly that it would be no bad thing if the fellow of the bullet fired by Pierre Bonaparte should strike his Imperial cousin. Pyat, of course, had been hiding romantically in a coal-barge on the Seine, and was by now well away to London.

The Opposition, however, split again. Flourens was furious with Rochefort for his sensible refusal to lead the crowd on Paris ; and Rochefort temporarily lost the leadership of the militant Republicans. In revenge, he quite unjustly accused Vermorel of being a police spy, than which there could be no fouler suspicion under the Second Empire. Thus began a bitter wrangle which tortured Vermorel until his death on the barricades of the Commune.

The Government had not the sense to exploit these dissensions. Piétri did, in fact, precisely the opposite by attacking Rochefort and making a martyr of him. Police arrested him at a seditious meeting, ostensibly a lecture on Voltaire, at the *Marseillaise* hall in La Villette, right in the heart of his own country.

Flourens, ever generous in the cause of freedom, rallied to him at once. Drawing an immense sword, and brandishing a revolver, " Citizens," cried he, " I call upon you to take up arms and march against the Empire in defence of the laws and universal suffrage, violated in the person of our Deputy, Rochefort ! "

That was a wild night. Flourens ended, fitly enough, in the " props " room of the Belleville Theatre, frantically searching for the dummy rifles used by the supers. At the point of his great pistol he held a captured constable, who frequently reminded the hero that he did not wish to die, as he had a wife and five ailing children. When Flourens emerged, his army had dwindled to one small urchin.

On February 8 and 9, the first barricades for many years were raised, in the Temple quarter. On the 11th, a workman, Mégy, shot a policeman who entered his room before the legal hour to arrest him for his share in the riots. His lawyer, the Blanquist Protot, was arrested, equally irregularly, a few days later.

Pierre Bonaparte's trial began at Tours on March 21. Witnesses and members of the public openly insulted the Government and the Court. Pierre was sentenced to 25,000 francs compensation. Obviously a Bonaparte could not yet be tried as an ordinary criminal.

Rochefort's arrest had been deliberate provocation. The next step, naturally, was to unmask a " plot." On April 10, therefore, it was duly announced that a vast conspiracy against the Emperor's life had been discovered: 450 Left leaders were arrested, but 379 had to be released for lack of evidence. Still, 70 conspirators was not a bad haul. The " plot," however, was a mere fantasy of Piétri and Flourens.

Flourens had retired to London to meditate new adventures. He thought, erroneously, that Bradlaugh might help him. In London he met one Beaury, in whom he believed he saw " the heart of an Agesilas Milano," the Neapolitan tyrannicide.

Beaury's plan, as Flourens describes it, was quite simply " to seize the Tuileries one night by means of intelligences within the Palace, and, laying low the Bonapartists, should they attempt to resist, by the aid of the formidable engines of destruction placed by Science at the service of oppressed Peoples, to paralyse by sheer force of audacity all the supporters of Tyranny, however terribly armed; and, with a few men of enormous energy, to liberate from its chains a great and impatient People; such was the plan which could not fail to seduce any brave and ingenuous spirit."

Beaury, whom Flourens had " convinced of the grandeur, the sacredness and the necessity of the deed," spent the money for the " formidable engines " on his mistress, who promptly sold him to the police.

The object of this police provocation was to provide fresh
" Red menace " propaganda for the provinces. Napoléon
had decided to put his popularity once more to the test of
one of those plebiscites the secret of which he so well knew.
France was asked to approve the new Liberal Empire, the
" crowned edifice."

No one in Paris was deceived; but the provinces were
carefully fed by the prefects with appropriate information.
Ollivier, the Liberal Premier, warned the Emperor that it
would be advisable to postpone the trial " in order that an
involuntary coincidence may not resemble an election
manœuvre." But the scare alone, as exploited by the
Governmental Press, did its work.

The plebiscite of May 8 was once more an overwhelming
victory for the Emperor. The Opposition had not been able
to agree whether to boycott or vote against it. The Liberal
Empire received 7,358,786 votes against 1,571,939 and
1,894,681 abstentions.

The vote was little less favourable than those of 1851 and
1852. Even in Republican Paris, the Opposition received
a bare majority of 45,000 in an electorate of 323,000.
Significant, however, was that nearly 15 per cent of the
armed forces voted against the Emperor, over 50,000 anti-
Bonapartists. There were negative votes even in the Imperial Guard itself.

Granted a comparatively free hand once more, the Empire
was able to give fresh compensations to the interests upon
whose tolerance its existence depended. With the slowing
down of industrial expansion, the employers had already
started to attack the workers' standard of living. Gradually
organised by factory conditions and by the unions permitted
by the Cæsarian Emperor, the workers struck. The most
important and typical of these strikes was that at the Le
Creusot steel-works (not yet armaments) on January 17,
1870.

Led by a handsome and eloquent southerner, Alphonse
Assi, and supported by the International's propaganda
contributed by Malon to Rochefort's *Marseillaise*, the strike

won considerable sympathy for the workers and the International.

For the first time, too, the real meaning of the Emperor's pseudo-Liberal labour policy was shown. It became obvious that while the workers were honestly fighting for reasonable improvements in their living standards, the owners, supported by the Government, were callously exploiting the struggle for their own purposes.

Creusot's owner, Schneider, owed his favoured position to the fact that he had backed Napoléon in 1851. He had displaced Rouher, another friend of the Emperor, in the presidency of the Corps Législatif. Rouher was closely connected with a Gregory Ganesco, " the foul Rumanian," as Marx calls him. Ganesco's paper, *Le Parlement*, suddenly came out strongly in favour of the strike, although hitherto it had been anything but sympathetic to the workers. Finally, Government troops broke the strike and Schneider kept his post.

The prestige of the International, the new tendencies in the Paris branch of this once-harmless Proudhonist organisation, and its recovery since the 1868 prosecution, combined to induce the Government to strike at it again. Flourens's " plot " had been a mere political manœuvre: the International prosecution was of definite social importance. On June 22, thirty-eight members were put on trial for founding a dangerous secret society.

Thanks to a fighting defence, probably composed by Rochefort, read by Chalain, the prosecution completely failed to win public approval.

Chalain, speaking for the whole society, told the Court quite plainly that " the proletariat was sick of resignation, victimisation by parasites, condemnation to hopeless toil, the sight of their claims for freedom fobbed off with petty concessions." What was the answer to their complaints ? Always force ! " We suffer from crises, unemployment, wage-cuts, speed-up: you meet us with the economists' *laissez-faire*. If we demand better conditions, you meet us with force. When you do not employ force, you insult us, call us looters, levellers. Looters, levellers, we who cannot read yet pay taxes for the Higher Education ! Who are taxed for land-expropriations and are flung out by stock-jobbing and trusting into foul hovels without air, space, light, on the edges of your great cities ! Who pay taxes of our own blood to defend against ourselves the property of those who enjoy the odious privilege of living without labouring !

" What can you gain by preventing the workers from studying the reforms which would regenerate society ? You will simply intensify the crisis, make the remedy more radical by postponing it. What the people want is the right to govern themselves without intermediaries, above all, without dictatorial ' saviours '; the abolition of usury, monopolies, the bureaucratic wages-system and the standing army; universal education : the reforms which will introduce equality of conditions. . . .

" We shall remain faithful to the International," he ended, " and you will see by the results of your sentence that it contains an Idea and a Force which cannot be vanquished by the slanders and persecutions of Reaction, because its foundations are Truth and Justice. It is invincible, because, from this day on, it is the expression of the ultimate form of human society : the Social and Universal Republic ! "

The confusion of doctrine inside the International was brought out in cross-examination. Héligon declared that no member of the association was more heartily opposed to Communist Collectivism than he was, while Malon stated that he was proud of his Communist opinions, but that the Association did not entirely share them. The Communist Combault disagreed with the Mutualist Murat. But all were emphatic about their unswerving devotion to the International and to their mutual friendship. The International stood above personal opinions. Its internationalism was symbolised by the Hungarian Jew, Franckel, delegate of the German section in Paris, who replied to the sentence of the French Court with " *Eppur si muove !* " in Italian with a strong German accent.

Although heavy sentences were inflicted, the popular success of Chalain's defence showed that the plebiscite had been in reality a failure. Nothing was left to Napoléon but the gambler's last throw. On July 15, France declared war upon Prussia.

The workers had been warned. On the 12th, the Paris branch had declared that " war for dominion or dynasty can be regarded by the workers as simply a criminal absurdity."

Many other branches published similar manifestos. The Berlin branch " adhered heart and soul." A huge demonstration at Brunswick proclaimed their solidarity with the French workers. Delegates representing 50,000 Saxon workers declared at Chemnitz: " We are happy to clasp the hand of brotherhood held out to us by the workers of France. Faithful to the slogan, ' Workers of all the world, unite!' we will never forget that the workers of *every* land are our *friends*, the despots of *every* land our *foes* ! "

But they did forget. " It is with deep grief and pain that we see ourselves compelled to suffer a defensive war as an inevitable evil."

Marx, however, was alive to the immense importance of the manifestos. Addressing the London branch on July 27, he said: " The mere fact that, at a moment when official France and Germany are plunging headlong into fratricidal war, the workers of France and Germany are exchanging messages of peace and goodwill, this great fact, unparalleled in past history, opens up the perspective of a better future. It proves that in the face of the old society with its economic misery and political furies a new society is arising, the law of whose international relations will be *Peace* because its national legislator will be everywhere the same, *Labour* ! "

Bourgeois French and German opinion was no less hostile to the war. The French Republican deputies unanimously refused to vote the war-credits : and some even openly suggested in the Chamber that it was nothing more than a Stock Exchange racket.

Even Thiers, lifelong Jingo, opposed the war, for reasons which won applause from the Government's own supporters. France, he declared, should have awaited the " legitimate opportunity," for then all Europe would have approved. " There is one point I have noted about our times," he lectured, " and that is that it is no longer possible to declare war arbitrarily. The nations, looking on at a war like seconds at a duel, must support you with their esteem and good wishes. It is absolutely essential to have the world's opinion on one's side; and it would have been proper to have waited until Prussia, by making fresh unjustifiable demands, had given us as allies the threatened nations and the indignant world."

Piétri thought it necessary to disguise his men as patriotic workmen and parade the Boulevards shouting " To Berlin ! " But when they entered the working-class districts, the real workers set on them and dispersed them.

Nevertheless, the fatal war-fever swiftly gripped Paris. A crowd broke Thiers's windows. The " Marseillaise," released by the censorship after eighteen years, was sung with frantic enthusiasm. Ceremonial swords were issued to both armies for the triumphal entry into the respective capitals.

Observers, however, noticed that the spirit of the departing troops was not good. At certain places, they seemed almost hysterical. There were sporadic mutinies at the stations.

Thiers was right. The French army was not prepared. The officers were corrupt with years of service at Court. Many were worse than corrupted by guerilla experience in Mexico and Algeria. " The French who go to Algiers," de Circourt told Nassau Senior, " are denationalised. The soldiers turn Bedouins, the officers Arabs. None of them preserve the least respect for law or the least sympathy for civil government." Havelock Ellis has noted the prevalence of perversion in the Algerian army.

Unlike the Prussian General Staff, the French command had learned nothing of the new strategy based upon the modernisation of armaments and transport. Sadowa had taught them precisely nothing. The Chassepot rifle, which had " done wonders " at Mentana ten years before, lost half its effect by ignorance of its tactical uses. The *mitrailleuse*, adopted in the strictest secrecy in 1864 and endowed with a fabulous reputation, was soon hopelessly outclassed by the mobile Prussian field artillery.

The usual army contracting frauds were carried out on a huge scale. Profiteering was scandalous. Schneider made ten million francs in cash alone, besides modernising his factories, now definitely turned to arms production.

The French army was as hollow and corrupt as the Empire it served. The Emperor himself, attempting to revive the legend of the Little Corporal (and also conscious that he looked mean and top-heavy on foot), was so tortured by the stone that he could hardly sit a horse, much less transform incompetent half-hearts into irresistible heroes by the magic of his personality.

At first war, and the excitement of being at war, absorbed Paris's whole attention. The trial of Flourens's " plot," before the Supreme Court at Blois, on July 18, passed almost unnoticed. The scare had done its work and the trial was a farce. Stoolies like Beaury were given nominal sentences. Mégy was given twenty years' hard labour. Prominent militants were fairly severely treated. The Blanquists Cournet, Razoua and Ferré were acquitted for lack of evidence. Ferré distinguished himself by his threats to the Court.

There was small sympathy for revolutionaries in the midst of the war-fever. All efforts were bent upon beating the Prussian. But Paris knew nothing of how badly things were going out on the eastern frontier. Palikao, Minister of War, starved the city of news, on the principle that no news is good news and bad news is revolution. Consequently, Paris obtained its news from wild rumours.

On August 6, the false announcement of a great victory, later believed to have been spread by a group of Bourse speculators, filled Paris with delirious excitement. Next

morning, Palikao could not suppress the fact that Mac-
Mahon had been seriously checked at Reischoffen, and,
the following day, badly defeated at Forbach.

There was an immediate outcry. The Government
resigned on August 9, to be replaced by a new combination still determined to uphold the Empire. Thiers sacrificed
his scruples and joined the Cabinet. But the Ministerial
crisis confirmed the universal impression that the Empire
was finished. There were rumours current next day in
Bordeaux that the Emperor had already abdicated.

That the Second Empire could survive just a little
longer in the hope that it might yet win the war was shown
by the complete fiasco of a Blanquist attempt on August 14.
The conspirators made a sudden descent upon the fire-
station at La Villette, where some arms were stored. After
a scuffle, they marched right through the heart of Belleville, the revolutionary working-class quarter. They were
unmolested; but their cries of " Long live the Republic !
Death to the Prussians ! " met with no response whatever.
The police, of course, waited until the heavily armed
rioters had gone, then savagely attacked the crowd.

The attempt was significant. It showed that Paris had
not yet accepted the idea of the Revolutionary Republican
War of 1793. It also showed the complete absurdity of
Blanquist tactics. Blanqui calmly admitted that the rising
was " inopportune." It should, he wrote, have been made
the previous Sunday, the 7th, when Paris was still agitated
by the news from Reischoffen. " The only reply possible
is that the leader of the enterprise, surprised, passportless,
at Brussels, by the stunning news from Alsace, was compelled to cross the frontier on foot during the night of
August 11–12." The enterprise was, in all probability,
forced upon the Old One against his better judgment by
the heady Eudes and the generous Granger, who provided
the 300 revolvers and 400 daggers carried by the hundred
or so insurgents.

Blanqui, Eudes and Brideau, denounced by an amateur
stoolie, together with four others who had had little hand

in the affair, were sentenced to death, in absence. Their friends persuaded several eminent Liberals, including Michelet and George Sand, to intervene on the grounds that the Blanquists had acted in mistaken patriotism: which was quite true. The sentences were suspended.

In the last days of August, Paris knew that the Emperor and MacMahon, attempting to join Bazaine at Metz, had thrown themselves into Sédan. The news of the surrender filtered through to the silent Government on the evening of September 2.

On the afternoon of the 3rd, Palikao announced disaster to a packed, apprehensive House. It was beyond all forecast bad. The junction with Bazaine had failed; MacMahon's army had surrendered; the Marshal himself was wounded, perhaps dead.

Jules Favre, leader of the Opposition, rose, long, bearded, melancholy, to voice the one dominating question: " Where is the Emperor ? Is he in communication with his Ministers ? " " No ! " snapped Palikao.

Palikao both spoke the truth and lied. It was eighteen hours since he had received a telegram: " The army has been defeated and captured. I myself am a prisoner. Napoléon."

It was twenty minutes after one o'clock on the morning of September 4 when Palikao at last let Paris hear that the burden of eighteen years had been thrown off by a foreign enemy. While the city slept uneasily, or did not sleep, men were pasting on the walls the first proclamation of the new era :

" FRENCHMEN !

    " After three days of heroic struggles by Marshal MacMahon's army against 300,000 enemy, 40,000 of our men have been taken prisoner.
    " General Wimpffen, replacing Marshal MacMahon, who is seriously wounded, has signed a capitulation.
    " This cruel reverse cannot shake our courage.
    " Paris is to-day in a state of defence.

" The country's military forces are organising.

" In a few days, a new army will be beneath the walls of Paris, and another is forming on the banks of the Seine.

" Your patriotism, your union, your energy will save France.

" The Emperor has been taken prisoner in the struggle.

" The Government, in conjunction with the public authorities, is taking all the steps demanded by the gravity of the situation.

" THE COUNCIL OF MINISTERS."

The fall of an Empire in one line at the foot of a shifty poster !

Paris demanded more: the Fighting Republic, the Revolutionary War of 1793, the Great Commune.

# CHAPTER II

# THE GOVERNMENT OF NATIONAL DEFENCE

" Ce n'était pas la peine assurément
De changer de gouvernement."
*La Fille de Mme Angot*

ON AUGUST 27, Palikao had wired to MacMahon: " If you abandon Bazaine, we shall have revolution in Paris." This wire did much to hasten the catastrophe of Sédan.

All day on September 4, a crowd, bourgeois and workers mingled, pushed around the Corps Législatif, singing the " Marseillaise," waving the tricolour, shouting for the Republic: No barricades, no police, no bloodshed. A pacific, happy crowd.

At last they pushed into the Chamber itself. They simply did not know what to do. Régère, a popular club-orator, later a member of the Commune, clutched Thiers's arm: " We have made a revolution; you ought to know what to do with it, you who have upset a Government or two in your time ! " Jules Favre, Lamartine revived, diverted the crowd to the Hôtel de Ville and there proclaimed the Republic. Not a word had been heard of the social revolution. The sole martyr was a bricklayer who fell from a scaffolding outside the Corps Législatif.

A Provisional Government was formed by acclamation, with the title of Government of National Defence, to be ratified by elections as soon as possible. It was composed simply of the Liberal Deputies of 1869, lawyers, professors, publicists. Certainly no revolutionaries, except Rochefort, appropriately appointed President of the Barricades

Committee, an uncomfortable colleague, just released from prison with the other political prisoners. Jules Favre, Vice-President of the Council and Minister for Foreign Affairs, the real head of the new Government, made the best of an inclusion irresistibly demanded by the Left: "Anyway we'd rather have him inside the Government than outside it."

The new Government had simply slid into the vacant seats. The real power was reserved for notorious Royalists, or, if not open Royalists, reactionaries. President of the Council and Military Governor of Paris was Trochu, a Breton with a Jesuit education imposed upon an innate stupidity; Victor Hugo called him "*participe passée du verbe 'trop choir*' " —"past participle of the verb 'to fail too much' "; he had promised the Empress to die on the steps of the Tuileries in defence of the dynasty. The police went to another Breton, Kératry. The Ministries "for talk" were reserved for the Liberal lawyers. Jules Favre, Foreign Affairs, might have been taken for one of Daumier's legal caricatures: indiscreet, verbose and lachrymose. Jules Simon, Public Instruction, well-meaning, lukewarm Radical, with a pleasant prose in which he had related with some success the woes of a washerwoman. Ernest Picard, Finance, elegant *boulevardier* and *boursier*, ever hostile to the Emperor's demagogic gestures towards the workers. Jules Ferry, Mayor of Paris after the early resignation of the aged and scholarly Arago, an inconclusive person, seeing in the class-war the root of all evil, a compromiser with fits of energy deprecated by everyone. Dorian, Public Works, philanthropic Saint-Simonian ironmaster, a name always thrown as a sop to the workers, with whom he kept his popularity. Gambetta, Dantonesque and energetic, soon left for the provinces in his famous balloon to raise new armies with his whirlwind oratory and set up a small dictatorship of conscription at Tours.

Thiers refused to participate in a Government with no legal standing. But his personal position was incomparable. He had friends in the Government, notably Jules Favre, as well as among the provincial Conservatives. The Monarchists he had attached by his Orleanist past and his manners; the remaining Bonapartists approved his refusal to recognise the Government which had overthrown them; the Conservative Republicans were reassured by his refusal to sabotage the Republic, " the Government which divides us least," and by his declared hatred of Socialism. He had dared to voice disapproval of the war and had been justified by the event, yet had not refused his co-operation in the defence. He was the one man who stood so well with every party in France that he could command with the Powers the oblivion of his jingoism of thirty years before and guarantee the authority of his personal word.

The Government of National Defence was a poor thing from the start, the long-awaited revolution something of an anticlimax. The fever of war, reinforced by pressing danger, had distracted all attention. The Prussians were drawing ever closer, almost without resistance from the disorganised French armies. Defence was the first necessity. Paris, thought the Jacobins, would at last have the chance to show itself not unworthy of its great ancestor, the Revolutionary Commune of 1793. Relieved of the incubus of the Empire, Paris would be irresistible. " *They* won't dare come now that we've got *it* ! " a workman said to Ludovic Halévy.

With a fresh enthusiasm, all parties rallied to the defence of Paris, living symbol of the Republic. Blanqui, at last able to walk his native streets in safety, immediately started a paper, *La Patrie en Danger*, the old revolutionary slogan; and in the first number, over the signatures of a dozen of his followers, appeared a manifesto supporting a Government composed of men he had so long hated: " In the enemy's presence, no more parties, no more divisions. Co-operation with a Government that was betraying the nation was impossible. The Government created by the movement of September 4 represents republican thought and national defence. That is enough. All opposition, all contradiction must vanish to make way

for national security ! " The melancholy Favre struck a
Dantonesque attitude: " We will not yield one inch of our
territory, one stone of our fortresses ! "

In private they knew that this was mere rhetoric. " Resistance is an heroic madness," said Trochu, head of the
Government and Military Governor. Blanqui reminded his
readers that " Paris is no more impregnable than we were
invincible." But Paris was determined upon the heroic
madness, resistance à outrance, to the bitter end. On
September 20, the city was invested by the Prussian armies.

Now there began that terrible epic of Parisian bravery
and suffering, the Prussian Siege. For one hundred and
thirty-five days, five long months of the worst winter known
for years, Paris endured terrible things, gathering hatreds
and despairs that could find an outlet only in open revolt.

It was all the misery of an economic crisis concentrated
into half a year and set to the unceasing thunder of the
great guns: morbid inaction and frantic action, a long
nightmare with brief and violent awakenings.

" The stifling atmosphere of siege," Hanotaux sum-
marises, " the enthusiasm of the first days, the confidence in
the new men, the common resolution and the sacrifices for
which all were ready; every man to the walls, ' M. Victor
Hugo's képi symbolising the situation.' The Government's
proclamations, read at first with enthusiasm, then with
irony. The general and continuous demand for the mass
sortie. The leaders' hesitation, the Governor's famous
Plan, the increasing disappointments. The extremists'
violence, discord settling down over the besieged city, the
gradual decline of popular reputations.

" Then the tension, the hopes ever on the alert and ever
disappointed; the eyes turned skyward awaiting the arrival
of the carrier-pigeons, messengers of delivery or victory; the
microscopic letters read and reread by groups, saying so
little and always too much: Bazaine, Faidherbe, Chanzy,
Bourbaki. Acclamations one day, silence the next. The
night-roar of the first shells announcing incredible bombardment, the indignation, the sombre exultation, the

children running after shell-fragments in the streets. Paris flocking each Sunday to the quarters upon which the shells were raining, the evacuation of all the Left Bank, the bombardment of hospitals and public buildings, shells on Saint Sulpice, the Salpétrière, the Panthéon. Hunger and strange meats: cat, rat, the elephant from the Zoo. The price of food, black bread, long queues outside the butcher and baker; the fuel-shortage, the trees of the Bois and public squares felled, streets black at night. Epidemics, the growing mortality, ten thousand men laid low, the old and the young struck down first—and how many there were that dragged out a long agony in the midst of their families!—the fury and the despair of feeling that one was doing nothing, that perhaps one could do nothing.

" The impotent convulsions of the last agony, Champigny, Buzenval; imprudent slogans: ' Dead or victorious,' ' The Governor of Paris will not surrender.' And the final rancour of the surrender, with the vague feeling that so many efforts and so many sacrifices had been in vain."

In the midst of this " obsidional fever," as contemporary observers call it, the spirit of the Parisians was splendid. Provincial prefects were unstinting in their astonished praise: " From one day to the next, these Parisians, so gay, so carefree, so facile in the commerce of life, have become Spartans, grave, sober, ready to look death in the face. Without constraint and without effort they have entered into the epic. . . . Paris will not succumb; but if in spite of her heroism she is reduced to burying herself beneath her own ruins . . . it will be the task of France to avenge her."

Almost the whole of the able-bodied male population of Paris was enrolled in the National Guard by a proclamation of the Empress-Regent on August 12. This citizen-militia, created by Lafayette on the morrow of the taking of the Bastille, had played a great part as a revolutionary body-guard, defending, as Robespierre put it, " the citadel of the Revolution and the pure and upright citizens who conduct the revolutionary chariot." It had been democratic under the Restoration, had been suppressed and revived with a more bourgeois composition, had taken part in the June Days, the bourgeois battalions on the side of " order," the workers beside the insurgents. Napoléon III had once more reorganised it on a bourgeois basis and had allowed it to decay into ridicule and neglect. Now, in the hour of need, it was revived once more; a dangerous proceeding for the Empire which should have remembered the prophetic words of Lafayette when he presented to the Assembly their revolutionary tricolour cockade: " I bring you, gentlemen, a cockade which will go round the world and an institution at once civic and military which will change the tactical system of Europe and reduce absolute Governments to the alternative of defeat if they do not imitate it or overthrow if they dare to do so." The Empress's reorganisation, based on the laws of 1851, provided that existing battalions should remain and that officers should be chosen from among ex-soldiers; a credit of 50,000,000 francs was opened to cover arms and pay.

After the fall of the Empire, the National Guard immediately set about reconstructing itself upon more democratic lines. It had been organised by districts, the battalions of each district forming a " Legion "; the Legion Commanders were under the orders of a Commander-in-Chief appointed by the Minister for the Interior and working in close connection with Military Headquarters in the Place Vendôme and with the armed Gendarmerie at the Police Prefecture.

The workers' battalions suspected that this arrangement had been made to use them as a subsidiary police. The battalions, therefore, elected four delegates each to form Vigilance Committees in each district and meet to discuss questions of common interest. Thus was constituted a central body known as the Central Committee of the Twenty Arrondissements (districts).

Inevitably, this Committee took an interest in politics, for the Vigilance Committees acted as much as overseers of civic virtue as of military capacity. It declared its pro-

gramme on September 14. Its aim was to " take measures
for the security of the country as well as for the definitive
foundation of a truly republican regime by the permanent
co-operation of individual initiative and popular solidarity." It presented a programme of measures, vainly submitted to the Government: suppression of the police and
magistracy and their replacement by elected municipal
authorities chosen by each district and by the National
Guard; the expropriation of all necessary food-stuffs
against bonds repayable after the war; the election of
committees " in every street or at least in every quarter "
to see that this measure was carried out; the assurance to
every citizen and his family the lodging indispensable to
his needs; immediate and more efficient measures for the
defence of Paris; the *levée en masse*, universal conscription.
Of the forty-seven signatories fifteen were later members of
the Commune.

This civic militia was enthusiastic rather than efficient;
but the inefficiency was not entirely its own fault. The
wretched Government was well aware that the workers
were suspicious, if not actively hostile, and was naturally
unwilling to train and arm a force which might at any
moment use that training and those arms against itself.
It was a vicious circle: the more the proletarian battalions
were neglected, the more they felt themselves slighted and
the more hostile to the authorities they grew.

At the same time, the National Guard was loaded with
absurd eulogies: " Be terrible, O patriots," cried Victor
Hugo from beneath his own *képi*, " stay only when you
pass by some simple hut to imprint a kiss upon the brow of
a little sleeping child ! " Such lapses were not taken very
seriously by the bearded, pipe-smoking militia, whose
bravery was not denied even by their most sceptical
superiors once they were given an opportunity to prove it.
But they were not well fitted for action in the open country;
behind a barricade and in defence of their own quarter, the
National Guards could fight with splendid discipline; but,
since they were organised on the local basis of districts, they

were unwilling to leave their homes save for some desperate and glorious exploit.

Every Parisian was, at first at any rate, anxious to serve in the National Guard. Soon, they were more or less compelled to do so. With the siege, almost all forms of employment had ceased, increasing the unemployment which had already become common among the thousands of workers who had migrated to Paris before the war. Thirty sous (about 1s. 3d.) a day was allowed to every man in possession of a gun, and this provided a form of unemployment dole. The Parisian unemployed had been increased by the 200,000 inhabitants of the suburbs brought into Paris at the beginning of the siege. When the Provisional Government authorised the creation of 60 new battalions on September 6, 194 answered the call, raising the numbers from about 90,000 to something over 300,000. That the thirty sous was not then the attraction, however, is shown by the fact that this pay was not decreed until September 12.

The military proper was composed of three distinct bodies: the regular troops of the line, the Mobiles, young bourgeois reservists, and the famous Francs-Tireurs, irregular volunteers raised by private individuals, of which Garibaldi's troop in the Vosges was perhaps the most famous. To the regulars, war was a profession, discipline hierarchic, politics indifferent; to the Mobiles, a patriotic duty executed with individual bravery and customary discipline; to the Francs-Tireurs, an adventure: by all three, the National Guard were despised and envied; despised as civilians, *pékins*, envied for their comparatively warm and comfortable homes, warmer at least than the pitiful huts on the fortifications to which the army was condemned. The National Guard, only too anxious to see some real fighting, was furious at this contempt; and all through the siege there was hostility between the regular and the civilian forces.

This distrust of the proletarian Paris National Guard extended to the nearer provinces. The provincial troops and

Mobiles were on the whole loyal to the Empire and to the Provisional Government. There was, however, some disaffection at the garrison town of Châlons at the beginning of August. On August 5, the prefect of the Doubs Department sent an urgent and confidential telegram from Besançon : " News is spreading here that three battalions of the Paris National Guard are being sent to Besançon. The respectable population is appalled, and the good officers of our Garde Mobile of the Doubs are *all* ready to resign for fear that contact with the Parisian battalions, whose acts of indiscipline at Châlons camp are already known to all, may spoil our good rural Mobiles who ask no more than to be permitted to behave well and to submit without murmuring to military life." After Reischoffen, friction arose at Châlons between the haggard and retreating soldiers and the frivolous reservists ; and when the Emperor arrived from Verdun, on the 18th, strictly incognito in a third-class carriage, he was greeted by dead silence. But there was practically no political movement among the troops outside Paris, except Bazaine's involved intrigues at Metz and the conspiracy of his officers, Cremer, Rossel and others, to defeat his treachery or his dictatorial ambitions.

Owing to their fear of the workers' battalions, numerically far superior to the rest, the Government neglected their armament ; and this was one of the National Guard's bitterest complaints. This scarcity of arms did much to attach the Guard to what rifles they had, an attachment very important in its future consequences.

There were six different sorts of rifles in use, and of course the ammunition was always getting mixed up : Sniders, Remingtons, Springfields and Spencers, in very small quantities, arms of special quality ; Chassepots, the regular army rifle, not many ; and old muzzle-loading muskets, somewhat improved by rifling the barrel. There were also the most fantastic and suicidal antiques : sporting-guns, ancient carbines, even the prehistoric ramrod-loading musketoon ; anything that would fire was given to the

National Guard, and those who remained in Paris exchanged their Chassepots for the inferior weapons of those who were going to the walls. Later in the siege, any signal bravery was rewarded with a Chassepot.

The Government was perpetually bombarded with requests for decent arms. One battalion sent in a petition signed by 200 of its members: the muskets delivered to them had already been declared useless by the State and had been sold as such; the battalion did not expect Chassepots or breech-loaders, but did ask for either old Chasseur carbines or even ramrod-loaders if they were rifled. " In the present circumstances, the muskets delivered to us (1822 model) would certainly be far more dangerous to ourselves than to the enemy." Curiously enough, their battalion commander was so indignant at this reasonable complaint that he replied that " the renewal of such a demand would provoke his resignation." Flourens tells passionately, in a private letter, how indignant he was at seeing " beautiful Chassepots " in the hands of dolts when they might have been so much better given to his Belleville boys. The officer reporting the musketry practice of the 204th Battalion on October 21 signals three accidents due to the recoil of suicidal weapons; one man was likely to lose an eye; and there would have been more casualties had not the 208th turned up six hours too late to take part in the exercises. On October 14, the 99th, 732 men from Vincennes, were armed only with flintlocks. The Remingtons stored at the main arsenal, the Ecole Militaire, had given out by October 5.

There was an impression after the fall of the Commune that the insurrectionary battalions had been better armed than the others, and some mayors were accused of yielding to pressure in the distribution to curry favour with the mob. There seems to be some justice in this accusation: the workers' battalions were more pressing because they were more eager to march against the enemy. For the same reason, some of the volunteer Franc-Tireur corps were well armed because they were equipped by hot militants at

their own expense. Thus Flourens had a body of 60 men of
Belleville armed with Chassepots out of his own pocket,
ready to follow him through hell against the Prussians or
the Hôtel de Ville. His friend Tibaldi, an ex-Garibaldian,
had a corps of 150 men, 30 of whom he had recruited in
London despite the ban of the Government which feared
international complications.

Besides the regular siege artillery, mostly naval guns
brought in by the sailors who played so large a part in the
defence of Paris, there were a great many new guns founded
by public subscription; and the workers, having paid for
them by scraping together their last halfpence, were
passionately attached to them. Some superficial observers
defined it simply as a " mania for guns "; but it was far
more: both honour and purse were involved. The
majority of these subscribed guns were collected in the
great battery on the hill of Montmartre and carefully
watched over by the Montmartre Vigilance Committee of
the Central Committee of the Twenty Districts, sitting in
Scribe's old villa, Number 6 rue des Rosiers.

Paris had spontaneously reorganised itself into a miniature federal body. Distrusting the Central Provisional
Government, the districts tended increasingly to take
matters into their own hands. Committees abounded; some
to attend to local matters, more to watch the other local
committees and see that they did not compromise the
revolution. All the leaders of the revolutionary opposition
under the Empire found administrative posts on them or
at the head of battalions of the National Guard, since this
body was organised on a local scheme. Consequently, they
acquired some administrative experience which was to be
extremely useful in organising the Commune. The germ of
the federal system of the Commune, indeed, grew up
spontaneously during the siege.

The *mairies* (borough-halls) became important centres for
the distribution of supplies, regulation of lodgings, pay of
the National Guard, even the local police. The workers' districts naturally demanded a more democratic organisation.

A meeting of National Guards' delegates on October 3 formulated a typical programme: (1) autonomous constitution of the *arrondissement* group; (2) election by universal suffrage of a municipal council by *arrondissement*; (3) mayor and assistants to be taken from this council and chosen by it; (4) a general council composed of two to four members elected from each municipal council to administrate the City of Paris as a whole. This was the elective principle, at one remove, of the Commune. Naturally, the Ministry of the Interior would not permit such an encroachment upon its powers of control.

The mayors who came to office after September 4 were mostly Liberal-Democratic bourgeois: most of the local government of Paris had always been opposed to the Empire in its later days. The wealthier districts were naturally represented by Conservatives, Republicans hostile to the social revolution.

After the elections of November 5, the most important of these reactionaries were Tirard of the IInd district, Vautrain of the IVth, Vacherot of the Vth and Desmarest of the IXth, with the Assistants Méline of the Ist and Chéron of the IInd. Greppo, Mottu, Dubail, Henri Martin and Clémenceau, of the IVth, XIth, XIIth, XVIth and XVIIIth respectively, were less reactionary, rather Radicals of the school of Ranc.

The revolutionaries had Delescluze, for a time, as Mayor of the XIXth, and Ranvier, a notable militant, of the XXth (Belleville). They were fairly well represented among the mayoral Assistants with Léo Melliet in the XIIIth, Jaclard in the XVIIIth, Miot in the XIXth, Millière and Flourens in the XXth; Tolain in the XIth and Héligon in the XIVth were non-revolutionary members of the International; Malon in the XVIIth, Dereure in the XVIIIth, Oudet in the XIXth and Lefrançais in the XXth were active Socialists. In general, the residential west of Paris was solidly reactionary or " reasonable," the commercial centre Radical but not revolutionary, the proletarian east solidly insurrectionary or Socialist.

The revolutionary Assistants kept up a close communication with their comrades on the local committees, on Opposition newspapers and in the National Guard. They favoured the creation of vigilance committees, civil as well as military. Raoul Rigault, for example, who had for a short time after September 4 managed to get a post at the Police Prefecture under Kératry (who from force of habit he always insisted upon calling Piétri), and had spent his time copying the agents' dossiers for future use, organised a counter-police in Montmartre. One of his reports has survived, well showing the close supervision to which the authorities were subjected during the siege: " The delegates are all at their posts and are acquitting themselves of their task with intelligence. On the whole, they are seconded by the goodwill of the population generally. Nevertheless, the reaction continues its intrigues. The rumour has been spread at the doors of certain bakeries that in other districts the ration has been raised to 400 grammes and that if it is kept at 300 in yours, it is your municipality's ault. This fact was remarked notably at the door of Citizen Nersey, 98 rue des Martyrs, just as I was leaving the house. Two individuals of suspicious appearance whom I easily recognised as former police-spies were saying: ' You elected Clémenceau and you only get 300 grammes; that's fine.' A good citizen immediately replied: ' Cresson (then Chief of Police) has taught you your lesson well but he forgot to change your faces, go and recite his composition elsewhere.' The people threw the blackguards out and they ran away as fast as their legs could carry them. The scoundrels probably belonged to the Lodgings-Inspection Service [Service des garnis]."

Beside the local committees, there increased in power another popular institution, the political club. These clubs, addressed by revolutionary favourites such as Rochefort and Flourens or, more often, by popular orators, had become common in the last years of the Empire, fulfilling for the workers the functions of the political café among the students and journalists. During the siege, when most of the theatres and regular entertainments were closed for lack of fuel and lighting, when the long, idle winter evenings brought the need for some other outlet for excitement, the clubs increased in number, in influence and in the extravagance of their discussions. Some were undoubtedly useful, debating the measures to be taken by the local committees; such was that run by Louise Michel, the anarchist schoolmistress, a group of women revolutionaries seriously engaged in drawing up a concrete programme.

More common were the wild harangues of such people as Jules Allix, later member of the Commune, a rather typical figure of the extremer clubs. Allix was quite harmless if a little mad. In 1850, he had invented a remarkable system of telegraphy by means of " sympathetic snails "; in 1853, accused of seditious rioting, he vehemently counter-accused the Government of preparing a sinister plot to rase the Butte Montmartre; Belleville was so much impressed by his extraordinary eloquence that it elected him Republican Deputy. During the siege, he was chosen as honorary member of the feminine club at the Gymnase Triat—the tall scraggy figure with the venerable beard and wild glare of the crazy prophet was just the sort of solitary male a women's club *would* elect !—and to them he exposed his brilliant plan for saving Paris from the Prussians; the " Paraviol." It would be most appropriate, he remarked, to use prussic acid in killing Prussians, and this might be done by means of little india-rubber thimbles tipped with a small pointed tube full of the acid; if an amorous Prussian should venture too near a fair Parisienne, she would merely have to stretch out a finger and prick him; he would drop dead on the spot ! " No matter how many of the enemy assail her," cried Allix enthusiastically, " she will simply prick them one after another and we shall see her standing, still pure and holy, in a circle of corpses ! " " At these words," a witness reports, " many of the women in the audience were moved to tears, but the men laughed heartily." But the Paris crowd loves a *blague*, which does not in any way contradict their fundamental seriousness especially in the matter of revolution. People like Allix were useful as a personification of the jesting with which a Parisian worker fights and dies for a serious cause.

The Government of National Defence was desperately placed. It had no legal standing even in Paris. Gambetta had gone off to Tours to lead a dictatorial triumvirate charged with raising new armies. In Paris the task was equally impossible: to stave off the social revolution by prolonging a defence which had no hope of succeeding, for the Parisian people which had set up the Government to defend them would hear no talk of surrender until hunger had made further resistance impossible. Chance of military success there was none. Army after army was raised in the provinces, fought splendidly, was annihilated.

The provinces were at first so enthusiastic for Napoléon's war that incidents like that of Hautfaye were not uncommon. In August, the peasants of Hautfaye, in the Dordogne, had burnt a young man alive because it was said that he had cried " Down with the Emperor ! " One peasant had lit his cigar from the flames. The clergy, too, had been exemplary; only in the Loire-Inférieure Department were they reported to have preached against the war. But those who had disliked Paris and the Republic even more than the Emperor in peace-time soon lost enthusiasm for a war both republican and disastrous. The harvest was ruined, their land was invaded. Prussian requisitions were a burden. They were soon ready for peace, and they blamed Paris for prolonging a hopeless and unnecessary war. From them the provisional and only half-recognised Government of National Defence could expect little support.

There was even less to be hoped from foreign mediation. Thiers had been sent off on a diplomatic mission to the Courts of St. James's, Vienna, St. Petersburg and Florence, on September 12, " at the pressing instances of Jules Favre and the whole Government, including M. de Rochefort." An Engineers officer blew up the bridge at Creil after his train had passed, cutting off Paris from the world.

Thiers's mission was a complete failure. Gladstone and Granville would not risk more than pious good wishes; Austria, beaten at Sadowa, was beginning to find a racial consolation in Prussia's Germanic progress; and Russia was carefully manœuvring for the support of both France and Prussia against England at the coming Black Sea Conference. All Thiers could get from Gortchakoff was a reception at the Winter Palace which tickled his parvenu vanity and a safe conduct through the German lines to go and discuss an armistice with Bismarck.

The Government could thus rely upon no outside help. But, even from their patriotic point of view, to resign would have been to precipitate disorders of which the Prussians would have taken full advantage. Their only hope of preserving at once the military situation and their own bourgeois republic against the Monarchist provinces and Socialist Paris was to attempt to bring the Parisians to the realisation that surrender was inevitable.

The Government was sufficiently realist to see that it must be a war of capitulation, but it had not the courage to admit it in face of the desperate courage of a people resolved to fight *à outrance*. Trochu simply continued the tactics of Palikao : starved Paris of all news, keeping even the mayors in ignorance of his policy, with the result that they lost a great deal of influence to the more belligerent spokesmen of the popular clubs. Trochu had a " plan " : that was all Paris knew and, in Trochu's opinion, that was all Paris needed to know. Bad news was at once attributed to the manœuvres of Prussian spies. But nothing practical was done, could be done : Trochu's plan became an object of derision.

There had at first been little talk of the Commune. On September 4, the red flag had been flown for a short time on the Parliament building, a few shouts of " Long live the Commune ! " heard. It was frequently discussed in the more social-revolutionary clubs, most of which broke up with the cry. But on the whole this meant rather a desire to conduct the war as it had been conducted in 1793 than any immediate hope of the social revolution.

Blanqui, who had more or less abjured Socialism in favour of Jacobinism and had been giving the Government admirable lessons in strategy in the editorials of *La Patrie en Danger*, and Flourens, blazing with impatient martial indignation, had held a meeting of nineteen commanders of National Guard battalions on the evening of October 5. In the afternoon, Flourens, unable to wait longer, had led his faithful Belleville corps to the Hôtel de Ville, and had only been pacified by an affecting address of Jules Feery's which reduced Flourens's lieutenants to tears. At the evening meeting, it had been proposed to set up the Commune and proclaim martial law to maintain it, a typical bit of Blanquism. They had got some support from the Central Committee of the Twenty Districts, whose authority, however, even within the National Guard, was still vague. Another attempt upon the Hôtel de Ville, on the 8th, came to nothing. The mass of the population, besieged for less than a month, still condemned such adventures as unpatriotic. The only tangible result was that Kératry resigned from the Police Prefecture and was replaced by Adam, a dull and fairly efficient official.

But dissatisfaction with Trochu's plan grew all the month with the waning of the hope of rescue, the tightening of supplies. Delescluze, Pyat, Blanqui harried the Government's slackness in eagerly read articles; the clubs and committees became loud in complaint; the National Guard demanded action. At the end of October, dissatisfaction came to a head, naturally through the agency of Félix Pyat.

On October 28, Pyat announced in his *Combat* the fall of Metz and the surrender of Bazaine, the failure of the last hope. He claimed to have had the news from Rochefort, member of the Government, who in turn had had it from Flourens; Flourens had heard it from an ambulance man working near the Prussian outposts during a truce and had passed it on to Rochefort, " as concerning the *salus populi*," as he put it. Such indirect information was at least suspect; although if Rochefort had it, the whole Government must know. The Government, however, made the fatal mistake of denying it categorically, claiming that Bazaine " had not ceased harassing the besieging armies with brilliant sorties." A furious crowd wrecked the *Combat* offices, and Pyat of course went into hiding.

On the same day the Paris forces made an important sortie in the direction of Le Bourget. As usual, no proper communications with the front were kept up. Paris was in an agony of suspense throughout the 29th and 30th.

On the evening of the 30th, Thiers returned from his vain errand with only Gortchakoff's safe-conduct to go to Bismarck at Versailles to discuss an armistice after consultation with the Paris Government. Passing through Versailles on his way in to Paris, he had seen the news of the fall of Metz posted on every wall.

At a midnight sitting, the Government gave him full powers to negotiate an armistice: Paris was to be revictualled and free elections should be held throughout France to regularise the Government and to decide whether the war should be continued.

Sitting at lunch with Favre on the 31st, Thiers heard only vague rumours of what Paris thought of the " deliverance and peace " which he considered he was bringing to the besieged city. As he crossed the river at Sèvres, in a wild storm of wind and rain, later that afternoon, he received some news of " disturbances in Paris." But the aged historian was meditating upon the historical picturesque: the fact that the fate of France was entrusted to a little cockleshell of a boat rowed by a small boy amid the falling shells.

Paris, waking after two days of feverish apprehension, found tidings of three disasters: the failure of the Bourget sortie, confirmation of Bazaine's surrender at Metz and Thiers's negotiations for the surrender of Paris. With strange lack of tact, the Government had placarded Thiers's arrival and Bazaine's failure side by side as compensating " good " and " bad " news.

The whole population came out furiously into the streets. Clémenceau, as Mayor of Montmartre, publicly expressed the opinion of his district, which was that of all

Paris: " The Municipality of the XVIIIth District indignantly protests against an armistice which the Government
cannot accept without betraying its trust ! " A huge crowd
demonstrating outside the Hôtel de Ville in the pouring
rain, invaded the building. Pyat reappeared, heaping coals
of fire upon the Government's head. Flourens strode up
and down on the council table, tearing up its baize with his
spurs, demanding a Committee of Public Safety. All the
revolutionary leaders were there. Pyat, protesting, for form's
sake, against the illegality of election by acclamation, then
proclaimed the Commune. The Provisional Government
was held prisoner in a side-room. Several lists were hurriedly
drawn up for the new Government, some of them headed
" Commune of Paris ": Pyat, Louis Blanc, Victor Hugo,
Dorian, Ledru-Rollin, Flourens, Blanqui, Delescluze were
the commonest names, for the most part simply the
" Glories " of the Forty-Eight: a very Jacobin Commune.

Everything was in complete confusion. The crowd
hustled about the great square outside. Blanqui took the
lead, tried to restore order. Rochefort even attempted, in
his own way, to defend Thiers: " I don't know Citizen
Thiers and I don't want to know him; I don't know if the
Government has charged him with a mission or if he has
taken it upon himself, but . . ." The crowd howled him
down: Thiers was an agent of the Orleanist Royalists,
working for the duc d'Aumale.

The Governmental troops had time to rally. Some
" loyal " battalions of the National Guard and two battalions of Breton Mobiles penetrated into the Hôtel de Ville
through the underground tunnel from the Lobau barracks
opposite. From sheer exhaustion, the end came at three in
the morning. Blanqui and Flourens reached some sort of
agreement with Tamisier, reactionary Commander-in-
Chief of the National Guard, and came down the steps
with him between them; partly as protection. Municipal
elections were to be held at the earliest possible date and no
proceedings would be taken against any of the insurrectionaries.

The crowd went slowly home. An attempt made by the Blanquists at a regular *coup d'état* with the capture of the Ministry of the Interior, Police Prefecture and National Printing Works failed completely.

The Government of National Defence immediately violated its pledges, secure in the knowledge that Paris on the whole disapproved of such diversions from the business of defence. Instead of elections, they reverted to the bad old Napoleonic system of plebiscite. On November 5, they received 557,996 votes of *yes* against only 62,638 *no* on a vote of confidence. Changes took place in the municipal offices. Adam was replaced at the Police Prefecture by a miserable lachrymose detective, Cresson; and Tamisier yielded his command of the National Guard to Clément Thomas, noted for his brutality in suppressing the insurrection of June 1848. Rochefort resigned from the Government.

Twenty-four warrants were issued, also in contravention of Tamisier's agreement, against the leaders of the insurrection; but only fourteen were executed. Some of the leaders made personal arrangements with members of the Government, notably with Ferry, Mayor of Paris, who had ambitions towards a sort of moderate Jacobin dictatorship. Others took refuge in the workers' districts, where they were so popular that to attempt to arrest them would have been to provoke a new insurrection. The Government, itself the result of an invasion of Parliament and elected by popular acclamation, was in an awkward position about the trials. As Hémar, the Solicitor-General, pointed out, the possibility of a comparison between October 31 and September 4 " could not fail to create considerable embarrassment in the Assize Court and might very well lead to an extremely distasteful debate."

Thiers's negotiations with Bismarck were ruined by the insurrection. The Prussian declared that there was no responsible Government in France capable of giving guarantees for the execution of the terms. Even as early as September 13, Bismarck had spoken, in a note transmitted to Thiers by Gladstone, of " the existing Government in

Paris or those which will probably succeed it." He used the opportunity to present unacceptable terms. On November 5, Thiers, who dared not come to Paris, met Favre and General Ducrot secretly at Billancourt, in a ruined hovel which reminded the aged historian of Pompei. Favre was ready to accept any terms, but Ducrot stiffened him into refusal. Thiers returned to Tours perched on a railway tender, more determined than ever to give France a responsible Government qualified to make peace, the paramount consideration. He arrived on the 8th. Next day, Gambetta, who had proclaimed after the fall of Metz, " So long as an inch of the sacred soil remains beneath our feet we shall maintain the glorious flag of the French Revolution ! " won a temporary success at Coulmiers. The war went on.

The siege, too, went on. Food grew shorter, the queues outside the food-shops longer. It was terribly cold, and fuel was very scarce. The wealthy could just live ; the poor could not. Shells began to fall on the suburbs ; the bombardment of the city drew ever closer. And still the Government did nothing.

The National Guard sat around the wine-shops, sole diversion ; wine was cheap, replaced food. By the middle of January, " Long live the Commune ! " was to be heard everywhere. In all the east of Paris, the Xth, XIth, XIIIth, XIVth, XVIIIth, XIXth and XXth districts, the red flag was flown openly. On January 6, appeared a "Red Poster," drawn up by Tridon and Vallès and signed by 140 names drawn from every opposition group, moderates of the Union Républicaine and Radical democrats of the Alliance Républicaine beside Jacobins and Socialists : " The policy, strategy, administration of the Government of September 4, a mere continuance of the Empire, are condemned. Make way for the people ! Make way for the Commune ! " Trochu was forced to issue a stupid counter-proclamation : " The Governor of Paris will never capitulate ! " He had known for four months that that was a lie.

Trochu was growing worried. Naturally, he had no result

to show from a plan which did not exist. But the National Guard, which he as a regular soldier despised and as a reactionary feared, demanded action. At a council on January 10, he spoke out: " If 20 or 25,000 men were left on the field in a great battle beneath the walls, Paris would capitulate; the National Guard will consent to peace only after losing 10,000 men." A general reminded him that it was not easy even for him to get 10,000 men killed. Clément Thomas, commander of the National Guard, doubted whether they would even appear in the field.

To carry out this plan, a great sortie in the direction of Buzenval was begun on January 19. The National Guard behaved with their usual valour and confusion; no military advantage was gained owing to a complete mismanagement of supplies and communications; and no more than 3,000 dead and wounded were left on the field.

Trochu, attempting to avoid responsibility, resigned and was replaced by Vinoy, a Bonapartist cavalry officer of brutal energy.

Suspicions that the sortie had been deliberately sabotaged stirred up a new riot. This time it was carefully planned by the Blanquists Sapia, Vaillant, Leverdays, Ferré, and Tridon who financed it, acting together with the central organisation of the National Guard. On the night of January 21, a crowd forced the doors of Mazas prison and released Flourens, Melliet, Brunel and other leaders imprisoned for their share in the October 31st riot. The XIIIth, XIVth and XVIIIth districts prepared to rise.

Blanqui himself, told of the plan only on the morning of the 22nd, strongly disapproved, considering that the Government would be only too glad to hand over its responsibilities; and, indeed, when Jules Simon, in desperation, offered the command that evening to anyone who could propose a plan, he found no takers. Once again the Old One's young lieutenants had forced him to embark upon an adventure for which he had no taste but which they were sure could not succeed without him: it was to be his last.

The plan was not a success. The bourgeois Alliance Républicaine wanted peaceful compromise. Cresson's police got wind of the arrangements and had the Hôtel de Ville fortified and occupied by the redoubtable Breton Mobiles, some marines and the municipal constabulary under Gustave Chaudey, Ferry's assistant.

A large but pacific crowd demonstrated on the muddy square in front of the Hôtel de Ville. When Sapia brought up the 101st Battalion, the crack revolutionary force, the situation became more threatening. Leverdays went off to try to persuade the gunners in charge of a battery outside Notre-Dame to train their guns on the Hôtel de Ville; but they refused.

Old Blanqui sat in the Café de la Garde Nationale opposite the Hôtel de Ville—it is still in existence—watching the demonstration of which he did not approve. It was his last insurrection; in a few weeks he was to disappear into his cell for another nine years; and after his release the classic days of insurrectionary conspiracy were over. From his café table, the sinister old man, " very short, slightly bowed, very short white hair, thin short white beard, bald forehead, nose pinched and pointed, owl-eyes, stoat-like," as the police-warrant described him, watched the deputations enter the building and return unsatisfied. Chaudey was playing for time.

Cresson burst in upon a session of the Ministry to offer his resignation; he told them, with tears, that Flourens, the terrible, the irresistible Flourens, had been released from jail by a vast and infuriated mob and he was moving down on the Hôtel de Ville at the head of his awful Belleville ruffians; the Police Prefecture was surrounded; the police powerless. The Ministers were panic-stricken.

Suddenly, a fusillade broke out on the square. Crouching in the mud, the 101st replied to the volleys poured upon the crowd by the Bretons posted at the mattressed windows. A fresh Governmental force took the insurgents in the rear, clearing the square before Flourens could bring up his men. When the firing was over, Sapia, a cane in his hand, lay

dead, with six National Guards beside him. Twenty more,
Guards and civilians, had been wounded: the Government
troops had one dead and two wounded. By 5.30 that
evening, Ferry was able to report that order had been
restored: " by the crime of a few our glorious and unhappy
Paris has. not been spared this sad extremity." It was
believed that Chaudey had given the first order to fire; it
now seems that he favoured milder repression by a cavalry
charge.

The riot of January 22 was the last protest against Paris's
surrender; it was the first real effort to bring in the insurrectionary Commune. Paris was still in an uproar. Vinoy,
Military Governor, replied energetically by suppressing
seventeen Radical papers and closing down the clubs. Even
as late as January 27, there was a small demonstration of
300 officers of the National Guard against the surrender and
what they called the Government's treason.

Jules Favre, after five days of negotiation with Bismarck
at the Rothschilds' property of Ferrières, during which the
cynical Chancellor humiliated the lawyer to tears which he
did not fail to advertise widely on his return to Paris,
brought back an armistice: twenty-one days' truce for the
election of a National Assembly to settle the peace terms;
the revictualling of Paris, which had food for only four more
days; the surrender of the northern and eastern Paris
forts, and the occupation of the others until an indemnity
of 200 million francs (about £8,000,000) had been paid,
within fifteen days; the disarmament of the 250,000 troops
in the city except the 12,000 National Guards, who, by
Article 7, were to retain their arms and maintain order in
Paris.

The armistice was signed at midnight on January 27.
It was the hundred and thirty-fifth day of the siege. Next
day, the Government of National Defence resigned to make
way for a National Assembly to be elected at Bordeaux.

# CHAPTER III

# THE NATIONAL ASSEMBLY

" Provoke the insurrection while you still have the power, in order that
you may crush it for good."

BISMARCK *to Jules Favre*

" We do not want it to come to a fight; but if it does, we'll hit without
mercy."

THIERS *to General Susanne*

THE ELECTIONS for the Bordeaux National Assembly
took place on February 8. In Paris a list was drawn up by
the International, the Federation of Syndical Workers and
the newly constituted Central Committee of the National
Guard: " the list of candidates presented in the name of a
new world by the party of the disinherited. France is to be
constituted anew; the workers have the right to find and to
take their place in the order that is preparing. The social
revolutionary candidatures mean: the refusal to allow
anyone to call the Republic in question; the affirmation of
the necessity of the political accession of the workers; the
overthrow of Governmental oligarchy and industrial
feudalism." Candidates were: Blanqui, Tridon, Vaillant,
Ranvier, Vallès, Lefrançais; another list contained the
names of Garibaldi, Gambon, Malon, Pyat, Tolain, the
older generation.

But the social-revolutionary workers were in a minority.
The petty-bourgeoisie and even a large number of workers
had been stampeded by the failure of the insurrections of
October 31 and January 22: the Republic was sufficient.
The Government of National Defence was, of course,
utterly discredited, but Paris was not ready yet for the
" party of the disinherited." The forty-three new Deputies

were entirely Republican, but the majority were the known revolutionaries of the Forty-Eight, the *Gloires*.

Louis Blanc emerged from obscurity to head the list with 216,000 votes, followed by Victor Hugo, Gambetta, Garibaldi; then a few prominent opponents of the Empire, Delescluze, Pyat, Rochefort; Thiers came 20th on the list; and Jules Favre, the only member of the Provisional Government to be elected by Paris, was almost at the bottom. The " disinherited " were barely represented; Blanqui received only 52,000 votes. Thus, only a minority in Paris favoured the social revolution at the beginning of February 1871.

To the horror and amazement of Republican Paris, the provinces, except a few larger towns, went solidly Royalist. It had been known that the Royalist influence had been strong in opposition to the Empire; but Paris had supposed that at least the heroic defence would have given it the right to lead opinion. Provincial prefects had been so lavish in praise: " Ah, we loved her well, our Paris," gushed a note added to a public and generally circulated protest against the Prussian bombardment. " We were proud of her greatness, of her beauty, of her wealth moral rather than material, of her glory. May she be blessed, our Paris, exhausting herself, sacrificing herself, dying to save France!" But, towards the end of the long-drawn-out agony, the tone had changed: on January 30, the Prefect of Finisterre, far out of touch with events, wrote that he had news of a mysterious treaty (in reality, the armistice), but was reassured because it was signed by Favre, not by Gambetta: " I can see only one explanation: Paris is at bay. But then, why have waited until now ? "

It was the fear that Paris might denounce the armistice which swung the anti-Republican vote. The provinces were heartily sick of a war that had lost its meaning when Napoléon III abdicated. The Bonapartist Party had vanished, with the Empire, overnight. The small agriculturalists, fearing nothing so much as the domination of the industrial towns, reverted to the support of Monarchism, chiefly to the Orleanist moderate party. They had not forgotten, too, the stupid agrarian policy of the Second Republic; and to the farmers one republic was indistinguishable from another: such mistakes, they thought, were inherent in the nature of republics. Above all, they wanted peace; the return of their sons and brothers from Prussian prisons for the spring sowing. To vote Monarchist was the only alternative, to them, to war and Parisian anarchy. They did not even believe in Thiers' " Conservative Republicanism " (" the Republic must be Conservative or nothing "), although Thiers was personally extremely popular as the chief advocate of peace, the adversary of the chief of the Republican war party, the *fou furieux* Gambetta, and as the former Minister of Louis Philippe. His stinging defeat in Paris, where he could collect hardly 100,000 votes, was compensated by 2,000,000 in twenty-six departments; he opted, however, for Paris, his constituency of 1869.

Of the 630 members of the Assembly, some 420 were Royalists. Two princes of the House of Orleans were elected. The distribution of the parties was roughly: Extreme Right, 200 Legitimists; Right Centre, 200 Orleanists; Left Centre, 30 Bonapartists; Left, 20 Republican Orleanists and 80 Radicals; Extreme Left, 20 revolutionaries, mostly veterans of 1848 and Deputies of Paris.

The Assembly practically unanimously elected Thiers Head of the Executive Power, for he was the one outstanding personality suitable for the post. Only after great efforts on his part, rather suspiciously resembling Cæsar's refusal of the crown, did they submit to adding the words " Of the French Republic." The word " Republic " was not popular at Bordeaux, but, as Thiers continually reminded them, they had been elected simply to decide upon the peace terms, not as a constituent assembly to settle the form of French government.

The Government which Thiers chose was a nice balance between Conservative Republicanism and Monarchism. Four ex-Ministers of the Government of National Defence, elected by the provinces who hardly knew their record:

Favre (Foreign Affairs), Picard (Interior), Simon (Public Education), Le Flô (War); then the Monarchists Dufaure (Justice), Lambrecht, de Larcy, Admiral Pothuau; and even one Bonapartist, at the Treasury, Pouyer-Quertier, heavy industrialist and protectionist, an old colleague of Thiers.

With this very grudging support, Thiers had founded his Conservative Republic; it remained for him to conclude his peace. It was a ticklish affair and one which needed firmness and speed. Bismarck, now a sick man and working under considerable pressure from Court circles, wildly excited by the recent elevation of the King of Prussia to the Imperial dignity and determined to humiliate France to the uttermost, had clearly hinted that he could treat only with a responsible Government. Any disorder in France he would use to blackmail Thiers for more exorbitant terms. Thiers, therefore, had to control at once Paris, bitterly hostile to the armistice, and the Assembly, equally bitter against Paris and ready to unleash civil war at any moment. It was an unenviable eminence, but Thiers, for all his complaints about the Assembly's " animal stupidity," secretly delighted in this opportunity of appealing direct to that " Tribunal of History " which he had so often invoked: so, " *O fortunatam natam me consule Romam !* " Thiers and Bismarck began to discuss the peace preliminaries on February 19 at Versailles.

Paris, disgusted by the capitulation, was appalled by the Assembly. There was now no longer any fighting to distract men's attentions from political and economic grievances. So long as the National Guard retained their rifles, they were assured of their thirty sous; but that was a poor consolation for an entire lack of work. Vinoy had bottled up opinion: repressed, it became only more furious, more dangerous. Scuffles took place in every corner. The theft of arms from the arsenals, the looting of armourers became ever commoner. There was no system in it; every man for himself; but it was none the less dangerous for that.

Terrified by the disorder and longing for release from the

stifling siege atmosphere, most of the bourgeois families who could afford to do so left Paris to visit their relations in the provinces: it is estimated that nearly 100,000 abandoned Paris. The forces of bourgeois moderation were thus greatly weakened. To balance this emigration, there came to fill the streets the demobilised soldiers, ragged and haggard, huddled up in their sheepskins, squatting in huts up on the Boulevard de Clichy, ready to exchange their guns for a litre of wine or a crust of bread. Their collecting-boxes rattled a grim accompaniment to all Parisian activity.

So threatening was the situation that on February 4 General Valdon, Chief of Staff to the Army of Paris, sent a circular to the sector commanders: " New circumstances oblige me to modify the orders given. Suspend absolutely and until further orders the disarming of the troops and establish at all your magazines reliable armed pickets, capable of defending them at need. Exercise the most entire and serious vigilance in this matter." There was, as yet, no open revolt; but Paris was only waiting for the spark to touch it off. On January 29, there had been a slight affair, significant only in that it was organised directly by the National Guard, not by a political group. Brunel, " General in Chief of the National Guard," and Piazza, his " Chief of Staff," elected to these posts by thirty-five battalion commanders, attempted to set up the military dictatorship of the National Guard at the Hôtel de Ville, but were arrested by Cresson, always well informed by his spies and for once energetic, while Dorian persuaded Flourens not to march. Tried by court martial on February 11, they were each condemned to two years' imprisonment for usurpation of functions—an unusually mild sentence.

The authority of the police and the official command of the National Guard were less and less respected. In certain districts, such as the XXth, Belleville, where the Mayor, Ranvier, had been jailed after October 31, the local administration was carried on by a revolutionary com-mittee. The regular police perpetually came into conflict with the local extra-legal counter-police. Discipline was breaking down among the regular troops. When two soldiers of the 118th of the Line " permitted themselves to answer their captain in the most improper and impolite manner," the outraged officer could find no one to arrest them. The bourgeois battalions of the National Guard were spontaneously disbanding. By February 26, the 2nd Battalion of the XVIIIth Sub-division (Faubourg Saint-Honoré) could count upon only 400 men out of an effective of 1,200: 300 were absent, and of the rest some were ill, others were " seriously occupied in their affairs and no longer showed all the eagerness in taking up arms that could be desired." The 3rd Battalion had from 560 to 580 men left, but could count upon at the most 350 to 400; at one roll call only about 300 arrived out of the 544 summoned.

A mysterious authority began to make itself felt in Paris, baffling the police. Clément Thomas's orders from Headquarters in the Place Vendôme were unaccountably countermanded. Headquarters increasingly lost touch with the battalions. Actually, there was nothing mysterious about this organisation save to the conspiracy-hunting imagination of the police; its posters were on the walls, signed in full; its meetings were accessible; it was simply the Central Committee of the Federated Battalions of the National Guard.

Despite the initiative of such bodies as the Montmartre Vigilance Committee, the old Committee of the Twenty Districts, composed mostly of bourgeois notables, had not functioned very efficiently. Local battalion commanders had always had far more authority. A new federation was founded to draw up a programme for the National Assembly elections at a meeting at the Palace d'Hiver on February 6. This skeleton committee adhered to the International and Syndical list already quoted.

A much larger meeting was held at the Tivoli-Vauxhall dance-hall on the 15th. Here was voted a preamble in which it was stated that it was the committee's duty to advise the citizen-electors in such a way that " the working man, the producer, is equally called upon to represent the nation." It is clear that at least the ideas of the International Socialists had a strong influence upon the committee from the start; and the incursion of the National Guard into politics is highly significant. A commission was appointed to draw up the general statutes of the new Federation.

At the next meeting, also at the Tivoli-Vauxhall, on the 24th, these statutes were adopted and the Central Committee formed. It was to be composed of one delegate from each company, without distinction of rank, and of elected battalion commanders. They were to be always revocable by their electors. Each company was to meet once a fortnight in Company-Circles to discuss immediate concerns and also general propositions which they might desire to bring up before the Battalion-Circle or the Central Committee, and, inversely, to discuss the decisions of the Central Committee and the Battalion-Circle. These Battalion-Circles were to be composed of five delegates from the Company-Circle unit, one of whom was to sit on the Central Committee, and were to discuss the larger immediate concerns of the whole battalion. The Grand Council of the Committee was to be composed of three members from each district elected by the Central Committee. One-third of the council was to be renewed every three months. It was to share a Bureau with the Central Committee: a president, a vice-president, four assessors, two secretaries and a treasurer, elected by the General Assembly every six months. The council's functions were to expedite current affairs, summon meetings of the Central Committee, to see to the execution of the Central Committee's decisions. A Supervisory Commission, of five members from the Grand Council, was to see that the Central Committee's decisions were carried out and examine the accounts. During election-time, the Central Committee should sit continuously until it had drawn up a list to be proposed *in the name of the Central Committee of the Delegates of the National Guard*. A monthly subscription of at least five francs per company was to pay the expenses of the Federation.

This constitution provided an elective body, at once rigid and flexible, completely democratic, and, most important, completely in opposition to the official organisation with its officers appointed by the Government and responsible not to their men, but to the Minister for Internal Affairs.

While Paris was organising against reaction, Thiers was being forced by Bismarck into a position where a clash with Paris became inevitable. The peace preliminaries were finally drawn up on February 26, two days after the federation of the National Guard in Paris. The terms were more severe than Thiers had expected and than Bismarck himself had desired; the cession of Alsace-Lorraine, an indemnity of five milliards and, most fatal, the technical occupation of Paris by the Prussian troops. This last was the crucial point, and for it Thiers was directly responsible. Bismarck had given him an alternative: the cession of the *rayon* round Belfort.

To yield Belfort would be to infuriate the military party who were, indeed, anxious for peace at the moment but were equally eager for " security " in which to prepare the *Révanche*. But to allow the Prussians to enter Paris, even merely a small quarter and merely as a gesture, might well provoke a mad resistance which Bismarck would consider a renewal of hostilities. This dilemma reduced Thiers to despairing tears. Bismarck himself was not eager to enter Paris, but the Court militarists were insistent. After a week's haggling, the terms were drawn up rather unsatisfactorily. " M. de Bismarck," Thiers recalls, " dominated by his savage temperament, wished to hurry matters, taking little care for a revision which he was certain that he could turn to his advantage later on." The definitive peace was to be negotiated by an Ambassadorial Conference at Brussels.

The signing of the peace preliminaries coincided almost exactly with the annual celebration of the " martyrs " of the February Revolution of 1848. From the 24th onwards, the Place de la Bastille was thronged with great crowds of pilgrims, excited and solemn. Soldiers, sailors, National Guards marched past the Bastille Column. They marched with drums, bearing great red and black wreaths which they laid at the foot of the Column. The red flag and the tricolour mingled. For the first time for twenty-three years, the red flag waved from the hand of the Goddess of Liberty. Trumpeters sounded the charge from each corner of the great pedestal, from which orators harangued the huge crowds. The Government withdrew its troops to the Left Bank, leaving the ground to the National Guard. With the Prussian invasion imminent, they could not rely upon the soldiers not to fraternise and disband, combining exasperated patriotism with the realisation that they too were workers.

There were, however, two distinct movements in different parts of Paris during these critical days. At the Bastille had gathered those workers from the adjoining districts who were for the social revolution. Near the Champs-Elysées, where the Prussian entry was expected, was gathered another great crowd of workers and bourgeois, united now simply as patriotic Parisians. The Central Committee published in the leading papers on the 25th a resolution carried at their meeting on the previous day : " At the first sign of the Prussian entry into Paris, every Guard pledges himself to assemble at once in arms at the usual rallying-place and to march thence against the enemy invader." On the night of the 26th, while Thiers was signing the treaty at Versailles, 40,000 men and women marched at midnight up the Champs-Elysées. But it was a false alarm and the demonstration dispersed quietly.

The Bureau of the Central Committee, however, sitting nearer the Bastille at the Place de la Corderie, was influenced by the wiser counsels of the International and the Syndicates. It advised against resistance, which would be simply to invite the sacking of Paris by foreign soldiery. The Prussians, they pointed out, would, if attacked, merely do the work of the French reactionaries by " drowning the claims of social reform in a sea of blood."

A highly significant demonstration of the united front against the Prussians, the contrasting but converging elements of which render this whole situation so complex, was the action of the Passy Battalion of the National Guard, a distinctly reactionary corps composed mostly of wealthy *rentiers* and professional men. On the afternoon of the 26th, acting directly on the Central Committee's orders, they seized 227 guns and some machine-guns abandoned by the Government in the artillery-parks of Passy and the Place Wagram right in the path of the expected invasion. It is more than probable that the authorities had simply forgotten them; but the National Guard and Paris opinion generally believed either that it was another instance of the Government's " treachery " or that it was a trick to disarm the National Guard. It was considered that the action was no seizure but the recapture of the Guard's own property; for many of the guns had been founded by public subscription during the siege. The treaty, too, had agreed that the National Guard was not to be disarmed; and the Tivoli-Vauxhall meeting on the 24th, even before the treaty had been signed, had protested unanimously against any attempt at disarmament. The Passy battalion was certainly thinking only of its prestige; but the guns were taken to the parks in the revolutionary quarters— Montmartre, La Villette, Belleville and the Place des Vosges.

The parallel revolutionary agitation at the Bastille continued. On the 27th, a crowd forcibly released the popular Brunel from Sainte-Pélagie prison, where he had been held for his activity on January 29. The sailors quartered in the Pepinière barracks broke out and fraternised with them. On the 28th, a police-spy, Vincenzoni, recognised in the Place de la Bastille, was flung into the canal and stoned all the way down to the Seine beneath the approving gaze of thousands of men and women.

In spite of the continued patriotic enthusiasm, the Bureau had now enforced its decisions on the Central Committee as a whole; and, on the 28th, it, together with the International and the Syndicates, published a black-bordered poster forbidding resistance and ordering instead a complete boycott of the invaders. So great was its moral authority throughout Paris that when the Prussians entered at last, on March 1, and rode down the Champs-Elysées, they were assailed only by the gibes of gutter-snipes. The statues on the Place de la Concorde were veiled in black. Not a shop nor café was open. No one spoke to them. A silent, mournful crowd glowered at them as if they had been a pest of vermin. A few barbarian officers were permitted a hasty visit to the Louvre. They were isolated as if they had been lepers. When they glumly retired, on March 3, a great bonfire was kindled at the Arc de Triomphe to purify the soil fouled by the invader's tread. A few prostitutes who had consorted with Prussian officers were beaten, and a café which had opened its doors was wrecked. The Central Committee had united all Paris in a great moral victory; even more, it had united it against the Government which had inflicted this humiliation.

In the next period, pure coincidence of date doubles the effect of the events which were to intensify the crisis and lead straight to revolution, just as the fortuitous crimes of Troppmann and Pierre Bonaparte hastened the fall of the Second Empire. March 3, the day of the Prussian evacuation, was the ordinary date for the Central Committee's meeting. Exalted by its moral success, but maintaining its general line, the Committee decisively asserted its claim to sole command of the National Guard. Viard passed with acclamation a proposal that if Headquarters should issue orders contrary to those decided upon by the Committee, the Guard should be prepared to arrest the General Staff. Varlin proposed the immediate re-election of officers dismissed by Headquarters for no reason other than their political activities. Another delegate demanded, amid applause, that the Seine Department (that is, Paris) constitute itself an independent republic should the Bordeaux Assembly deprive Paris of its rank as capital of France.

The Central Committee was now, it is clear, a decisively revolutionary federalist organisation completely controlling the city.

Simultaneously, the Bordeaux Assembly and the Government began to provoke Paris beyond bearing. The debates had been stormy. Republican Deputies had been insulted and howled down. Garibaldi himself, respected by all Europe irrespective of political prejudices, was hooted by the " backwoodsmen," as the Radical Marseillaise journalist, Crémieux, called them. Exasperated by this treatment, Gambetta, Hugo, Rochefort, Ranc, Tridon, Razoua, Malon and Félix Pyat, a quarter of the Paris representation, resigned from the Assembly. Although they were the Radical fraction, all Paris resented the insult to its honour as embodied in its Deputies, and apprehension of the Assembly's intentions increased.

Still, on March 3, General d'Aurelle de Paladines, victor of Coulmiers but reputedly responsible for the defeat at Orléans, arrived in Paris to take up the command of the National Guard to which he had been appointed on the 2nd. D'Aurelle had been an enthusiastic Bonapartist and was famous for his brutal energy. It was said that such a man would not have been appointed if a *coup d'état* were not in prospect. The Franco-American adventurer, Cluseret, who had been confusing the revolutionary issue all over France since September 4, wrote a silly but effective letter to the National Guard from Bordeaux on the 6th, declaring that " there is not an honest man in France who could serve under the orders of a Paladines." The battalion commanders of the chief revolutionary districts interviewed d'Aurelle on the 8th to receive a declaration of his Republican sentiments, but he refused to publish his assurances in an open proclamation.

March 11 was a day of cumulative provocation. In the afternoon, the court martial set up, in direct contravention of the Provisional Government's pledge, to try the leaders of the October 31 riot, sentenced Blanqui and Flourens, in absence, to death. They immediately published, from hiding, firm, dignified and reasonable protests which gained them much sympathy, especially as they pointed out that the Provisional Government itself had at that time no more legal existence than their afternoon's regime. The general indignation blazed up when Vinoy attempted to gag it by suppressing, the same evening, almost the whole of the Left-wing Press: Rochefort's *Mot d'Ordre*, Pyat's *Vengeur*, Vallès's *Cri du Peuple*, Vermesch's *Père Duchêne*, Grousset's *Bouche de Fer* and Pilotell's *Caricature*.

The culmination was a measure of the Assembly which was in effect a brutal attack upon the livelihood of the Parisian middle classes, rousing them far more effectively to active opposition than any political, military or patriotic provocation could have done. This was the news of the voting on the previous day of the famous *loi des échéances*— the law on maturities. A great deal of business in Paris was then, and is still, done by promissory notes, often for very small sums, payable at the offices, shops or homes of the payees. The siege had naturally brought business to a standstill, and the Government of National Defence had decreed a moratorium on all such paper. The National Assembly decided to regularise the situation, especially as a large amount of these bills had become concentrated in the hands of a few brokers who were eager to get their money in to take full advantage of the post-war business revival and the profitable reconstruction and reparation loans about to be floated. In spite of the desperate protests of the Chambers of Commerce and the National Union of Commerce and Industry, the Assembly now decreed that all bills which had fallen due between August 13 and November 13, 1870, the original moratorium, be payable with interest exactly seven months after the date when they were originally due; bills which had fallen due between November 13, 1870, and April 13, 1871, would be payable with interest from June 13 to July 13, 1871.

The law, passed on the 10th, was reported in Paris on the 11th and would actually come into force on the 13th, the day upon which payment was due. It meant utter ruin for thousands of small traders. Between March 13 and 17, 150,000 bills were protested in Paris.

A parallel measure proposed was a law enabling land-lords, many of whom had fled the hardships of the siege, to collect immediately all rents on land and buildings which had been prorogued during the war. The poor were faced with eviction, and even the largest tenants could not find the money to pay so suddenly.

This economic attack threw the middle class into the ranks of the workers. Socialist expropriation could be no worse than this foretaste of a Royalist restoration. The salvation of the bourgeoisie lay, it was clear, only in a democratic republic which they could control. Once again, as in 1848, the policy of the middle class was of necessity an alliance with the workers against the provincial squires, with a mental reservation in favour of turning against their allies should they go inconveniently far towards encompassing their own Socialistic aims.

The provocations on this fatal March 11 were not yet complete. A final humiliation gathered all the separate social and economic grievances into one united moral protest. The Assembly decapitalised Paris.

It was obviously no longer possible to keep the seat of Government marooned in remote, overcrowded and uncomfortable Bordeaux. Thiers found the lack of contact with important persons and events in Paris intolerable. He needed, too, to be in the closest possible touch with the Peace Conference in Brussels. Communications were still rudimentary. Foreign politicians and financiers, whose help would be so indispensable in the reconstruction of France, refused to travel the distance. A Government squatting in the depths of the country lacked dignity as well as convenience.

Big business in Paris felt this inconvenience even more, conscious that it was at the mercy of riots or of " d'Aurelle's inclination towards *coups d'état.*" The Governor of the Bank of France wrote to Thiers: " We cannot yet feel the directing hand, the rallying unity, the decision which sets uncertainty at rest. Paris, too, somewhat agitated and, especially, humiliated, wishing to return to business and gaiety, must not be allowed to think herself neglected and fail to profit by the instincts and needs she has to satisfy in the restoration of security and work." Thiers replied with some heat: " For heaven's sake don't pester us with stupid complaints such as, for example, that the directing hand is not making itself felt. The directing hand is not idle, and if you do not feel it, it is because we are four hundred miles away and every force loses some of its visible energy at a great distance."

Thiers himself did not underrate the difficulties of returning to the capital. " The disturbances in Paris," he wrote, to his Ambassador in London, " are more of a nervous disease than anything else." But this was merely for diplomatic consumption. He had already written to Susanne, temporary War Minister in Paris, with instructions to pick his officers and men carefully, to keep them busy and contented—above all, not to let them mix with the civil population; to occupy and put in order the forts evacuated by the Prussians, especially Mont-Valérien. Three divisions of repatriated prisoners, he announced, were on the way to Paris, and " we shall have to get together rifles for them; the disarmament [of the National Guard] would be a means, and it would be a good argument for it as well."

Thiers was not only intending a *coup* to disarm the Paris National Guard, he was actively preparing it. On March 5 he sent 30,000 troops to Favre, who already had 18,000 and the police, " so that you will be able to restore order little by little if it does not come to a fight, or immediately should a rising take place "; these troops, however, were not in good condition and must on no account be allowed to mix with the Parisians. In a postscript, Thiers adds: " It is not my view that we should take the offensive against the agitation; with a large military force in hand, a firm attitude and a little patience, there is a good chance of getting off without a fight. If we have to fight, we shall fight, and, if we do, without quarter."

It is clear that Thiers had no immediate intention of bringing the seat of Government back to Paris itself, although Paris, as he wrote to Favre, was his ultimate aim. Into Paris, anyhow, the Assembly simply would not go. With a seat near Paris, Thiers could keep an eye simultaneously upon the agitation in the city and the intrigues of the Assembly; a military force guarding the Assembly could easily become an offensive force against Paris. It could also, if necessary, be used against the Royalist manœuvres of these " backwoodsmen " who were growing restive under his cavalier treatment. He could still sway them by his astonishing rhetoric, by sheer force of personality, but he dare not take his eye off them for a moment. When he writes to Rouland that he works twenty-two hours a day, and " if I were to fall ill, which might well happen at any moment, I do not know what would become of everything. . . . The Assembly is devoted to me for the moment, but I don't know how long it will last," Thiers is for once not exaggerating. The Assembly would follow him and him alone; but not into Paris.

He opened the debate upon the removal on March 10. It was one of his greatest successes in parliamentary tactics. In spite of proposals of Bourges and Fontainebleau, of rumours of a typhoid epidemic at Versailles, and the feeling that " to succeed the Prussians would be odious," Thiers carried his point. The Assembly voted by 427 to 154 in favour of meeting at Versailles on March 20.

The authorities were seriously alarmed at the possible results of this provocation. On the night of the 11th, the troops stood by. An order from the Commander-in-Chief of the Paris forces ran: " In presence of the decision taken by the National Assembly to sit at Versailles, the condemnation of Blanqui and Flourens, the suppression of five [sic] of the papers which are most extreme in urging revolt against the Government, I think it prudent to advise you to take precautions to maintain order in your districts."

On the previous day, the Central Committee had fore-

seen a provocative act and had issued an appeal to the
regular troops:

" Citizen soldiers, will you obey the impious command
to shed the same blood as flows in your own veins ?
Will you rend your own entrails ? No ! You will never
consent to become parricides and fratricides !

" What are the desires of the people of Paris ?

" It desires to keep its arms, choose its own leaders
and dismiss them when they no longer deserve its
confidence.

" It desires that the army on service shall be sent back
to its hearths that the family may regain its heart,
labour its arm, as soon as possible.

" Soldiers, sons of the People, let us unite to save the
Republic.

" Kings and Emperors have done us harm enough.
Do not sully your lives.

" Discipline does not absolve you from the responsibility of conscience.

" Embrace us before the eyes of those who to attain
a rank, to acquire a position, to restore a monarch
would make us cut each other's throats."

This moving appeal was not required on the 11th, nor
were the Government's special precautions. Paris was not
yet at the limit of endurance.

Things, indeed, were rather too quiet. Cresson, Police-
Prefect, was, for him, surprisingly optimistic: " The agitation," he reported to Thiers, " seems to be coming to an
end "; on the 12th: " The guns are more and more slackly
guarded." An incident on the 11th seemed to justify him.
The delegates of the 61st Battalion of the National Guard,
posted at the Montmartre battery, reported to the Mayor,
Clémenceau, that they were willing to hand over the guns,
" certain that it is in this the interpreter of the whole of the
National Guard of the XVIIIth district." But the 61st was
rather too certain; they were a bourgeois battalion, under
the influence of the old Central Committee of the Twenty

Arrondissements with its shady leader, Raoul du Bisson.
Getting wind of the proposal, the local Vigilance Committee, the Blanquists Ferré and Jaclard and the Internationalists Dereure and Jean-Baptiste Clément, author of
the once-famous ballad, " Au Temps des Cérises," at once
vetoed the resolution and forced Clémenceau to retire.

Such incidents completely misled Cresson, whose agents
were not in a position to penetrate into the really revolutionary quarters owing to the activity of the local counter-
police. It was perfectly true that many of the Parisians
were worn out with excitement and the discomfort of
guarding the guns through the snowy March nights. But it
was not true that the revolutionaries had adopted a
gradualist policy. What gradualism there was was almost
entirely the effect of sheer fatigue. There were enough
Vigilance Committees ready to call the workers into the
streets at any hint of serious attack; and these Cresson—
and therefore Thiers, who relied almost exclusively on
Cresson's reports—seriously underrated.

Meanwhile, the main body of the opposition, the Central
Committee, was finally organised, on March 15. It had seen
with disapproval the formation of a rival Republican
Federal Committee under the shady Raoul du Bisson,
based upon representation by one delegate of each rank
from each battalion. This it considered less democratic, but
admitted that it might be more practical. A compromise
was reached in order to form " a great Association affirming
its existence in complete publicity by acts which would be
constantly submitted to examination by its constituents; an
Association strong in that it groups in the interests of
common security all the members of the great family to
which we belong."

This Proudhonist " family " was dangerous since it let
in possible *provocateurs* of the du Bisson type; but it was
undoubtedly necessary in face of the threatening offensive
from the Government. Several members of the International, which as a body tended to distrust the Committee's Jacobin tendencies, served on it, notably Varlin.

The International's organ, Vallès' *Cri du Peuple*, was its semi-official paper; and the two organisations had close personal contact, since they shared the same offices.

The Blanquists Duval, Faltot and Eudes were elected Chiefs of the XIIIth, XVth and XXth District Legions. Other appointments now made were those of Lucien Henri as Chief of the XIVth District-Legion, Lullier as Commander of Artillery, and the absent Garibaldi as General-issimo, an honour which he declined with thanks.

The new combined Federation now included 215 out of the 270 battalions of the National Guard, the delegates representing 1,325 companies. The cash balance on March 15 amounted to 571 francs 20 centimes (rather less than £25).

That evening, Thiers arrived in Paris to prepare for the opening of the Assembly at Versailles on the 20th. He had less than a week in which to restore enough order in Paris to guarantee the safety of the Deputies sitting not ten miles from the city. The forces at his disposal were by no means brilliant, and had not been improved by the measures recently taken by Vinoy and Le Flô. At the date of the capitulation, the forces under arms in Paris had amounted to some 275,000 men. The peace preliminaries had permitted 40,000 beside the Paris National Guard. With the uncertain transport facilities, the demobilisation of five-sixths of the armed forces meant in practice their dispersion haphazard among the civil population. Vinoy's one great anxiety had been to remove this potentially turbulent element from Paris. Many of them, particularly the Mobiles of the Seine department, were disbanded practically without pay. By March 15, almost all who could had gone. The last contingents of sailors, the backbone of the defence during the siege, left for Rochefort on the evening of the 17th.

Vinoy had retained only one division, Faron's, which included some companies of marines and had been brought up to full numerical strength by including disarmed troops. On the 10th, he had received ten more regiments from

Bordeaux. In the second week in March, Vinoy had, besides these, four battalions of Chasseurs, some miscellaneous cavalry and engineers, 2,400 marines, the Garde Républicaine and Gendarmerie. Some 20,000 men in all. Thiers imagined that he had also 18,000 " loyal " National Guards; but in the event he found that he had no more than three battalions.

The 20,000 troops were in a deplorable state. They were sick of soldiering, disappointed at not being demobilised, hated the police and Gendarmerie, and were only too anxious to fraternise with the Parisians. Except for Faron's division, they were mostly young conscripts from the provinces whose whole desire was to go home to their families.

The prospects of reducing Paris with these resources were not bright. But it was necessary to settle the affair at once. The Assembly had to be pacified. The financiers were urgent. " You will never get any financial business done," they told Thiers, " unless you make an end of those scoundrels, unless you take their guns from them." This was really disturbing to Thiers, for in effect it was a threat to sabotage the payment of the first half-milliard which the Prussians demanded as the price of their evacuation of the Somme and Oise departments, the right bank of the Seine and its forts.

On the 16th, the workers prevented another attempt to take their guns, this time at the Place des Vosges, by raising barricades in the rue des Tournelles. Paris was seething with rumours of a coming *coup d'état*. Foreign correspondents sent home the most alarming reports. The Central Committee, although itself on the defensive, did not check individual initiative. There were scuffles round the arsenals and thefts of arms and ammunition. A band of armed men seized a house in Montmartre and defied the police.

Late in the evening of the 17th, Thiers summoned Vinoy, d'Aurelle, the Ministers, the Mayor Jules Ferry, and M. Choppin from the Prefecture to a council of war. No other authorities had been informed of what was in the wind. The local mayors knew nothing. Even the police commissioners had only been told that the daily reception by the Prefect would not be held on the 18th.

Thiers unfolded his plan: the four hundred-odd guns were to be seized between three and four that morning by 15,000 regulars and 3,000 gendarmes; the National Guard would cover their retirement to the Ecole Militaire. Only Ferry supported the idea. The rest were appalled. D'Aurelle had just obtained the opinion of the commanders of forty of his most reliable battalions: they had been unanimous in declaring that their men could not be trusted. Vinoy, knowing well enough that his troops were inadequate for so vast an enterprise, nevertheless, covered by Thiers's responsibility, yielded: " I am a soldier; give your orders ! " Thiers, eloquent as ever, carried his point.

There could be hardly a hope of success; but if the guns could not be removed, it was probable that the insurrection thus provoked could be easily suppressed, once and for all. Thiers stood to win either way, provided only that these calculations were correct. To the historian of the Consulate and Empire the suppression of a mere Paris riot seemed simplicity itself. He would enormously enhance his prestige with the Assembly and abroad, might, like Cavaignac who had insulted him so grossly more than twenty years ago, " deserve well of his country." Whether he gained the guns or decimated Paris, he would attain his final objectives: peace with Prussia, defeat of Royalist reaction, the constitution of the French Republic, the Republic of Adolphe Thiers.

# PART II

# CHAPTER I

# THE EIGHTEENTH OF MARCH

" Well, M. Thiers, you were wrong about Paris on March 18th. . . ."
" I have never been wrong about Paris ! "
" You have admitted it yourself."
" I have never admitted it, never ! "
" What, never ? Here is the *Moniteur*. . . ."

FALLOUX: Mémoires d'un Royaliste

" I could accuse one or two people, but I will not do so, although people have very often not been so tender of *my* feelings. I will not tell you the cause of the mistake, if, indeed, mistake there was."

THIERS: Enquête sur le 18 mars

THE TROOPS set out about three in the morning of March 18. The night was cold and foggy, and snow had fallen only a few days before. Save for the men of Derroja's and Faron's divisions, the soldiers were raw provincial levies suddenly brought into Paris, thrown on the city's hospitality, excited and intimidated by the silent monstrosity of the icy, dumb streets as they marched to attention, forbidden to talk or smoke, without rations, coffee or brandy, marching on a night expedition whose object, if they guessed, they disapproved.

La Mariouse and Faron led their men to the Buttes-Chaumont and Belleville in the east, Wolff to the Bastille, Derroja to the Hôtel de Ville. Other columns spread to the Invalides, the Luxembourg, the Place Saint-Michel, the Temple : to every quarter where there were guns.

The hardest task was reserved for the divisions commanded by Paturel and Lecomte : the capture of the 171 guns at the great battery crowning the Butte Montmartre.

There could hardly be a *coup* more hazardous than one

directed upon the Butte. The topography and the population were equally redoubtable. To make matters worse,
Thiers had sent there not his best men, Faron's infantry and
marines, but the 88th Regiment, already notorious for their
indiscipline. Neither Thiers nor Lecomte knew beforehand
that the guns were so encumbered that they could not fire
effectively and that they had no serviceable ammunition.
Thiers had visited the battery himself a few days before
and had persuaded himself that here lay the strength of his
opponents. He had been correct, at least, in a way he had
not realised : the Montmartre Vigilance Committee was the
moral and political centre of resistance.

Lecomte reached the Butte unperceived. The sentry,
Turpin, alone, awake, greasing a bayonet, was shot and
wounded. The guard-post in the rue des Rosiers had time
to fire before they were rushed, captured and shut up in the
cellars of the Tour Solférino restaurant. It was all over by
four. The natives, accustomed to nocturnal shooting, had
not roused.

Lecomte's men stood to their arms around the guns and
waited for horses with gun-carriages. But the horses did not
come. Lecomte rode up and down in the freezing mist.
Still no sign of the indispensable horses. Paturel's Division,
behind them, had captured the guns at the Moulin de la
Galette with equal ease. But there, too, horses were lacking.

At Headquarters, after an agitated exchange of telegrams, Valentin, Commander of the Mounted Police,
reported to Vinoy at last, at 5.55, that Wolff and Henrion
had successfully occupied the Bastille and the Cité ; at 6.20,
that Belleville, too, was in the hands of the troops. Satisfactory reports continued to come in from all over Paris.

About eight, however, a slight note of anxiety began to
creep into the telegrams. There was some criticism of the
provocative action to be heard from the residents at the
Place Saint-Michel. At 8.15, two barricades were raised in
front of the *Marseillaise* hall, the popular rallying-place in
the rue de Flandre at La Villette. They were almost opposite
the police station, and the local commissioner began to

grow worried, though not seriously alarmed. At eight, too, news came in that Montmartre had been successfully occupied and that horses and gun-carriages were on the way: four hours too late. At 8.20, Montmartre reported the capture of 400 prisoners, a gross exaggeration. At 9.10, Faron's marines had torn down the red flag on the Bastille Column.

About 8.30, Ferry, at the Hôtel de Ville, had received from Valentin a thoroughly reassuring summary: " Reports in general satisfactory at the moment. Seem to be preparations for resistance with barricades at the *Marseillaise* hall. Montmartre seems to have been occupied after a very slight engagement; Belleville, too, with certain points of resistance. General demand for disarmament of rebel districts."

Suddenly, the sound of gun-fire broke across their satisfaction. Duval, Commander of the National Guard in the XIIIth district, had fired blank from the Gobelins battery; it was known that he had munitions ready for his fifteen guns which commanded the Avenues and the Place d'Italie. " The quarter," ran the scared report, " is almost without troops and entirely in the hands of the self-styled General Duval, who is recruiting the local urchins and giving them shovels with which to dig trenches." But half an hour later the Mayor of the XIIIth reassured Ferry: the ammunition was now all damp and useless.

Duval's signal had been heard. The XIth began to rise. Barricades sprang up in the rue de la Roquette, cutting the Bastille from Père-Lachaise. The troops at the Place de la Bastille were fraternising. From La Villette, the police wired, at 10.25, that the situation was becoming ridiculous: a score of persons were inside the *Marseillaise* hall and had shut the doors; the troops were in the street and making no attempt to get in; "if this goes on, the troops will be foiled."

Five minutes later came the worst news of all. At 10.15, the Prefecture had sent out a circular telegram reporting the occupation of the Butte Montmartre and the encirclement of the Vigilance Committee in the rue des Rosiers. Now the

Prefecture wired urgently: " Very bad news from Montmartre. Troops have refused to act. Butte, guns and
prisoners recaptured by the insurgents." Within a few
minutes the disaster was confirmed by the thunder of three
salvos of blank from the Butte. The affair had been long
settled; but, as usual, communications had not been kept up
during this critical period.

Lecomte's men had been standing to arms for three hours
in the cold. There had been no breakfast. There had been
no sign of the horses. They had waited with growing discomfort, while Lecomte and his staff rode desperately up
and down trying to pierce the raw fog which veiled Paris.

Meanwhile, the Government's posters were spreading
over the walls. Verbose and tactless, they spoke highly of
the hated d'Aurelle, " so worthy to be at your head "—
almost a calculated ironic provocation. They treated the
Parisians like naughty children. They distinguished between
" good " and " bad " districts. They spoke of " order,"
indissolubly linked in Parisian minds with the 2nd of
December: " Parisians, we address you thus because we
value your good sense, your wisdom, your patriotism; but,
after this warning, you will approve a recourse to force, for
it is necessary that, at all costs and without a day's delay,
order, the condition of your welfare, be restored, complete,
immediate and unshakable." There could not have been a
more provocative ultimatum.

The early-rising Montmartrois began to come out for
milk, bread, water from the communal pump. Soon a
crowd, puzzled rather than hostile, began to gather round
the troops, offering them breakfast, shaming them for
connivance in a Royalist plot. The soldiers, cold and
weary, embarrassed by this good humour, answered timidly.
The sun was rising, warm and cheerful. It hardly seemed
the day for the bloody work of " order."

The crowd pressed around the soldiers, breaking their
ranks. Lecomte, his staff and the police, who had long not
dared to show their faces in Montmartre, were powerless.
Garbed as a National Guard, Louise Michel, leader of the

revolutionary women Socialists, was tending the wounded Turpin. Clémenceau, the Mayor, arrived about eight o'clock, examined the wounded man professionally, began to make arrangements to have him transported to a more suitable place. A police-sergeant stopped him. Clémenceau applied to Lecomte. " No," replied Lecomte, " I know the effect of carrying a wounded man through a riot." Clémenceau remarked that he was, after all, Mayor of Montmartre. " Well, get to your *mairie* then ! " Lecomte ordered brusquely. Leaving the responsibility to the military, Clémenceau retired. Louise Michel, too, ran down the hill, calling out that there was treachery afoot.

The National Guard had now realised what was happening. At the post in the rue Doudeauville they found two drums which had not been smashed, and ran through the streets beating the fall-in. The drums filled the narrow alleys, menacing, alarming. Guards, half-asleep, ran out of their houses, slinging their rifles. None of them had received Vinoy's orders to fall in at six. By eight, there were nearly 300 of them on the Boulevard Ornano.

Here they suddenly ran into a detachment of the 88th of the Line. There was a moment of suspense. Then the soldiers turned up the butts of their rifles, fraternised. Arm-in-arm they walked along to the rue Muhler, the widest approach to the summit of the Butte on that side.

The rest of the 88th were guarding this approach, Lecomte's rear. Seeing their comrades fraternising, they waved to them to come up. Lecomte caught sight of this, had them arrested and thrown into the Tour Solférino cellars, replacing them by police. But the momentary distraction was fatal. A crowd of women, children and National Guards swept up the farther side of the Butte, breaking down the troops' half-hearted resistance.

Lecomte lost his head. Commanded his troops to fire on the crowd. A pause filled with terrible suspense. Lecomte again ordered his men to fire ; and again. Then the troops turned up the butts of their rifles, and, amid the wild joy of relief, handed them to the crowd in exchange for a mug of wine, a kind word, a fraternal embrace. " Long live the Republic ! " they shouted; and the crowd replied " Long live the Line ! "

Furious gestures surrounded Lecomte. They took him for Vinoy himself. Dragged him from his horse. The 88th, released from their prison, were for shooting him out of hand. Saner members of the National Guard simply arrested him, as well as some sixty police. They took the police off to the *mairie* in the rue des Abbesses, Lecomte himself to their headquarters in the rue des Rosiers.

A raging crowd howled round the little house. The 88th were clamorous for his blood. Inside, Lecomte was forced to scribble a pencilled order for the evacuation of the Butte; but this was quite unnecessary, for all the troops had long gone over to the crowd and the officers and police had slunk away as best they could.

It was imperative to get Lecomte away. The 88th especially, furious at their arrest, were getting ready to besiege the house, although the civilians and the Guards seemed satisfied with their triumph. Finally, Lecomte was escorted through the howling mob down the hill to a music-hall in the rue de Clignancourt, called the Château Rouge, once a pavilion built by Henri IV for Gabrielle d'Estrées. Here he, together with some other captured officers, was placed in the keeping of a genial old whiskered Jew, Captain Meyer, who made himself responsible for their safety, hoping to smuggle them out under cover of darkness. By ten o'clock, the Montmartrois were again masters of the Butte, and at 10.30 the three volleys of blank announced the recapture to Paris.

Paturel had fared no better at the back of the hill. He had managed to get a few horses together and had begun to move the guns down the narrow, precipitous rue Lepic. But the street had suddenly become solid with people, and it was impossible to force a way through without a massacre. The soldiers fraternised; the gun-traces were cut. The unfortunate General, pelted with vegetables from a barrow, fell off his horse, slipped away. The crowd hoisted the guns, by hand, back to the Moulin de la Galette, then joined the others on the Butte.

So far the incident had passed off with good humour. But down on the Place Pigalle, Susbielle had been faced by a very different enemy: the swell mobsmen and prostitutes of the Outer Boulevards, the sinister carrion of the edges of a great city. There was a scuffle, a few shots, before the troops went over. A few people were wounded. A Chasseurs captain spurred his white horse into the press, swinging his sabre. A couple of shots felled him and his horse. Half an hour later, there was not a trace of the animal left. It had been cut to pieces by the women, who had conserved this jackal trick from the Prussian Siege. The savagery brought into the temper of the revolt a new element which was to have its full consequence on the hill later that day.

Thiers's *coup* had failed completely. Its last hope had vanished when the troops had fraternised. He had counted upon 18,000 loyal National Guards: when the fall-in sounded at six o'clock, some fourteen men from each battalion appeared, not 600 in all. The rest, not even warned for duty, since the Council of War the previous night had broken up too late for the order to reach them, did not know at all where to meet, and, confused by the opposing drums, carried along by the hurrying crowds, dispersed, or simply returned home to await events. Thiers himself admitted later: " I must say, for I wish to be just, that even if the best measures had been taken to seize the guns, to cross Paris with 250 gun-carriages, for there were 250 guns to transport, was an operation of the greatest difficulty and the greatest risk." So great a risk, indeed, that the dispositions made by a man who, even discounting his own estimation, was no fool, cannot escape the suspicion of deliberately provocative intention.

The insurgents were, so early in the morning, as confused as the authorities. Every quarter for itself was the watchword. No one had the least idea what was happening, save a confident feeling that some sinister Royalist or

Bonapartist *Coup d'État* had been foiled. *It* had come at last: another new era of fraternity.

None of the organisations or parties had any idea of canalising or exploiting the outbreak. The Blanquists, in the absence of the Old One, arrested the previous day from his sick-bed in the South, were quite unprepared. The International knew nothing and was ready for nothing. The only authority left was the Central Committee of the Federation of the National Guard, the " occult committee " so dreaded by the police and the regular powers, but in fact endowed with the merest simulacrum of command when it came to direct action.

The Committee had met the previous evening in a school in the rue Basfroi, behind the Bastille, for the Place de la Corderie had lately become dangerously infested with police spies. The sitting had lasted well into the night, and the last members had left, very tired, about half past three in the morning—just too early to see the troops moving. The next sitting had been fixed for eleven o'clock that evening, so that it is plain that no one at all expected Thiers' move. When the guns announced the recapture of the Butte, Ferré of the Montmartre Vigilance Committee found Bergeret, appointed, last evening, Commander of the Montmartre Legion, and sent him post-haste down to the rue Basfroi, where he was joined a little later by Assi, Géresme, Bouit, Lavalette and a few more. None of them had the least experience of directing an insurrection, except Assi of the Creusot strike, and Bouit, Blanqui's secretary. They had no plan ready. Events had moved far beyond their capacity. They discussed and argued, while one of them held, in the school-yard, a vague examination of the various prisoners continually brought in.

Barricades were rising everywhere. The rue de la Roquette was blocked. The whole XIIIth was in the hands of the National Guard. The tricolour hoisted on the Bastille Column by Faron's men, early that morning, had been torn down and replaced by the red flag. Isolated commanders were gathering their battalions in their districts:

Faltot in the rue de Sèvres, Brunel and Ranvier in the XXth
and Xth, Duval at the Panthéon, which he had carried
without a blow, Pindy in the IIIrd, Varlin, after much
confusion, in the Batignolles, Arnould a mixed crowd of
Guards and mutinied soldiers in Montmartre. But as yet the
battalions refused to leave their own districts, making
preparations to resist the troops who were actually retiring
fast upon the Ecole Militaire from every point in the city.
As yet, too, there was no central direction whatever.

D'Aurelle distinguished himself by a pompous announcement of victory which he sent round to the papers, some of
which were unwise enough to print it. At noon, the Government posted another provocative proclamation, drawn up
by Picard : " The Government has decided to make an end
of an insurrectionary committee whose members represent
only communistic doctrines and wish to deliver Paris up to
pillage and France to the grave." Nothing in fact could have
been further from the thoughts of the Committee than pillage or even Communism. Even now they were discussing
in the rue Basfroi how civil war might be at all costs
avoided.

Soon after midday, everyone went off to dinner. The
photographers were busy " shooting " National Guards,
well-bearded and heroic, in sublime postures against the
barricades.

At the Château Rouge, prisoners and captors sat down
together to a meal which must have been at least tolerable,
for it cost no less than 86 francs. Lecomte was restive. He
kept demanding to be taken before this committee of which
one heard so much, instead of remaining quietly till dark
behind Simon Meyer's bayonets. The crowd outside were
shouting that he should be taken before the committee.
But what committee ? Paris was full of them. No one knew
where the Central Committee was sitting, or whether it was
sitting at all so early in the day. But the word " committee "
seemed to possess some magic authority. Meyer, pressed on
both sides, by the mob and by Lecomte himself, decided
that the Montmartre Vigilance Committee would be best :

it was influential locally and, above all, it was near. It would have been terribly dangerous to transport a general through the riot to the rue Basfroi, half across Paris.

The crowd in the rue de Clignancourt had changed since the early morning. Then it had been composed of Montmartrois natives, rough but not vicious, aglow with patriotism and brotherhood. Now there were mixed with them the sinister persons who had mangled the horse in the Place Pigalle and the now thoroughly demoralised deserters of the 88th. Lecomte's position was really dangerous.

Under a strong escort, commanded by one Lagrange, Meyer evacuated his prisoners. They fought their way by main force back to the rue des Rosiers. The mob, climbing the Butte after them, stormed round the little house. The Vigilance Committee was not there. By an acute irony, Jaclard, Ferré and Bergeret had met a few doors from the Château Rouge just before Lecomte had left. At half past three, they heard of the critical situation there and sent word to Meyer to redouble his precautions. It was just too late.

Down on the Place de la Bastille, the storm-centre, crowds were moving excitedly but aimlessly, shouting, " To the Hôtel de Ville ! " but hesitating to go there without a lead. A huge barricade had been completed in the rue de la Roquette. Another was building in the rue Neuve de Lappe. Detachments of National Guards were marching past with guns and prisoners for the Committee in the rue Basfroi, saluting the red flag on the Bastille Column. Then there was a different, a solemn, drum-roll ; a hush. A funeral cortège, a short procession, walking slowly. Behind the coffin a tall, familiar figure, hatless, in the cloak of the Romantic Age. The Guards presented arms. It was Victor Hugo, following his son Charles to Père-Lachaise. Many fell in behind. The old Revolution died as the new was born ; and the birth was on the consecrated place of Paris revolutions : the Bastille, the martyrs of July and June ; and those, soon to follow, of May. Solemnly drummed, the procession passed on to the great cemetery, soon to hold the last stand of the Commune.

William, first Emperor of the united Germans, victor of Paris, was at that moment entering Berlin in triumph.

The Ministers sat in agitated consultation at the Foreign Office. Vinoy had relapsed into doubts. Thiers, behind his twinkling spectacles, remained impassive. The man who had made 1830 and 1834, who had narrated the Consulate and Empire, knew what he wanted and how to get it. All was by no means lost. Ferry had forty-eight hours' provisions at the Hôtel de Ville, and was covered by Derroja's men in the Lobau barracks opposite. The Ecole Militaire, the Trocadéro, Auteuil, Passy were still loyal. The bourgeois of the Bourse quarter asked only to be supported by armed force. A resistance could be organised, even an offensive attempted; and this would have deprived the scattered insurrection of its chief strength, its onward urge. At the least, the action could have been maintained until uncontaminated troops arrived from outside the city. This had been Cavaignac's plan in 1848; but Thiers, perhaps recalling the Dictator's snubs, refused to take it. His own plan was crueller, more certain. He decided to practise now what he had suggested to Louis Philippe in February, to Cavaignac himself in June, a plan which had been successfully carried out by Windischgrätz at Vienna. He would retire from the city in order to retake it and " restore order for a generation."

The Ministers and the generals were astounded. They considered that the insurrection of October 31 had been far more serious, and it had ended in fiasco. Without the Hôtel de Ville, which was in no immediate danger, the riot could not aspire to the dignity of a revolution. They were appalled by the responsibility for civil war implied in Thiers's decision, underrating his power of distortion for propaganda. Vinoy, as usual, protested and, as usual, took cover in his military obedience. Thiers signed the order for the total evacuation of Paris.

A chance incident removed the Ministers' last scruples. An insurgent battalion from the Gros-Caillou district passed along the Quai d'Orsay on their way to the centre. For a moment it seemed as if the whole Ministry would be seized. " We are done for ! " cried the Minister for War, making for the back-stairs. But the battalion went on, never suspecting how close they had been to a valuable haul. Thiers, too, slipped down the back-stairs, more slowly; he climbed into a cab, and, escorted by General Vinoy and a few cavalry, drove hell for leather to the Pont de Sèvres. He stopped for an instant, pencilled confirmation of the order to evacuate; and then the cab hardly drew rein until they were safe in Versailles. It was just four o'clock.

At this precise moment the crisis had come in the house in the rue des Rosiers. Meyer had been joined by Herpin-Lacroix, Garibaldian Franc-Tireur, a great bull of a man. The mob was milling round the house, soldiers thrusting their rifles through the window. Herpin-Lacroix flung his huge body across the passage. In the narrow garden, Lagrange's huddled platoon looked like a firing-squad.

Kadanski, a Pole, who had arrived from Autun that morning and, mingling with the curious sightseers, had been recruited by Jaclard of the Montmartre Vigilance Committee, quite casually, because he looked like a reliable officer, thought of trying to save the prisoner by the parody of a court martial in a room upstairs. It was recognised there that Lecomte had only been carrying out the orders of his superiors when he commanded his men to fire on the crowd. Kadanski shouted this decision from the window, but the mob's howling drowned his voice.

Lecomte might yet have been saved, for the National Guards at least were beginning to sober. Suddenly everything was ruined by an unfortunate accident. About half past four, Herpin-Lacroix was swept aside by the inrush of a new mob from the sinister Outer Boulevards, dragging with them a tall white-bearded old man in frock-coat and silk-hat : it was Clément Thomas.

Paris had long cherished a particular hatred of this " butcher " of 1848. More recently, he had openly declared that the Buzenval sortie had been undertaken only to let a little of the National Guard's hot blood, and had publicly insulted their delegates after its heroic failure. With ill-timed curiosity, he had mounted a small barricade in the Place Pigalle to see what was happening. Recognised, he was at once seized by the mob, ridiculously accused of spying, and dragged off to the rue des Rosiers.

This final inrush broke down the last resistance. Herpin-Lacroix was dragged from his hold. Kadanski, his epaulettes wrenched off, vanished in the crush. They ran Clément Thomas through the house and into the garden. A shot knocked off his top-hat. As he caught it up, correct unto death, he was flung against the wall and riddled with bullets. The firing continued long after he was dead. Seventy bullets were found in his body.

Lecomte had no further illusions. He took leave of the other officers, who saluted as he passed into the garden. He fell on his knees; some say, shot from behind—in the neck. They propped him up beside Clément Thomas's corpse; and it was done. It was soldiers that fired this time, and fewer of them.

After an explosion of hysterical glee, the crowd seemed to realise what they had done. The house was deserted. Silent men slunk down the street. The bodies lay under a blood-stained sheet beneath a dead peach-tree. A few children on the wall squabbled for a view of the corpses.

In the restored quiet, Simon Meyer escorted the surviving prisoners back to the comparative safety of the Château Rouge. The crowd stood hostile but silent. The escort crossed Clémenceau, pale-faced. He had been guarding the gendarmes imprisoned at the *mairie* and had only just heard what was happening on the Butte. He had arrived too late. Not that he could have done anything against the mad-dened mob. Now they growled: he was suspect, a Deputy, the Mayor, one of the authorities. He pushed his way back to his *mairie* at the mercy of a shout, a shot. It took him nearly an hour to make the few hundred yards back to safety.

The news of the murder spread rapidly through Paris.

At once the riot became serious. To the " Men of Order "
addressed by Thiers's proclamations the Central Committee
became automatically " assassins," and so, by the logic of
political jargon, " bandits " : the most horrid excesses were
to be feared from them, and were, indeed, already credited.
But the horror was not potent enough either to rally a loyal
resistance or to check the insurgents' advance. Armed men
were pouring downhill upon the centre at last, from the
Buttes-Chaumont in the east, the Butte-aux-Cailles in the
south and the Butte Montmartre in the north.

The Committee had at length begun to organise the
insurrection. Four members sat as a permanent executive
committee in the rue Basfroi. One by one, all the main
strategic positions were falling before the forces converging
upon the Hôtel de Ville, the key to political and strategic
control of Paris.

Inside the building, the Mayor, Jules Ferry, still sat under
the protection of some four-score of Derroja's regulars in
the Lobau barracks. He had received repeated orders to
evacuate, repeatedly refused, incredulous that the Government should have decided to abandon Paris to a riot less
apparently formidable than that of October 31. Faron's
sailors were holding the western bridges. A strong defence
of the Quais might still cut the insurrection in two and
save the Hôtel de Ville. But almost all the rest of the troops
had already retired to the Ecole Militaire, preparatory to
falling back on Versailles. Thiers's orders had been formal.

The insurgents were close now. Brunel had occupied the
Napoléon barracks and that essential instrument, the
National Printing Works. At 7.30, he joined up with Pindy
from the Quartier Saint-Antoine and Ranvier from Belleville, and moved on the Hôtel de Ville, running up a few
barricades on the Place de Grève and at the corner of the
rue de Rivoli to protect their flank from counter-attack.
They still hesitated to attack the building, believing that
it must be held by a large force. But Ferry, deserted by his
gendarmes, was telegraphing in vain for reinforcements,
refusing to leave. It was nearly ten o'clock before Derroja

finally decided that he dare disobey orders no longer. The insurgents were cautiously creeping into the building as Ferry fled through the underground tunnel to the Lobau barracks. At half past ten, Brunel at length occupied the whole Hôtel de Ville for the Central Committee, ran up the red flag, and illuminated the whole frontage with the gas-flares used for triumphal celebrations.

Ferry escaped to the *mairie* of the Ist district, hurriedly informed a gathering of frightened Mayors of the fall of the Hôtel de Ville, and leaped through a back-window, with Brunel's men hot behind him. He hid for the night at a relative's and was away to Versailles in the morning.

The Mayors had met at the *mairie* of the IInd district that afternoon, where they had learnt for the first time of Thiers's decision to evacuate Paris. Some Ministers had joined them. Vautrain of the IVth and Vacherot of the Vth, both strong Conservatives, were in favour of resistance, but Picard, Minister for the Interior, would take no initiative against Thiers's orders. Terrified by the burden of responsibility laid upon them as the only legally constituted authority left in Paris, in whom alone was vested the power of negotiation which might still avert civil war, the Mayors had exceeded their strictly municipal functions by replacing the lamentable Cresson at the Police Prefecture by Edmond Adam, who had been forced to resign after the riot of October 31, and d'Aurelle by a certain Colonel Langlois, a puffy, pompous renegade from the International. At nightfall, a deputation had taken these proposals to the council of Ministers sitting in the rue d'Abbatucci. Among the delegates, Jules Favre had noticed the Radical Deputy Millière, who had had Favre himself in his power for a few minutes on October 31 and had later raked up some scandals in his private life for Pyat's paper, at the time of the Assembly elections. Favre interrupted the Mayors' spokesman: " Is it true that some Generals have been shot ? " Then, with one of his grand rhetorical gestures: " There can be no parleying with assassins ! " The Mayors, anything but assassins, had to retire unsatisfied. Jules Favre

had made the first move in Thiers's policy of sabotaging
conciliation and provoking civil war.

After the short session at the *mairie* of the Ist, interrupted
by Ferry's spectacular passage, the Mayors returned to the
IInd, whither Picard's secretary brought confirmation of
Langlois's appointment. Langlois, swelling with his new
title, quite arbitrarily promised to replace Ferry by Dorian,
the popular Saint-Simonian ironmaster always brought out
to save the Government's neck on such occasions; and also
to propose to the Assembly immediate elections in Paris.
Then he sent to the *Journal Officiel*, which was still in the
Government's hands, an announcement of his appointment
so braggart that Favre and Picard had to telegraph urgently:
" Suppress in Langlois's announcement the words, ' Relying upon the courage and patriotism of M. Langlois, Member
of the Assembly.' " After this, Langlois, accompanied by
the Deputies Lockroy and Cournet, proceeded to the Hôtel
de Ville in all the pride of his new rank.

The Central Committee was now completely master of
Paris. Duval had occupied the Prefecture, Varlin and
Bergeret the General Headquarters in the Place Vendôme.
Great barricades had been built to repel counter-attacks
upon these two key positions; another was building in front
of the Hôtel de Ville. But the precaution was needless. All
the troops, except one regiment left behind at the Luxembourg in the confusion, had retired.

The Committee sat in the Hôtel de Ville in the utmost
perplexity. They had never had the slightest idea that they
might be called upon to act as a Government, at least as
legal as that of September 4, rival to the National Assembly.
Their political claims had been purely local; their activities
hardly more than those of supervision. None had any
political experience. A few were members of the International, notably Varlin, an efficient co-operative and
union organiser. Brunel and Duval were good soldiers, but
not actually Committee members. The rest were a collection
of mere delegates, personally vague. The only man who
had some realisation of their task was a young commercial

traveller, Edouard Moreau, who quite suddenly emerged from complete obscurity to lead their deliberations.

The first thing to be done was to appoint a commander of the National Guard. At this opportune moment arrived the Commander of the Artillery, Charles Lullier. A picturesque and magniloquent drunkard, four times jailed by the Empire for riotous behaviour, but with a good service record during the siege, he at once was acclaimed for his impressive appearance. Brunel, who had captured the Hôtel de Ville and had been prominent all day, might have seemed a more logical choice; but he lacked the braggadocio of Lullier, who afterwards produced a pre-posterous tale of how he had more or less run the revolution single-handed.

When, therefore, Langlois, the Mayors' nominee, arrived at two in the morning, he was met with a curt denial of his competence, and retired to Versailles to confirm his resignation of a post he had never held. It was the Committee's first check to the Mayors. Favre had already anticipated them. The Mayors were being forced into the uneasy position between two fires which they were to occupy throughout the week of the Government of Monsieur Assi.

The troops were still retiring. " In good order," Thiers wrote next day. They straggled through the dark, dragging the step, cursing the gendarmes whom they accused of " framing " them. According to Thiers's instructions, all the forts had been abandoned, including the key to the Paris-Versailles road, Mont-Valérien. Vinoy had tele-graphed to Daudel, at Fort Bicêtre, at 7.55 p.m. to retire his whole brigade on Versailles, leaving only two battalions at Mont-Valérien; commanders, pickets, engineers and gunners alone were to stay in the other forts. The Staff was aghast at the order, but their instructions were peremptory. The commander of Mont-Valérien, however, was intelligent enough to play for time with the emissaries sent by the Committee next day.

At Versailles, Thiers, who had learned of the generals'

murder at late supper, slept the brief sleep of affairs and age in the bed which the German Emperor had vacated only a few weeks before. Two huge Chasseurs stood sentry at his door all night. At three in the morning, his companion-housekeeper, Mademoiselle Dosne, woke him to urge, at the Staff's insistent request, the reoccupation of Mont-Valérien. Sulkily, he assented. With that sleepy order he had won his war.

In Paris, the tocsin, pealing from Saint-Merri and Notre-Dame, boded gothically a new Terror.

# CHAPTER II

# THE GOVERNMENT OF
# MONSIEUR ASSI

"A Republican of yesterday and before yesterday, a Republican at school, in the workshop, in the study, I shuddered in terror at the Republic's approach. . . . What were we to do with the Revolution? What was to become of us all when there was no one above or below who possessed its secret, its conception? . . . I fled before the monster of democratic socialism, the riddle of which I could not unravel; and an inexpressible terror froze my soul, depriving me of very thought, . . . Contrary to all experience, contrary to the order of historic development hitherto invariably followed, the fact was to come before the idea, as if Providence had, this time, struck deliberately without warning."

PROUDHON, *on the Revolution of February 1848*

THAT SUNDAY OF MARCH 19, 1871, was the perfect beginning of yet another new era in Paris. The day shone brilliant and mild. Paris indulged in all those excesses of the Continental Sunday which shocked the last of the retreating English tourists. Comic barricades were built haphazard, and comic National Guards posed in an orgy of photography. Politics were briefly forgotten. Even on the shocked boulevards, Edmond de Goncourt's lively curiosity noted only "a stupefied indifference, occasionally an ironic foreboding, mostly the consternation of elderly gentlemen with hands lifted in despair and a prudent glance around them." Most of the bourgeois had given at least a tacit approbation to the revolution: unwilling themselves openly to revolt, they were not ungrateful to this "occult and unknown Committee" for taking the initiative against the stupid and ruinous Assembly.

The Central Committee was unknown simply because its members were mere delegates from the federated

battalions. That they could not be truly called an anonymous conspiracy, as Thiers's propaganda alleged, was
shown by their posters, signed in full, even with some of
their addresses.

Some of them, too, were popular characters in their own
circles. Everyone knew Babick—or Babicki, for he was of
Polish extraction—the " perfumer of the rue de Nemours,"
an eccentric but harmless " character," devotee of a strange
religion called " Fusionism," a mixture of the elements of
many odd cults (" to fusion " was a favourite word of his
in the Committee's debates), a spiritualist who spent much
of his time in graveyards conversing with the ghost of Saint-
Simon's disciple, Père Enfantin. Blanchet, alias Stanislas
Pourille, was a familiar Latin Quarter figure, a black-
bearded, half-paralysed, limping skeleton with the loud
thin voice of the Sue conspirator : renegade Capucin novice,
bankrupt silk merchant, private tutor to some innocent
girls, finally secretary to the Police-Commissioner of Lyons.
But the fools and knaves were not typical of the Committee
as a whole. It included men of considerable talent : Assi,
the handsome little leader of the Creusot strike ; Jourde, a
tall, slim Auvergnat, clerk at the Banque de France ;
Eugène Varlin, efficient organiser of the Bookbinders'
Union and a chain of co-operative restaurants ; Bergeret,
energetic in spite of his incredible vanity, forced by an
accident during his early career as a stable-boy to lead his
men in a cab. The rest, less well known, were a fairly
representative cross-section of the Paris which composed the
Federation. They were, indeed, in the truest sense representatives ; and the bourgeois did not know them simply because they knew nothing of Paris east of the Hôtel de Ville.

There were rogues, too, who had swaggered in to collect
the spoils of a revolution they did not quite understand.
These centred round the new Commander of the National
Guard, Charles Lullier. Lullier himself was in the pay of
Versailles : it is, however, less certain whether he really
intended to give value for the money. His knavery was
almost indistinguishable from his accustomed drunken folly.

His immediate *entourage* was both bogus and dangerous, the condottiere of the many guerilla wars which had accompanied the " penetration " of colonial and backward countries. There was Ganier d'Abin (not an aristocrat; Abin was his native village), who claimed to have been Generalissimo of the Siamese army, with a medal-smothered chest which " rang like a tocsin " as he strode round the Place Vendôme. There was the *provocateur* Raoul du Bisson, who may or may not have been a count, but had certainly been a Royalist; Carlist in Spain, Legitimist under the Second Empire, general under Bomba, tyrant of Naples, finally aiming at a throne of his own by a shady expedition to Abyssinia. Around this precious trio a motley crowd of Garibaldians, Zouaves or pseudo-Zouaves, Irishmen, Poles and Americans presented a picturesque spectacle as they spurred through the cheering streets in the blue tunic and breeches, black patent boots, gold-bedizened cuffs and epaulettes, broad red revers and sash of the General Staff.

Other famous characters brightened the streets that Sunday. *The* Garibaldian, in his red shirt and blue breeches and field-grey cloak, revealing expanses of gold braid, the whole surmounted by a huge slouch hat adorned with a great drooping feather. And his rival, the " Moldo-Wallachian Citizen," pacing slowly up and down the boulevards on a superb white charger, outshining the Garibaldian with red-plumed slouch hat, scarlet cloak and scarlet sash, simply bristling with revolvers of every calibre. Paris was amused with its new toy of a revolution.

The Central Committee's first proclamation, posted during the day, recalled the Parisians to seriousness:

" *To the People:*

" Citizens,

" The People of Paris has shaken off the yoke which it was attempted to impose upon them.

" Calm, impassive in their strength, they awaited, without fear and without provocation, the shameless madmen who would have assailed the Republic.

" This time our brothers of the Army refused to lay hands upon the ark of our liberties.

" Thanks be to all ; and may Paris and France together lay the foundations of a Republic acclaimed in all its consequences, the only Government which will close for ever the era of invasions and civil wars.

" The state of siege is raised.

" The people of Paris is summoned in its sections to hold its communal elections.

" The security of every citizen is assured by the co-operation of the National Guard.

" Hotel de Ville, this March 19th, 1871.
            " *Signed :*

" ASSI, BILLIORAY, FERRAT, BABICK, MOREAU, C. DUPONT, VARLIN, BOURSIER, MORTIER, GOUHIER, LAVAL-ETTE, JOURDE, ROUSSEAU, LULLIER, BLANCHET, GROL-LARD, BARROUD, GERESME, FABRE, POUGERET."

Another proclamation, addressed to the National Guard, was no less moderate :

" You charged us with the organisation of the defence of Paris and your rights.

" We are conscious that we have fulfilled this mission. Aided by your generous courage and your admirable coolness, we have driven out the Government that was betraying us.

" Now our mandate has expired and we hand it back to you, for we do not claim to take the place of those whom the popular breath has overthrown.

" Prepare therefore to hold your communal elections at once, and give us our reward, the only reward for which we have ever hoped : that of seeing you establish the true Republic.

" In the meantime, we will continue to hold the Hôtel de Ville in the name of the People."

The Versaillese Government had got out an edition of the *Journal Officiel* in the morning, just before the offices were taken over by the Committee. It contained a proclamation simply unintelligible to peaceful Paris. But such rhetoric was intended, as the event soon showed, simply as propaganda for Versaillese and provincial consumption. " The Government had exhausted every means of conciliation. . . . A committee calling itself the Central Committee has murdered in cold blood Generals Clément Thomas and Lecomte. Who are the members of this Committee? Communists, Bonapartists or Prussians ? "

This was sufficiently absurd in itself, but it told certain elements officially what they privately wished to believe. The Committee had a crushing rejoinder on the walls early in the afternoon: " The blood and mud with which they are trying to soil our honour are an ignoble infamy. Never has a sentence of execution been signed by us; never has the National Guard taken part in the execution of a crime. . . . Our conduct shows what we are. Have we solicited salaries or honours ? If we are unknown although we have obtained the confidence of 215 battalions, is it not because we have disdained propaganda ? Notoriety is cheaply earned : a few hollow phrases and a little baseness is enough : the recent past has proved that." Once again the Committee addressed the people: " Here is the mandate with which you entrusted us : where personal interest might begin, our duty ends ; do your will. My master, you have made yourself free. Obscure a few days since, we shall return to your ranks as obscure, and show to Governments that one can come down the steps of your Hôtel de Ville with head held high and the certainty of finding at the foot the clasp of your trusty, sturdy hands." Were these men " Communists, Prussians or Bonapartists, murderers or bandits " ?

The first session of the " Government of M. Assi " was held in the Hôtel de Ville on the morning of this Sunday, March 19. Assi did preside, although he was of practically no importance after the first meeting ; but the name struck the humour of English journalists especially—naturally, *Punch* could not resist the pun ; and it came to be adopted for the period of the Central Committee's rule, March 19–26.

The first business of the new Government was to reorganise the public services thrown into disorder by the withdrawal of most of the civil servants, expressly ordered by Thiers to sabotage the revolution. Varlin and Jourde were appointed to the financial business; Combaz, a Garibaldian Franc-Tireur, to the Post Office; Moreau to the National Printing Works; Eudes to the Ministry of War; Duval and Raoul Rigault to the Prefecture of Police, the hated name of which they palliated by calling it the " *Ex-*Prefecture "; Bergeret was confirmed as Lullier's Chief of Staff.

Most of these executive officials were not actually elected members of the Committee but local commanders recommended by their activity on March 18 or by their reputation. They were far more revolutionary in temper than the Committee, which, however, made itself responsible for their extremist policy by appointing them. The military and police were, under Eudes, Duval and Rigault, entirely in the hands of the Blanquists. Thus there arose the paradoxical position of a fundamentally " gradualist " Government served almost exclusively by a " physical-force " executive. The Committee was consequently drawn more and more into an intransigent attitude which it originally had every intention of declining. This contradiction is the sense of the whole period of Monsieur Assi's Government.

The conflict became apparent at the very first sitting. Eudes and Duval were clamorous for an immediate attack on Versailles. It might well have been successful, for Thiers's army was utterly demoralised and Lullier had assured the Committee that he had occupied Mont-Valérien, the key to the Paris-Versailles road. But the Committee simply would not realise that civil war had been made inevitable by Thiers's evacuation of Paris; they would not realise that they were a revolutionary Government. They were, as they proclaimed, entirely preoccupied

with preparing elections to regularise the position they had
not sought. Never had a revolutionary Government been so
anxious to abdicate; and it is not strange that Versailles
and the partisans of Versailles in Paris should have been
somewhat sceptical of this unheard-of self-abnegation.

With the Central Committee, with the Mayors and
even with Thiers the desire to avoid open responsibility for
starting civil war loomed large; not so with the Assembly.
The Central Committee especially, raised so unexpectedly
to a power which they had never even contemplated, were
terribly anxious to remain within the limits of strict legality
in order not to provoke civil war. They could not see that
Thiers had only not already openly contravened legality
simply because his army was not yet ready. They could not
see that the Assembly did not care about legality in the
slightest, were, in fact, in their preparations for a Royalist
*coup d'état*, making far wider breaches in legality than they
themselves could possibly have done. Above all, they could
not recognise that, however little they had meant to arrive
at the Hôtel de Ville, their presence there was, by every
canon, and especially by Versaillese canons, tantamount to
armed insurrection; and despite the urgings of the more
energetic executive members such as Eudes and Duval,
trained Blanquist insurrectionaries, they simply could not
see the first rule of insurrection, patent to all those who had
understood the Forty-Eight: never play with insurrection
unless you are fully prepared to face the consequences, for
the defensive is the death of every armed rising. Engels had
formulated those simple rules back in 1852. Well might
Marx storm at the " Parisian gentlemen with their heads
filled with Proudhon's emptiest phrases "; well might
Thiers, Talleyrand's pupil, doubt the Committee's sincerity.
With every chance of marching upon Versailles, scattering
the Assembly and dictating their own terms, even though
those terms might be the emptiest Proudhonist phrases, the
Committee contented itself with fixing the elections for
the Commune at the earliest possible date: Wednesday,
March 22.

With all their passion for strict legality, the Committee exceeded the attributions of a municipal government at this first sitting. The abolition of the court martial, the raising of the state of siege, an amnesty for all political and Press offenders were rather the property of national government. But these measures were harmless enough, even reassuring. The raising of the state of siege in particular was an extraordinary measure for a revolutionary government to take on the morrow of coming to power: it meant the abandonment of the elementary precaution against counter-revolution. Nothing better proves the Committee's pacific intentions.

A more immediately practical question was that of the murder of the two generals. Obviously, the Committee was in no way responsible, but it had in effect taken over the whole revolution, whether it wanted to or no, including its liabilities. " Take care not to disavow the people," said one member, " lest they in turn disavow you." Another pointed out that the revolution had been made by the workers and the bourgeoisie together; the bourgeoisie must be conciliated to secure the elections. " Well," was the reply, " abandon the people to gain the bourgeoisie: the people will withdraw, and you will see whether it is with the bourgeoisie that revolutions are made." The Committee compromised: the article in that evening's *Journal Officiel*, the first issue published by the revolution, defended the " executions " maladroitly enough. Thiers was permitted to stigmatise the Committee, in his despatches to the provinces, as a handful of ruffianly assassins.

The remainder of the session was devoted to the elections. They were to be held on a new basis: one representative for every 20,000, or fraction of over 10,000 inhabitants in each district. The former system, three representatives from each district irrespective of population, ranked the thinly inhabited residential quarters equally with working-class agglomerations where the population was three times as large—in effect, a plutocratic principle. The new system was thus far more democratically representative.

The registration was to be based on that of the November 1870 plebiscite. But the population had been considerably modified since then: nearly 60,000 people had died during the siege, another 60 to 100,000 of the wealthier had left Paris after the capitulation, and a large number more had left or were leaving for Versailles. On the other hand, some working-class districts had increased: the XIXth, for example, from 88,930 to 113,000, so that it was to elect six representatives instead of three. A more representative electoral system, therefore, would necessarily bring in a more proletarian municipal council.

The Mayors' assent was absolutely necessary if the elections and the Commune were to be unimpeachably legal. The Mayors were the only regular and legal authorities left in Paris, had been commissioned by the Minister for the Interior to mediate between Paris and Versailles, and held the electoral registers and ballot-forms. The only revolutionary among them was Ranvier of the XXth. Clémenceau of the XVIIIth tended to follow Ranc and sympathise with revolution if successful. Mottu of the IXth had personal ties with Delescluze, some sympathy for workers.

The reactionary group, headed by Thiers's confidant, Tirard of the IInd, included notably Vautrain of the IVth and Vacherot of the Vth. Desmarest of the IXth and the *restaurateur* Bonvalet of the IIIrd fell increasingly under Tirard's sway.

With them in their conciliatory efforts acted most of the bourgeois-Republican Paris Deputies: Louis Blanc, Henri Martin, Lockroy, Schoelcher, Greppo, Floquet, Tolain, Millière. They divided much in the same way as the Mayors, the Radicals and even the Socialists of the Forty-Eight, becoming far more reactionary than the younger men.

The Committee's simple, if misplaced, good faith in the negotiations was hardly matched by the Mayors'. Thiers had impressed upon their leader, Tirard, that it was necessary to gain time while the army was being reorganised at Versailles. Their task was to be twofold: to distract the

Committee with concessions which Thiers could easily refuse to ratify, and to encourage the reaction in Paris by every means: slander, sabotage, effective assistance. Many Mayors really desirous of conciliation unconsciously lent themselves to this policy.

The Mayors met at Bonvalet's at two o'clock on Sunday afternoon. With them were the Paris Deputies and the commanders of 50 reactionary battalions " of order," mostly from the Ist and IInd. The position was that, although they considered Thiers's policy fatal from every point of view, political, financial and diplomatic, he did represent the forces of order against anarchy and the defence of the Republic against Royalist reaction; so that, while he was not the ideal of moderate Republicans, he ought to be supported until some better leader could be found. This reasoning found general assent. The battalion-commanders declared their solidarity with the Mayors.

At another meeting, at the *mairie* of the IInd, Picard delegated full powers in Paris to Tirard. The Deputies resolved to go to the opening session of the Assembly next day to demand the most urgent reforms. Meanwhile, the Committee had occupied several more *mairies*.

The Mayors' next business was to get in touch with the Committee. At ten o'clock that Sunday evening, the Deputies Héligon and Malon, of the International, with Bonvalet and Murat, also sympathetic to the workers' movement, left Bonvalet's for the Hôtel de Ville. At the same time there arrived four delegates from the Committee—Arnold, " too well-dressed, latest fashion," Jourde, " violent talker," Moreau, " mild character in appearance," and Varlin, " the most amenable to reason," as Chéron, Tirard's Assistant, characterised them.

The debate rapidly became heated. The position of the Committee was stated by one of the delegates with admirable precision and concision. " The Central Committee has received a regular, imperative mandate. This mandate forbids them to allow the Government or the Assembly to touch their liberties or the Republic. Now, the Assembly has never ceased putting the existence of the Republic in question. It has placed a dishonoured general at our head, decapitalised Paris, tried to ruin her commerce. It has sneered at our sufferings, denied the devotion, the courage, the self-sacrifice Paris has shown during the siege, hooted her best-loved representatives, Garibaldi and Victor Hugo. The plot against the Republic is evident. The attempt was begun by gagging the Press; they hoped to terminate it by disarming our battalions. Yes, our cause was one of legitimate self-defence. If we had bowed our heads, there would have been an end of the Republic."

Varlin defined the claims of Paris: " We want not only the election of the municipal council, but real municipal liberties, the suppression of the Prefecture of Police, the right of the National Guard to name its chiefs and to reorganise itself, the proclamation of the Republic as the legal Government, the pure and simple remittance of the rents due, an equitable law on overdue bills, and the territory of Paris forbidden to the army."

The disputes dragged on far into the night. Arnold left at one o'clock, entrusting to Varlin a draft agreement. Thereupon Tirard, who presided over the meeting, declared that the delegates of the Committee were nothing but rebels, and that it was only his horror of bloodshed that decided him to accept the conventions unofficially, but that, officially, he did not mean to recognise them in any way. This unreasonable line of conduct roused Jourde's Auvergnat temper, and he was with difficulty soothed by Varlin, always calm. At 3 a.m., Chéron, according to his own account, got Jourde and Moreau to leave, and Varlin, exhausted, alone signed a rough agreement an hour later. It was agreed that the *mairies* and the Hôtel de Ville were to be restored to the Mayors, on condition that they proceeded immediately to hold municipal elections. The Hôtel de Ville was to be handed over to Bonvalet and Murat at ten that morning. Tirard had Thiers's promise of a general amnesty in his pocket, but refused to make use of it. The Mayors were visibly worried by their situation,

foreseeing more dangers. Chéron himself heroically proposed to constitute himself a hostage for their good faith,
but Varlin had no mandate to accept such a proposition,
as Chéron was undoubtedly aware.

The whole agreement was, in fact, highly irregular; only
one of the four delegates from the Committee had signed the
conventions, on his personal responsibility and without
submitting it to ratification. When Bonvalet and Murat
arrived next morning, the Committee, which had no cognisance of the treaty, refused to carry it out. The Mayors were
profoundly shocked by this apparent breach of faith, and
Thiers made great capital out of it; but, actually, it was no
more flagrant, but merely more public, than the behaviour
of Tirard. Henceforth, with the meeting of the reactionary
Assembly at Versailles, the struggle lay no longer between
the Mayors and the Committee, but between Versailles and
Paris: the unfortunate Mayors were caught between two
fires, and their position became increasingly untenable.
It was now the turn of armed resistance by the Friends
of Order in Paris, the comedy of Admiral Saisset and the
Grand-Hôtel conspiracy.

J. M. J. T. Saisset was a typical elderly vice-admiral, a
fiery old gentleman of sixty, stubborn, foolhardy, fearless;
as Schoelcher declared to the Commission of Enquiry into
the events of March 18, " neither encouragement nor dis-
couragement has any effect upon the Admiral when once he
is set upon what he conceives to be his duty." He had acquired
a reputation almost legendary by his exploits on the eastern
fortifications during the siege; but the whole character is
somehow almost legendary; his testimony at the enquiry
was so wildly improbable and so preposterously naïve that
it alone of some sixty depositions aroused the laughter of
those grim Commissioners. The Admiral's *Putsch*, as seen
by himself, was irresistibly comic. Throughout, he acted
with a sort of benevolent bad faith.

He seems to have begun intriguing for the leadership
of the forces of order very early on the 19th. At 12.45
p.m. Calmon, Under-Secretary of State for the Interior,

telegraphed to his chief, Picard, suggesting Saisset, who had just put himself at his disposal: " He would be well at the head of the National Guard." Calmon repeated his suggestion in two more urgent telegrams before one o'clock, reporting that Saisset guaranteed to restore order. The Ministry of the Interior was occupied by the insurgents at 1.15.

About two o'clock, a crowd of " elderly gentlemen with hands raised in despair " were pacing the boulevards in great agitation, full of thoughts of military resistance. One of these gentlemen, a lawyer, M. Lortat-Jacob, met the Admiral outside the Café du Helder, where retired colonels used to sit reading the *Military Gazette*. Soon they were surrounded by a crowd of the Admiral's admirers. They held a council in the café, and Saisset, saying nothing of his activities with Calmon that morning, was persuaded by his friends to go to Versailles to get a commission to organise the resistance of the Friends of Order in Paris. A delegation of notables went off to Versailles, saw Jules Favre, in the absence of Thiers, and returned that evening with the Admiral's appointment hidden in M. Lortat-Jacob's boot. The Admiral demanded sixty men to make an immediate attempt on the Elysée, for no particular reason, since there was hardly anyone there. But the required number could not be found, and so action was postponed till the Monday, Saisset meanwhile setting up his headquarters at the Grand Hotel.

The Admiral went to Versailles next day, the 20th, to consult with Thiers and to receive the confirmation of his mission. He received a verbal commission, almost unintelligible in its vagueness, probably designedly so: " I do not order you to go to Paris," said Thiers; "I am glad of your project. I recommend you to take all necessary steps to obtain the release of General Chanzy. Do all that you can by means of your popularity to try to avoid the horrors of civil war. I have no instructions to give you; the Mayors of Paris have received full powers from me." Saisset's mission, then, was in effect confined to negotiations for the

release of Chanzy, who, with General Langourian, had been
arrested by the National Guard on his arrival at the Gare
d'Orsay on the afternoon of the 18th, a chance capture of
no particular importance. As for the organisation of resistance, Thiers was under no illusions about its probable
failure. If it were to succeed, he could take the credit; if not,
he could disclaim all responsibility.

The Admiral arrived in Paris again on the 21st and took
stock of the men at his disposal. The situation was not
brilliant. Accredited agents of Versailles and officious
Friends of Order had already bought up some hesitating
National Guards and disorganised soldiers. The dubious
Captain Bonne had been particularly active in this work.
Lullier and his staff were for sale. The *mairies* of the VIth
and IXth districts were in the hands of moderates, hesitating and on the defensive. The *mairies* of the IInd and
IIIrd were still in the hands of the Friends of Order. The
students of the Polytechnic and some from the Latin
Quarter had gone over to the side of Order in considerable
numbers, and were flocking to the *mairie* of the IInd and to
the Panthéon. In addition to the students, there were two
battalions of " loyal " National Guards in Passy, under
Dr. Marmottan and Bouteiller, the whole force available in
that district; but these could not be relied upon to act
outside their own quarter. Besides these there was a considerable body of Friends of Order thronging the boulevards, fiery old gentlemen, ex-officers, journalists, swells,
*boulevardiers*, inhabitants of the wealthier districts shocked
by the intrusion of " men with faces such as were only seen
on days of revolution ": some 11,500 in all.

This considerable force, however, was sadly deficient in
discipline, cohesion and equipment. There were no supplies.
They were armed with five different types of arms: Chassepots, Remingtons, Sniders, muzzle-loaders and muskets
*à tabatière*; there were only about twelve cartridges per
man. There were no regular officers, since most of them had
resigned in disgust equally with the Assembly and the
Committee. The men were frivolously disorganised. When

the Admiral, to test their efficiency, raised a false alarm of a night attack on the Grand Hotel, the guard refused to turn out, but went on sitting at " little X-shaped tables such as you see outside cafés " and singing the " Marseillaise "—" *Une vraie scène de truands,*" as the indignant Admiral put it.

This conduct produced in the Admiral reflections hardly favourable to the warriors at his disposal. " Everyone has his own point of view," he reflected. " Well, I take it that I am a man of action, energetic and resolute; only, I have never been beaten in my life. I do not like the idea of being beaten, and when I decide to fight, I want to know if my men are capable of seconding me."

Sceptical of the value of the " heroes " who were to " cover themselves with glory at his side," Saisset returned again to Versailles to make his report; but first he drew up a very typical poster announcing his arrival in Paris:

" I have no other title to the honour of commanding you, my dear fellow-citizens, than that of having defended to my utmost and until the last minute the forts and positions placed under my command; besides an irreparable misfortune, the loss of my only son, ship's lieutenant, killed by the enemy at the age of twenty-four in the defence of the bastions of Fort Montrouge. Firmly resolved to give my life for the defence of order, the respect of persons and property, supported by the elected heads of our municipal franchises, I hope, by persuasion and wise advice, to succeed in operating the conciliation of all parties on the neutral ground of the Republic. Group yourselves around me; give me your confidence, and the Republic will be saved. My device remains that of the Navy: ' Honour and Country.' "

Saisset really believed that he was addressing the majority of Paris, and that the Committee's influence was limited to a small band of criminals, mostly escaped convicts; that they were all mad. But what was more curious, he found, was that they all said that it was he who was mad. For the moment there was nothing more to be done: he left the Mayors to their work of conciliatory negotiation.

That afternoon Paris was lively. Encouraged by the resistance of the Mayors, the threatening attitude of the Assembly, whose first session had taken place at Versailles on the previous day, by a notice in all the Conservative Paris newspapers exhorting their readers to boycott the elections, fixed for the 22nd, and by the Admiral's arrival, a crowd of the more bellicose Friends of Order held a demonstration on the boulevards and marched towards the Place Vendôme, where they were easily scattered by Bergeret's National Guards. The demonstration, although futile enough, was sufficiently successful to raise the hopes of the reaction: it proved that there was a strong nucleus of resistance to the Committee to support the " loyal " battalions of the Guard, and that a demonstration, working in concert with them, might have some chance of success. The Friends of Order agreed to meet again on the following afternoon outside the Grand Hotel to renew the attempt.

The evening was stormy on the boulevards; not a café was open from the Chaussée d'Antin to the Faubourg Montmartre, and furious arguments laid many a top-hat in the dust. The demonstration was not without effect upon the Committee. It obviously did not fear any serious military developments from the proposed renewal of the demonstration, for no additional precautions were taken and Bergeret did not even see that the two guns which commanded the rue de la Paix were provided with ammunition. Nevertheless, it was certain that the elections fixed for the next day would be marked by scenes of disorder, and, therefore, postponed them to the 23rd.

Even the more reactionary of the Mayors were carried away by this enthusiasm. The Deputies returned from Versailles at midnight on the 20th. At a sitting at Vautrain's, early in the morning of the 21st, Chéron developed a plan for organising the *arrondissements* and grouping them together under a General-in-Chief. Already, on the 20th, he had organised the defence of the IInd with nine battalions under Colonel Quéreaux, of the 149th, unanimously elected. By the evening of the 20th the district was under arms. Chéron himself went from house to house to " stimulate the apathetic," and thus prevented the battalions from entering the Committee's Federation. But even so, he had found " many arguments, but few men of action."

Chéron's proposal, discussed but not adopted at the midnight sitting, found more favour late next afternoon. Clémenceau, Lockroy and Schoelcher had gone to the Hôtel de Ville to report on their progress at Versailles. They had been kept waiting for an hour and had then been more or less thrown out without a hearing. It had been an intolerable insult to their dignity. Schoelcher was " indignant," Lockroy " furious and very violent against the Central Committee." It was decided that no more attempts at conciliation should be made. Saisset was adopted as Commander-in-Chief of the forces of order. But the only member of the Mayor's council who imitated Chéron's initiative was Méline, in the Ist. Even in the IInd, Tirard, who had full powers from Thiers and Picard, left all the work to Chéron.

On the 22nd, the Mayors began to organise a movement parallel to that of the Friends of Order. Héligon, Dubail and Tirard formed a permanent central committee of Mayors and Deputies. The IInd district was the centre of the resistance. At the request of the Mayoral Council, Lemaître organised the legal police. He had scornfully turned down an odd proposal made him by Rigault and Grousset early on the 20th, offering to have him appointed the Commune's police chief.

The nine battalions faithful to Chéron published a poster which they had drawn up on Monday evening, after the Mayors had agreed to his proposals:

" CITIZENS,

" The deputies of Paris, in concert with the Mayors and Assistants, have resolved to protect the Republic against all comers by maintaining first of all the tranquillity of the city.

"The Municipality of the IInd district and the battalion commanders associating themselves with this resolution have organised a service of protection and surveillance in this district. Every citizen devoted to the Republic owes them his assistance. Every abstention in the present circumstances is a civic crime. We make, therefore, a vigorous appeal to all our comrades to second us in the work of conciliation, whose principle is order."

The second, and larger, demonstration of the Friends of Order duly took place next day after lunch. The idea was certainly Saisset's; but he was rather carried away by his followers' enthusiasm, taking the attitude of Ledru-Rollin on a somewhat similar occasion in June 1849: "*Je suis leur chef: il faut que je les suive!*" Some alleged eye-witnesses reported that he had been at the head of the procession, supported by his standard-bearer with the tricolour. The Admiral himself, however, always denied this.

Saisset had good reason to disown this farcical and tragic adventure. Some have seen in it a tactical effort to cut insurrectionary Paris in two by forcing the Place Vendôme and joining up with the "loyal" battalions at the Bourse, the Louvre and Passy, thus isolating the Hôtel de Ville. This is to exaggerate even Saisset's scatter-brainedness. Even he could hardly have hoped that a miscellaneous rabble of elderly gentlemen, armed only with sticks and revolvers, could march with impunity down a broad street covered by rifles and machine guns and force barricades defended by artillery. The organisers did, however, overestimate the moral effect of a demonstration as such, which, it must be remembered, was still comparatively uncommon at that time.

They marched, some thousand strong, down the rue Neuve Saint-Augustin, uttering fierce and provocative shouts; overpowered and beat a couple of sentries at the top of the street; and poured tumultuously into the rue de la Paix. Bergeret and some two hundred Guards met them at the entry to the Place Vendôme. The Committee had been so careless or so confident that it had not even strengthened the ordinary pickets.

Ten times Bergeret read the usual *sommation*, ordering the rioters to disperse. For five minutes nothing could be heard but the drums. The crowd replied with a howl of insults, and pressed closer. Suddenly there was a fusillade, two, perhaps three, volleys, answered by revolver shots. In a moment the crowd simply melted away, leaving some twenty on the ground, ten of them killed outright. An English journalist " eye-witness " wrote, with the genial exaggeration of his trade, that the Place Vendôme was a " sea of blood." A witty ball, as Lissagaray nicely puts it, struck one of the most pugnacious of these amateurs, Henri de Pène, editor of *Paris-Journal*, in the rear. Bergeret had two killed and seven wounded. From the nature of the wounds on both sides it would seem that the confusion and the suicidal form of musket used had been more deadly than the fusillade, which must have been aimed high, otherwise the closely packed mass would have suffered more damage. It is impossible in such scuffles to say who fired first; in spite of Bergeret's denials, Raoul du Bisson, Lullier's shady Chief of Staff, got himself passed a vote of congratulation, a step which reinforces the suspicion that it was he who was responsible for the inadequate provision for the defence of the Place Vendôme, the obvious stupidity of which can be explained only by the machinations of an *agent-provocateur*.

Chéron is a boaster, but, on the whole, not a deliberate liar. According to his account, there now took place a very curious incident which put the whole insurrection for a moment in danger. According to Chéron, then, Bergeret was simply terrified by the responsibility for the bloodshed in the rue de la Paix. He sent an emissary to the Mayoral Council in the IInd district, Andrieu, of the International, " an illiterate and unintelligent young worker." From his confidences, Tirard concluded the presence of Bonapartist agents among the insurgents. Chéron returned with Andrieu, and, after crossing " puddles of blood," entered the Place Vendôme. The Place was very strongly guarded, the interior " terrifying." Bergeret sat surrounded by pistols: on the table at which he was writing, on the mantelpiece, on the bed—everywhere; armed men stood all around him. He was very worried; denied giving the order to fire, accusing the demonstration of firing first. Chéron was there to assure him that the forces of order would not attack the Place by night, as Bergeret feared. A secret truce was drawn up between the two of them. " I wished to profit by his emotion; for a moment, I had the brilliant idea of capturing the Place Vendôme all by myself. Bergeret was young, seemed honest. I was gaining him; he wept; I was on the point of succeeding; he had already an order from the Central Committee in his pocket; decided not to execute it. I congratulated him. I had almost attained my object when suddenly there entered Jourde, Varlin and a charming young man, Chalain, of the International, semi-literate. All was lost. Varlin and Jourde were intoxicated by their position. I tried to disabuse them. They answered me by complaining of the Mayors, whom they called sophists, hair-splitters. They had had news from the provinces, which were rising in their favour; they were full of audacity and confidence." Chéron therefore abandoned Varlin and Jourde, and attempted to win over Chalain. " He seemed affected, pressed my hand in an expressive manner. I promised him that his life would be spared, etcetera. But Jourde began to look askance, and I reflected that the first word spoken would be my condemnation and execution; and so I retired before these unfortunate intruders, but carried with me at least the assurance that civil war had been postponed to the 24th, thanks to my independent action." The incident is at least curious for the light it throws on Bergeret. From Chalain, the orator of the Third Trial of the International, it seems unlikely that Chéron would have extorted a betrayal, in spite of the " expressive handshakes." But, if this is true, the Commune owes one more debt of gratitude to Jourde and Varlin.

The failure of the demonstration, its tragic outcome and the Committee's tacit approbation of its repression had the effect of bringing all parties to a more definite attitude. The really determined " loyalists," reduced now to about 30,000 more or less efficient National Guards, with a sprinkling of regular officers, strengthened and fortified their military positions, especially at the Saint-Lazare railway station, thus securing their line of retreat on Colombes and Versailles. Millière, Malon, Jaclard and Dereure, Deputies and mayoral Assistants, impatient of the Mayors' temporising, seceded from their Council. The International, which had hitherto kept aloof from the Committee, distrusting its efficacy to better the conditions of the workers, and merely sending four delegates to observe its proceedings, proclaimed its definite adhesion on the 23rd, formulating a programme of moderate social reform: communal autonomy, free and compulsory secular education, the organisation of credit and exchange and the right of association.

The elections were now fixed definitely for Sunday, March 26. The Committee, although driven more and more on the defensive, still proclaimed its desire for con-ciliation: " Paris does not wish to reign, but to be free; it is ambitious for no other dictatorship than that of example; it neither claims to impose its will nor is it willing to abdicate it; it is no more anxious to issue decrees than to undergo plebiscites. . . . It drives no one by violence into the way of the Republic, contenting itself with being the first to enter upon it." The Assembly replied by a fresh series of violent insults, applauding Favre's ferocious denunciation of the wicked city.

Saisset, walking that evening with Schoelcher to a meet-ing of the reactionary Mayors at the *mairie* of the IInd district, summed up the situation very justly: " This is a curious adventure; I have had many. I have a taste for the unknown, but I should never have believed that I should find myself in such a situation." In spite of their resolute attitude, none of his men were ready to attack; his attempts to inspire them with warlike sentiments had ended in cheers and embraces.

After the shooting affray in the Place Vendôme the most frightful stories were believed about the desperadoes of the Hôtel de Ville. Saisset heard one that evening at the *mairie* of the Bourse. Incredible and untrue though it is, it is a good specimen of what was currently believed, and is worth repeating in the Admiral's own words, for the myth is always, at the time, more important than the fact. This is the story which the Admiral told the Commission of Enquiry some months after the fall of the Commune. He was sitting in an ante-room in the *mairie* of the IInd, when suddenly " an individual " rushed in and flung a bundle of bank-notes on the table, crying: " I can no more ! Let them leave me alone; they are nothing but assassins ! " It was Lebreton, the " Paymaster-General of the Commune," he said; although there was no Commune at that date. " It is frightful," continued the wretched individual. " I dined with Assi yesterday. They are shooting each other in there; they shot twelve before my very eyes. Assi had invited me to dinner. He said to me: ' You will dine with me, I want to talk to you.' I dined with him, and it was an excellent dinner. At the end of dinner, he said to me, ' A paymaster always has some money, you know.' ' No, no ! ' said I, ' I have none.' ' You are Paymaster-General; you must have got still more money than an ordinary paymaster. You have got to give me 300,000 francs, because the moment has come for me to make for Belgium. If you do not give it to me, I will kill you.' ' You are joking,' I said. ' I have not got it; do what you like about it.' The door opened, and an individual with a glass of champagne in his hand came in reeling and singing. It was M. Lullier. Assi said to him, ' What are you doing here ? ' and kicked him out. A minute later, I saw six Garibaldians armed with Chassepots line up behind me. One of them told me: ' We have orders to execute you if you do not give Assi the money.' "

Lebreton managed to escape at last with his money, and

Saisset, struck by his shocking tale, gave him 450 gold francs to escape to Belgium. One cannot help feeling that the generous Admiral was victim of a hoax, and a costly one at that; but such stories were generally believed among the Friends of Order and the inhabitants of Versailles, nourished upon Thiers's alarming propaganda and Favre's rhetoric; even worse, they were believed by the provinces, and, to some extent, by Europe. The Mayors, however, were sceptical of Saisset's scare-stories and scandalised by his approval of the Assembly; and so the military side of the reaction henceforward received less and less support from them, while they found themselves increasingly isolated between the Assembly and the Central Committee.

In concert with Tirard and those Mayors who had now definitely taken the side of Versailles, Admiral Saisset, confirmed in his appointment as Commander-in-Chief of the National Guard, with Langlois as his Chief of Staff and Schoelcher as his Commander of Artillery (a few *mitrailleuses* at the *mairie* of the IInd), offered, on the 23rd, the regular pay of 30 sous a day to those Guards who should rally to the call of order at the Bourse. Unfortunately for Saisset, this sensible step came too late. The Committee had perfectly realised that the 30 sous were all that most of the population of Paris had to live on, and that only the continuation of this pay could ensure the loyalty of their troops. There was a considerable sum left in the coffers of the Ministry of Finance, but, in the delicate state of negotiations at that moment, and with their excessive regard for legality, they preferred not to requisition this money. On the 20th, therefore, Jourde and Varlin, appointed to the administration of the Committee's finances, applied first of all to Rothschild for the loan of the very moderate sum of half a million francs. Rothschild granted the loan against a bill on the City of Paris's account at the Banque de France.

Jourde's next step, however, was far more important: the demand of a million francs from the Bank of France. This was not actually a requisition, as the City of Paris had a credit of 9,400,000 francs on the books, but it was hardly within the province of a *de facto* Government to levy the money of their fellow-citizens without their consent. The Committee, however, could, and did, appeal to the necessity of the situation and pointed out that the money was essential for the preservation of order and the prevention of looting. There was an element of comedy in this interview: as Jourde avowed later, he felt very uncomfortable when faced with his former chief, old M. Rouland, the President of the Bank. Rouland, however, was perfectly amiable, remarking that the Bank always expected the visit of the new Government on the morrow of a revolution. At the same time, he stressed the neutrality of the Bank as an independent commercial concern which could not be treated as a State department. He answered for its security by means of a garrison of armed servants of the Bank, and for its impartiality; and, indeed, beyond some 300,000 francs somewhat unwisely advanced to Saisset and the removal of a quantity of bullion to Versailles, the Bank did little more than hold its own, vainly trying to sabotage the revolution by paying out as slowly as possible. It would have been dangerous to send any large sum to Versailles from Paris; and Versailles gave the Bank almost no support or even instructions.

The Marquis de Ploeuc, who took over after Rouland had retired to Versailles, continued his policy of slow payment. Rouland had agreed to a levy of another million. When Jourde and Varlin came on the morning of the 23rd to fetch the first instalment, 350,000 francs, de Ploeuc refused, procrastinated. The delegates sent a strong letter of protest at noon, arrived with a couple of battalions in the evening. The money was paid.

Jourde, and Beslay, who replaced Varlin later as the Commune's delegate at the Bank, have been blamed by Socialists for not at once expropriating this essential tool of government, the best weapon and hostage offered them. It was against the whole nature of the essentially legal-minded revolution to do so; the revolutionary error is implicit in the whole character of the Commune; and it is

not correct to isolate or emphasise this single aspect of it.
It is more a matter of revolutionary principle, for in actual
fact little practical disadvantage resulted from this policy:
the Commune easily paid its way under Jourde's wise
management and the Bank gave no effective aid to Versailles. It was, until the very end, essential, from mere
numerical considerations, to keep the support of the petty-
bourgeois shopkeepers and artisans; and to them the Bank
of France represented stability of existence. The Communards had not yet learned the necessity of completely
smashing capitalist structure, and, although many of their
measures did so in effect, these measures arose from the
needs of the situation far more than from any revolutionary
doctrine. The old Proudhonist, Beslay, defended this revolutionary error by an argument which seems representative:
" Is it not established that the Bank, as the depository of
wealth and the centre of credit, represents the national
patrimony, whose vitality is a matter of interest not only
to France but to the whole civilised world ? For to-day
capital, credit and commerce no longer possess frontiers,
and the disappearance of the Bank would have shocked
the world." It is no use to reply that Beslay's Proudhonist
economics are absurd from any revolutionary point of view
and that it *was* the Commune's business to shock the world.
As a model, the Commune's policy was lamentable; but the
Commune was not then concerned with setting a revolutionary example but with justifying and defending its
existence. The seizure of the Bank would certainly have
had a fatal effect upon French securities; it would have
recalled the anarchism of the *assignats*; and the Commune,
hoping to gain the sympathy of the provinces and of Europe,
and not in any urgent need of money, could not then afford
to take any risk that was not absolutely essential to its
existence.

The Committee was particularly anxious to gain foreign
sympathy. Courbet, the famous painter, later member of
the Commune, even hoped for formal recognition. But
Paschal Grousset was quite incompetent as Delegate for

Foreign Affairs. There was no official news-centre for foreign correspondents; Longuet's careful explanatory articles in the *Journal Officiel* were hardly inspiring; and correspondents were left to gather their news from Versaillese propaganda and the Commune's " yellow press," especially Vallès's clamorous *Cri du Peuple* and Vermesch's *Père Duchêne,* extremely popular but so foul-mouthed that its *grandes colères* and *grandes joies,* however enjoyable, were simply untranslatable. Vallès himself was shocking for a different reason. As Goncourt explains: " France is so classical that the literary theories of this man of letters have already harmed the new Government as much as the social theories of his colleagues: a Government of which a member has dared to write that Homer ought to be thrown on the rubbish-heap and that Molière's *Misanthrope* lacks gaiety seems to the bourgeois more alarming, more subversive, more anti-social than a Government which were to decree on the same day the abolition of inheritance and the replacement of marriage by free union." On the whole, however, the English Press at least was fair in its accounts. The Commune even gave the London *Times* special facilities. It was not their fault that their three or four columns of well-written " story " tended to be overshadowed by the all-absorbing Tichborne and Purchas cases.

Grousset marked his first dealings with a foreign power by a bad *gaffe.* The Committee's *Officiel* of March 21 had declared that, as a purely municipal council, it was firmly resolved to respect the conditions of peace negotiated by the Assembly. On the 23rd, the *Officiel* published an exchange of notes between Major-General von Schlotheim, commanding the 3rd Prussian Army Corps occupying the northern forts, and Grousset: " To the present commander of Paris: The undersigned takes the liberty of informing you that the German troops occupying the forts to the north and east of Paris . . . have received orders to preserve an amicable [*amical*] and passive attitude so long as the events of which the interior of Paris is the scene do not assume with regard to the German armies such a hostile character as to place them in danger, but are kept within the limits prescribed by the peace preliminaries. But should these events assume a hostile character, the City of Paris will be treated as an enemy." Grousset replied that the Central Committee was in no way aggressive towards the Prussians.

The attitude was explicable, the word " amicable " not. Grousset had made an easy slip in reading German script: he had taken *friedlich*—pacific, for *freundlich*—amicable. The curious thing is that the mistake did not strike the editors of the *Officiel*; a proof, emended in another minor point by Boursier, Grousset's fellow-delegate for Foreign Affairs, is still in existence; and the word *amical* is not queried.

The mistake naturally caused intense indignation, since the causes of the revolution had originally been largely patriotic; while Thiers made so much capital out of this slip that the simple-minded provincial Versaillese troops were persuaded that by annihilating the Communards they were in some measure revenging their defeat by the Prussians upon an ally of the hated foreigner. As Goncourt, speaking as a Conservative intellectual, points out, " If the Commune, instead of showing itself more complaisant to Prussian exigencies than Versailles itself, had broken the treaty for which it blames the Assembly; if it had declared war on Prussia in a fury of heroic madness, it would have been impossible for Thiers to open his attack, for he could not have worked for the reduction of Paris with the assistance of a foreign enemy." But this was for the Commune simply the same choice as that before Paris at the Prussian entry: annihilation lay in either decision; and the Communards preferred to die for the social revolution rather than to vindicate the honour of a " France " which merely meant industrial slavery to exploiters with French instead of German names.

The tension of this first period came to its peak on this Thursday, the 23rd, both in Paris and at Versailles. The Blanquists at the Prefecture and Ministry of War were strengthening their influence. The Committee began to realise its power. Even Lullier made some show of energy to compensate for having allowed the 69th Line Regiment, which had been left, half-starving, at the Luxembourg, to escape to Versailles. The capture of the Saint-Lazare station by Saisset's men was neutralised by the occupation of the Batignolles junction. Delegates, backed by the threat of armed force, were sent to the *mairies* of the IIIrd, VIth, Xth, XIIth and XVIIth districts, where the Mayors were still hesitating. Only the Ist and IInd now remained to the reaction. A notice was inserted in the *Officiel* dismissing all civil servants not back at their posts by March 25. Papers too loud in denouncing the Committee were threatened with the ordinary law of libel. The mutinied soldiers wandering about the streets, penniless, aimless and disorganised, at the beck of the bribes of any Captain Bonne, were incorporated in the National Guard with the regular thirty sous pay.

On the 24th, the treacherous and drunken Lullier and his flashy Staff were replaced by Eudes, Duval and Brunel until Garibaldi should come to take up the command offered him. The old fighter, however, while thanking the Committee for the compliment, declined on the 28th. A young Italian who attempted to assume command, pretending to be Menotti Garibaldi, was unmasked as an imposter. Lullier and Ganier d'Abin were arrested—not for any particular fault so much as for general inefficiency and strong suspicions of worse. The Ministry of the Interior was strengthened by the replacement of Grêlier, an unimportant and intriguing little man, by Vaillant, scholar, Internationalist and trusted friend of Blanqui.

The Committee, with increasing confidence in its executive, was no longer in the mood to stand much more procrastination in the matter of the elections. Nevertheless, it still confined itself to strictly municipal affairs and maintaining order in Paris.

Eudes, Duval and Brunel, however, although the Committee would not allow them to march upon Versailles, issued a proclamation expressing the new attitude: " The time for parliamentary devices is over. We must act. Paris will not permit public order to be disturbed with impunity. All who are not with us are against us."

This attitude was strengthened next day, the 24th, by unexpected help from outside: the proclamation of the Commune in several large towns, Saisset's blundering behaviour and the continued provocations of the Assembly at Versailles.

# CHAPTER III

# THE COMMUNE

*" They* won't dare to come now that *it* has arrived ! "
A WORKMAN, *on September 4, 1870.*

For five days the Central Committee had behaved
with exaggerated moderation; but, driven not only by the
energetic demands of its Blanquist executive but also by
the whole development of events, it had come to exercise
an obstinate authority which, although still directed
towards eventual abdication, claimed now to dictate its
terms. Much of the responsibility for this hardening lay
with the mistakes and provocations of its adversaries.

On Friday, the 24th, Admiral Saisset, whose position
had been at least tenable on the previous day, succeeded
in ruining the hopes of his supporters by publishing an
incredibly stupid proclamation:

" Dear Fellow-Citizens,

" I hasten to bring to your knowledge that, in agreement with the Deputies of the Seine and the elected
Mayors of Paris, we have obtained from the Government of the National Assembly:

"1. The complete recognition of your municipal
franchises;

" 2. The election of all the officers of the National
Guard, up to and including the Commander-in-Chief;

" 3. Modifications in the law on maturities;

" 4. The proposal of a law on rents, favourable to
tenants, up to and including rents of 1,200 francs."

There was not a word of truth in all this. So far from according modifications in the laws on maturities and rents, the Assembly had twice refused to listen to Millière's desperate attempts to make them act at once. The other measures were equally improbable. Such a dubious proclamation at once seemed a dangerous manœuvre; a mistake was unthinkable. Yet it is not improbable that the Admiral himself was not acting with deliberate treachery; at the worst, he wished to bring matters to a head.

The circumstances in which this strange document were published are not very clear; and there were no less than seven different versions of it. The proclamation seems to have been drawn up at the beginning of Saisset's mission, with a view to eventual capitulation; the verbs, which should have been put in the future, were thus put into the past tense; by the indiscretion or the trickery of some of the Mayors, the poster was printed and published without Saisset revising the proofs. Saisset accused Mottu, Mayor of the XIth, whom Choppin, Prefect of Police, declared to be absolutely under the influence of his Assistants, notably of Tolain, of the International. It is true that Mottu had some sympathy with the International and was under a personal obligation to Delescluze, but he had nothing to gain from such a manœuvre; and the accusation is the more improbable since Saisset had a personal grievance against him, which must deprive such testimony of value. The effect aimed at was to discredit the Committee by showing that it no longer had a reason for existing, and thus to make conciliation impossible if it persisted in holding the power. Tirard, Thiers's chief agent in Paris, had a far greater interest in this policy than had any other of the Mayors.

The immediate result of the proclamation, however, was to discredit the Mayors finally in the eyes of both Paris and the Assembly. The wealthier middle classes, hitherto the backbone of the opposition to the Committee, asked why the law on rents should have been fixed so low as 1,200 francs (£50); it seemed to them that the Assembly, not the Committee, were the " levellers," the Communists.

It was, too, unpardonable in the Assembly to have " par-leyed with the insurrection," a thing which Jules Favre had denounced as unthinkable. The more reactionary felt that they had been betrayed by the Assembly; the more moderate saw no reason for further opposition now that an agreement had been reached on all important points and the position of the Central Committee had been regularised. The supporters of the Committee, on the other hand, saw only a fresh example of the treachery of Versailles and the Mayors in announcing an agreement which, they knew, was quite chimerical. Saisset's proclamation, there-fore, brought almost the whole of Paris to support or to acquiesce in the rule of the Committee; and this solidarity remained almost undisturbed until after the election of the Commune.

The Committee was not disposed to stand much more procrastination on the part of the Mayors. The elections were announced definitely for the 26th. The Committee held almost all the *mairies*, with or without the consent of the Mayors; Bonvalet had given them a room; Vautrain had been expelled by force; two companies had occupied the IXth, and Desmarest dared not attempt to reinstall himself, although the districts were mostly anti-Committee in temper. The only two which held out were the Ist, with Méline, and the IInd, with Chéron.

The IInd, indeed, was still in a state of siege. Lemaître's police were functioning, disarming refractory Guards, filling the temporary jails. They were busy compiling dossiers, and had swept into their net all sorts of irrelevant persons: several released convicts, three of Lagrange's Bonapartist police spies, whom the Committee would have been equally glad to catch. On the previous day they had captured an ammunition-wagon in the rue de Valois, after a scuffle in which one of its guards had shot a man. Armed students from the Polytechnic were camped in the main hall of the *mairie*. During the night, *mitrailleuses* had been transferred from the Ist district, and the *mairie* was now a small fortress.

This was too much for the Committee. Brunel was sent with a company of the Belleville Guards and two *mitrailleuses* to occupy the *mairies*.

He went first to the *mairie* of the Ist, where Méline, urged by all the officers of his battalion, consented to receive him. Thence Brunel, Protot and Lisbonne, with a crowd of officers, marched to the IInd, and were received by Schoelcher, with the consent of all the municipal officers present: Tirard was then at Versailles. Méline explained that he had come to ask for help: half his battalions belonged to the Federation, and the district, threatened from the Quais and the rue de Rivoli, could not be defended; he had been forced, therefore, to receive Brunel, who brought news of the public desire for conciliation. Méline had previously consulted Thiers as to the elections: Thiers had fixed April 2; Méline, expressing the opinion of the Mayors, had agreed with Brunel to compromise for March 30.

After they had heard Méline's report, the Mayoral Council at the IInd, " considering that they had the practical certainly that the Government would consent, and that, in any case, it was to avoid civil war, which M. Thiers wished to avert as much as they did," came to terms and ratified Méline's agreement with Brunel. The elections were fixed for March 30, and a naval officer, aide-de-camp of Admiral Saisset, insisted on their acceptance of this solution, offering to sign it in the Admiral's name. Lisbonne, as member of the Committee, engaged his signature, as did Brunel. Protot declared that the people he represented also desired the right of electing their general of the National Guard. Schoelcher replied that the measure was dangerous and anti-democratic, as putting too much power in the hands of a single individual and facilitating a *coup d'état*. However, some of the Mayors signed this second convention also; a few, including Schoelcher and Chéron, refused. But they all signed the agreement about the elections.

The news quickly spread along the boulevards. There

was an outburst of universal enthusiasm. Battalions of
Order and battalions of the Federation embraced, shed-
ding tears of manly joy. A cheering crowd waved green
branches, shouting that peace had been made at last;
urchins rode astride the *mitrailleuses*.

Unfortunately, this generous enthusiasm was inaccep-
table to the authorities on both sides. At the exact moment
of the transaction, Tirard was interviewing Thiers at
Versailles to ask him for a regiment of gendarmes to occupy
the Batignolles railway-tunnel and another to hold the
Porte de Passy and support the loyal battalions of that
district. " I have not got four men and a child to give you,"
replied Thiers. " I am very sorry not to be able to do what
you ask : I understand its importance as well as you do,
but it is absolutely impossible. Confine yourself to gaining
time for me." At this moment, the news of the agreement
between the Mayors and the Committee was brought in.
" I will not sign that ! " cried Tirard. " Do not sign, if
you do not want to," replied Thiers, " but do not disavow
your colleagues; sign without signing; publish a proclamation approving them; let the elections be." Saisset, when
they went to him for the confirmation of his signature,
was no less sly. He too had the mission of temporising until
Thiers's army should be ready to crush Paris from outside.

The Hôtel de Ville was no more enthusiastic than
Versailles. The organised resistance of the IInd district had
inspired them with no great faith in the Mayor's peaceful
intentions. Brunel had exceeded his mandate. He had been
ordered simply to occupy the building in order to prepare
the elections for the 26th. The Committee had refused to
ratify the agreement made by Varlin on his own initiative
on the 20th; similarly, they could not permit the efforts oɪ
individuals, however praiseworthy, to pledge them as a
body on the 24th. On the 20th, they had been too shaky to
engage themselves lightly : on the 24th, they were too firm.

The insurrection of Paris had suddenly become the
revolution of France. News had just arrived of revolt in the
provinces. Lyons, the most traditionally revolutionary of all

French cities, had been in an uproar since the news had arrived from Paris, and had raised the red flag on the 22nd, dispersed the Municipal Council, and arrested the brutal prefect, Valentin. At Marseilles, Gaston Crémieux, a Radical journalist, had demanded the adhesion of the Council to the " Government of Paris." Narbonne had proclaimed the Commune on the 24th; Cette and Perpignan were in an uproar. Farther north, Toulouse and Limoges had risen on the 22nd and 23rd. In the east, Saint-Etienne and Creusot were the scene of riots.

The provincial movement, deprived of adequate support from Paris, supplied with inefficient agitators, starved of news, was short-lived; the last stand was made at Marseilles on April 5; all the other insurrections had fizzled out even before the proclamation of the Commune in Paris. But these revolts, short-lived and sporadic though they were, generalised the struggle: it passed beyond the limits of the Paris *mairies*. The Central Committee, conscious of its position as leader of a full revolution and eager to encourage the provinces by the speedy proclamation of the Commune, could not permit any further delay. They refused, therefore, to ratify Brunel's agreement.

The debate dragged on at the Hôtel de Ville for hours. Ranc, Ulysse Parent and Paul Dubois went to the Committee and were received by Ranvier and Jaclard. Ranvier pointed out that the moderates were no longer masters of the Committee and would be accused by the majority of attempting to draw back. Chéron, who was ready to believe the worst, went off with a report of the Montmartre battery ready to bombard Paris with petrol-bombs, of 40,000 men with cannon and *mitrailleuses* surrounding the rich district of the Bourse in the hope of pillage, etc. At 3 a.m., Ranvier came back to the *mairie*. He had obtained no concession. The Mayors capitulated finally, only Chéron and Héligon, die-hards to the last, refusing to sign. Ranvier had brought back the text of the original agreement, which they solemnly tore up.

The afternoon's enthusiasm had had its effect, and

everyone was impatient for the elections without further delay. The Mayors had lost all authority, and the Committee could maintain its own only by keeping at least its official word. The apparent breach of faith alienated much of moderate republican sympathy: happily for the Committee, the Assembly, by its outrageously stupid behaviour, did even more to forfeit what little adhesion it still owned in Paris.

The Assembly at Versailles had been appalled by Saisset's proclamation, seeing in it a subtle move of Thiers to use Paris as a lever to overthrow their Monarchist aims. The Deputies were now in a state bordering upon hysteria. Their first session, on Monday, the 20th, had at once shown their attitude towards Paris and towards Thiers: they peremptorily refused to consider a proposal introduced by Millière to bring in an immediate measure to alleviate the distress caused by the law on maturities; and they set up a Council of Fifteen, all violent reactionaries, " to represent the collective sense of the Assembly and to work in concert with the executive power in order to act as circumstances dictate." The working in concert, of course, meant in fact the continuous surveillance of Thiers's behaviour.

At the first sitting, too, they had been alarmed and inflamed by a denunciation of Paris by Trochu, the first of a series which culminated in the really remarkable curse of Favre on the 21st. Some of this harangue is worth quoting as a specimen of the anti-Parisian rhetoric upon which the " backwoodsmen " were nourished. Favre began on a note of reason, of confidence—a gentlemen-of-the-jury note. Gradually he worked up and up to a thunder of denunciation. " The honest citizens of Paris accept only with a shudder the shameful yoke imposed upon them by a handful of scoundrels, against whom they have had the courage to protest ! " Here he read out the list of those Conservative papers which had called for the boycott of the elections proposed by the Central Committee. They were received with cheers. " And there are more to come ! " cried Admiral Saisset. Then Favre turned upon the insurrectionary Press:

" I should blush were it necessary for me to repeat to you the insults and outrages which these enemies of the public weal pour upon the legitimate authority of universal suffrage, setting above it I know not what sanguinary and rapacious ideal." (*Shouts of " True ! True ! Bravo ! "*)

Then a most curious philosophic sophism, extremely impressive in its obscurity : " What they have desired, what they have realised, is an essay in that ominous doctrine which, unfortunately, has had illustrious adherents, of good faith perhaps but ignorant of the import of the opinion in which they had gone astray—an opinion which may be called, in philosophy, individualism and material- ism, and which is called, in politics—to use a term which I have heard employed here—the Republic placed above universal suffrage ! " (*Hear ! Hear ! Enthusiastic applause and fervent agreement.*) This casuistry was too much for even Langlois, who was at least a Republican Deputy of Paris : " I demand the floor ! " But Favre swept on over him, over the applause. " To-day, how can we hesitate, how can it be that the serious, the absolute obligation should not impose itself upon our conscience to take the most energetic measures to wipe out at last such a disgrace inflicted upon civilisation ? Perhaps, they would say, there was serious risk of civil war : what, then, *was* the present state of Paris ? Was it not civil war open and unashamed, accompanied by dastardly murder and pillage in the dark ? But let the insurrection be sure that if the Assembly was at Versailles, it was with the intention of returning to combat the in- surrection, and to combat it resolutely. All the provinces were absolutely repelled by the ideas of Paris. They could, then, afford to wait, but to wait while one-third of their departments were still occupied by the enemy, to wait while the whole population suffered, to wait when the Minister who had the honour to be addressing them had spent days and nights debating questions of detail between the enemy and those upon whom that enemy lay so oppres- sively ! For such was the work in which the Committee at the Hôtel de Ville had come to interrupt him—[*sensation*]—

making, however, to him and to the honourable M. Thiers a proposition which he would call grotesque, were not the word improper at that tribune : facilities for the continuance of negotiations with Prussia ! [*Exclamations.*] The question, then, was simply this : whether they would repress the insurrection at once and by themselves, or whether, by temporising with it, they wished to give the right to repress it to the foreigner ? " [*Enormous sensation.*] Saisset, quite carried away : " There you have it ! Make your choice ! "

Such furious rhetoric incited the Assembly to even more provocative behaviour. They refused to write " *Vive la République !* " at the foot of their proclamations; they appealed to the provinces for volunteers to reduce the city of brigands and assassins, declaring openly : " Do not fear from us those moral weaknesses which would aggravate the evil by treating with the guilty," and howled down Millière when he attempted to point out the danger of such phrasing. On the evening of the 23rd they hooted the Mayors, who had come solemnly to the Trianon Theatre to present their solution, shouting " *Vive la France !* " in reply to the Mayors' " *Vive la République !* " There could be no doubt of their temper : Paris was the mortal enemy, and any attempt at negotiation with the city treason.

Their natural fury was reinforced by fear. They were in perpetual apprehension of an attack from Paris. Thiers had only 20,000 men, disorganised and ill equipped, although he announced to the provinces that he had 45,000 in excellent order. The Assembly suspected the truth, although most of the troops were isolated at the camp at Satory in the process of reorganisation. The Deputies were kept in a state of terror by the most alarming stories of atrocities in Paris, where many of them had relations, friends or business interests. They were demoralised by physical discomforts, overcrowded lodgings, expensive food, the confusion of a small town suddenly filled with officials and refugees. Some sixty of them were sleeping actually in the Council Chamber in the Château, and it was no uncommon sight for a scarlet nightcap to rise up suddenly in the midst of a debate. The Hôtel des Réservoirs continued to reap the rich profits which it had enjoyed under the Prussian occupation by selling its meals to the patriotic Deputies and generals at siege prices. The Deputies were irritated too by the attitude of Thiers, who treated them as recalcitrant schoolboys, and by what they looked upon as the wanton interference of the Mayors and other conciliators. There was danger and annoyance within and without.

Saisset's proclamation acted as a spur to their resentment. The Monarchist Council of Fifteen resolved to overthrow Thiers at the evening session, when the propositions of the Mayors were to be examined in the light of Saisset's announcement. There was talk of bringing back a Royalist prince, Joinville or d'Aumale. Thiers got wind of the plot. So too did the Paris Deputies, through the indiscretion of Jules Simon. Thiers exercised all his parliamentary skill, mounted the tribune, and, declaring that an ill-considered word might provoke torrents of blood, forced the President of the Council, Grévy, his creature, to hurry through the sitting in ten minutes, without hearing the Mayors. Once more the logic of the situation, the fatal coincidence in time of a personal plot against Thiers and the most critical moment of the negotiations, drove Paris and Versailles inevitably to civil war.

The rumour of this Royalist plot ended the opposition in Paris. Saisset sat alone in the Grand Hôtel, issuing orders to an army which no longer existed. Lullier, Ganier d'Abin and other suspect traitors were in prison. The Mayors, repulsed both at Versailles and at the Hôtel de Ville, gave way. There was nothing more for Saisset to do but " the most manly act of his whole life, to tell everyone to return home."

He posted a last proclamation : " The Deputies and Mayors of Paris, having accepted the electoral conditions imposed by the Central Committee, have recognised this power *de facto*. I declare that it is the duty of all officials who are resolved, like me, to recognise only the Assembly sitting at Versailles, to retire before the officials of the Central Committee."

At 3 o'clock, Saisset finally disbanded himself—it was all he had left to disband—and retired in disgust to Versailles. Tirard, too, issued a proclamation supporting the elections. Thiers had said to him that morning: " There is nothing more to be done for the moment. I am reorganising the army. General Clinchant is in the north with General Ducrot. I hope that in two or three weeks we shall have a force strong enough to deliver Paris."

The Central Committee had served its purpose; it was now ready to give way to the Commune. Its preliminary work had been sufficiently remarkable. On the 20th, all the public services had been completely disorganised, in accordance with Thiers's plan to allow the insurrection to perish of its own weakness. Most of the regular civil servants had retired to Versailles, taking with them the mechanism of their services; others remained to carry on the work of sabotage. In six days the public services were working almost normally. Combaz had reorganised the Post Office, except the telegraph; the lines of the provinces had been cut, and even for the internal telegraph it was difficult to train operators quickly enough, and so the administration was farmed out to private companies; but the regular postal service was restored. Cafés and theatres were open as usual: there were even two first nights—a revue, *P.L.M.*, at the Folies-Bergère on the 20th, and a vaudeville, *Difficile à Marier*, at the Folies-Dramatiques on the 23rd. Six thousand sick, abandoned in the hospitals without attendants, were immediately cared for.

Thanks to the money obtained by Jourde and Varlin from the Bank of France, added to the receipts from the *octrio* and 1,200,000 francs found in the municipal treasury, the services of poor and sick relief at the *mairies* worked as efficiently, or inefficiently, as usual; and the pay of the National Guard was distributed on the whole satisfactorily.

The respiratory and digestive apparatus of the great organism functioned without disturbance. After the first few days, the circulation of traffic was restored by the demolition of most of the barricades. Provisioning went on, as usual, by way of the neutral zone to the north, protected by the Prussian garrison in the forts and at Saint-Denis.

Although the forts on the south—Ivry, Bicêtre, Vanves, Montrouge and Issy—had been occupied on the 19th and 20th, and although it was believed, in reliance upon Lullier's declaration, that the key-fort to the Paris-Versailles road, Mont-Valérien, was in the hands of the revolution, the gates were hardly guarded, and communications between Paris and Versailles were not difficult. It was always comparatively easy, though not very dignified, to obtain a pass through the Prussian lines. Public order had never been so little disturbed. The mohawks of the Empire had retreated to Versailles or gave vent to their spirits by sharing in the excitements of the Saisset adventure. Crimes of violence were few; robbery decreased notably. A proclamation on the walls of the Hôtel de Ville decreed death to thieves. The streets were quiet.

Rigault, however, began to show his mettle by an enormous number of arrests, which did cause some terror among the bourgeois, who, nourished upon the wild Versaillese propaganda, firmly believed that arrest meant instant execution. Actually, arrest was a farce. No less than 431 persons were taken up between March 18 and 28; but of these 227 were released sooner or later. No charge was formulated for 333 of these arrests; the others included: espionage, theft (only two), suspected Prussian subject, defacing the Committee's posters, holding a dance on the day of the capitulation, suspects (4), incitement to civil war, member of the Bonapartist police, etc. Several magistrates and officials were held temporarily, including Clémenceau, his Assistant Lafont, and a former Deputy of the Forty-Eight, Glais-Bizoin. By a pleasing irony, Claude, self-confessedly last of the master-detectives, was easily caught by his former subordinate, Rigault, who had served under him for a moment at the Prefecture after September 4.

Claude very nearly became an official of the Commune.

Rigault had appointed the engraver Cattelain, an old *confrère* at the Café Théodore, head of the detective service, simply because Cattelain had explained that, not being of a warlike temperament, he felt that he had qualifications as head of the detective service or the public assistance. Treillard had already been appointed Director of Public Assistance, so Rigault gave Cattelain the succession of Claude. Cattelain could find no staff and, far worse, no lunch when he came to his office. Finally, he collected three men, one who was fishing in defiance of the close season, two more " with drunkard noses," and gave them each five francs: upon which they vanished. Poor Cattelain, completely at his wits' end, wanted to employ Claude; but both Claude and Rigault refused point-blank. Cattelain did, however, employ some of the old police agents, and even found some virtues in them. But Rigault, who hated them all, kept arresting them. Cattelain was annoyed, for he was a good fellow at heart, as befitted a true Montmartrois; his police took up a collection for widows of war-victims, declaring: " Widows know no flags ! The Republic has bread for every poor person and kisses for every orphan ! "

A great many priests were arrested, for, as Rigault said, " the priests are the most powerful agents of propaganda." It was part of the general anti-clerical policy of all fractions of the Commune. There was one rather amusing incident at Easter, when the market-women rose in fury to protest against the arrest of their favourite *curé*, the Abbé Simon of Saint-Eustache. Old Beslay joined them and gave the *curé* a certificate of good citizenship. Rigault had to release him.

The arrests were mostly retrospective rather than for any new crime. There was no statute of limitation. On March 28, at the very moment when the Commune was being proclaimed at the Hôtel de Ville, the grandson of Pommier, one of the four sergeants of La Rochelle executed for conspiracy in 1822, recognised and denounced Bignon, who had then informed against them. Bignon, therefore, was arrested for an act committed nearly half a century before. Curiously enough, the Sergeant Bourgeois shot with Ferré and Rossel by the Versaillese on November 28, 1871, belonged to the Four Sergeants' regiment, the 45th of the line.

Both sides suspected the presence of large numbers of convicts in the ranks of the insurrection. The prisons had been frequently stormed to release political prisoners, and numerous criminals had taken advantage of this. Claude, who certainly exaggerates everything, put the number as high as 12,000: 4,000 freed or on ticket-of-leave during the siege and 8,000 who had flocked back to Paris after the capitulation. Of course, Claude's estimate ranks political and common-law offenders together. Before March 18, Picard, Minister for the Interior, had requested the Mayors to set up a commission because of the number of convicts suspected in the ranks of the National Guard. But this commission could get no information from the Prefecture.

The Central Committee also suspected their presence, and, to cover themselves in case of any disorder, published a proclamation in the *Journal Officiel* of March 21: " Numerous ticket-of-leave men who have returned to Paris have been sent to commit attempts against property, in order that our enemies may have further chance of accusing us. We recommend to the National Guard the greatest vigilance in its patrols. Every corporal should take care that no stranger concealed by the uniform slips into the ranks of his detachment." In the same way, the Committee covered itself in an unpleasant incident on March 24: " The Committee learns that men dressed in the uniform of the National Guard and recognised as former gendarmes and police-agents have fired on the Prussian lines." It was not, however, a very convincing apology for its failure " to bridle its absurder elements."

The Central Committee was ready to " come down the steps of the Hôtel de Ville with head held high." Its remarkable advice to the electors was posted up on Saturday morning:

" Citizens, our mission is ended ; we are about to yield
our place in your Hôtel de Ville to your new representatives, your regular mandatories.

" . . . . If our advice may claim some weight in your
resolutions, permit your most zealous servants to tell
you, before the ballot, what they expect of the day's
voting.

" Do not lose sight of the fact that the men who will
serve you best are those whom you choose from amongst
yourselves, living your life, suffering your ills.

" Distrust the ambitious no less than the upstart : both
consult only their own interests and always end by finding
themselves indispensable.

" Distrust also talkers, incapable of translating words
into action : they sacrifice everything to a speech, an
oratorical effect, an empty phrase. Avoid too those whom
fortune has too highly favoured, for only too rarely is he
who possesses fortune disposed to look upon the working-
man as his brother. . . .

" In short, seek men of sincere conviction, men of the
people, men resolute and active, men of sense and recognised honesty. Give your preference to those who do not
ostentatiously solicit your suffrages : true merit is modest,
and it is for the voters to recognise their men."

Paris went to the polls on Sunday, March 26. The results
were to be announced formally on Tuesday, the 28th. The
voting was completely free. A few battalions of the National
Guard were stationed at points where disturbances might be
expected, but there were no serious complaints of violence.
Probably there has never been an election in Paris that
passed off so freely and tranquilly. Some of the Friends of
Order in the Ist, IInd and IXth districts followed the time-
honoured electoral custom of hiring bullies, but few
scuffles resulted.

A notice posted at midnight recalled that, in view of the
decreased number of voters, an eighth of the votes recorded
would suffice for valid election, on the basis of the electoral

laws of February 18 and March 15, 1849. As there was to be only one ballot, a clear majority was not to be expected in most districts.

While Paris went cheerfully and peacefully to the polls, the Assembly continued its provocations. It decreed a day of public mourning for the murdered generals, their public funeral at Versailles Cathedral, a public monument to their memory, the adoption of Lecomte's family by the nation and a pension to his widow. Having thus spent a good deal of the nation's money, the Minister for Finance economised by shelving once more Millière's proposals to alleviate the Paris rent crisis. On a motion by 80 members, the Assembly declared the Paris elections invalid in advance. Thiers, in a circular to the provincial Prefects, disowned the Mayors' "capitulation." The army was being satisfactorily re-organised, the overthrow of Paris a matter of a few days. Versailles felt almost secure.

The Commune was elected by 229,167 voters from a register of 485,569. This was a heavier vote than appeared. The number of voters for the Government of National Defence in November had been only 322,000. The difference can be largely explained by absence, flight to Versailles, deaths during the Prussian Siege and the wholesale emigration of the wealthier inhabitants after the capitulation. It is quite untrue to say, as Thiers telegraphed to the provinces that evening, that the elections had been boycotted by the Friends of Order. The very diversity of the candidates elected, the large proportion of bourgeois republicans, proves exactly the reverse.

In the Ist (Louvre) district, four anti-Communards were elected; four more in the IInd (Bourse); five in the IXth; two in the XVIth: all these districts were solidly against the revolution. The VIth (Luxembourg) elected three anti-Communards, together with the Proudhonist moderate Beslay, and only Varlin as a real revolutionary. Thus the whole of western Paris, with its bourgeois residential and business population, voted solidly against the Commune. Murat in the IIIrd, Lefèvre in the VIIth and Fruneau in the XIIth were also hostile. Altogether, nearly a quarter of the new representatives belonged to the Opposition.

It is interesting, however, that revolutionaries received a large number of votes even in these predominantly bourgeois quarters : Pillot, Miot and Vésinier in the Ist, Serrailler, Durand, Pottier and Johannard, all members of the International, in the IInd; even in the XVIth, Pyat received only 600 votes less than Bouteiller, with Victor Hugo another 60 behind. In the IXth, the revolutionary vote was considerable but much split: Delescluze followed two more Liberals, Dupont de Bursac and the historian Avenel, at some distance. In the revolutionary IVth (Hôtel de Ville), on the other hand, Louis Blanc and the reactionary Mayor Vautrain had each a fairly large vote.

The other districts voted solidly for known revolutionaries. Varlin was elected in three districts, A. Arnould, Delescluze, Flourens and Blanqui in two. Blanqui's name figures on the lists of at least 13 districts besides the two (XVIIIth and XXth) in which he was elected; he beat Hugo in the bourgeois IXth.

With six double elections, the Communal Council was composed of 92 members. The 21 anti-Communards resigned within two weeks, and were replaced at by-elections on April 18th. Individual members, like the whole body, held such a confusion of views that it is hard to draw up any regular " party-scheme "; besides, the Commune was not a parliament. Some points, however, emerge. There was at first a definite opposition group, 6 radical republicans or Gambettists and 15 Liberals. The Central Committee had, in the spirit of their proclamation, not " ostentatiously solicited suffrages," and were left with only 16 seats on the Commune; and of these at least 7— Assi, Bergeret, Brunel, Eudes, Grousset, Jourde, Varlin— were elected rather for their general militant activity than as representatives of the Committee. The International had 17 representatives. There were 8 Blanquists, besides the absent Blanqui. The rest were more or less well-known individual revolutionaries.

The Commune was not by any means entirely proletarian in composition, although those elected certainly represented the workers. There were 21 workers on the Commune; 30 professional journalists, writers, painters and intellectuals generally; and 13 clerks, small tradesmen and miscellaneous. Thus, while the Commune cannot, owing to the undeveloped state of Paris industry at the time, be called truly proletarian, it contained enough workers and representatives of workers to make it something entirely new in the way of governments. So much so, indeed, that, whatever its immediate aims, and whatever the contradictions in its final objects, its measures demonstrated the nature of the proletarian dictatorship which was implicit in its very existence.

One thing united the members of the Commune and distinguished them from the Assembly: their youth. In the Versailles Government there was not a Minister under fifty, and three of the most important were over seventy; their average age was about sixty-two. Delescluze, it is true, was sixty-two, Pyat sixty-one and Beslay seventy-five; but the average age of the first Executive Committee, even including Pyat, was only thirty-seven, and of the first Committee of Public Safety, also with Pyat, forty. Ten members of the Commune taken at random gave an average of 37.4 years. The company of the 77th Battalion of the National Guard defending Fort Montrouge had an average of 32.5, and 40 per cent of them were only twenty-one or under. These figures can be taken as representative of the Communards as a whole.

The Commune was installed at the Hôtel de Ville on Tuesday, March 28. It was a perfect day. " Bitter winters for foreign wars, admirable summers for civil wars, that's our rule," remarks Halévy. The great square before the old Hôtel de Ville, so recently the scene of the fiasco of October 31, the massacre of January 22, was packed with thousands of Parisians of every class come to salute their new world—

Parisians who had seen the proclamation of so many new worlds cancelled in blood. But this day, like all those other days, seemed really the turn of history, the inauguration of the reign of justice. Even the bourgeois flung up their silk hats amid the thousands of caps and *képis*. Paris had carried its just demands; civil war had been averted by timely and harmless concessions; and any Government at the Hôtel de Ville was better than none, than mob-violence and civil war.

Paris was free at last. The guns of the Old Commune roared a salute. The sun reflected the gleams of a quarter of a million bayonets. Great tribunes had been built before the building to receive the elected of the People of Paris. The whole façade was swathed in red flags. On the platform, scarlet chairs; a bust of the Republic in the centre, wreathed in scarlet. Over the main door the equestrian statue of Henry IV had been hidden by scarlet draperies. Red flags everywhere, red flags streaming from the naked bayonets of marching battalions, red scarves encircling the people's representatives. Blood-red. And the memory of blood, too, in the traditional songs of the Great Commune—the " Ça ira," the " Carmagnole," the " Marseillaise."

The newly elected members of the Commune appeared on the platform, joined by the Central Committee about to resign its functions to the regularly elected Government of the people. Assi made a brief speech, inaudible in the tumult. Ranvier rose—tall, thin, ill—to say: " Citizens, my heart is too full of joy for me to make a speech. Permit me only to thank the people of Paris for the great example they have given to the world." Boursier, a member of the Central Committee, beside him, read out the list of the elected. The drums beat a salute, the crowd broke into the " Marseillaise." Ranvier, in tears, had the honour to shout, unheard, " In the name of the people, the Commune is proclaimed ! "

The two hundred and fifteen battalions of the Federated National Guard marched past all afternoon and far into the evening; when they passed the bust of the Republic, the officers saluted with drawn sabre, the flags dipped. Brunel managed the parade very cleverly, so that all the battalions which could not find room on the square crossed it and saluted the Commune in the process of filing off. His proposal for a general illumination of the city, for which he seems to have had a passion, was not, however, carried out.

Gradually, the great square emptied. A few bivouac fires smouldered in a silence broken only by rare shouts of " Long live the Commune ! " The firelight gleamed on the bayonets of the stacked rifles.

In London that afternoon Queen Victoria had formally opened the rotund Albert Hall.

# CHAPTER IV

# WAR

" The defensive is the death of every armed rising; it is lost before it measures itself with its enemies. Surprise your antagonists while their forces are scattering, prepare new successes, however small, but daily; keep up the moral ascendancy which the first successful rising has given to you; rally those vacillating elements to your side which always follow the strongest impulse, and which always look out for the safer side; force your enemies to a retreat before they can collect their strength against you; in the words of Danton, the greatest master of revolutionary policy yet known, *de l'audace, de l'audace, encore de l'audace* ! "

FRIEDERICH ENGELS: *Revolution and Counter-Revolution in Germany.*

" The royalist conspirators have ATTACKED ! "
*Proclamation of the Commune, April 2, 1871*

IN THE EVENING, after the proclamation of the Commune, some fifty of the newly elected members met in the corridors of the Hôtel de Ville. Everything was dim confusion. They stumbled over National Guards, smoking, sleeping, drinking, who could tell them nothing of their whereabouts. Nothing had been prepared for them, not even a room for their meeting. No member of the Central Committee to hand over the administration. The sixteen elected to the Commune had not appeared. At last, Arnould, who had been a municipal official since September 4, remembered the old Municipal Council-room, and, after a locksmith had forced the door, they installed themselves in the gloom and dust of the huge amphitheatre.

Following the tradition, the oldest member, Charles Beslay, was elected president of the session. The aged Proudhonist defined the new regime in a way which won approval even from bourgeois Republicans outside. It was to be a form of local federalism, a harmless Proudhonist idea long out of date in Paris. " The enfranchisement of the Commune of Paris is the enfranchisement, we cannot doubt, of all the communes in the Republic. . . . Your adversaries have said that you have struck the Republic; we reply that if we have struck it, it is as one strikes a pile, to drive it deeper into the ground. . . . The Republic to-day is not what it was in the great days of our Revolution. The Republic of '93 was a soldier who, in order to fight for its defence at home and abroad, needed to centralise in its hands all the forces of the country; the Republic of 1871 is a worker who above all needs liberty in order to fertilise peace. *Peace and work!* there lies our future! There lies the assurance of our vindication and our social regeneration, and, understood in this sense, the Republic may yet make of France the support of the weak, the protector of the toiler, the hope of the oppressed of all the world, the basis of the Universal Republic. . . . The Commune will deal with local affairs; the Department with regional; the Government with national. And let us proclaim it aloud: the Commune that we are founding will be the model Commune. There, in my opinion, citizens, is the path to follow; enter upon it boldly and resolutely. Let us not exceed the fixed limits of our programme, and the country and the Government will be happy and proud to applaud this revolution, so great, so simple, the most fertile revolution in our history!" It was, old Beslay declared, the happiest day of his life. But the proud and happy Government was even then carefully drilling its soldiers, preparing its guns to clap at the revolution.

Personal disputes began to trouble even this first session. In the dust and gloom, tired voices squabbled bitterly. Someone proposed the abolition of the death penalty; he was accused of wanting to save Vinoy's skin. Vallès demanded that members of the Commune who were also Deputies to the Assembly should choose between their mandates. Tirard asked for no better opportunity of resigning with ironic politeness. Cournet and Delescluze threw in their lot with the Commune. Delescluze, old and ill, wished to retire altogether; but they persuaded him to stay: they could not do without his courage, experience and prestige. A few hours before, he had scribbled a hasty note to his friend Quillot: " In a couple of hours, we install ourselves at the Hôtel de Ville and the Commune will be set up at last. It will not have been without difficulty. In October what is happening to-day would have saved France. Will it be so to-day ? I hope and believe so. The provinces are coming out for us or will come out. . . . Burgundy will send us volunteers to take Versailles in the rear. . . . I am a little better, but I am still very poorly and I need a great deal more care than the situation allows." Delescluze knew that he was probably condemning himself to death by taking up his seat on the Commune.

Next day, Clémenceau also resigned from the Assembly, and Lockroy and Floquet on April 3, none of them sympathetic to the Commune, but unwilling to associate themselves with the attack of a Monarchist Assembly upon Paris. Méline, who had just been much impressed by re-reading Proudhon's *Principe Fédératif*, shirked open support even of Beslay, and sent in a resignation pretending ill health. Delescluze, dying, had stayed.

A more important question was that of the secrecy of the sessions. Grousset carried his motion, in spite of the protests of Arnold, Theisz, Jourde. " We are a council of war," he cried; " we must not let the enemy know our decisions ! " Unfortunately, it also kept friends in the dark, and there seemed real justification for Thiers's accusation that the revolution was being run by an anonymous conspiracy. After two weeks of silence, such wild reports of the session filtered into the Press that the Communal Council was forced to publish its debates, much censored and curtailed, in its *Journal Officiel*.

The first session of the model Commune wrangled until after midnight; broke up amid general dissatisfaction.

The next day the Commune's work was divided up into nine commissions, rather too obviously upon the lines of bourgeois organisation. The general Executive Commission was composed of Tridon, Vaillant and Lefrançais, Blanquist Internationalists, with Duval, Eudes and Bergeret to maintain close relations with the military administration, and naturally Félix Pyat, ever at the head of a victorious revolution. Compared with the military men and Pyat, the others were moderates, more concerned with Socialist legislation than with executive action; consequently, they acted as a necessary but untimely check at a moment when the Commune's salvation lay in immediate attack upon Versailles. The Military Commission included, besides Duval, Eudes and Bergeret, one other " activist "— Flourens; the rest, the Internationalist Pindy, the Blanquist Chardon and the social-revolutionary Ranvier, were at this time also lacking in aggressive audacity, tragically too sensible.

Internal administration was carried on by four commissions. The Internationalists Varlin and Victor Clément, the old Proudhonist Beslay, with Jourde and the revolutionary orator Régère acted on the Financial Commission. The International, which had always made this its special interest, controlled the Commission for Labour, Industry and Exchange with Malon, Franckel, Theisz, Dupont, Avrial, Eugène Gérardin and Puget, with Loiseau-Pinson, a moderate Radical bourgeois who soon resigned. The Commission for Education was composed of a very mixed lot of moderates, journalists, schoolmasters and Socialists: Dr. Goupil, Leroy, Robinet and Lefèvre resigned, leaving Verdure and Vallès, journalists, Urbain, a shady ex-schoolmaster, and Demay, a Socialist workman. The Public Services were run by a nondescript group, and hardly functioned: Billioray, J.-B. Clément, Martelet, Mortier, Ostyn, Rastoul. Ostyn and Clément also worked on the Commission for Supplies with Dereure, Champy, Parisel, Emile Clément, Henry Fortuné, but this Commission, too, had little to do.

Grousset and Arnaud, from the Central Committee, remained on the Foreign Affairs Commission, with Delescluze,

Arnould, Charles Gérardin, and Ranc and Ulysse Parent, moderates who resigned. This commission did little but draw up appeals to the provinces; and let itself in for a hoax about pretended recognition by a bogus Ecuador Legation.

The Commission for Justice was manned by some of the most intelligent of the " activist " revolutionaries—men honestly striving to set up a decent revolutionary code: Protot, a dissentient Blanquist lawyer well known for his defence of revolutionaries under the Empire; Vermorel, the pamphleteer; and Léo Melliet, somewhat hampered by the mild lunatic Babick and the nonentity Ledroit; Ranc, the most efficient of all, resigned from the Commune, although remaining in close touch with Protot.

The Commission for Justice came into perpetual conflict with the " Ex-Prefecture " of Police. Here the Terrorist Raoul Rigault was supreme, with his friends and fellow-Blanquists Ferré, Cournet, Oudet, Gérardin and the Internationalists Assi and Chalain. They had long dreamed of a Red Terror more efficient than the White Terror of the Empire: a sort of Tcheka; necessary enough to a revolution, but childishly violent under Rigault. The " Ex-Prefecture," indeed, tended to become more and more independent of the Commune's control.

Unfortunately, the attributions of these commissions were never properly defined; and the minor conflicts between the commissions, instead of being bureaucratically smothered, as in a bourgeois administration, were fought out in the open Communal Council as matters of principle. Undoubtedly they were that, but the Commune had a more important affair on hand: the defence of its very existence. The real executive powers, as was inevitable in a Government at war, were still vested in the military and the police, headed by unconstructive Blanquists and Jacobins. Socialist reorganisation had to take a subordinate place.

The early sessions of the Commune were as curiously unrelated to reality as the first had been. The generals—

Eudes, Duval, Bergeret—and their men were blazing with eagerness to march on Versailles. But even now, the Commune, whose very existence was an offence to the Assembly, could not see that civil war was inevitable, that the Commune's only chance lay in striking first. They went on as if nothing had happened : " To-day the decision about rents ; to-morrow about the bills ; all public services reformed and simplified ; the National Guard, henceforth the only armed force in the city, reorganised without delay : such will be our first acts."

They decreed the remission of all rents for the October 1870, January and April 1871 quarters ; all sums paid during these nine months were to be deducted from future rent ; all leases might be cancelled at the tenant's wish for the next six months ; all notices to quit should be prorogued for three months. Another decree suspended the sale of pledges at pawn shops until a fresh decree should be drawn up preventing the worker being separated from his tools and so deprived of further chance of employment. Rigault at the " Ex-Prefecture " suddenly became puritan and banned all games of chance and gambling, " whereas a pernicious example is given to the people by the *chevaliers d'industrie* who encumber the public way and incite patriots to every kind of game of chance, and whereas it is immoral and against all justice that men should be able to suppress the little well-being that wages can bring to the family hearth by the turn of a die and without difficulty, and whereas gaming leads to all vices, even to crime."

Such had been the first decrees : purely municipal, even admirable. No provocative interference in national affairs. Suddenly Pyat jumped up " like a jack-in-the-box " and proposed the abolition of military conscription. A perfectly senseless proposal, since Paris had now no control whatever over the army, it having just been decreed that the National Guard was to be the sole armed force in Paris. The Commune was absurdly compromised : " Commune in the morning, Constituent Assembly in the evening ! " This folly still mattered very much, for war was not yet declared, the position of the Commune, blessed by the Mayors, still perfectly legal.

At the same time, Pyat was clamorous in his paper, the *Vengeur*, that the Commune should march on Versailles: "Poor Versailles ! It has forgotten October 5 and 6, 1789, when the Commune's women alone sufficed to catch its king ! " Pyat does seem to have been acting with a sort of frenzied Jacobin good faith, trying even by provocation to stimulate the tragically legal-minded Commune to attack. All Paris except the Communal Council was wild for the *sortie torrentielle*. The odds seemed in their favour. Pyat assured them that the Versaillese army would not fight. The imprisoned Lullier had sworn that a garrison at least sympathetic to the Commune held Mont-Valérien. But a treacherous attempt might be expected from Versailles: one of the last proclamations of the Central Committee was a warning against bands of disguised Versaillese, resolute and armed with revolvers, marching upon Paris.

The army at Versailles was indeed in a pitiable state, although discipline was being slowly restored by careful isolation. Thiers telegraphed to the provinces on April 1 that " the organisation of one of the finest armies that France has ever possessed is being completed. Good citizens may then take heart and hope for the end of a struggle which will be sad, but short." At the moment, Thiers had actually only about 35,000 disorganised men, 3,000 horses and some 5,000 gendarmes hated by the regular soldiers. The police reported a considerable improvement in the soldiers' discipline, but room for considerably more. The troops were the object of an active pacifist propaganda; the contagion in Paris and the hardships undergone in the provinces had had a deplorable effect upon the raw levies; the defections on March 18 had set a very bad example.

From the conversations picked up by the police-agents who watched the troops closely, the feeling seemed unanimous: the troops had had enough of fighting, they would not fire upon Frenchmen, they had had enough of hardship, they wanted to return home. There was no trace of

revolutionary ideas; simply inertia and apathy. The
officers, disgusted with a war without glory, waged for the
profit of lawyers and profiteers, set a deplorable example:
the open exhibition of numerous officers accompanied by
public prostitutes produced a bad effect every evening.

But Thiers was cunning. The troops were well fed, kept
busy. Demands for leave into town notably decreased. The
troops in cantonments were given extra field-rations and
an extra allowance of 50 centimes a day; the officers also
had extra rations and an indemnity on the basis of the Paris
garrison scale. This was indeed necessary: prices had
quadrupled at Versailles, where the good inhabitants were
determined to get their bit for doing their bit.

The Versaillese could not rely upon the villages outside
Paris in the line of any main action. When Vinoy enquired
on the morning of April 1, the police were forced to admit
that Courbevoie, Nanterre and Puteaux were definitely
sympathetic to the Commune, a fact of which the Communards never took full advantage; these villages guarded
Neuilly, the key position to the north-west route to Versailles above the Bois de Boulogne. Suresnes and Garches,
agglomerations of bourgeois country villas nearer to Versailles, would support Versailles. Rueil would rally to the
stronger side. At Sceaux, the workers gave " dangerous
advice " to the Versaillese troops.

Thiers was well informed of the agitated state of Paris.
The population was at fever heat. The moderate elements,
who had rallied to elect the Commune, were falling away.
Their representatives were resigning from the Council.
Irresponsible National Guards were carrying out requisitions with a frequency which amounted, in the eyes of
terrified shopkeepers, to pillage; they had a habit of ordering large meals and charging up the bill to the Commune.
Actually, the system of *bons* of requisition had been much in
vogue during the siege; but this continuation in a nominal
time of peace, especially after the Commune had, by decree,
raised the state of siege, was alarming. Rumours of an
approaching attempt upon Versailles were becoming

increasingly consistent as early as March 30. Everyone knew that it would be made by the three main routes to Versailles, and the leaders claimed that they would meet only a feeble resistance, that the regular army would come over to them.

Thiers, who had no scruples about opening the hostilities that were quite obviously inevitable, and armed with the excuse that he was initiating not a civil war, but a legal repression, was determined to forestall this attempt by the Commune, which, if even slightly successful, would have a fatal effect upon the timorous Assembly and upon his reputation and the reputation of the Republic of Order, in the provinces, where revolution was still smouldering in the larger cities.

On April 1 he held a Council of War; the conversations have remained secret, but the atmosphere must have been that of the fatal Council of March 17. Vinoy spoke of it many years later to General de Sesmaisons: as before, the Generals pointed out the risk of marching with such disorganised troops; as before, Vinoy, after some hesitation, " felt his sense of duty revolt," but demanded the personal responsibility. On April 2, Palm Sunday of the year 1871, began the second, and the vaster, siege of Paris.

The right wing was formed by troops from the Army of the Loire and a regiment of marines, under Admiral Bruat; the left by Daudel's brigade, the 113th and 114th of the Line; the extreme left by the cavalry of General Galliffet. Of the Marquis de Galliffet much will be heard in this struggle; he is nearer in character to this kind of irregular war than the other, the regular, generals; might, in fact, have almost been a Communard of the stamp of Raoul du Bisson. He had been a very typical figure of the swash-buckling Second Empire; he was, later, to be the intimate friend of Edward VII of England. The Marquise de Galliffet had been one of the Tuileries beauties, ambitious and intriguing, closely connected with the set around Morny and the Empress. She had got her husband, " Dodore," a post and the rank of general in the Mexican affair; and

here, faced with the guerilla tactics of Berriozaba and
Juarez, he had learnt their kind of war and used it against
the irregulars of the Commune; it was a war which perfectly
suited his method of taking no prisoners.

The Commune was dogged by ill luck from the beginning. The Federals held the Rond-Point of Courbevoie,
ambushed in the few houses there. They saw a figure cross
the open; he wore five broad gold stripes on his sleeve,
seemed at least a general; they fired, killing him outright.
Unfortunately, it was Dr. Pasquier, the chief military
surgeon attached to Vinoy's staff. Of course, Thiers made
great capital out of the mistake, cried to heaven about this
breach of the usages of civilised warfare in general, the
Geneva Convention in particular.

The next evening, Galliffet shot five prisoners, who were,
it is true, technically deserters from the regular army; but,
since Versailles had attacked first, they could have at least
pleaded self-defence or major compulsion on the part of
the Commune, as Lecomte had pleaded compulsion on the
part of Vinoy. At the least, they had the right to trial before
a court martial. Galliffet did not hesitate to boast of his
action in a communication to the Versaillese *Journal
Officiel*. It was the beginning of the bloody " reprisals "
which were to end with the shooting of priests guilty of
nothing but their calling and children guilty only of
Parisian birth.

The Versaillese were at first badly repulsed. A battalion
of the 74th fled, communicating their panic to the rest.
Vinoy, according to the custom still honoured only sixty
years ago, put himself at the head of some marines, with
words more suitable to the occasion than to print. The
Rond-Point was captured by assault. The Communards
fled. The Avenue de Neuilly was black with fugitives. A
couple of shots from a battery which had been brought
up, and a vast white blank reached as far as the Porte
Maillot. The troops captured the bridge at Neuilly almost
without a blow. Later in the evening, they were withdrawn
again: Thiers had given formal orders not to follow up the

success. Perhaps he was not ready for a too-easy victory; perhaps he dared not empty Versailles of troops, leaving it exposed to a sortie by the southern route. At any rate, this check, without serious results, had an enormous psychological effect on Paris.

The Executive Commission published an alarming proclamation that same evening. All day, the Parisians had heard the familiar rattle of gunfire without knowing exactly what was happening. The proclamation was addressed to the National Guard:

" The royalist conspirators have ATTACKED.

" Despite the moderation of our attitude, they have ATTACKED.

" Unable to count upon the French army, they have ATTACKED with the Pontifical Zouaves and the Imperial Police.

" Not content with cutting our communications with the provinces and with making vain efforts to reduce us by famine, these madmen have wished to imitate the Prussians to the last detail, and to bombard the capital.

" This morning, the Chouans of Charette, the Vendéans of Cathelineau, the Bretons of Trochu, flanked by the gendarmes of Valentin, covered with shot and shell the inoffensive village of Neuilly and engaged in civil war with our National Guards.

" There are dead and wounded.

" Elected by the population of Paris, our duty is to defend the great city against the culpable aggressors. With your aid, we shall defend it."

This talk of Chouans, Vendéans, Bretons and Pontifical Zouaves was, unfortunately, though picturesque, untrue: it was French soldiers that had attacked. But the Commune still hoped that the regular army would not oppose a sortie, would turn against this miscellaneous crew of Royalist ruffians. Mont-Valérien had not fired. There was still great hope for the morrow. Paris had not yet realised that it was

to be a serious civil war which could only end in annihilation. This was a mere skirmish: the Versaillese had three
killed (including Pasquier) and seventeen wounded, including one officer; the Communards had lost twelve killed
and a considerable number wounded. The Versaillese had
taken numerous prisoners; twenty-five reached the Dis-
ciplinary Chamber of the Avenue de Paris Quarter at
Versailles.

Paris was in turmoil. It was uncertain what had happened, but it was certainly serious. The barricades at the
Hôtel de Ville and at the Place Vendôme were fortified.
Troops got out of hand; the 83rd Battalion fell into a panic;
a free corps named the Vengeurs de Paris became riotous,
terrorised the IVth district, and tried to disarm the troops
at the Célestins barracks; demonstrations assembled on the
boulevards and could not be dispersed by Rigault's police;
several battalions parading on the Champ de Mars refused
to obey orders.

But the general spirit was excellent. Goncourt noted
" a hidden satisfaction, a sly joy " on the faces of his bourgeois friends, but there were 100,000 men ready to fight
at once. In the Executive Commission, the generals—Eudes,
Duval and Bergeret—demanded an immediate sortie. The
majority, headed by Lefrançais, kept some sanity; demanded
a review of their resources first. Pyat remarked, sensibly
enough, that one does not set out on such an expedition
without cannon, cadres and leaders. Duval retorted violently, asking why, in that case, the *Vengeur* had been
clamouring for a sortie for the last three days. With some
hope of carrying their point the Commission appointed a
new Delegate for War, Cluseret.

Gustave Paul Cluseret was a somewhat shady figure. A
pure adventurer, he had been mixed up in most of the
revolutions of the past half-century, never very particular
upon which side he held his command. He had served in
the French army, was indeed a Saint-Cyrien; had shot
down the workers in the Forty-Eight, carrying single-
handed eleven barricades and receiving as reward the cross

of the Legion of Honour; fought in the Crimea, twice wounded in action; transferred to Algeria, was drummed out of the army for a mysterious affair in connection with the disappearance of stores. Undaunted, he served in Sicily under Garibaldi, then in the American Civil War, first under Fremont, then with McClellan, who made him a major-general in 1862. He stuck to Fremont for a time in his presidential campaign after Lincoln's death; turned up in Mexico about 1866; was back in New York in '67, conspiring with the Fenians. America temporarily too hot to hold him, he came to France, mingled with the International, and, as he had been naturalised an American citizen, was deported. At the time of the Blois trial, he wrote to Varlin an extremely typical letter which made some stir at the time: " The Empire will soon fall. We must be ready both physically and morally. On that day it will be ourselves or nothing ! Until then, I shall probably remain quiet, but when that day comes, I affirm it, and I never say yes meaning no, Paris will belong to us or Paris will cease to exist." After September 4, Cluseret appeared again in France as an emissary of Bakunin, stirred up a riot in Lyons, tried to do the same at Marseilles, and came to Paris at the beginning of March, with a recommendation from Gambetta, having received over 20,000 votes in Paris at the elections for the National Assembly.

Thoroughly an officer of McClellan, he despised the show and dash of the Flourenses, the boasts of the Bergerets of the Commune. His men, who never appreciated this lack of *panache*, called him a mere civilian. Cluseret for his part had no use for any but regularly trained soldiers, and, except in principle, was thoroughly contemptuous of democratic patriotic enthusiasm. He had his own vanity and his own bravery; was a thoroughly tough American freebooter, like his friend and adviser in Paris, General Sheridan, who had been with Moltke at Gravelotte. All the revolutionary movements of the age had employed men like him beside their more picturesque and more passionate heroes. One is rather reminded of Disraeli's Captain Bruges in *Lothair*.

The most characteristic thing about Cluseret was his
enormous laziness—the laziness of a veteran adept at avoid-
ing fatigues. Added to his vanity and unscrupulousness,
this indolence made him an unreliable, though sensible,
military leader. He thoroughly disapproved of the sortie
proposed by Duval and Bergeret, whom he despised, but,
appointed too late to have to undertake its responsibility,
he did nothing either for or against it, relying on its certain
failure to consolidate his own position.

There was never a stranger muddle than the great sortie
of April 3–4. The majority of the Communal Council had
not definitely forbidden it; Pyat had contented himself with
saying doubtfully, " Well, if you think you can do it . . ."
The battalions were kept marching about in a cold fog,
ordered and counter-ordered. There were no provisions for
reinforcement, for reserves, for communications. There were
no standing orders. Half the men did not know where they
were going. Never was a sortie more *torrentielle*.

Yet the plan was simple and indeed obvious. There are
three main routes to Versailles from Paris: on the right
bank of the Seine, via Neuilly and Rueil to Bougival, due
west, and then at right-angles due south; on the left bank,
via Meudon and Chaville, south-west, the shortest route;
or, thirdly, via the plateau of Châtillon and passing Plessis-
Piquet, due south and due west, in much the same line as
the northern route. Bergeret and Flourens were to make
a strong demonstration in the direction of Rueil, while
Eudes would try to force Meudon, and Duval, in order to
protect Eudes' flank, Châtillon.

Bergeret moved off early on the morning of the 3rd,
arriving about 3 a.m. at the newly evacuated bridge of
Neuilly with about 10,000 men. Here he rested his troops
and sent off a famous telegram : " Bergeret *himself* is at
Neuilly."

At dawn, he moved on. It was an odd army. They
marched in sections down the middle of the road, without
scouts, preceded by Jules Bergeret himself in a Phrygian
cap, seated in a carriage drawn by a pair of horses. They

walked on cheerfully, cheerfully breasted the slope of the
Plateau des Bergères, when suddenly a shell burst in their
midst. It came from Mont-Valérien, that battery which
Bergeret himself had assured them would not fire. A few
more shells followed; not very accurately aimed. A frightful panic broke out; there were the usual cries of treachery.
The column was cut in two, the rear half scattering into
the fields or fleeing straight back down the road to Paris.
The Prussian Siege had seen no defeat quite so radical.

Some 1,200 men stayed with Bergeret, mostly of the 91st
battalion, and effected a junction with Flourens at Rueil,
whither he had arrived by way of Asnières: they had perhaps 3,000 men with them, although the Versaillese supposed them to number at least 7,000. Flourens, sword and
red beard waving, pushed on to Bougival, after putting to
flight some of Galliffet's cavalry at Malmaison.

Vinoy, taken somewhat by surprise after the success of
the previous day, did not arrive with the 114th until about
ten o'clock. The National Guards' position was by no
means hopeless. Colonel Boulanger, whom Vinoy ordered
to retake Bougival, had only 1,400 men out of his whole
regiment, and his orders were formal; they might easily
have been overwhelmed by numbers. But the Communards had no guns, and under fire from a 12-pounder posted
on the heights of La Jonchère, their position became untenable. They were totally unable to stand under artillery
fire in open country. Boulanger was able to recapture
Bougival, Rueil and Malmaison at the ridiculously small
cost of one killed and three or four wounded.

Flourens and a few men refused to quit Rueil. They were
completely exhausted. They went into a small inn. Flourens
took off his tunic, laid aside his sword-belt and *kêpi*, and
was preparing to rest. Some mounted gendarmes rode up
to the door. Flourens came out, pistol in hand. The leader
of the squadron, Desmarets, without waiting for a word,
smashed in Flourens's head with one ferocious swing of his
sabre. The gendarmes did not recognise the body, but,
supposing it to be that of an officer of importance, sent it

back to Versailles in a dung-cart. Four days later, the body
of Gustave Flourens, revolutionary and romanticist, was
recovered by his mother, widow of a professor, and quietly
buried in Père Lachaise with due rites of clergy: Flourens
had been a lifelong atheist.

The columns under Eudes and Duval fared little better.
As there had been no cohesion in the movement, they set
out separately, without any notion of what was happening
at Rueil in the north. Duval reached the plateau of Châtillon with 6 or 7,000 men, bivouacked for the night in the
redoubt, which the Prussians had left in a fairly defensible
state. Naturally nothing was done to improve it. Derroja's
brigade attacked at dawn, turned their flank by way of
Plessis-Piquet, and compelled most of them to surrender.
Duval and what was left of his column retired to the plain
of Châtillon, where they held out all day under the attacks
of Derroja, reinforced by the newly organised division of
Pellé, some 800 more men.

Eudes, with Ranvier and Avrial, were equally futile in
the centre, although they might easily have covered Duval's
retreat. They drove some gendarmes out of Les Moulineaux,
but were halted by La Mariouse's regulars strongly entrenched in Meudon. At 6 p.m., they retired again to
Moulineaux, under the guns of Issy, commanded with some
effect by Ranvier. Issy, indeed, as Versailles officers point
out, was the real hindrance to the Versaillese movement
and could have been used more intelligently. But the supply
of munitions was so inefficiently handled that the artillery
was practically useless.

Duval had spent a troubled night without cover on the
plateau of Châtillon. At eight o'clock he was surrounded.
The National Guards, some 1,200 in all, surrendered on
condition that their lives were spared. All Duval's men who
still wore the regular uniform were shot on the spot by their
captors. The rest were marched towards Versailles. At
Petit-Bicêtre, the column met Vinoy. He was for shooting
all the officers, but, reminded of Pellé's promise, had to
content himself with asking for their leader. Duval came

forward: " I am General Duval." His Chief of Staff, an officer wearing the uniform of an infantry battalion-commander and the Military Medal, also left the ranks. " Shoot them," said Vinoy, recalling, no doubt, his military honour. They died simply and without ostentation, crying " *Vive la Commune !* " A captain tore off Duval's boots and rode round waving them as a trophy: it was that sort of a war. The official report runs: " Another of their generals [besides Flourens], M. Duval, was killed by our men at the moment of the assault."

At nine o'clock, a counter-attack from Issy and Vanves began to harass the Versaillese and continued for the rest of the day; and a couple of guns at the head of the Clamart cutting rendered Châtillon untenable. But no forward movement could be attempted.

General Pellé was wounded by a stray shot from a house in Clamart, but was consoled by his nomination, next day, as Grand Commander of the Legion of Honour. The Versaillese losses had been moderate: 25 killed and 125 wounded, including 12 officers. The Communards' losses were very high, especially in prisoners.

The most remarkable thing about this sortie is the state of Paris while it was going on. The sortie had really been almost spontaneous. There was no service of regular news from the scene of action. The Commune was fighting its most decisive battle under the walls of Paris, and no one knew at all what was going on. The wildest reports circulated, uncontradicted by the Commune, which, overborne by the generals, had almost washed its hands of the affair.

Pyat, more responsible than anyone for the tacit approval Duval had assumed, spent the evening session demanding the abolition of the cult budget—that is, the official disestablishment of the Church. This had been for years the commonplace of all Republican programmes, whatever else might be their tendency. Obviously the measure would be one of the first that the Commune would adopt as soon as it had definitely thrown overboard its idea of acting solely as a municipal Parisian council, but Pyat's proposition, coming from such a person at such a moment, seems a little misplaced.

Pyat continued his irresponsible behaviour next day. The orator who, the day before, had pointed out the folly of an unorganised outburst against the enemy, now called upon the agitated citizens to rush off pell-mell to Versailles; six times he repeated in the *Vengeur*: " To Versailles, if we do not want again to resort to balloons ! To Versailles, if we do not wish to fall back again upon pigeons ! " etc. The Executive Commission reported success: the junction of Duval and Flourens at Courbevoie. The evening edition of Maroteau's *Montagne* got out huge headlines: " Victory ! General Duval and General Eudes are at Meudon and Châtillon. Long live the Commune ! Mont-Valérien is ours. Flourens is marching on Versailles."

The bourgeois were frightened. Goncourt declares that a single confirmed success, however slight, would have convinced them of the final defeat of Versailles. Three hundred women, who had gathered at the statue of Strasbourg in the Place de la Concorde, originally in order to go to Versailles to try for conciliation, marched, instead, up the Champs Elysées behind a red flag demanding to be led against the enemy. The Prussians at Saint-Denis, alarmed at the possible results of the decisive victory of either side, began to take precautions, turning their guns on the city and entrenching the northern railway line. The whole day Paris lived in anticipation of victory.

The Communal Council published a decree which gives the measure of the unreality in which they were living. Voted on the evening of the 2nd, it appeared in the *Officiel* of the 3rd :

" Whereas the Versailles Government has ordered and begun the civil war, attacked Paris, killed and wounded National Guards, soldiers of the Line, women and children; whereas this crime has been committed with premeditation and treachery against all right and without provocation, the Commune decrees: (1) MM.

Thiers, Favre, Picard, Dufaure, Simon and Pothuau shall be indicted. (2) Their property shall be confiscated until they have appeared before the justice of the people."

It recalls Pyat's offer, during the war, of a sword of honour to the man who should kill the King of Prussia. It recalls, too, de Tocqueville's bitter observations upon the revolutionary Assembly of 1848: " The imitation was so manifest that it concealed the terrible originality of the facts; I continually had the impression that they were engaged in play-acting the French Revolution far more than continuing it." Meanwhile, no attempt was made to see about the sending of reinforcements and provisions to the troops fighting outside Paris.

The awakening was terrible. Fugitives began to crowd into the city during the evening of the 3rd; the full extent of the disaster was known only at midday on the 4th. The news of Flourens's death was received with fury and consternation; his Belleville sharpshooters formed themselves into a free company dedicated to his memory, the " Avengers of Flourens "; Duval, too, had his " Avengers." The indignation was heightened by a proclamation of Galliffet to the Versailles papers; he had shot a captain, a sergeant and a Guard, taken prisoner on the morning of the 3rd, at Chatou; he declared: " It is war.without truce or pity that I declare on these assassins." The excitement was increased by the solemn funeral of Commandant Henry, killed at Nanterre beside Bergeret; there were funeral speeches by Tibaldi, Jules Vallès and Bergeret himself, who broke down in the middle.

Indignation ran high, but, curiously enough, it was almost entirely directed against Versailles. There was no question whatever of a riot nor of an attack on the Hôtel de Ville, as after the equally disastrous sortie against the Prussians on January 22: it was, as Cluseret had said, the Commune or nothing. The defence of Paris became more obstinate for the reverse. Lissagaray speaks of the " Parisian malady " which was epidemic at this moment,

and defines it well: " This was a fever of faith, of blind devotion and of hope—of hope above all. What rebellion had
been thus armed ? It was no longer a handful of desperate
men fighting behind a few paving-stones, reduced to loading their muskets with slugs or stones. The Commune of
1871, much better armed than that of 1793, possessed at
least 60,000 men, 200,000 muskets, 1,200 guns, 5 forts; an
*enceinte* covered by Montmartre, Belleville, and the Panthéon
over-towering the whole city, munitions enough to last for
years, and milliards at her bidding. What else is wanted to
conquer ? Some revolutionary instinct. There was not a
man at the Hôtel de Ville that did not boast of possessing
it."

Reports of the treatment of the 1,200 prisoners taken to
Versailles inflamed the fury aroused by the murders of
Duval and Flourens. They had been led through the streets
in the midst of a howling mob of civilians, Versaillese and
refugees from Paris. The bourgeois had been badly scared
and their savagery was proportionate to their terror.
Well-dressed and respectable gentlemen and ladies spat in
the faces of the prisoners, beat them with sticks and
umbrellas, covered them with the foulest insults, howled
for their death. The troops had the greatest difficulty in
getting the prisoners through. They had been under fire
all day, they were enraged enough by the resistance of the
Communard irregulars; but they were even more disgusted
by the bestiality of the citizens for whom they were supposed
to be fighting. There was nearly a mutiny that night at
Satory.

Chardon officially reported the killing of Duval at the
evening session of the 4th. Defeated outside the city, the
wilder members of the Council began, true Jacobins, to
seek for objects of vengeance within; but, in this first stage
of the civil war, the enthusiasm for the Commune itself
was still such that they did not, like the Jacobins of 1793,
set to destroying one another, but concentrated their
vengeance upon those of the enemy's party upon whom they
could immediately lay their hands.

There were a number of gendarmes, alleged spies and so forth already in the Commune's jails: to these were now added the regular hostages. The taking of hostages had been a not uncommon feature of the Franco-Prussian war, when leading citizens of occupied towns had been detained by the invaders as guarantees for the good behaviour of their fellow-citizens; so that the Commune was not initiating any new method of terrorism. At the same time, this imitation of Prussian " barbarity " created the worst impression upon moderate opinion in France and abroad.

Rigault had already arrested some notabilities on the 2nd: his object seems originally to have been to negotiate an exchange for Blanqui, without whom, Rigault was firmly convinced, nothing could be done by the Commune. The most important was Bonjean, ex-President of the Cour de Cassation, a Republican, Voltairean magistrate, strongly sympathetic to democracy. He also arrested Jecker, that enigmatic Swiss, originator, with Morny and the Empress, of the Mexican expedition, type of all the swindling financiers of the Second Empire, but cheated at the last by his own associates.

On the 4th, Rigault began to arrest priests, starting with the Archbishop of Paris himself, Mgr. Darboy. About half past four, some thirty National Guards arrived at the Archbishop's Palace in the rue de Grenelle. Darboy and his Vicar-General, Lagarde, were taken to the Prefecture, where they were received by Rigault, in the uniform of a commander of the National Guard, and his secretaries Slom, Da Costa, Levraud, Chardon, Henry and Ferré. The Archbishop advanced towards them, exclaiming, " My children . . . " " There are no children here," said Rigault coldly, " only citizens." The Archbishop was accused of counter-revolutionary conspiracy. He tried to answer. " All right," Rigault interrupted him. " You have been doing it for eighteen centuries now. It won't go on. Since you deny all conspiracy, justice will enquire into it. Meanwhile, I shall hold you. You will be questioned later."

The arrest of the Archbishop led to a general round-up of clergy. A number of Jesuits were arrested at the Ecole Sainte-Geneviève in the rue des Postes. " What is your profession ? " Rigault asked one of them. " Servant of God." " Where does your master live ? " " Everywhere." " Take this down," said Rigault to one of his secretaries; " So and so, alleging himself to be servant of one, God, vagrant." Besides some minor clergy, Rigault also arrested Deguerry, Curé of the Madeleine.

The news of the shooting of prisoners by the Versaillese directed attention to the hostages. Some of the Commune were for immediate reprisals upon the hostages, since the Communards had taken no prisoners. (It is remarkable that during the whole operation, from April 2 to May 28, only 183 of the Versaillese troops were reported missing, and of these by no means all were captured by the Communards, while the Communards were taken prisoners literally in thousands.)

The saner of the Communal Council would not yield to mere terrorism. Rigault demanded the immediate execution of the hostages; another member was for throwing them to the lynch-law of the mob; but Protot, Delegate for Justice, checked this dangerous violence. " We must act legally," he said; " draw up, discuss and adopt, if we approve it, a proposition instituting a mode of reprisal, still keeping within the bounds of the law." Lefrançais and Delescluze supported him; and the Commune invited the delegate for Justice, " the most competent in questions of law," to draw up the decree.

Protot drafted the " Law of the Hostages " as he sat at dinner at the Père Tranquille. As a conservative paper, *L'Avenir*, pointed out, it was the old revolutionary Law of Suspects " carried to its maximum intensity." Considering " that the Government at Versailles openly trampled underfoot the laws of Humanity as well as those of War; that it had shown itself guilty of horrors with which even the invaders of the soil of France had not stained themselves," the Commune decreed:

"Art. 1: Every person suspect of complicity with Versailles shall be immediately indicted and imprisoned.

"Art. 2: A jury shall be set up within twenty-four hours to take cognisance of the crimes referred to it.

"Art. 3: The jury shall render its decision within forty-eight hours.

"Art. 4: Every accused person detained by the jury shall be the hostage of the People of Paris.

"Art. 5: Every execution of a prisoner-of-war or partisan of the regular Government of the Commune shall be immediately followed by the execution of a triple number of the hostages detained by virtue of Article 4, to be chosen by lot.

"Art. 6: Every prisoner-of-war shall be brought before the jury, which shall decide whether he is to be immediately released or detained as a hostage."

The hostages were safe for the moment. Indeed, they were never regularly executed by a decree of the Commune. As some of the extremer members pointed out when execution was deferred time after time, the Commune was acting absurdly: either the Commune should have entirely abjured revolutionary terror or it should have adopted it resolutely, since the only sanctity recognised by revolution is the preservation of the revolutionary idea, just as its only justification is its success. Yet the decree about the hostages was the only way in which Protot, Delescluze and Lefrançais, the Communards whose sense and integrity is the least open to doubt, could save them: a decree which was deliberately intended to remain a dead letter. Even now, they could not believe that Thiers was quite ready to sacrifice an archbishop to the interests of his propaganda; while Thiers certainly calculated that the Commune would not dare to carry out the decree: as usual, he stood to win both ways.

Both sides were now committed to war à outrance, for neither could afford to yield. Offers of conciliation were politely turned down by both sides. There was nothing more to be got from " legal " negotiations.

Cluseret, leaving operations outside Paris to the Military Commission, at once began to reorganise the National Guard on a fighting basis. The condottiere had no use for amateurs, however much inspired with revolutionary ardour. Irregulars, yes ; but disciplined irregulars such as he had commanded in the States. His ideas were something of a shock to the Jacobins who still believed the legend of the Spontaneous Commune of 1793; and perhaps they estimated their fellow-citizens more correctly. By attempting to introduce a centralised militarism, Cluseret set himself against the Central Committee's federalism, lost their willing co-operation. It was a dilemma : to form an efficient fighting force was to deprive it of its main fighting spirit.

An addition to the Commune's decree abolishing military conscription had laid it down that every able-bodied citizen of Paris *ipso facto* was a member of the National Guard. On April 4, Cluseret called up all fit men between the ages of seventeen and thirty-five; thus excluding, in accordance with his dilemma, the less fit but more revolutionary veterans of the Forty-Eight. This call alarmed the bourgeois, who were sympathetic only so long as they were not themselves called upon to act; and many of them emigrated through the Prussian lines to Versailles. Only the Alsatians and Lorrainers, who had lost their homes to the Prussians, were exempted.

On the 9th, Cluseret, in a long circular, proposed to reorganise the active battalions. The functions of each unit were to be kept distinct : battalion committees, legion councils and Central Committee delegates. Only the legion commanders might issue general orders, sign proclamations, summon the battalions; and their personal responsibility for such orders was absolute. This was a great change from the Central Committee's atmosphere of " the great family "; and it was not popular. It began that conflict between the Military Commission, the Commune and the

Central Committee which did more than anything else to destroy the revolution.

There had been an affecting scene when the Central Committee had come to place command of the city in the hands of the new Commune on the morrow of its proclamation. The Commune had not wished to disavow the force which had made the revolution: it had permitted it to remain as the "great family council of the National Guard." It had been well represented on the first Military Commission by Eudes, Duval and Bergeret; and they had been responsible for the April 4 disaster. Duval was dead, Bergeret in prison, Eudes an individualist. The Committee as such was hardly represented on the Commune. The arrest of Bergeret and a general distrust of civilian delegates and of Cluseret encouraged the Committee to remain on the watch, sitting now in the rue de la Douane, ready to take over when the Commune had proved its inefficiency. Professional jealousy rather than greed for power. Their leader, Edouard Moreau, the real maker of the revolution, delegated to the military report and Press service at the War Office, was in close touch with Cluseret, watched every move, reported to the Committee, waited for one false step.

There was also political conflict between the Committee and the Commune. The Commune was composed largely of theorists and romantic Jacobins, revolutionary petty-bourgeoisie: the Committee represented the workers, not very enlightened, not thinking constructively except in so far as they were influenced by the Proudhonists and the International, but conscious of their position as workers. It was the Committee that proclaimed the real sense of the struggle against Versailles:

"Workers, do not be deceived: it is the great struggle: parasitism and labour, exploitation and production are at death-grips. If you are sick or vegetating in ignorance and squatting in the muck; if you want your children to be men gaining the reward of their labour, not a sort of animal trained for the workshop and for war, fertilising with their sweat the fortune of an exploiter or pouring out their blood for a despot; if you want the daughters whom you cannot bring up and watch over as you would to be no longer instruments of pleasure in the arms of the aristocracy of wealth; if you want debauch and poverty no longer to drive men to the police and women to prostitution; if, finally, you desire the reign of justice, workers, be intelligent, arise ! and let your stout hands fling beneath your feet the foul reaction !

" Citizens of Paris, merchants, industrialists, shop-keepers, thinkers, all of you that labour and seek in good faith the solution of social problems, the Central Committee adjures you to march united in progress. Take your inspiration from the destinies of our country and its universal genius.

" The Central Committee firmly believes that the heroic people of Paris is about to immortalise itself and regenerate the world.

" Long live the Republic ! Long live the Commune ! "

There was as yet no open conflict between the Committee and the Commune; but there was terrible confusion between the Military Commission and the dozens of small committees, sub-committees, municipalities and local interests, soon complicated by the rivalry of the Commune's civil delegates, all only too anxious to help in the work. The real trouble was that each leader was serving at a dozen posts at the same time, and could not possibly keep in continuous touch with the work of any one of them. Even the Central Committee was helpless here.

Cluseret, spasmodically energetic but appallingly lazy, had got the Commune's forces into some sort of shape by Easter Sunday, April 9. Versailles believed that the National Guard had 8,466 officers and 205,403 men. Cluseret's report of April 5 gave 41,500 of all ranks besides 12 to 15,000 in the forts and front-line. Cluseret believed in pitching his estimates too low in order to stimulate recruiting; actually, it had the reverse effect, aroused alarm and defeatism. On the other hand, a later roll, of May 3, reporting 6,507 officers and 162,250 men is as exaggerated as that of Versailles which, in turn, had been exaggerated in order to increase the repute of Thiers's achievement, to terrify provincial opinion into acquiescing in the most extreme measures of repression and to excuse the increase of his army by begging Bismarck to repatriate the prisoners of war.

Even Cluseret's modest estimate could not be entirely depended upon for an offensive action. The disaster of April 4, the deaths of Duval and Flourens, the relegation of Brunel and the arrest of Bergeret had removed the chief inspirers of the *sortie torrentielle*. Cluseret was under no illusion that attack could be contemplated for a long time; and the longer he deferred it, the smaller grew the enthusiasm, the better organised the Versaillese forces. There were 145,000 men inscribed in the National Guard: probably no more than a quarter were willing to march; but this quarter, mostly workers, were ready to march through hell.

There was a plentiful supply of guns in Paris: some 1,740, scattered about the city. But only about 320 were ever used. The local committees exaggerated their " mania for guns," would not let them be moved. There were 5,600 artillerymen, excellent mechanics and of legendary bravery, devoted to their pieces; but acting under the orders of an almost independent Central Artillery Committee, they refused to serve away from their positions. There was an unlimited supply of munitions, but here, too, local committees were obstructive and the distribution appallingly inefficient.

There were practically no military engineers; no cavalry, in spite of a decree by Cluseret requisitioning all horses not already monopolised by the excessive mounted staffs against which he fulminated in vain. Communications, provision-supply, ambulance-service were in complete disorder; and the *intendance* one vast squander. There was an enormous amount of work to be done before the Commune's army would be ready to fight efficiently.

Nevertheless, with even a passable central organisation, Paris might have held out indefinitely. It seemed incredible that a French force would bombard Paris, a thing from which the " barbarian " Prussians had shrunk. Even so, the fortifications, Thiers's own work, were, according to Thiers, impregnable. Paris could not be starved, since there was a regular supply through the Prussian lines; and Thiers, as Goncourt had pointed out, could not risk the odium of openly allying with Prussia against Frenchmen. Only treachery and disorganisation could serve Thiers; but he had always counted on those allies.

The front-line Communard troops were capable and determined; but they were hopelessly neglected by the higher command. They were killed cheerfully for a city which had almost forgotten them. Some battalions were not relieved for three weeks under incessant fire; some were wiped out without the knowledge of Headquarters. Appeals for reinforcements were met by haggling debates. The home-service battalions refused to serve in the forts. Life in the city went on, and for two months Paris was defended by heroes known to it only by their splendid funerals.

Yet their commanders were personally remarkable. Cluseret, efficient, vain and lazy; without ostentation, refusing to wear his general's uniform, lounging about under the heaviest fire with an eternal cheroot between his teeth. He even decreed the abolition of the general's title as undemocratic, and tried to check the ostentation of Communard uniforms. Here again, with all his sense, he conflicted with the spirit of the Communard troops. They liked their leaders to look like leaders. Uniforms were a terrible drain on the *intendance* expenditure. Varlin, investigating, stood one morning in Godillot's, the military tailors, and saw no fewer than eight young fellows arrive in one hour with vouchers for complete staff uniforms. As

Varlin explained to that enquiring Englishman, Albert Vandam : " It is really done to please the National Guard; they distrust those who remain in mufti; they attribute their reluctance to don the uniform to the fear of being compromised, to the wish to escape unnoticed if things should go wrong "; also, " to the Latin races the wisdom of Solomon lies in his magnificence." Cluseret did not please the National Guard : he was no Latin.

Cluseret's Chief of Staff, Nathaniel Rossel : his antithesis. A strict Protestant, son of a pastor, an ex-officer of the regular army, involved in the Metz conspiracy to prevent Bazaine from surrendering. Young, idealist, earnest and terribly pure, a Robespierrean " pure "; sacrificing a brilliant military career to join an insurrection in which he saw only a patriotic protest against the shameful decadence of the elder leaders of France, whether of Napoleon and Bazaine surrendering to the Prussians or Thiers surrendering simultaneously to Royalist " backwoodsmen " and a Paris riot. In the Commune he detected the germ of new vitality. He declared to his executioners after the fall of the Commune that he had fought for France and the soldiers' civil rights. An inflexible disciplinarian, so impatient of disorder that he was willing to intrigue for his own dictatorship to create order out of chaos. Temperamentally he could not stand Cluseret, that cynical Yankee. He would have been willing, and the *Père Duchêne* group of Jacobins tried to persuade him, to set up his dictatorship to save Paris from Cluseret's errors.

His coldness did not attract his men. He had begun badly. Elected Legion-Commander on his arrival in Paris, he had been abandoned by his troops in his first affair, a march on Courbevoie with his one intimate friend, Gérardin, and Malon; two battalions were blind drunk, five more simply dispersed. Rossel was arrested for a short time for attempting to restore discipline, an undemocratic proceeding, they thought. But he soon acquired a reputation for scrupulous efficiency in his important but subordinate position. Even Cluseret found him indispensable, and the Central Committee highly approved of him.

The rest of the command needed a considerable purging, which did not please the Central Committee. Assi, Commander at the Hôtel de Ville, and Bergeret, at Headquarters, spent most of their time now in celebrating their exploits with heavy meals; it was necessary to remove and arrest them. Madame Eudes had to be expelled from the Ministry of War where she paraded an Amazon uniform, a bunch of pistols and an hospitable table.

Bergeret was superseded by a Pole, Jaroslaw Dombrowski. At first, Dombrowski was looked upon with so much suspicion by the indignant Central Committee that the Commune had to invent a legend for him, that he had led the last Polish insurrection and had commanded in the Caucasian War. But it was known that Garibaldi had particularly wanted him to serve with him in the Vosges Army in the war; and the cool daring of this charming, courteous and efficient soldier in his first engagement immediately created another and truer legend around him.

The defensive positions round Paris were apportioned. On the right wing, Dombrowski, holding Neuilly and supported as far as Saint-Ouen by his brother, Ladislas. South of him, another Pole, ex-captain of Francs-Tireurs, Okolowicz. Then Colonel Laporte, a rather shady person, as far as the Point-du-Jour salient in the south-west. From the Seine to the Bièvre, behind the southern forts, Eudes and La Cécilia, mathematician, linguist (he was the only member of the Commune who could talk to Dombrowski in his own language) and ex-officer. On the extreme left, from the Bièvre to Charenton, another Pole, Wroblewski. An extremely able set of commanders, experienced in insurrection and guerilla warfare, with excellent material under them; but neglected by a central command rent by futile conflicts.

The success on April 4, due more to the Communards' inefficiency than to Versaillese strength, had worked wonders to the morale of the Versaillese armies. This moral effect was carefully reinforced by good treatment: they were flattered, well fed, well housed, isolated at Satory from the civil population, and received the doubtful pleasure of visits from the Head of the Executive Power himself.

The Versaillese forces had the supreme advantage of a single command: that of Thiers himself. The nominal command was entrusted by him to Marshal MacMahon, the failure of Sédan. Thiers, with his usual foresight, had left his card at the Marshal's house on the fatal 3rd of September. The aged and discredited Marshal was now to have the opportunity of retrieving against fellow-Frenchmen the legendary glory of Magenta and Malakoff ("*j'y suis, j'y reste*"). The first review held by Thiers and MacMahon was carried out with the greatest secrecy; but none of the apprehended demonstrations took place. Thiers kept all the threads in his own hands. Every morning, he gathered the Military Staff round him and convinced them, as he could convince anybody, that his was the right plan of campaign. The aged historian enjoyed himself hugely in this imitation of Napoléon: the Staff not so much.

The troops were not favourably impressed by the Assembly, which had made itself somewhat ridiculous on April 4 by solemnly proposing to visit the heroic wounded and finding that no heroic wounded had yet been brought in. A few days later, they applauded a fierce duel between the War Minister and the President of the Council, both denying responsibility for having omitted to collect the Deputies to accompany General Besson's funeral. But, on the whole, the soldiers, once convinced that the Parisians were a sort of Prussians, took little interest in politics.

The army was now composed of three army corps of three divisions each; the first under Ladmirault, one of the best generals of the unfortunate Rhine Army, the second under de Cissey, an excellent organiser who had distinguished himself at Rezonville, the third, entirely of cavalry, under

Du Barail. Two more divisions of repatriated prisoners were being reorganised at Cherbourg, Cambrai and Dijon, the 4th under Douay, formerly in command at Châlons camp, the 5th under Clinchant, who had struggled so heroically but vainly with the Eastern Army. A reserve of three divisions was commanded by Vinoy, consoled for his obscurer post by the Grand-Chancellorship of the Legion of Honour.

At the evacuation of Paris, Thiers had only 22,000 men. He had denuded not only the southern forts but even the key to the Paris-Versailles road, Mont-Valérien. Luckily for him, this fort was commanded by an intelligent officer, who dismissed all his disaffected troops, prevaricated with the Central Committee's envoys and held the fort with a dozen men until reinforced from Versailles. With Mont-Valérien safe and conditioned for offensive bombardment, Versailles was protected and the attack could begin.

The peace preliminaries allowed the Army of Paris to retain 40,000 men: Thiers thought he needed at least 150,000. During the first days at Satory, the 22,000 were brought up to the permitted 40,000. On March 24, Favre applied to Bismarck for permission to increase to 80,000. Bismarck consented, but reserved in return the right to terminate the convention " as soon as Prussia might consider her interests compromised." Thus Prussia " exercised a sort of usurious blackmail to force on the definitive peace, since the occupation was very onerous." " By March 18, all the conventions so laboriously worked out in the past two weeks were beginning to be put into execution; France was returning to life. The Prussians were disposed to withdraw their armies promptly. . . . The insurrection at Paris awakened all the fears and all the distrust of Prussia; it put in doubt the existence of the Government of the Assembly and, consequently, the execution of the peace preliminaries. . . . The Prussians immediately took precautions against all the inconveniences that might result to them; at the same time they put themselves in a position to profit from the new advantages that the Paris sedition gave them over the French Government. They stopped their evacuation; and fearing that the soldiers returning from Germany might support a triumphant revolution and recommence hostilities, they suspended the repatriation of prisoners of war on March 21."

The position was delicate. Thiers could not too openly ally himself, even against revolution, with enemies whose very presence was a humiliation. Grousset's mistake about " amicable " relations had caused uneasiness. The Prussians, believing in the possibility of a united front of a reconciled Paris and Versailles, which would deprive them of their splendid opportunity for blackmail, had regarded the Mayors' efforts with disfavour. On March 26, Fabrice had written to Favre: " In any delay public opinion will see the hesitation of the French Government to assume governmental responsibilities until it has come to an agreement with the dissident party in Paris. The Chancellor thinks that by acting in such a way as to destroy this suspicion the French Government would powerfully contribute to the re-establishment of its authority." Thus Bismarck definitely incited Thiers to civil war.

Once the war had begun, Bismarck resumed the repatriation. He allowed Thiers to increase his army, first to 80,000, then to 150,000 men. But this increase was set off by fresh exactions in the peace terms. " Every advantage obtained to the profit of social order was paid for by a retreat on diplomatic ground. This was the general character of the Brussels negotiations, and it was one of the most deplorable results of the Paris sedition."

Thiers's plan of attack was simple enough. As he, the builder of the fortifications, well knew, the weak point was the salient in the extreme south-west, on the right bank of the Seine, the Point du Jour. It was commanded by the Mont-Valérien, Meudon and Montretout batteries; the protection afforded by Forts Issy and Vanves could become an enfilade after their capture. A force entering the city in this quarter would have the advantage of the

assistance or acquiescence of bourgeois Passy and Auteuil.
The scene of battle would be large gardens and sparse
streets, unfavourable to barricade fighting, as far north as
the Trocadéro and east as the Champ de Mars.

The campaign, therefore, began with a fierce bombardment. Ladmirault was to divert the Federals' attention
by a daily demonstration against Neuilly, backed by continuous artillery fire. Vinoy's reserve, in the centre, was
to dominate the Bois de Boulogne and wait until de Cissey's
corps had mastered the southern forts by a regular artillery
and entrenchment operation. On the south, du Barail's
cavalry, extending as far as Longjumeau, was to cut
communications between the Seine and the Bièvre and
guard the Orléans railway.

Thiers, enjoying to the full his tactical game, was insistent
that it be carried out pedantically. Halévy recalls a conversation he heard at Versailles at the beginning of May.
Someone remarked to him : " In my opinion, we could have
entered Paris by surprise a month ago." Thiers was twenty
yards away, but had, it seems, a sharp ear for talk of the
Paris fortifications. He turned upon the speaker in an
absolute frenzy : " So, my dear sir, you are one of those who
think that Paris can be entered by surprise ? You can be
quite certain that that is an error. By surprise ! It is easy to
talk ! You take command of the army and enter Paris by
surprise ! By surprise ! I, perhaps, know something of the
question. The Paris fortifications are an immense work, a
work of the first order. They held the Prussians for six
months. They would have held them for five years, for
fifty years, had Paris not lacked food. And the Commune
does not lack food : it can get what food it needs through the
Prussian lines. Believe me, the Paris fortifications are no
small matter. It is a colossal, a gigantic enterprise. We shall
not be able to carry it through without a vast general operation, an immense military effort, worked out in great detail
and with great care. Ah ! the Paris fortifications ! I know
them better than anyone, the Paris fortifications ! "
Halévy's friend commented : " Yes, M. Thiers wants to

enter Paris and he will enter, but it would displease him to
see his fortifications fall too quickly and too easily. It must
be fully demonstrated that M. Thiers alone was able to
take a city rendered impregnable by M. Thiers. ' *Amour-
propre d'auteur !* ' "

# CHAPTER V

# CLUSERET

" I have seen many organisations and many insurrections in the course of my life; but never have I seen anything comparable to the anarchy of the National Guard in 1871. It was perfect of its kind, and Proudhon would have been satisfied with the fruits which the tree he planted in 1848 bore in 1871."

CLUSERET: *Mémoires*

" Some American citizens told me: ' You are sure worth a million.' "

*Report of Commission of Enquiry into the Affair of Citizen Cluseret: Accus.4.*

BY EASTER SUNDAY Paris was enjoying a too-familiar spectacle: bombardment. On April 6, Mont-Valérien, rearmed with heavier artillery, had begun to fire on Courbevoie. After holding out for six hours, the Federals had been driven back behind the great barricade on the Neuilly bridge. Here they had stood for another day under the cover of the Porte Maillot battery; but, despite the artillerymen's legendary heroism, they had been forced back and back, leaving their emplacements a smoking ruin.

Next day, without warning, the whole village of Neuilly was smashed by devastating fire. The inhabitants crept into their cellars, where these respectable tradesmen and *rentiers* were held, starving and maddened, for more than two weeks.

The Versaillese followed up the bombardment with a fierce assault, carrying the Neuilly bridge-head; but Thiers's express orders checked the pursuit.

The Commune had counter-attacked, retaken Asnières and the north-eastern part of Neuilly. The southern front was protected for the present by an armoured train on the Issy viaduct. From Sèvres, Communard gunboats fired upon the Versaillese emplacements in Meudon.

The front was now very much the same as it had

been before April 3; but the bombardment of Paris itself marked the beginning of the next stage in the war. The Versaillese, already reorganised for victory, had passed to the offensive. The Commune had finally missed its one chance of military success.

Paris was not alarmed. Crowds of strollers thronged the Champs-Elysées to watch the shells break in the clear sky over the Arc de Triomphe. Goncourt sat comfortably in a café at the Rond-Point. Men and women were sipping their beer with the calmest air in the world, listening to an old woman playing one of Thérésa's airs on a violin.

Someone had posted up a copy of Thiers's former appeals defending his fortifications: " It would be calumny to suppose that any Government might one day seek to maintain itself by bombarding the capital. What ! After riddling the domes of the Invalides and the Panthéon with its bombs, after devoting your families' homes to the flames, could it then present itself to you and ask you to confirm its existence ? " And again, from a protest against the bombardment of Palermo in 1848: " You have all shuddered with horror on learning that a great city has been bombarded for two days. By whom ? By a foreign enemy exercising the rights of war ? No, gentlemen ! By its own Government ! And why ? Because this unfortunate city demanded its rights ! Permit me to appeal to the opinion of all Europe ! It is to render a service to humanity to pronounce, from perhaps the highest tribunal in Europe, some words of indignation against such misdeeds ! "

Thiers's agents were completely deceived by the calm. " Paris," they reported, " was unusually gloomy on Sunday; the boulevards and the usual resorts were completely deserted; there is terror in every face one meets; the passers shun each other, so mistrustful have people become." Certainly the boulevards were deserted: their usual crowd of idlers had long ago scuttled off to Versailles: the centre of Paris life had moved east, to the workers' quarters; and the remaining Friends of Order had reason for their mutual and terrified distrust.

Rigault was particularly keen against both the immorality and the counter-revolution he suspected in the boulevard cafés, and razzias were frequent. Several English correspondents were arrested one night at Noel-Peters, Rigault explaining that they had only themselves to blame if they would frequent such dubious haunts. The Café de Suède, on the south side of the Boulevard Montmartre, was always a notorious haunt of what was left of the counter-revolution; but its conspiracies were very puerile.

The Communards had other distractions: the revolutionary clubs, held in the deserted churches; the committees; the service in the National Guard. The Commune had its public ceremonies, the splendid revolutionary funerals it gave to its defenders.

The first of these was held on April 6. Three catafalques, each carrying thirty-five coffins veiled in black and draped with red flags, drawn by eight horses, passed slowly along the boulevards to Père-Lachaise. Trumpets and a squadron of the Avengers of Paris preceded them. Delescluze and five other members of the Commune led the procession, bareheaded and girded with their red-and-gold sashes. Thousands followed. " What an admirable people ! " cried old Delescluze. " Will they still call us a mere handful of sedition-mongers ? " At the grave, Delescluze spoke: " I will not say many words; already they have cost us all too dear. Justice for the families of the fallen ! Justice for the great city which, after five months of siege, betrayed by its Government, still holds in its hands the future of humanity ! Let us not weep for our brothers who have fallen heroically, but let us swear to continue their work, to save Freedom, the Commune, the Republic ! "

Four days later, the Commune officially adopted the widows and children of all citizens who fell in the defence of the people's rights, granted a pension of 600 francs to such widows, 365 francs and free education to every child, legitimate or not, of every National Guard killed in action, and pensions of 100 to 800 francs to dependants.

It by no means suited Thiers that the provinces should

know of the complete calm in Paris. He continued to flood the country with sensational " red terror " propaganda. He had the local prefects, sole source of information, carefully in hand; and the agents of the Commune, Bastélica and Paul Lafargue, could make little headway.

On April 6, the Commune attempted to repudiate these slanders. In a proclamation to the provinces it protested against the accusation that Paris wished to set up its dictatorship over France, that robbery and murder were the order of the day. Never had the streets been quieter. Not a murder nor a robbery for three weeks. " Paris aspires only to found the Republic and to obtain its communal franchises, happy to furnish an example to the other communes of France. If the Commune of Paris has exceeded the sphere of its normal attributes, it is with great regret and only in reply to the state of war provoked by the Government at Versailles. Paris aspires only to its autonomy, respecting fully the rights of other French communes."

A few days later, Malon and André Léo (Léodile Champseix) issued a parallel proclamation to the peasants, explaining in simple and moving terms what the social revolution meant to the agricultural labourer, as exploited as the worker: for his freedom too Paris was fighting: for " the land to the peasant, the tool to the worker, work to all."

But the movement in the provinces came to nothing. At Narbonne the revolutionaries had abandoned their leader on March 31, when troops came up from Toulouse. At Limoges, the National Guards had dispersed, after disarming a detachment of soldiers going to Versailles. At Marseilles, the Commune set up by Crémieux had been hemmed in in the Prefecture and had been forced to evacuate under bombardment from the heights of Notre-Dame-de-la-Garde. General Espivent's sailors had assaulted the empty building; " and do you know how ? " Thiers had asked the Assembly. " With boarding-axes ! " [*Profound sensation.*] Espivent's repression had been as bloody as Thiers's. Order reigned over France, and Paris was once more isolated.

The Moderate Republicans and several non-political bodies had not yet lost hope of finding some agreement which would put a stop to the horrors of civil war. On April 4, the *Temps*, Conservative journal, suggested that both the Assembly and the Commune should simultaneously resign; on the 6th, that this solution should be carried out by Thiers and Louis Blanc, neither actually involved in the Assembly nor the Commune. At the same time, the National Union of Syndical Chambers, representing 56 organisations with nearly 7,000 Paris industrialists and merchants, brought forward a conciliatory plan; and some republican Deputies and ex-Deputies of Paris, Corbon, Pichat, Lockroy and Clémenceau, under the leadership of Ranc, founded the Republican Union for the Rights of Paris, demanding recognition of the Republic, municipal franchises of Paris and recognition of the National Guard as the military force in Paris.

But, after the demonstration of the Friends of Order on March 22, all activity coming from such quarters seemed to the Commune suspect. The defeat on April 4 had made tempers even more intransigent. A meeting of the conciliators summoned at the Bourse on April 6 was banned by the Executive Commission: " Reaction assumes every sort of disguise, to-day that of conciliation. . . . Conciliation with *Chouans* and police spies ! In such circumstances, conciliation is treason ! Every demonstration likely to disturb public order and provoke internal dissensions during the battle will be rigorously repressed by force."

Two days later, the Freemasons joined the efforts for conciliation, despite the disapproval of the Council of the Grand Orient. The Freemasons at that time were neither political nor suspect of sinister conspiracies, and it is remarkable that, in spite of their adhesion to the Commune, they were never seriously accused of having plotted the revolution. Several members of the Commune itself were Freemasons. A deputation of 7 FF∴ MM∴ went to the Hôtel de Ville, were received by F∴ M∴ Melliet on the 8th and invited by him to a consultation next day. Here they found Vaillant, Tridon, Delescluze and Cluseret. The delegation met with a " kind and almost cordial welcome," but the Commune was sceptical of their success and emphasised that the Commune could not yield any of its legitimate claims. The following day, the delegation met Jules Simon and Pouyer-Quertier at Versailles; here, too, the reception was very cordial, but the Versailles Government refused to treat with the insurrectionary Government. The Freemasons, checked for the moment, determined to continue their efforts.

The siege of Paris was proceeding slowly but methodically. The first object of the Versaillese was to consolidate the positions gained on April 4, especially on the southern front, extending their line eastwards from the heights of Meudon to enfilade Fort Issy and isolate it from Fort Vanves. The action took the form largely of an artillery duel, with rare but fierce attacks and counter-attacks. On April 11, the Federals retook Neuilly, after fighting all day hand-to-hand under a murderous bombardment which almost annihilated the village. On the 17th, the Versaillese rushed Asnières and Bécon, but were driven out again. On the 21st, Dombrowski broke through the tightening line of encirclement, held the crossing of the Seine at Clichy, and hung on somehow to shattered Neuilly.

The Versaillese advance was slower than had been expected, not only because of the surprisingly fierce resistance of the Communard troops, but also because their own morale was still shaky. On April 14, the 76th and 110th of the Line in the trenches at Châtillon were almost mutinous, and the 20th battalion of Chasseurs was noticed by the ubiquitous police as showing " a very bad spirit." The 55th had been very discontented at being brought to Versailles from Sathonay; several of them had given cartridges to workers at Essonnes; with the 67th, they had listened favourably to agitators at Longjumeau, and some thirty of them, led by three sergeants, had deserted. A squadron of Hussars had found eighteen of them in the Verrières woods and shot them on the spot.

The villages round Paris were doubtfully loyal to Versailles. The Vincennes National Guard rallied to the Commune, but Saint-Mandé refused. Rueil, Nanterre and Bougival came over to Versailles after April 4: " Is it because of the presence of our troops or of the crimes committed in Paris ? " the police wondered somewhat naïvely. When the Commune issued an " Appeal to Frenchmen " on April 22, and sent copies to the local Mayors, Maisons-Alfort, Creteil, Saint-Maur, Champigny, Vincennes were not enthusiastic; Bonneuil, Aubervilliers and Pantin refused to post it up.

By April 21 the siege of Paris entered upon its second phase. Consolidation was completed, and Versailles opened the attack, which was to last until May 8, on the key-position of Fort Issy. The Versaillese line now held almost all the points which had been occupied by the Prussians in the first siege: from Asnières by way of Courbevoie and the Bois de Boulogne to Meudon, Clamart, Châtillon and Bourg-la-Reine. They were advancing steadily on Issy, which covered the Point-du-Jour, their final objective, and Vanves, which covered Issy. Forts Montrouge, Bicêtre and Ivry had not yet come into play, but reconnaissances were frequent along the Orléans railway towards Choisy-le-Roi and Vitry, which covered Ivry.

The Communards' first line was the forts; behind them, they were strongly entrenched at Bagneux, on the Montrouge road, covered by Forts Montrouge and Bicêtre; at the Hautes-Bruyères redoubt, between Bourg-la-Reine and Villejuif, covered by Fort Bicêtre; and at the Moulin-Saquet redoubt, between Choisy-le-Roi and Vitry, covered by Fort Ivry.

The Communard troops had been terribly neglected by Cluseret, engaged in reorganising the National Guard in Paris whenever he could trouble to do anything at all. An appeal for relief by the 176th battalion at Hautes-Bruyères is typical. " This is the 26th day that we have been in the redoubt and the men are very tired, since no leave is granted, and a large number of the Guards of my battalion are boys, and they cannot get a clean change of clothes. They are beginning to be attacked by vermin and scurvy. I beg you therefore to be kind enough to have us relieved and send us home for a day or two to rest our men a little; after this rest, we shall be at your disposal, ready to go wherever you think fit."

The front-line fighters were a band of determined and desperate citizens, for no one else would undertake their service. One commander received some reinforcements with this characteristic introduction: " Citizen, we are sending you the Bastille Column Battalion. Splendid fellows but awful blackguards. Excellent for outpost service and assaults. Take care of their rations and pay. Their post will be in front of Villejuif."

The front line was holding out with extraordinary herosim in conditions far worse than those suffered by the regular troops during the first siege: under intenser bombardment, in weather almost as foul—sleet and rain all the time, and little shelter.

Cluseret did try to restore some sort of order in the services, but his supercilious regular-army manners alienated the Commune, the Central Committee and his own men. The Commune dared not leave his proclamations uncensored. A typical example is a notice in the *Journal Officiel* of April 20, as compared with his original version: " For some time there has been an excessive (*ridiculous*) consumption of munitions in the forts; Vanves alone has consumed 16,000. Besides the impropriety of burning powder uselessly, of spending the people's money to pure loss and arousing anxiety in people's minds (*throwing them into terror*), this (*stupid and entirely Monarchist*) practice shows more enthusiasm than coolness (*is ridiculous in the eyes of men of war*). (*It is only poltroons that are so little masters of their emotions that they cannot control their actions themselves.*) The Delegate for War warns the National Guard and the commander of the fort (*forts, Fort Vanves in particular*) that in future no requests for munitions beyond the number of shells allocated to each fort for its defence will be granted."

Cluseret sent the original draft to the Executive Commission with a curt note to post it up. Pyat noted on it that there was no reason to publish, and Debock, Delegate to the *Journal Officiel*, sent a hurried message to suppress the phrase " this stupid and entirely Monarchist practice," which seemed really dangerously brutal.

The frictions latent in the Communal Government were already coming to a head. The two controlling powers of the fighting forces, Cluseret and the Central Committee, quarrelled with each other and with the civil power, the Commune, itself internally divided. The Central Committee was behind Cluseret's appointment, but their nominee had very soon broken loose from their control. They had been antagonised by the arrests of Bergeret and Assi; they were dissatisfied with Cluseret's cavalier methods of dealing with the National Guard. Although they did not actually bring about an open quarrel, they kept a strict control over him. They constituted eleven special commissions within the Delegation for War and kept Moreau at the military report service. They retained control of supplies and the *intendance*. They proposed the complete control of all measures undertaken by the Delegate for War, although he was nominally responsible to the Commune and revocable by it.

A further step in this struggle was the creation of the court martial. The shooting of prisoners by Galliffet and his brutal glorification of his action, published in Paris on April 9, had been the immediate cause of the Decree on the Hostages. It was now reported that Dufaure, Thiers's Minister for Justice, had carried a proposal to hasten the procedure of the courts martial: the Minister for War was to bring the accused before the Council of War without preliminary investigation, and sentence should be executed within forty-eight hours. The Communard *Journal Officiel* advised the Parisians on no account to surrender: the fate of prisoners was now sealed.

As a counter-measure, a Council of War, originally intended to check the indiscipline of the National Guard, was set up on April 11. But this Council worked too slackly.

On the 16th, therefore, Cluseret, acting with the Commune's Executive Commission, formed a provisional court martial. Some members of the Commune viewed this creation with distrust: it looked as if Cluseret were trying to set up an independent power, for he wished both to bring the accused before the court and to preside over it. The Executive Commission decided that he should rather appoint a president. Under pressure from the Central Committee, he chose his Chief of Staff, Rossel, in whom the Committee already saw his possible successor. The court was packed with committee-men; Henry, Chief of General Staff; Razoua, Commander at the Ecole Militaire; Collet, Eudes's Chief of Staff; Boursier of the Central Committee; and Chardon, Military Commander at the Ex-Prefecture of Police to keep up the liaison between Rossel and Rigault. Thus a military police, distinct from the Commune's civil police, was growing up; and in a state of war might well supersede it, if it could come to an agreement with Rigault, whose friends on the *Père Duchêne* already hoped for Rossel's dictatorship to restore order in the services. And Rossel, eager for power, detesting Cluseret's lazy contempt for the purity of revolution, waited.

But Cluseret dined calmly at the Café d'Orsay with his American friends, or lay on his back on the soft sofas of the Ministry of War, his eternal cheroot between his teeth, surrounded by a crowd of importunate office-seekers into whose antecedents he never troubled to enquire, giving orders which no one carried out.

The Commune, too, had suffered serious internal quarrels, but the sessions were not reported until April 13, and then in so garbled a version that they left room for the uneasiest conjectures. A split was growing wider between the extreme Jacobins, who were all for reviving the forms of 1793 under completely different conditions, and the Socialists, who saw in this revolutionary romanticism only a hindrance to real social reforms. This antagonism first came to a head over the relatively unimportant matter of the by-elections on April 16.

Owing to resignations, double elections and deaths, there were thirty-one vacancies on the Communal Council. Although all the best revolutionary forces were at the front, and although it was no time to test the temper of the city under such unfavourable conditions, it was decided to discover whether the Commune had lost or gained ground in Paris. The Commune was naturally anxious for a large vote, and most of its papers reprinted an appeal published in Rochefort's *Mot d'Ordre* : " We appeal to the people to go to the polls. Vote for whomever you wish : for Chaudey in prison or Father Gaillard in charge of the barricades : but vote ! The essential is that we oppose a large vote to the maunderings of the Versailles papers. The insecurely established Thiers who rules the Anti-National Assembly has declared that the Paris insurrection was made by twenty thousand convicts. The only answer to make is to prove that it is being made by two hundred thousand citizens."

The revolutionary municipalities and committees carefully chose their candidates. The International, which had viewed the Jacobin predominance with alarm, was particularly active. Special polling-booths were set up in each battalion. But the result was disappointing : only 53,680 votes were cast, as compared with the 229,167 for the Commune on March 26.

Three districts out of the fourteen called upon did not vote at all : the IIIrd, VIIIth and XIIIth. The Ist (3,271 votes as against 11,056 on March 26) elected Cluseret, Vésinier, Pillot and Andrieu ; the IInd (3,601 as against 11,143) Pottier, Serrailler, Durand and Johannard ; the VIth (3,469 as against 9,499) Courbet and Rogeard, the third representative required not being elected ; the VIIth (1,939 as against 5,065) Sicard ; the IXth (3,176 as against 10,340) only Briosne out of five representatives to be elected ; the XIIth (5,423 as against 11,328) Philippe and Lonclas ; the XVIth (1,590 as against 3,732) only Longuet from the two necessary ; the XVIIth (4,848 as against 11,282) only Dupont from two necessary ; the XVIIIth

(10,068 as against 17,443) Cluseret and Arnold; the XIXth
(7,090 as against 11,282) Menotti Garibaldi; the XXth
(9,204 as against 16,792) Viard and Trinquet.

Only twenty of the thirty-one representatives to be elected
had been returned, and only twelve had obtained the
majority of one-eighth of the registered voters which had
been the electoral principle of the Commune. Cluseret had
been elected twice.

There were five workers among the new members, four
of whom were cobblers, already well represented on the
Commune: Serrailler, active member of the International
in England; Sicard, a violent one-eyed person; Trinquet
of Belleville, a square, energetic little man; and Durand, a
comparative nonentity; the fifth worker was the decorator
Johannard of the International, a magnificent figure, the
best billiards-player of the Commune, and a very useful
man. Of the rest, the most famous was Gustave Courbet,
the " realist " painter, friend of Proudhon, now a rather
violent and untidy old drunkard, who had joined the
Commune to be with his old friends of the revolutionary
cafés. Pottier, active in the International, had been a friend
of Henri Murger, had often exhibited designs at the Salon,
and, later, composed the International anthem. Then
Andrieu, a fat, jovial, one-eyed professor; Rogeard, author
of the *Propos de Labiénus*, which had caused a sensation
under the Empire; Longuet, who had been editing the
*Officiel*, active in the International; Vésinier, nicknamed
" Racine de Buis," a vindictive little hunchback hating
everybody in general and Longuet in particular; Briosne,
Socialist club-orator; Dupont, an amateur chemist; Viard,
nephew of a wealthy varnish manufacturer—" young but
practical," he claimed; Arnold, an architect employed by
the Paris municipality; the rest were nonentities. Menotti
Garibaldi, like his father, refused with thanks.

The new members did not change the alignment of
parties in the Commune. Andrieu, Arnold, Courbet,
Longuet and Serrailler joined the minority Socialist group
composed of the Internationalists and Vallès, Vermorel,

Ostyn, Arnould, Tridon, Jourde, Babick and Verdure. The rest joined the Jacobins.

The question arose whether the nine elections which had received insufficient votes should be counted as valid. Rogeard and Briosne refused to take their seats. The point was debated in a violent session of the Commune on the 19th. Should the revolution be efficient or respectable ? As Varlin pointed out, it was a question whether the Commune could afford to be consistent or must conform to the democratic electoral law of 1848: some similarly situated candidates had been declared valid at the original Communal elections. In actual fact, if the question had not been so emphatically raised, Paris would not have greatly cared either way; it had not been sufficiently interested even to vote. The elections were declared valid by 26 votes to 13.

A group of Internationalists, Franckel, Jourde, Malon and Varlin, their best men, supported the Jacobins for once, to uphold the consistency and prestige of the Commune; on the other hand, some Jacobins—Géresme, Miot and Verdure—opposed the motion. Besides these three, the minority consisted of Arnould, Avrial, Beslay, Clémence, Victor Clément, Langevin, Lefrançais, Rastoul, Vallès and Vermorel.

The division had passed off amicably, for it did not seem that any basic principle was at stake. At the session on the 21st, however, Pyat suddenly found all sorts of conscientious scruples, and sent in a letter offering his resignation. The old romantic thought it a good opportunity to get a personal vote of confidence. He had not been at the debate, being detained at the Ministry of War. His chief argument was speciously Jacobin: that the elected had no right to replace the electors, that they could not take upon themselves the functions of the sovereign people; this he could not reconcile with his revolutionary democratic conscience. There had been resignations offered before this, by members overburdened by several functions, but this was the first on a matter of principle. Régère and Amouroux, usually the mildest of men, attacked furiously this attempt to evade responsibility; and the Commune decided to keep Pyat at his post, ignoring his offer.

Matters were coming to a head with the opening of the general attack of the Versaillese armies. Some of the Commune, notably Vallès, thought that the War Delegation was acquiring too much independence. Cluseret realised that the main attack was developing, but had to carry on the struggle for the organisation to meet it both against the Commune, which feared his predominance, and against the Central Committee, which blamed his slackness.

The Committee had obtained the release of Assi and Bergeret. Lullier, too, had escaped from prison, and, his pockets bulging with revolvers, had recruited a private bodyguard and was intriguing with his old shady friends, Ganier d'Abin and the provocateur Raoul du Bisson. Assi had prevented the election of Lullier to the Commune, but the Central Committee had been so unsuccessful in securing their own representation that they might well join forces with such elements. To meet this danger, Cluseret fell back on the Commune as the lesser evil. The Council decided to reorganise.

The situation of individual members had become intolerable, and the original Commissions could hardly function. The Executive Commission was never to be found at the Hôtel de Ville, since its members had to work on all sorts of other committees as well. At that very debate, Ranvier sent in a letter apologising for his absence: he had not yet been replaced in the command of his battalion and he had also to attend a public funeral in his district that afternoon. The districts preferred their leaders to attend to local affairs and had little confidence in the Hôtel de Ville.

Delescluze proposed the formation of nine new Commissions, with a Central Commission of Delegates from them, to replace the useless Executive Commission. The question of their personal responsibility was the core of the debate. It was essential that decisions taken by individual delegates should not compromise the Commune as a whole; on the other hand, no member would accept a delegation if his

actions were to be continually interfered with, as had
hitherto happened. There was also the danger that the
Council of the Nine Commissions might become a dictatorial
oligarchy. Billioray proposed that a superior Supervisory
Commission should be formed to examine the activities of
the Executive Commission and report on them to the Commune, a form of Committee of Public Safety, although he
did not yet bring up that name. Finally, it was decided
that nine Commissions of five members each should be set
up, each with a delegate subject to their supervision and
revocable by them after consultation with the Commune.

The Delegates from the nine Commissions were to form
the executive body of the Commune, were to meet each
evening to decide, by a voting majority, decisions concerning their departments, to inform the Commune in secret
committee of their decisions each day, and let the Commune have the final word in the matter—a rather remarkable organisation, a complete break with parliamentarianism,
dictated not only by the necessities of the present situation
but by the whole revolutionary character of the Commune.

The new Delegates were:

War: Cluseret.
Finance: Jourde.
Supplies: Viard.
Foreign Affairs: Grousset.
Education: Vaillant.
Justice: Protot.
Police: Rigault.
Labour and Exchange: Franckel.
Public Services: Andrieu.

The new Commissions were:

War: Delescluze, Tridon, Avrial, Ranvier, Arnold.
Finance: Beslay, Billioray, V. Clément, Lefrançais, Pyat.
Police: Cournet, Vermorel, Ferré, Trinquet, Dupont.
Education: Courbet, Verdure, Miot, Vallès, J. B. Clément.
Supplies: Varlin, Parisel, V. Clément, Arnould, Champy.

Justice: Gambon, Dereure, Clémence, Langevin, Durand.
Labour: Theisz, Malon, Serrailler, Longuet, Chalain.
Foreign Relations: Melliet, Ch. Gérardin, Amouroux, Vallès, Johannard.
Public Services: Ostyn, Vésinier, Rastoul, Arnaud, Pottier.

Billioray's proposition for a tenth Commission—of Propaganda—was unfortunately shelved.

Régère had demanded that the guiding principle in the choice of members should be their aptitude for their functions; judging by their transference from the earlier Commissions to quite new duties, some of the delegates must have been remarkably versatile. Actually, the new Commissions grouped their members far more accurately according to their qualifications than had the first hastily elected organisation.

Jourde, Grousset, Protot, Rigault and Franckel had all had previous experience at their posts. Vaillant, an extremely brilliant scholar with degrees from several universities, was an admirable Delegate for Education. The Education Commission as a whole was in the hands of specialists, since it also included the functions of the old Ministry of Fine Arts. The Labour Commission was entirely in the hands of the International, who put through the Commune's most notable social measures although in a minority on the Communal Council.

But some of the key Commissions were very weak: that of Justice especially, where Protot worked practically single-handed against Rigault's encroachments. On the Finance Commission, too, Jourde and Beslay did all the work; it would seem that the other delegates, especially Pyat, who knew not the first elements of even Proudhonian financial schemes, were included simply to give them executive positions.

The newly elected members of the Commune were given a surprising number of posts: Viard and Cluseret were Delegates, and Arnold, Courbet, Longuet, Pottier, Serrailler, Trinquet and Vésinier all served on the Commissions.

There had been great changes in the most important of all—the Military Commission. Only Ranvier survived from the former Commission. Delescluze had come in from Foreign Affairs, Tridon from the Executive, Avrial from Labour; Arnold, a newly elected member, was a Central Committee man. Of the original Military Commission, Duval and Flourens were dead; Bergeret a suspect agitator of the Central Committee; Eudes was fighting; Chardon was on the court martial and at the Ex-Prefecture, together with Pindy. The new Commission was somewhat incoherent, although staffed by men of proved revolutionary ability. Cluseret could not, however, count upon much personal support from them.

Disputes broke out again next day, and once more Pyat was the storm-centre. Vermorel attacked him bitterly for the inconsistency between his journalistic utterances and the opinions he expressed in the Commune. As early as April 4, Lissagaray's *Action* had demanded the suspension of all papers hostile to the Commune. On the 18th, the Commune had acted; Rigault had suppressed four leading dailies, *Le Bien Public*, *Le Soir*, *La Cloche* and *L'Opinion Nationale*. Rochefort, whose ingrained scepticism made him as caustic a critic of the Commune as he had been of the Empire, found it " very odd " that Félix Pyat, a member of the Commune, should continue to edit his paper, *Le Vengeur*, " especially when this representative of the people, to whom he owes his whole time, presides daily over the suppression of papers he does not edit." The *Moniteur du Peuple* complained of the preferential treatment of the *Vengeur* in the supply of news: " Pyat (Félix), member of the Commune, communicates to Pyat (no less Felix), journalist, the decrees signed during the sessions at an hour when no other paper has received the official documents." Vermorel brought to the Commune's notice that the *Vengeur* of April 21 had vigorously blamed the suppression of papers, a measure which Citizen Pyat had approved and even to some extent initiated in the Commune; Vermorel found this immoral.

Everybody lost his head. Régère suddenly defended Pyat, attacked Vermorel so outrageously that Varlin, presiding, had to call him to order. J. B. Clément, noted for his good humour, absolutely lost his temper and demanded Pyat's arrest. Arnould fell on Clément, declaring that he found it monstrous that people should keep on talking about arrest for the expression of an opinion. Clément retorted by attacking Ostyn about a local matter. The lunatic Allix kept making proposals after the question had been settled.

At last the sinister Blanchet, who had been agitating for all sorts of absurd measures such as the changing of the name of the rue Bonaparte in his district, screamed in his high shrill voice a general denunciation of the Commune: " We are not employing revolutionary measures, and, meanwhile, reactionary assemblies are organising. Let us talk less and act more. Less decrees, more execution. . . . People are saying that the Commune is not revolutionary, and they are right. The reaction is gathering force. Citizens, we pass many decrees which are not carried out; we owe an account of our mandate to our electors; you saw that when you summoned the electors." Varlin protested: " Perhaps we do waste a lot of time here, but those who shout loudest are not those who do most."

Delescluze rose, and in the speech of his life, greeted with enthusiastic applause, brought the Commune to its senses with words to the sincerity of which his whole life bore witness: " You complain that our decrees are not carried out. Well, citizens, are you not yourselves somewhat accessory to this fault ? . . . When a decree appears in the *Journal Officiel* with thirteen negative votes and only eighteen affirmative and does not meet with the respect that this assembly deserves, can you be astonished ? There is a minority which has arisen against the Executive Commission. It is quite simple, citizens. You should have replaced us sooner. You have not the right to withdraw for a personal spite or because the ideal we pursue is not completely in accord with the project. Do you think that

everyone here approves of what is being done ? Well, there
are members who have remained at their posts, and will
remain until the end despite the insults with which we are
covered, and, if we do not triumph, we will not be the last
to die, whether on the ramparts or elsewhere. There has
been a latent conspiracy against this unfortunate Commission, which will perhaps be regretted later, because we
are trying to ally moderation with energy. We are for
revolutionary methods, but we wish to observe the forms,
respect the law and public opinion. If there are some dis-
cords, are they not caused by the quarrels about precedence
which divide certain leaders ? Here is a district, the XIth,
to which I have the honour to belong, and which weighs
considerably in the balance. This district has 45,000
National Guards. And it is full of bickerings ! And why ?
Because of jealousies and quarrels ! It is the military element that dominates and it is the civil element that should
always dominate ! [*Cheers.*] I tell you that, as far as I am
concerned, I am determined to remain at my post, and if
we do not see the victory, we shall not be the last to be
struck down on the ramparts or upon the steps of the Hôtel
de Ville ! [*Prolonged cheers.*] " But the rebuke had no lasting
effect.

Next day, there was another row. The swashbuckling
caricaturist, Pilotell, working at the Ex-Prefecture and,
somehow or other and much to Courbet's indignation, also
Director of Fine Arts, had arrested Gustave Chaudey, Jules
Ferry's assistant who was accused of ordering the shooting
on January 22, and had kept his watch. Vermorel and
Arnould took the opportunity of attacking Rigault's in-
discriminate arrests. The debate turned to a point brought
up by the old Forty-Eighter, Jules Miot, that members of
the Commune should have the right to visit prisoners held
*incommunicado.* Was Rigault maintaining this system, which
Arnould described as a relic of barbarism that the Commune should end ? Rigault was absent, and Miot's proposal was carried.

At the next session Rigault defended himself furiously,

held to the maintenance of the system, and offered his resignation if the Commune insisted upon relaxing it.

Most of the members had experienced its horrors under the Empire. " Solitary confinement," said Arnould, " is immoral. It is moral torture substituted for physical. Even from the point of view of security, it is useless : the prisoner can always find a means of communication. We have all been held in solitary confinement under the Empire and yet we succeeded not only in communicating with outside but even in getting articles inserted in the papers." Rigault replied that war was immoral too, yet they were fighting. Jourde declared that he was theoretically in favour of all liberties, but during a state of war it was no use having a " platonic theory." Theisz, speaking for the International, said they were sick of hearing that liberties would be granted " later." after the victory; if the measure were good, they should pass it now. Billioray, who was making himself felt in debate, summed up the argument: " In principle, I am for the suppression not only of solitary confinement but of all preventive detention. All of us here have had a taste of solitary confinement. There is no need for us, therefore, to make a profession of mere Liberalism; but it would be strange if we broke what weapons we have. Of two things one : either you will be victorious and will then be able to abolish solitary confinement and all other arbitrary measures, or you will be defeated through lack of precautions and they will use against you the system you will have abolished."

Billioray had made a particular question a matter of principle; and this was the chief characteristic of all the Commune's debates. Consequently, very little practical steps were ever taken. It was the result of the non-existence of any dominating group with a programme and theory worked out beforehand in the long period of opposition. These debates are, therefore, extremely instructive, but tend to lead nowhere. Even the point of principle was apt to become confused by personal recrimination, especially where so stirring a member as Rigault was concerned.

This happened now. The point at issue was not that of the abolition of solitary confinement but merely whether members of the Commune had the right to visit prisoners so confined. All the members were aware that Rigault might arrest any of their friends at any moment, with or without reason; if the motion were not passed, they could do nothing to save them. Yet the proposal struck at the root of the system of efficient revolutionary terror. As Rigault put it, " When one has not seen a prisoner's dossier, one may be softened by his appeals, by questions of family, of humanity, and help him to communicate with outside." Recriminations and threats of resignation poured in from every side. But Miot's proposal was carried, and Rigault and his fellow-terrorist Ferré at once resigned.

The Commune was shocked. They had no other efficient police chief. Cournet, a Blanquist militant and personal friend of Rigault, was elected to his place by 35 to 20 votes. It was then necessary to replace Cournet and Ferré on the Police Commission. Delescluze considered that, whatever might be Citizen Cournet's revolutionary zeal, it was essential for him to be aided by men with real qualifications for the work. There seemed no adequate reason for Rigault's resignation: let him at least remain on the Commission. Ferré too was re-appointed, and things were exactly as before, except that Cournet was now technically Rigault's superior. But on April 27 Rigault was at last given the post of his dreams—Public Prosecutor for the Commune—*Procureur de la Commune*—Chaumette !

The internal divergences of the Commune kept pace with the intensification of the Versaillese attack. The first phase in both had ended around April 21. In the Assembly, too, ultra-reactionary tendencies were becoming even more manifest. They had voted a proposal by Batbie, supported by Thiers, by which only communes of less than 20,000 inhabitants were allowed the right of electing their Mayors, thus keeping local administration in the hands of the magnates, while cities with a politically educated electorate were disenfranchised. On April 13, they had adjourned the

consideration of peace with Paris. On the 17th they completed the effect of the declaration of martial law in the
departments of the Seine and Seine-et-Oise, voted on the
6th, and of Dufaure's expedited courts martial, by giving
Thiers the right to declare martial law over the whole of
France, in order to check any demonstration of sympathy
with Paris. The provincial cities had remained republican
even after the suppression of the revolts there, still bitterly
opposed to the Royalist Assembly. They had already
addressed protests to Thiers and their hopes for the maintenance of the Republic and communal liberties: between
March 31 and April 10, Perpignan, Roanne, Valence,
Châlon-sur-Saône, Marmande, Besançon and Saint-Omer,
and now Lille, Mâcon and Lyons, with the Paris suburbs
of Sceaux and Saint-Denis. Their Delegates were preparing
a congress at Bordeaux to attempt a reconciliation between
Paris and Versailles. But moderate Deputies such as Chas-
sin, Meurice and Lockroy were arrested by Versaillese
troops as they were coming from Paris and taken off to
Versailles by mounted gendarmes exactly as if they had
been Communard prisoners. The Bordeaux Congress was
banned. Dufaure, in a circular to the District Attorneys
on April 23, ordered them to prosecute " the apostles of
conciliation who set on a level the Assembly elected by
universal suffrage and the self-styled Commune of
Paris."

Attempts at conciliation, however, still continued. On
April 19, the League for the Rights of Paris appointed a
commission to organise a common action with the National
Union of Syndical Chambers. On the 21st, 24 Syndical
Chambers, representing 107 associations and corporations,
adhered to the L.R.P.'s programme. The Freemasons also
began their efforts once more. The hour was critical. There
was still hope of averting the worst of the civil war.

The most that the League could achieve was an armistice
for the evacuation of the inhabitants of Neuilly. These
unfortunates, not partisans of the Commune, had been
under fire for nearly three weeks and were in a terrible

condition. It was agreed that both sides should cease fire on April 25 from 9 a.m. until 5 p.m.

The battle, however, was not to cease on the southern front. Cluseret afterwards maintained that this truce had been the fatal turning-point in the action, since it had given Versailles the opportunity of moving their forces from the north to Issy. This is obviously untrue: the Versaillese operations, carefully planned in advance, had not counted upon this advantage; and although it is quite true that they took full advantage of it, they had by now perfected their army and plan of attack so far that, aided by the logical internal disintegration of the Commune, they were ultimately irresistible. The Commune had lost its last chance of victory on April 4. To blame any one incident was now futile.

Old Beslay also fell into this error when, in a long open letter to Thiers placarded in Paris on the eve of the truce, he summoned his comrade of the Thirty and the Forty-Eight to resign in order to place the Assembly in a position where it would have to decide definitely for the Republic or for Monarchist restoration, for " a Cossack or a Republican France." But this voice from the past, telling Thiers that he himself was a man of the past and that France needed a man who represented the future, made not the slightest impression upon the Chief of the Executive Power.

Great preparations for receiving the wretched inhabitants of Neuilly went on throughout the 24th. The Commune appointed a special commission of five, Oudet, Johannard, Fortuné, Eudes and Bergeret, a notable predominance of Central Committee men, to supervise the evacuation. A special decree, proposed by Malon, requisitioned all empty lodgings for the refugees: a particular, not a general, measure, but one in accordance with a Socialistic programme. Thirty ambulances, provided by the International Ambulance Society and by some wealthy merchants, set out from the Palace of Industry. The Duval restaurants provided food. All Paris took a sympathetic and lively interest.

The evacuation took place without incident. A crowd of sightseers flocked to Neuilly. Many of them tried to seize the opportunity of crossing the front and taking refuge behind the Versaillese lines, but even these bourgeois deserters were checked by naked bayonets.

Neuilly had suffered beyond anything that had been seen during the first siege. There was hardly a house standing. Trees, street lamps, roads, were twisted, smoking ruins. Many of the inhabitants, who had lived for three weeks in damp cellars on mouldy food and waterless wine, had gone mad. Others had become so used to their prison that it was with difficulty that they were persuaded to leave. The strollers returned to Paris with great bunches of lilac. Not a mile away, the Commune's armoured train kept up an incessant fire at Asnières, and in the south the great siege-guns thundered and thundered.

In spite of this reminder of the hopelessness of effective conciliation, attempts continued; and the last delegation of the N.U.S.C. was waiting to see Thiers when the Versaillese armies were already in Paris.

The Freemasons tried one final effort. The day following the evacuation of Neuilly, they came to the Commune and declared that they would plant their banners on the walls of Paris; if a single bullet touched a single banner, they would join the Commune. Allix declared that the Commune was putting into practice what the Freemasons had long affirmed: the construction of the Temple was certainly, in this epoch, the reorganisation of Labour. Vallès gave them his scarf of office, and their leader, F.·. Thirifocq, promised that this emblem should be preserved in their archives as a memorial of this day.

The whole Commune greeted the Freemason procession from the balcony of the Hôtel de Ville. Pyat gave them one of his inimitable harangues. Beslay, amid great applause, embraced one of the Brothers. A Freemason claimed the honour of planting the first banner on the walls, that of " Perseverance," which had existed since 1790. Melliet gave them a red flag, " the flag of universal peace, of their

federal rights," to plant amidst the Masonic banners.
Several thousand Masons proceeded down the boulevards,
amid enormous enthusiasm. A balloon marked with the
ritual three points and inscribed " Commune of Paris "
floated above them. The marchers were gay with symbolic
ribbons, blue, green, white, red and black, with gold and
silver spangles, triangles, suns and trowels. Before them
went the great white banner of the Vincennes Lodge with:
" Let us love one another."

At 3 o'clock, in a shower of rain, and under the Versaillese
bullets which wounded one Brother, the Freemasons
planted their seventy banners from the Porte Bineau to the
Porte Maillot. Spokesmen interviewed the Versaillese commander, himself a Mason. He could do no more than cease
fire for a moment. Two delegates who went to see Thiers
were received without enthusiasm. The banners remained
under heavy fire. Next day, the Freemasons joined the
Commune; and, on May 2, decided to " defend in arms
the claims for municipal franchises."

The general attack had begun. Repulsed by Dombrowski
at Clichy in the north, the Versaillese captured Bagneux
in the south. The Communards counter-attacked next day,
but were repulsed by a murderous fusillade at close quarters.
Bagneux would have been untenable if Fort Montrouge
and the Hautes-Bruyères redoubt had converged their fire
upon it, but their commanders, after two weeks' inaction
under heavy fire and terrible weather, considered that the
time had come for infantry action. The Versaillese thought
so too.

On the 24th, Versaillese scouts surprised a party of
Communards at Bourg-la-Reine, capturing a red flag.
Thiers himself met the corporal who had captured the
flag and conferred on him the Military Medal. Thiers and
MacMahon went on to inspect the position, were received
by Colonel Hepp, Cissey's Chief of Staff. Thiers desired,
and MacMahon seemed to make no opposition, that they
should bombard Fort Issy violently, then attempt to carry
it by assault. Hepp wrote to Cissey next day: " You know

what my ideas are on this subject and how risky such an
enterprise seems to me . . . but I am trying to carry it out,
even against my opinion." Thiers knew best.

This part of the action, perhaps the most decisive point
in the whole war, was directed to the capture of Fort Issy.
It was a formidable position. Issy Park lay at the end of a
small plateau which could be approached up fairly steep
slopes from the Seine and the Valley of Fleury, but this
approach was exposed to the fire of the Point-du-Jour. The
attack, therefore, had to be made from the Clamart
plateau. This was divided in two by the railway viaduct
and an embankment which provided useful cover for
massing on the Meudon side. The embankment top was
protected by a trench which the Versaillese had just
joined up with the main communication-trenches between
Châtillon and Clamart. The trench left the railway-track
where it turned left towards Vanves, so that the glacis at
Clamart was completely under the Versaillese fire, and no
sortie from Fort Issy was possible in that direction. The
upper slopes of the plateau were covered by the fort's
outworks, but these could easily be put out of action. Issy
Cemetery, at the foot of the glacis on the Meudon side,
had been fortified by the Communards; but, once taken,
provided cover from the fort. There was a large quarry in
front of the cemetery, excellent cover. The Versaillese plan
was to join this quarry to the main line of investment by a
night-attack on the 25th; the artillery would silence the
fort, then break down its walls and the defences of the
cemetery. Meanwhile, action would be kept up all along
the line to distract the attention of the fort's defenders.

Versailles disposed of enormous forces to reduce exhausted and ill-supplied Issy: 53 batteries of all calibres,
60 naval guns, 45 regiments of infantry, 13 of cavalry, 2 of
gendarmes, 10 battalions of Chasseurs, 10 companies of
engineers, and a reserve of 60,000 men.

The Versaillese attacked Issy-les-Moulineaux, commanding the road between Fort Issy and the Seine at Billancourt
Island, on the evening of the 26th. The bombardment was

intense. In Fort Issy, a company of engineers became absolutely demoralised and refused to work. The 92nd, which
had hitherto been the mainstay of the defence, demanded
next morning to be relieved. The Versaillese investment was
creeping upon the fort. Redon, commanding in the absence
of Mégy, who had gone off to direct the artillery on the
walls, complained bitterly to the Commune that he had not
enough men and munitions nor heavy enough guns to
prevent it. Losses were heavy and there were not nearly
enough doctors and ambulances. The men's spirit was,
however, with few exceptions, admirable. An artilleryman
of seventy refused to leave his gun when wounded. But the
fort was almost in ruins and there were no engineers to
repair it.

Cluseret took no notice of Mégy's and Redon's urgent
messages, except to complain of the wrong use of certain
guns. He refused to believe that the situation was serious,
and sent only a tenth of the reinforcements demanded.

The next day, the Versaillese engineers opened a trench
only 550 metres from the fort, covered by a heavy bombardment. That evening there was an attempt on the
Communard barricade in front of the Bonamy Farm before
Châtillon, but the bombardment had been too weak, and
the Versaillese fled at the first shot, " owing to the fault of
a bad officer." But another company took Hautes-Bruyères
village without loss to themselves, capturing 13 Communards, and advanced from the village as far as the
redoubt trenches. By the 29th, the trenches were only 235
metres from the fort.

On the 29th, Issy Cemetery was taken at the point of the
bayonet, the château park, the railway cutting near Clamart and the advanced posts of the fort itself. Simultaneously, on the right wing, Lacretelle's division assaulted
the Bonamy Farm. The Versaillese were now at the foot of
the Fort Issy glacis.

This success finally confirmed the morale of the Versaillese troops. " The men are veritably transformed ; they
demand only to push on and finish off those scoundrels who

had called themselves their brothers and friends." The two companies, the 70th and 71st, that had so brilliantly carried the Bonamy Farm were summoned to Headquarters to escort their prisoners to the Commander-in-Chief. " Many of the soldiers of the division," ran the divisional report, " attracted by the spectacle, watched the insurgents file past and did not conceal their contempt for these prisoners, insolent when our generous soldiers hesitated to strike them, despondent and weeping to-day. There is a great contrast between these visages upon which are to be read the vilest passions and vices and the loyal faces of our young soldiers. The morale of our troops is henceforth assured, and our men now know that they are on the side of right and duty."

The Versaillese morale had shown itself a few days earlier. On the 25th, four National Guards had been surprised by 200 Chasseurs at Belle-Epine, near Villejuif. They had surrendered, and were being taken off, when a captain had ridden up to them and shot them in cold blood. One of them, badly wounded, had managed to drag himself back to his battalion and report the atrocity. On the other hand, on the 23rd, when a squadron of Chasseurs had ridden up to the Communard lines to surrender, the Guards, mistaking their intention, had opened fire. But the Versaillese shootings of prisoners *after* they had surrendered, on the grounds that these were technical deserters from the regular army, redoubled in fury. The commander of Fort Vanves sent an urgent message to the Commune asking for new uniforms, since volunteers, with the best will in the world, could not risk a sortie because they had no proper uniform and every man wearing Versaillese uniform would be shot at once, either by the enemy into whose hands he fell or by the Communards by mistake.

That evening, Wetzel, commander of the trenches in front of the fort, evacuated what was left of his men without saying a word to the fort. At ten o'clock, Redon had reported that the morale of the garrison was entirely satisfactory. At midnight, they suddenly heard the Versaillese trumpets sounding the charge. Then, nothing. The trenches were silent.

Next day they discovered Wetzel's evacuation. The enemy was only 200 metres from the fort. The garrison cried treachery. It was impossible to hold them back. Early on the morning of the 30th, Mégy, who had now resumed command, saw the Versaillese making towards the Seine, in order, he thought, to surround the fort. This turning movement was in reality simply a feint by a small detachment from Issy Park.

Leperche, commanding the Versaillese attack, had noted that " it would be imprudent to think of taking the fort by the aid of a panic among the insurgents; however, we must count upon good luck as well as bad. . . . I repeat, an improbable eventuality." But Leperche had his good luck. Mégy sent word to the Military Commission that he needed an attack by at least fifteen battalions to save the situation; unless 10,000 men came up to defend the abandoned trenches, he could no longer hold out. Cluseret despatched an order to La Cécilia, commander of the southern front, to send 1,500; but even this inadequate force never arrived.

Mégy could hold his men no longer. The evacuation was decided. The guns were spiked, but so inefficiently that it was easy to put them in order again the same evening. A few men refused to leave. In the course of the day, Leperche summoned them to surrender within a quarter of an hour under pain of immediate shooting. They made no answer; and the Versaillese, ignorant of the evacuation, dared not attack.

Under a pouring rain, Paris was full of rumours. News of the fall of Issy had spread, and whole battalions of the National Guard were coming to the Hôtel de Ville to find out whether it were true and whether the Commune had given the order for evacuation. The Commune itself, meanwhile, was solemnly receiving yet another body of conciliators, the Republican Alliance of the Departments. Municipal elections in all the provincial cities were to be held next day, and the delegates wished to assure their electors of the Commune's loyalty to the Republic. The rest of the session was occupied by a long wrangle about the *Journal Officiel*, everyone assailing the wretched Longuet, who was accused of not even writing decent French. The debate was growing bitter when the news of the evacuation of Issy was brought in. The session was at once suspended.

Cluseret, faced at last with a task he could do himself without the meddling of enthusiastic fools, at once collected a couple of hundred men and La Cécilia and hurried off to Issy. He stood there amid the bullets, in civilian clothes and slouch hat, without turning a hair, then simply strolled into the abandoned fort. There was no one left there except one small boy, Dufour, sitting on a powder-barrel with a box of matches in his hand, ready to blow up the fort and himself if the Versaillese approached. Reinforcements were hurriedly sent, the guns unspiked, and Issy, by this miracle, held out for another week.

But this taste of his quality did not now help Cluseret. The Commune, seriously alarmed by the military disorganisation, had, on the 23rd, voted an immediate enquiry into its causes. Two days later, they accused Cluseret formally of working with the Central Committee against the Commune. They complained that Cluseret never troubled to report to them on the military situation, although the Committee had full information from Moreau. Faced with this beginning of disruption, the Commune, incited by old Miot, had been arguing about the creation of a supreme Committee of Public Safety. Now, roused by the near-disaster at Issy, it determined to assert itself at last. On his return from the fort, Cluseret was arrested. The public was not officially informed until two days later.

Thus every decisive stage in the war was paralleled by a decisive move in the internal politics of the Commune.

# CHAPTER VI

# ROSSEL

" One day we were sitting in Rossel's office at the Ministry of War. Rossel went to the window, pointed to a group of the Committee's officers gesticulating and arguing loudly below, and, turning to us, cold-eyed, muttered between his teeth: ' If I were to have them shot, now, down there in the yard . . .' "

MAXIME VUILLAUME, *Mes Cahiers Rouges*

THE ARREST OF CLUSERET was merely the most sensational incident in a thorough reorganisation of the Commune which had already been under way for some days. The great question at issue was that of the predominance of the civil or the military authority, of the Commune or the Central Committee. The temporary capture of Fort Issy showed clearly that the position had become critical, if not hopeless. A last desperate effort to save the very existence of the Commune was essential, even if this meant abandoning nearly every idea which the revolution had developed since March 18.

Cluseret's obvious successor was his coldly puritan Chief of Staff, Nathaniel Rossel. He was an admittedly efficient officer, but he was obeyed without fervour. At least he was obeyed. It seemed possible that this young officer who had sacrificed a brilliant military career to his principles, first in the conspiracy against Bazaine's supposed treachery at Metz and then again by joining a revolution in which he saw chiefly an affirmation of the one living and regenerative force still surviving in France, might bring some sort of order into the chaos bequeathed him by Cluseret. It was true that, a native of Nevers, he knew little of Paris and understood less of the character of Paris revolution; that his sole revolutionary experience was what he had been able to acquire in three weeks on Cluseret's staff and from his friends on the *Père Duchêne*; but this very objective view might prevent his being too deeply involved in the Parisian situation itself.

His appointment was greeted with moderate approval. The Central Committee had been favourably impressed by his professional military capacities, and immediately installed delegates as his advisers in the Ministry of War itself.

Rossel had already come into conflict with the civil branch. One man, Girot, sentenced by him in his capacity of President of the Court Martial, had been released " in view of his democratic antecedents." The court's action had been suspended by the Commune to save Mégy, on trial for his evacuation of Issy.

On accepting his appointment, Rossel at once appealed to the Executive Commission for their support. " I accept these difficult functions," he wrote, " but I need your fullest support if I am not to succumb beneath the weight of circumstances."

The Commune submitted their new Military Delegate to a kind of qualifying examination. They had just decreed that candidates for staff posts should be chosen, in default of technical knowledge, for their " moral and practical value." Miot asked Rossel what were his " democratic antecedents." " I will not tell you," replied Rossel, " that I have made any deep study of social reform, but I have a horror of the society which has made this cowardly surrender of France. I do not know what the new order of Socialism will be. I have confidence in it, for it will always be better than the old order of society." " Your frank explanations," declared the old Jacobin Forty-Eighter, " have satisfied the Commune. You may be assured of its unreserved support."

Miot had already led the Commune to a reorganisation absolutely essential for the necessities of the defence but fatal to the role of the Commune as a first Socialistic dictatorship of the proletariat. In a final effort to assert the supremacy of the civil power he had suggested the creation of a Committee of Public Safety. It would consist of five members of the Commune appointed by it and responsible to it alone, with the widest authority over the Nine Commissions. Although the present Executive Commission would retain its powers, the Committee of Public Safety could in practice override its decisions.

The proposal was brought forward on April 28; and this most critical of all the Commune's debates lasted for three days.

On April 30 they discussed the name of the proposed Committee. This was of the utmost importance, for its name would be the declaration, both to the Commune and to the public, of its line of policy. Was it to be called Committee of Public Safety or Executive Committee? " Committee of Public Safety," whatever its defined functions, would connote a reversion to Jacobin Terror and the negation of modern Socialist Democracy. The voting was equal.

Next day's debate was decisive. The majority had arrived in full force, and included many members who had not the slightest sympathy for Jacobin revivals but did not wish publicly to split the Commune.

Members explained their votes. Ferré, Rigault and Pyat naturally advocated a full-blooded Jacobinism in the manner most characteristic of themselves. Rigault hoped that the Committee of Public Safety would " be in 1871 what it is generally but erroneously thought to have been in 1793." Ferré simply pointed out that he considered that he was acting logically in fulfilling the imperative mandate laid upon him by voting for the Committee. " Seeing that the words *Public Safety* are of exactly the same period as the words *French Republic* and *Commune of Paris*," Pyat explained his approval.

Vermorel protested impatiently against the name: " It is nothing but a word, and the people have been fobbed off with words too long." Longuet " believed no more in words

of salvation than in talismans and amulets." Tridon disliked " useless and absurd gear which, far from giving us
strength, takes away what little strength we have." Courbet,
surprisingly enough, stated the correct historical case
against the Committee: " The words *Public Safety, Mon-
tagnards, Girondins, Jacobins* and so on cannot be used in this
republican Socialist movement. What we represent is the
period which has passed between '93 and '71, with the
genius which should characterise us and spring from our
own temperament. This seems to me the more obvious in
that we are like plagiaries, re-establishing to our own
detriment a Terror that is not of our time. Let us employ
the words suggested by our own revolution."

The case which decided the issue was put by Franckel
and Vaillant, both members of the International and anything but Jacobins. " Although I do not see the use of this
Committee," said Franckel, " but since I do not wish to
give cause for insinuations against my revolutionary
opinions, and reserving every right of opposition to the
Committee, I vote in favour of it."

Vaillant approved of the motion simply because it
seemed a return to the more vigorous days of the first
Executive Commission, of which he had been a member.
" The Commune," he declared, " should begin by reform-
ing itself and stop being a talkative little parliament,
destroying one day what it created the day before, and
obstructing every decision made by the Executive Commission."

After a heated debate, the 23 members of the Minority
refrained from voting; and a majority of 45 set up the
Committee of Public Safety.

The members of the Committee now elected were surprisingly undistinguished, chiefly because many of the most
able men had opposed its creation, while others already
occupied other posts. Arnaud had shown himself vigorous
in debate and represented the Central Committee. Léo
Melliet was coming to the fore as an energetic and able
organiser. Charles Gérardin was Rossel's one intimate

friend in the Commune, and had connections with the
Ex-Prefecture. Ranvier was an old and tried militant,
extremely popular in Belleville, where he had long been
Mayor. Félix Pyat, of course, completed the number.

This crucial debate marked the first definite emergence
of a Minority opposition. It was composed of Socialists of
the International, Proudhonists, intellectual moderates:
Arnould, Andrieu, Avrial, Babick, Beslay, Clémence,
Victor Clément, Courbet, Eugène Gérardin, Jourde,
Langevin, Lefrançais, Longuet, Malon, Ostyn, Pindy,
Rastoul, Serrailler, Tridon, Vallès, Varlin and Ver-
morel. Later, they were joined by Franckel, Arnold and
Theisz.

Thus, most of those who had some idea of the Socialist
society at which the revolution should have aimed were
forced by the logic of the situation to oppose the only
measures which could, for the moment at least, stave off its
destruction. With the creation of the Committee of Public
Safety, the Commune had regressed a century; and its
final struggles could only assure it a place in the great
international proletarian epic.

Rossel immediately set to work to liquidate some of the
worst confusion. The problem had now become almost
entirely a military one. Owing to the regional basis for
the recruitment of the National Guard, the local Legion-
Commanders had by now acquired far more influence
than the mere battalion-delegates on the Central Committee. If the Central Committee itself were reluctant to
accept the directions of the Commune, especially now
when the Committee of Public Safety was attempting
to exercise the supreme military command, the Legion-
Commanders resented the central control even more
strongly. Here was the main centre of confusion.

Rossel, the regular soldier who could not appreciate the
fact that the central characteristic of the Paris National
Guard was its parochial loyalties, had the idea of organising
a regular fighting force by regiments, breaking up and
fusing the Legions.

Naturally, the Legion-Commanders were furious at what they considered an encroachment upon their rights and functions. Groups came to the Ministry of War to protest. There were small mutinies in the Legions, and the Committee of Public Safety's orders were deliberately disregarded.

Rossel's first proposal was that the districts should be organised in wards, each with a sub-delegation to distribute identity cards, report and prosecute National Guards—that is to say, any able-bodied Parisian—who refused to go on duty, draw up a list of available horses and vacant apartments and provide for munitions, arms and shelters against bombardment.

This raised a storm. Not only was it quite impossible to distribute such cards efficiently under the circumstances, but it seemed, too, an attempt of the Military Delegation to interfere with civil affairs. Rossel was openly accused of wishing to set up a military dictatorship.

At the Commune sitting, Rossel's proposals were met with a fury of disappointment and anger. It immediately raised the whole question of the position in which the Commune had placed itself by the creation of the Committee of Public Safety. The matter of principle was fought out in the open.

Avrial pleaded for some sense of realities : it was physically impossible for members of the Commune to do everything themselves : they could not be with the army, at the sessions, at the municipalities, at the delegations all at the same time; so that, whatever the principle involved, conditions must dictate behaviour, and a too-strict adherence to principle would merely multiply confusion.

The strain was really becoming too great for some members. Delescluze, a dying man, asked permission to resign from the Military Commission, but could not be spared.

Jourde, producing the balance-sheet of the Commune's finances, which Vaillant praised as " a real *tour de force*," also offered his resignation. The Financial Delegate could

not work with the Committee of Public Safety, since it
deprived him of all responsibility and thus prevented all
confidence in the Commune's financial policy, since any
measure taken by him could be countermanded by the
Committee. The Commune would have to raise loans.
Expropriation would be of no use, seizure of bonds still
less. The Prussians, for instance, would say: " You are in
the process of setting up a new, a Socialist, State; that is all
very well, but there is no reason why we should suffer the
consequences; your offer to us does not present sufficient
guarantees; we need ready cash." " I want, therefore,"
Jourde said, " to be allowed to re-establish credit, restore
the basis of ready cash. By means of economies, even if I
reduce the *octroi* charges by 50 per cent and double the
budget for public education, I could reduce the city's
budget by at least 50 millions a year." Jourde, therefore,
had cogent reasons against seizing the Bank of France.
There is no reason to doubt that he would have carried out
his promise; but the Committee of Public Safety, which
could have seized the bank, made no move, and simply
hindered the alternative financial policy. But Jourde could
not be spared, and was re-elected by 38 votes to 6.

The Central Committee was now determined to show
the Commune that they did not share their approval of
Rossel. Reorganised on April 27, they were furious at his
idea of breaking up the federal formation. They sent the
Legion-Commanders to the Hôtel de Ville to protest to the
Commune. Rossel heard of this and arrested one of them on
the way. The others arrived at the Committee of Public
Safety's offices but found no one there. They left a cate-
gorical note: " The Committee of Public Safety will
receive the Central Committee at 5 o'clock." Pyat found
the note on his return and rushed over to the Commune in
a fury of indignation. The Commune coolly replied that it
was the Committee of Public Safety's business to deal with
the Central Committee's insolence.

Pyat had no stomach for such practical responsibility.
His chance of backing down came next day. Grousset was

reporting to the Commune the result of the municipal elections in the provinces, where the most Radical list had passed except in a few towns where the Republicans had decided to abstain from voting, notably at Lyons, where this abstention had stirred up a new insurrection. There had been demonstrations of sympathy for the Commune abroad also, in Germany, Switzerland, Italy and England. He demanded that in view of this favourable situation all attempts at conciliation should be treated as treason. He was surprised to hear that the Committee of Public Safety had listened favourably to a fresh attempt by the bourgeois League for the Rights of Paris.

There was an immediate storm against the Committee. Tridon, Johannard, Vermorel attacked Pyat with especial bitterness. Pyat and Vermorel fought for an hour, piling upon each other the accumulated resentment of years. Vermorel called Pyat a " chamber-conspirator." Pyat replied with " bespectacled silkworm, polychrome butterfly battening on every sort of flower, royalty and republic." The Commune, although qualifying Pyat's offered resignation as desertion, seemed ready to accept it. Pyat, thoroughly alarmed, asked them to withdraw their censures and " he would keep no memory of this deplorable incident in his heart." They were fools enough to agree.

It was decided that this deplorable incident should not be reported in the *Journal Officiel*. It had not yet been settled whether the Commune's sessions should be public or not, a fundamental problem of democracy. There appeared to be no room at the Hôtel de Ville suitable for public sessions, and so the Commune was faced with a dilemma: either not to admit the public or to leave the Hôtel de Ville, the traditional and essentially symbolic home of Parisian democracy, of the Commune. The debate was at a deadlock, when Mortier, of the Central Committee, rushed in to report disaster.

Thanks to Cluseret, the Communards had reoccupied Fort Issy. But the Versaillese, unaware of the chance they had missed, had continued the siege methodically.

During the night of May 1–2, Paturel's marines and Foot Chasseurs had captured the Clamart railway-station, while Clinchant occupied the trenches between Issy and Vanves, and, after a hard struggle, captured the Château of Issy. The fort's supplies were thus cut off. Sixty Communards were captured at Clamart, 300 at the Château of Issy. On the 2nd, the Versaillese had occupied the railway-line as far as the redoubt beyond Clamart. Clinchant's 5th Corps was reinforced by Cissey's 2nd, and Cissey took over the general command on this front.

Meanwhile, the Versaillese had been trying to persuade the fort to surrender. Even before the evacuation, Colonel Leperche had sent a flag to the fort, then commanded by Lieutenant Lantara of the Turcos of the Commune, who replied, as the official *communiqué* of the Commune relates, that he would rather blow up the fort than surrender to the Royalists, or, more probably, as he was later accused before the Versaillese court martial, with the " *mot de Cambronne*."

Leperche had tried again on the 30th. Thiers had approved the suggested conditions: life, liberty and personal baggage, and, if absolutely necessary, permission to keep their arms and return to Paris. Leperche thought this last clause unnecessary. In spite of the white flag, firing continued on both sides. The summons was at last presented. Eudes sent it back to Rossel, who replied in a letter, which he published in the Communard Press: " My dear comrade,—Next time you permit yourself to send us a summons as insolent as your autograph letter of yesterday, I shall have your parliamentary shot, conformably with the usages of war."

The bearer of this letter was simply furious at the role he had unsuspectingly played; he was a respectable commercial traveller. He refused to return to Paris and sent a letter to Eudes announcing his resignation, and asking him " to permit him to tell him that when one has not got the courage to go and tell people what one thinks of them to their face, one certainly ought not to write to them."

The outraged Leperche sent a copy of this letter to Headquarters.

But Rossel had also struck just a slightly wrong note: Paris, while applauding his bravado, thought it hardly revolutionary of Rossel to address the comrade of Vinoy and Galliffet as his " comrade " too. On the 2nd, Rossel had defined what he considered the usages of war in this respect: " The sending of parliamentaries sometimes serves to cover a ruse. Therefore, fire must not be suspended to receive one, even if the enemy has suspended his." At the same time, he threatened with dismissal and a month's imprisonment any officer who published any document which might inform the public of the Commune's military resources and their method of employment.

After occupying Issy Château and Clamart station, the Versaillese had spent the following day consolidating their position. During the night of the 3rd–4th they had pushed on with two surprise attacks. On the left, Faron's division tried to cut communications between Vanves and Issy by capturing the railway cutting in front of Clamart station. They were repulsed by heavy fire from Fort Vanves, with 12 killed and 84 wounded—one of their worst checks. The troops were very much shaken and had to be rallied by their generals in person all the time.

On the right, however, they won a decisive success. The redoubt of Moulin Saquet was a key-position in front of Villejuif, protecting Fort Bicêtre. It was defended by about 800 men of the 55th and 120th battalions of the National Guard. Lacretelle set out with five companies of volunteer scouts and two battalions of the 39th Regiment. The attack was made in the deepest silence. Lacretelle's men marched between the elms and the houses on the Paris road under the full moon. They took to the fields to the right after Choisy and marched along the ditch, hidden from the Communards. Turning the outposts by way of Vitry, they suddenly fell upon the sleeping Communards in the redoubt. The defenders managed to resist bravely for half an hour. Of the 800 men, 250 were left on the field, 300 surrendered. The Versaillese suffered 36 casualties. They destroyed the redoubt and retired. It was intended as a moral more than a tactical success.

The Commune suspected that the surprise was the result of treachery; that Gallien, commander of the 55th, had betrayed the password; but the confidential Versaillese military report makes no mention of this.

The redoubt was reoccupied almost immediately by the 133rd, but the men were quite demoralised. Four days later, the 120th insisted on returning to Paris to reorganise, and the 133rd, transferred to the Villejuif barricade, refused to go out on reconnaissance. Not unjustly: no effort had been made to relieve troops so sorely tried. The Communards reoccupied Clamart station, and, next afternoon, set fire to Issy Château.

The moral effect of this disaster, crashing in upon the Commune's irrelevant discussions, was enormous. They at once went into secret session and summoned Rossel to account. He complained that the surprise was the fault of the Committee of Public Safety, which had caused intolerable confusion by transferring Wroblewski to the command at Issy. Dombrowski, too, had received an order, without Rossel's knowledge, to leave Neuilly and take over the general command. Pyat assured them that neither he nor the rest of the Committee had signed any military order.

At the evening session, Tridon, Vermorel and Arnould demanded an investigation. Next day, Arnould read a copy of an order sent to Wroblewski; it was signed Léo Melliet, A. Arnaud, Félix Pyat. Melliet defended himself somewhat irrelevantly by saying that the surprise was due to treachery, not to the order. Pyat was sent for. He declared that he had not the least memory of having signed it. He was confronted with the paper: " Is that your signature ? " " I did not think that I was signing an order to General Wroblewski by scribbling a couple of lines at the bottom of the note." J. B. Clément turned to him: " One should not suffer from loss of memory, Citizen Pyat; in my opinion, you ought to resign." Arnould read several military orders issued by the

Committee of Public Safety. Pyat again offered his resignation. But once more the Commune was not ready to allow him to desert his post: it was the whole Commune or nothing.

The Commune was gradually becoming more energetic, tending increasingly towards a Jacobin Terror in proportion as the Versaillese lines drew nearer to the walls. On May 4, Rigault, Procureur of the Commune, began to prepare his revolutionary tribunal by appointing Ferré, Da Costa, Martinville and Huguenot his substitutes, an old Jacobin term for judicial assistants.

On the 5th, Cournet suppressed seven more Conservative papers, the *Petit Moniteur*, *Petit National*, *Bon Sens*, *Petite Presse*, *Petit Journal*, *France* and the *Temps* itself. It was on this day that the Commune used for the first time the old revolutionary calendar, abolishing, on the " 15th Floréal, Year 79," ninety-two years at a stroke. Which was, however, no more absurd than the titles Louis XVIII and Napoléon III.

Rossel, too, began to attempt to tighten up the military organisation. Disgusted by the action of the Committee of Public Safety in the Moulin Saquet affair, he now persuaded the Commune to allow him to try to collaborate with the Central Committee so far as to let them have the control of all the military administrative services and the greater part of the organising services, owing to " the impossibility of recruiting in time the administrative personnel necessary for the service, the propriety of completely separating the administration from the command and the necessity of employing in the most effective manner not only the goodwill but also the high revolutionary authority of the Central Committee of the Federation."

The Committee of Public Safety confirmed this arrangement in the first of its proclamations, to be dated according to the revolutionary calendar (15th Floréal, 79). The War Delegation was definitely divided into a military direction commanded by Rossel and an administration by the Central Committee under the direct control of the Military

Commission of the Commune. But the bitterest struggles arose from this complicated division of labour and from the Commune's attempts to impose their direct control upon the Central Committee.

Under this new arrangement there were various changes in the command. Wetzel was recalled from Issy and replaced by La Cécilia; and when La Cécilia fell ill, on May 7, the command of the whole centre and left was entrusted to Wroblewski. Dombrowski was to direct the Right Bank of the Seine in person—Rossel was very emphatic about this. Bergeret and Eudes were to command the 1st and 2nd reserve brigades.

These generals were to have headquarters inside the city as well: Dombrowski at the Place Vendôme, La Cécilia at the Ecole Militaire, Wroblewski at the Elysée, Bergeret at the Corps Législatif, Eudes at the Legion of Honour.

Durassier, who had been commanding at Asnières, replacing Okolowitz, who had been wounded, was appointed commander of Fort Vanves. Léo Melliet, to atone for Moulin Saquet, took over Fort Bicêtre, where he was far more in his element than on the Committee of Public Safety. Fort Issy was entrusted to Captain Dumont, of the crack 101st battalion, " a man of cool energy," whose appointment " would put an end to the uncertainties and weaknesses which have compromised the defence of the fort for the last few days."

Varlin, who had replaced the Brothers May at the Military Intendance after they had " found means to insert in the *Journal Officiel* in the director's absence a panegyric of their actions which was false from end to end," was co-opted on to the Military Commission.

The aged cobbler, Father Napoléon Gaillard, was commissioned to build a regular second line of barricades inside the city, with three great fortresses at the Trocadéro, the Butte Montmartre and the Panthéon.

The Central Committee of the Union of Women for the Defence of Paris and the Care of the Wounded, under the leadership of Louise Michel and Dmitrieva, published a most eloquent manifesto declaring that they would organise women's battalions and go to the front. These battalions, however, never actually went, " having noticed," as Louise Michel relates, " the crowd of unknown and suspicious persons who had joined the few women of good faith " ; they did, however, fight most heroically on the barricades.

The Commune still discussed, and passed useful social measures; but it was becoming more and more unreal outside the special Commissions. Members began to lose themselves in their other occupations. At the session of May 7 there were not enough present even to form a quorum. The intrigues went on around the Hôtel de Ville.

Jourde came to the session of May 8 in a blind Auvergnat fury. Some quite unknown persons, members of the Central Committee, Lacord, Josselin, Papray and Piat, had left a note on his table calmly announcing that the Military Commission would hand over to them the administration of the ordnance. Even Rossel had not been informed. Apparently the Committee of Public Safety was privy.

Gérardin attempted to justify its collaboration with the Central Committee. Jourde replied heatedly that the Commune was superior to the Central Committee and had elected the Committee of Public Safety to defend its interests; here was the Committee of Public Safety joining with the Central Committee over the Commune's head; it was really intolerable. Varlin had been surprised to hear that Rossel had appointed the Central Committee to the military administration without at all consulting the Military Commission, and he had refused to make way for the Central Committee's delegate. Gérardin at last admitted that the Central Committee had really become dangerous. Pyat wriggled round as usual: " If Citizen Rossel has had neither the strength nor the intelligence to hold the Central Committee to its purely administrative functions, it is not the Committee of Public Safety's fault."

As a result of this debate, the Military Commission published an affirmation of its authority: " Seeing that the

decree which entrusts the military administration to the
Central Committee contains this restriction: ' Under the
direct control of the Military Commission,' the Military
Commission decrees that the Central Committee cannot
nominate to any post; it proposes candidates to the Military
Commission which has the final decision." However, the
Central Committee obtained the official appointment of its
leader, Moreau, as Civil Commissioner to the Delegate for
War.

Meanwhile, the Versaillese were opening the final general
attack upon the Paris defences. At ten o'clock on the morning of May 8 began the great general bombardment. From
the Château of Meudon, from Meudon station, Bellevue,
Brimborion, Sablonnière, Clamart, Fleury, the Porte de
Billancourt, Châtillon, Fontenay, Issy Park, no less than 80
great guns fired simultaneously upon Issy, Vanves, Montrouge, the Point-du-Jour. The great battery of 70 naval guns
at Montretout smashed the fortifications from the Point-
du-Jour to the Porte de Passy, so that in a few hours the
Grenelle district and half Passy became uninhabitable.
Thiers was particularly proud of the Montretout battery;
by employing civil engineers at high wages he had had it
constructed within a week, beating, as he boasted, the
military at their own game.

Thiers coupled the bombardment with a particularly
specious proclamation to the Parisians: " So far the
Government has confined itself to attacking the exterior
works. The moment has now come when, to shorten your
sufferings, it must attack the fortifications themselves. It will
not bombard Paris, in spite of what the Commune and
Committee of Public Safety will not fail to tell you. A
bombardment threatens a whole city, renders it uninhabitable, and has as its aim the intimidation of the citizens to
force them to capitulate. The Government will fire only to
force one of your gates, and will try to limit to the point
attacked the ravages of this war of which it is not the
author." He called upon the Friends of Order to rise against
the Commune, promising that the bombardment should

cease as soon as the Versaillese army had forced one of the gates. Naturally, no one in Paris took this quite absurd argumentation in the slightest seriously, at any rate until the Versaillese had entered the city and the bombardment did *not* cease. As the Commune pointed out when publishing it, it was intended solely for provincial consumption. The Etoile had been under fire since early in April.

The Communards had recaptured Clamart station on the 6th, but the Versaillese had cut the line from Issy to Vanves the same night. The line of investment was drawing ever tighter round the doomed fort. A ferocious bombardment made it almost untenable. No reinforcements arrived. When two battalion-commanders went to Rossel to ask for some, he replied that he had the right to shoot them for deserting their post and that, according to Carnot, of whom they had probably never heard, a fort is to be defended at the point of the bayonet. There were no more provisions, doctors, engineers. One by one the guns were dismantled by the enemy's fire. Eudes was nowhere to be found; the Versaillese thought he had been killed, but that was Wetzel, and some in the fort said that he had been shot in the back. An engineer, Rist, and the commander of the 141st battalion from the XIth district were left alone in charge. The prison, the corridors leading to it, the cells, were packed with corpses in piles six feet high. The bombardment did not cease for a moment. Six shells every five minutes came from Fleury. There was nothing to eat except the meat of killed horses. Three women did what they could for the wounded; one of them was killed.

Ranvier told the Commune of the fort's plight on the 6th. Parisel demanded that six 7's should be sent. The Commune objected that the Committee of Public Safety alone was qualified to give military orders, which it was not.

The next day, the fort was receiving ten shells a minute. The ramparts were a total wreck. All the guns but two or three were out of action. The Versaillese lines were almost level with the fort. It was " hermetically surrounded."

There was nothing to do but abandon it. The last defenders reluctantly retired.

The Versaillese dared not enter for a long time, so hot had been the resistance. At length, three " intelligent non-commissioned officers " of Paturel's division went in and found it empty. Their captures included " one battalion standard, of the 115th, white and red, a fine omnibus which had just come to fetch the 60th's baggage, 109 guns, 137 quintals of biscuit, 8 of rice, 1 of salt, 6 of bacon, 13 hecto-litres of brandy, partly pure, partly mixed with tobacco, 1,500 rations of bread, 7 quintals of oats "; such is the official Versaillese report of May 10; the provisions must have been brought up in the " fine omnibus " at the last moment.

The Versaillese had lost only 2 killed and 21 wounded. During the whole action from April 4 to May 8, the 1st and 2nd brigades engaged on this front almost continuously had lost only 3 officers and 58 men killed, 25 officers and 361 men wounded. The Communard losses are entirely beyond calculation, but cannot be below 500 killed and wounded and probably at least 1,000 captured.

A few hours after occupying Fort Issy, the Versaillese crossed the Seine and dug trenches in front of Boulogne, right under the bastions of the Point-du-Jour and only 300 metres from the walls. The Delegate for War and the Committee of Public Safety did not hear of it until next morning. A bridge was thrown over the Seine at Billancourt and a hastily constructed battery silenced the gunboats under the Point-du-Jour viaduct, driving them back to the city. The direct attack upon Paris had begun.

Strange things had been happening at the Ministry of War. Rossel lived in a perpetual state of nervous tension with only his icy resolution to keep himself pure amid the revolutionary confusion. The Central Committee officers swaggered past him in the corridors. Friends came from the police to suggest wild things to his lack of humour. The Legion-Commanders suspected this bureaucrat who was so obviously not of the Parisian people; suspected, too, that their commands, based on local popularity as much as on military qualifications, were in danger.

At last they decided to have it out with him. Rossel heard that they were coming to the Ministry. When they arrived, they found a detachment of armed guards waiting for them. " You are bold," said Rossel, tense. " Do you know that this platoon is here to shoot you ? " They were calm: " There is no question of boldness ; we have simply come to talk to you about the organisation of the National Guard." Rossel, who had not quite known what he was expecting— a miniature October 31 of which he had heard so much in the provinces, perhaps ?—relaxed. He admitted that he had practically no forces under him, but challenged them to show that they had any either. To prove it, he ordered them to gather 12,000 men at eleven o'clock next day on the Place de la Concorde. If the men were there, he would lead an attack by way of Clamart station. The Legion-Commanders agreed, spent the whole night rounding up their men.

Not that there was much hope of collecting 12,000. On the previous day, when Rossel had taken La Cécilia with him to attempt an attack at Petit-Vanves, they could not collect enough men even for a skirmish. Rossel, the former President of the Court Martial, had contented himself with a puerile gesture: he had cut off the left sleeves of the cowards' uniforms, and all the poor fellows had burst into tears.

The Central Committee duly paraded its men: only about 7,000 of them. Rossel rode rapidly down the lines, hissed to the Legion-Commanders that they had not kept their word, and galloped back to the Ministry of War.

Here he was met by the news of the fall of Fort Issy, abandoned fifteen hours before. In a fit of cold fury, he scribbled: " The tricolour flag floats over Fort Issy, abandoned yesterday by its garrison," had it immediately printed in 10,000 copies instead of the usual 6,000, and posted up on the walls.

Then he wrote a bitter resignation to the Commune:

" Citizen members of the Commune, I feel myself incapable of continuing to bear the responsibility of a command
which everyone discusses and no one obeys. When it was
necessary to organise the artillery, the Central Artillery
Committee discussed and took no steps. The Central
Committee discusses and has not yet been able to act.
During this delay the enemy was surrounding Fort Issy by
adventurous and imprudent attacks for which I should
punish him had I the least military force at my disposal. . . .
Thus the nullity of the Artillery Committee prevented the
organisation of the artillery; the hesitations of the Central
Committee hinder the administration; the petty preoccupa-
tions of the Legion-Commanders paralyse the mobilisation
of the troops. My predecessor made the mistake of trying to
liquidate this absurd situation. I retire, and have the
honour to ask you for a cell at Mazas."

At the Hôtel de Ville, Rigault and Vermorel were arguing
about the police administration. Suddenly Delescluze
broke in on the discussion: " You argue, and it has just
been proclaimed that the tricolour floats over Fort Issy !
I had hoped, citizens, that France would be saved by Paris
and Europe by France. . . . To-day the National Guard is no
longer willing to fight, and you discuss questions of procedure ! . . . It is the deplorable debates of the past week, at
which I am glad not to have been present, that have
produced this disorder. . . . And it is at such a moment that
you waste your time on questions of personal prestige !
There is a force of revolutionary feeling in the Commune
capable of saving the country. Throw away all your mutual
hatreds. We must save the country. The Committee of
Public Safety has not fulfilled our expectations. It has been
an obstruction, not a stimulus. I say that it must disappear.
We must take immediate, decisive steps. . . . We must find
in the heroes of March 18, and in the Central Committee
which has rendered such great services, the powers that will
save us. We must set up the unity of command. I proposed
the unity of the political direction : that will now be no use.
We arrived at the Committee of Public Safety. What is it

doing ? Nothing; except individual appointments instead
of common actions. It has just named Citizen Moreau Civil
Delegate to the Military Commission. Then what are the
members of the Military Commission doing ? Are we then
nothing ? I cannot admit it. We were appointed seriously
by the Commune and we will do our duty seriously. The
military administration pure and simple was entrusted to
the Central Committee. What has it done ? I do not know.
But if the Central Committee, accepting the situation, is
willing to help in the work of rallying the scattered elements
to the defence of Paris, the Central Committee is welcome.
Your Committee of Public Safety is annihilated, crushed by
the weight of the memories with which it is burdened, and
does not do the work of even a simple executive commission." The Commune applauded what was an expression
of personal opinion rather than a defence of the Military
Commission and went into secret session to discuss the
political question.

After several hours of heated debate, they decided to
renew the Committee of Public Safety, appoint a civil
Delegate for War, to meet only three times a week in future
except in urgent cases, to settle the new Committee of
Public Safety permanently at the Hôtel de Ville, the
members of the Commune remaining in their local *mairies*,
to set up a court martial, of which the members were to be
appointed immediately by the Military Commission, whose
first task would be to try Rossel.

The Commune met again in the evening. Pyat presided.
The Military Commission demanded the maintenance of
Rossel for another twenty-four hours, threatening their own
resignation if they were not satisfied. Pyat took advantage
of his position to insult Rossel in his absence : " I told you,
citizens, that he was a traitor but you would not believe me.
You are young, you did not realise, as our masters of the
Convention did, that military power is to be distrusted."

There was a tremendous row. Several members nearly
came to blows. The session was suspended to nominate the
new Committee of Public Safety. The Minority found them-

selves alone in the room. Growing impatient, they went to
look for the Majority, found them discussing their candidates behind locked doors; broke in and forced them back to
a general discussion. The Majority shouted for the arrest of
Rossel and the whole Minority. Pyat renewed his attacks.
Malon shouted at him, " You are the evil genius of the
revolution ! It is your influence that is destroying the
revolution ! " Arnold of the Central Committee added, " It
is the men of Forty-Eight who will destroy the revolution ! "
But the Majority list passed in full. The new Committee of
Public Safety kept Ranvier and Arnaud, added two
Blanquists—Gambon, a leader of the Forty-Eight, lieutenant
of Garibaldi and friend of Rigault, and Eudes—with
Delescluze, now the leading figure in the Commune. It was
an incomparably stronger body personally than the first
Committee.

The meeting broke up long after midnight. On the
proposal of Vésinier, who was actively intriguing for control
of the *Journal Officiel*, the Commune publicly announced :
" It is untrue that the tricolour flag floats over Fort Issy.
The Versaillese are not occupying it and will never occupy
it." They had been there since early the previous morning.

All day, Rossel had been receiving delegations. It was still
uncertain whether he were traitor or saviour. In his reten-
tion or in his arrest lay the solution of the whole problem.
In the afternoon, he went to a meeting of the Central
Committee, defended his conduct, carried them by his
regular-officer talent for the clear explanation of a military
situation.

After he had left, the Committee decided that the only
hope of saving both Paris and their own authority was to
make Rossel dictator. The proposal was carried by 22 votes
to 6.

Five delegates from the Committee caught Rossel as he
was going to dinner with Dombrowski and told him of his
appointment. He thought for a moment, answered, " It
is too late. I am no longer Delegate. I have sent in my
resignation."

Meanwhile, the Central Committee had demanded from the Commune full powers for Rossel. On his return to the Ministry after dinner, he was met by the Military Commission and Johannard. Avrial and Delescluze were their spokesmen. Delescluze had a warrant for Rossel's arrest in his pocket. Rossel almost convinced them that he was the man to save the situation. The delegation went into the next room to talk it over. Delescluze told them that he could not bring himself to arrest Rossel before the Commune had heard his defence. Rossel agreed to stay at his post for another day to give the Commission time to arrange matters, but refused to sign any engagement. The delegation went away, leaving Rossel under the supervision of Avrial and Johannard.

Next day all three went to the Hôtel de Ville in Rossel's carriage. The Commune were discussing general details. Delescluze had just been appointed Civil Delegate for War by 42 votes to 2. Rossel had thus been dismissed by implication. When Johannard came in to say that Rossel was waiting outside, the Commune was deciding upon a report by Courbet proposing the Marshals' Hall in the Tuileries as a public sessions-room. Delescluze demanded that Rossel should be heard by the Commune at once. " We have to judge him without hearing him here," said Paschal Grousset, who hated him. Pyat : " If the Commune does not repress the insolence shown in his letter, it is committing suicide ! " Dupont remarked that Cluseret had not been heard, so why should Rossel be ? By 26 against 16, they refused to hear Rossel in his defence. By 34 against 2, with 7 abstentions, they decided that he should be tried by court martial and sent to Mazas as he had requested. His crime was military, not political.

The Commune had passed to a *distrait* hearing of some proposal by Allix, who had been arrested for his peculiar behaviour in his district, when Avrial burst in to say that Rossel had disappeared, together with Charles Gérardin. Gérardin, Rossel's one friend and dismissed member of the first Committee of Public Safety, seeing the way the

debate was going, had slipped out to tell Rossel. Avrial
was tired by his long sentry-duty and had asked Gérardin
to relieve him. Gérardin noticed Avrial's revolver on the
table, remarked upon his conscientiousness. " I don't
suppose that this precaution is on my account," said Rossel.
" Anyway, Citizen Avrial, I give you my word of honour
as a soldier that I will not try to escape." Avrial went into
the session, leaving Rossel alone with Gérardin. While he
was gone, the two walked calmly downstairs and got into a
passing cab. At the Place Saint-Michel they separated.
Rossel reappeared only to be tried and shot by the Versaillese.

At two o'clock that same afternoon, Favre, who had gone
to Frankfurt on May 6, and had nearly been caught by the
Communards at Saint-Denis on his way, signed the Treaty
of Peace with Prussia. Immediately afterwards, he heard
the news of the fall of Fort Issy. But Bismarck had already
exacted his final terms. The annihilation of the Paris
Commune was now, to Favre and Thiers, a work of
patriotic revenge, the final defeat of the " Prussians of
Paris." It was to be the salvation of Thiers's " Conservative
republic."

# CHAPTER VII

# DELESCLUZE

" The Commune has delegated me to the Ministry of War; it has thought that its representative in the military administration should belong to the civil element. Had I consulted only my own strength, I should have declined this dangerous post; but I count upon your patriotism to render its exercise easier for me. The situation is grave, as you know; the horrible war waged against us by the feudal seigneurs leagued with the relics of monarchic regimes has already cost you much precious blood; yet, although I deplore these sad losses, when I look forward to the sublime future opening out to our children, even if it be not granted to ourselves to harvest what we have sown, I should still greet with enthusiasm the Revolution of March 18 which has opened to France and to Europe perspectives which none of us dared even hope three months ago. To your ranks, therefore, Citizens, and stand firm before the enemy ! Our walls are as stout as your arms, as your hearts; and you are not ignorant, too, that you are fighting for your freedom and for social equality, that promise which has so long escaped you, and that if your breasts are exposed to the shot and shell of Versailles, the prize assured to you is the liberation of France and the world, the safety of your homes, the lives of your women and children. You will conquer, then; the world that is watching you and applauding your great-souled efforts is ready to celebrate your triumph, which will mean the salvation of all the peoples. Long live the Universal Republic ! Long live the Commune ! "

CHARLES DELESCLUZE: *Proclamation
to the National Guard, May 10, 1871*

So LONG AS CLUSERET and Rossel had been at the head of the administration, the Commune had functioned in what may be termed a regularly revolutionary way—that is to say, its specifically Parisian, its Jacobin, characteristics did not entirely dominate. It was, of course, the gradualness of the emergence of these characteristics that made the domination of the two foreigners possible; and it was the impossibility of assimilating the two elements under the particular objective circumstances of the revolution of

March 18 that caused their fall. Inevitably, those elements which represented local reactions to local causes began to predominate over the elements which represented a revolution for which the economic and social preconditions had not yet been fulfilled. The Socialists were definitely submerged by the Jacobins; and of the Jacobins Charles Delescluze, the new Civil Delegate for War, was the most complete and convinced representative. Although this final return to pure Jacobinism destroyed the social significance of the revolution and in place of a programme bequeathed only a martyrology, in it lay the last chance of saving Paris, by giving to the Commune the basis for a united front of all those who, whatever their political and social aims, were primarily Republicans and Parisians. It was the last chance of uniting the Commune and the Central Committee, the civil and the military powers, in a common resistance to the enemy's final onslaught. The appointment of Delescluze and his line of action were the only possible course in the immediate situation. That alone could revive in the waning revolution the absolute determination to stake their lives upon a now hopeless cause.

It was really too late to do anything but prepare to sell their lives as memorably as they might. Delescluze himself, dying but indomitable, was the visible symbol of dying and indomitable Paris. He seemed to be preparing for Paris a revolutionary funeral, to be rehearsing the speech to be spoken over its tomb. They all felt it, and some of them became imbued with the same spirit, a defiant certitude that excluded all passive fatalism. It seemed that even before they had died they were united in death. But the Commune had still three more vivid weeks of existence.

The line of investment was drawing irresistibly closer. After the fall of Fort Issy, the piercing of the Point-du-Jour salient could only be a matter of time. On the left, Douay was extending his line right up to the back of the Butte Montmartre. On his right, however, Ladmirault was still held in check at Asnières and Neuilly, despite intense bombardment. In the centre, Clinchant had crossed the

Seine, encamped at Longchamp and opened up a line of entrenchment from the Lakes as far as the Muette Gates. The Billancourt battery had swept the Point-du-Jour viaduct in a couple of hours, sunk the gunboat *Estoc* and forced the others to retreat up the river to the Place de la Concorde. On the right, Osmont had cut communications between Vanves and Montrouge. Fort Issy had been reconditioned to fire upon the walls and Fort Vanves. Vanves was now the objective of the action in the south.

Protected by the bombardment, the Versaillese infantry advanced steadily upon the fort. It was by now almost untenable. Its commander, La Cécilia, had gone sick and had been replaced by Wroblewski with two battalions from the XIth district. On May 12, he repulsed a preliminary Versaillese reconnaissance with considerable loss. The Versaillese replied by capturing the Convent of Les Oiseaux at Issy. During the night, they surprised the Vanves school.

At noon on the 13th the Communards finally evacuated Issy village, a mass of ruins, with the loss of eight guns, some flags and many prisoners. The road to Paris was black with fugitives. The tricolour was hoisted on Issy town-hall and, according to the Versaillese, the inhabitants " welcomed the arrival of the troops with veritable enthusiasm." " The insurgents had left horrible traces of their passage at the Convent of Les Oiseaux: a number of nuns' graves had been violated and the limbs of the corpses scattered about the park "; such is the ordinary effect of artillery bombardment.

The Versaillese built a barricade in the main street of Issy, only 500 yards from the Porte de Vaugirard and two more on the Ile Saint-Germain, 1,000 yards from the Porte de Sèvres.

Rossel had entrusted the defence of the village to Brunel, who, after April 4, had been relegated to an unimportant command of reserves. Brunel had asked for artillery and reinforcements to relieve the 2,000 men who had been holding the village for 41 days; he was given no more than

200 or 300. On May 13, he went back to the Ministry of War, whither Delescluze had summoned him and Dombrowski, Wroblewski and La Cécilia to a council of war, the first held there since April 3. Dombrowski had spoken of the possibility of still raising 100,000 men. Wroblewski suggested the plan which should long ago have been adopted —that of transferring to the southern front the great numbers of men who were quite uselessly holding Neuilly. Nothing was decided, and the council had broken up before Brunel arrived.

After seeing Delescluze at the Hôtel de Ville, he went back towards Issy. At the Porte de Versailles he met the fugitives from Issy village clamouring to be let in. He went round to the Porte de Vanves to try to lead them back to the village. The guard, thinking he was trying to escape, would not let him leave the city. He rushed back to the Ministry of War, then to the Central Committee, begged for men, spent the night rounding them up, and got back to Issy only at four in the morning, and with only 150 men. It was too late. Brunel and his fellow-officers were sent before the court martial and imprisoned for their failure.

Fort Vanves was no longer tenable. During the night of May 13–14, the garrison, cut off on every side, fled through the underground tunnels leading out through the Montrouge quarries. They had to pick their way over heaps of corpses. Of some 6,000 fugitives, only about 2,000 ever came out. Weeks later, madmen were seen haunting the quarries, looking for something.

After some hesitation, the Versaillese entered the fort. " The state of Fort Vanves is still worse than that of Issy. The *escarpe* facing our attack is literally riddled with bullets, the casemates are smashed to pieces; the barracks are in ruins, the drawbridge broken down, the parapets torn up, the guns almost all bear the marks of our shells "; there were still about 50 guns in good condition.

On the 16th, the Commune held no position in the south from the left bank of the Seine to Petit-Vanves near Montrouge, where there were about 2,000 men under La

Cécilia and the actor-soldier Maxime Lisbonne. The Versaillese held a line along the whole of western Paris: from Vanves across the Seine, through the Bois de Boulogne to Neuilly and Asnières as far as the Prussian lines at Saint-Ouen.

The reconditioned Fort Issy was firing upon Paris and, after silencing the walls at Grenelle, joined in the bombardment of the Point-du-Jour. The whole of Passy was under fire. The fortifications from the Porte de Sèvres to the Porte de la Muette were hardly tenable. On May 16, Delescluze was informed that the artillerymen defending the walls from Bastion 64 (level with the rue Mirabeau) to the Point-du-Jour had been forced from their posts. Nothing was done to relieve them. Nothing could be done, for the men refused to go to certain death so far from their own districts.

Local loyalty was replacing loyalty to the Commune. All through the revolution, as during the Prussian Siege, local interests had predominated over general politics, the *mairie* over the Hôtel de Ville. Delescluze himself, believing fervently in the tradition of Paris street-fighting as he had known it himself in the June Days, rather favoured this inclination which he saw to be intensely natural to a Parisian insurrection. But, fatally, he believed too firmly in the spontaneous barricade. That could not help against an organised army with artillery. Cavaignac had proved that. Nothing was done to carry out Rossel's plan for a second line of barricades linking Montmartre, the Trocadéro and the Panthéon, although Father Gaillard, whose spectacular constructions were stigmatised publicly as " the infancy of the art," was dismissed and the work entrusted to the Director of Military Engineering, who was to " see to the continuation of the works begun in the measure which he shall think fit." Delescluze offered 3 francs 50 a day to professional masons to help in the work; but the Committee of Public Safety overbid him in a paragraph in the *Journal Officiel*, immediately below his, offering 3 francs 75.

A scientific delegation under Dr. Parisel studied chemical

methods of attack, about which much had been heard in
the Prussian war, gathering data about available quantities
of sulphur, phosphorus, etc., and buying up all the car-
bonic sulphurate possible. A Monsieur Borme was asked to
manufacture the famous and probably mythical *Feu Grégeois*,
but sabotaged the production. All sorts of " frightfulness "
were demanded daily by the clubs. There was much talk of
mining the sewers; but only talk. Vallès published a semi-
humorous threat in his *Cri du Peuple*: " Not a soldier will
enter Paris. If M. Thiers is a chemist, he will understand."
On May 12, Paschal Grousset replied to Thiers, who had
told the International Society for Help of the Wounded
that " the Commune not having adhered to the Geneva
Convention, the Versailles Government had no obligation
to observe it," that the Commune officially declared its
adhesion and had never violated a single article. On the
16th, however, he pointed out that this did not mean that
the Commune would abstain from using " the new engines
of war of which the Revolution disposes ": the Convention merely guaranteed the neutrality of military ambulances, but did not claim to regulate the use of scientific
methods of warfare.

The Delegation for Public Services ordered that all stocks
of petrol should be declared at the offices of the lighting
service, which has à sinister sound in the light of future
events, but was probably simply a precaution against a
failure of gas, since there had been considerable trouble
with the gas companies. As a matter of fact, the revolution
disposed of no " new engines " whatever.

The fall of Issy and the intrigues for Rossel's dictatorship
had greatly encouraged the Versaillese agents in Paris, who
had spent most of the time since the proclamation of the
Commune denouncing each other to the central agent,
Troncin-Dumersan, at Versailles, and attempting to extort
their pay in advance.

There were upholders of three main methods : insurrection against the Commune, sabotage of its services, plain
treachery by the purchase of a battalion or a gate. The

insurrectionists had little hope. Their leaders were Charpentier, commander of a reactionary battalion, former
instructor at the Saint-Cyr Military College, with some
bourgeois, Durouchoux, Demay and Gallimard. A rival
organisation, under a naval lieutenant, Domalain, later
joined up with Charpentier. They claimed that they had
6,000 men and 150 engineers, and received hundreds of
francs from Versailles. At the end of April, they suffered
serious competition from the leader of the sabotage method,
Le Mère de Beaufond, a former Governor of Cayenne, with
Laroque, a clerk at the Bank of France, and Lasnier, a
former officer in Schoelcher's legion. De Beaufond had
managed to buy agents at the Ecole Militaire and at the
Ministry of War itself, where Guyet, head of the artillery,
sabotaged the munition service. Lasnier and Laroque were
able to work the commander of the XVIIth Legion.

There were other sinister individuals working on their
own. That precious trio, Lullier, Ganier d'Abin and Raoul
du Bisson, were still at large and active. A more dangerous
person was the self-confessed *agent-provocateur*, Barral de
Montaud, who got himself appointed commander of the
VIIth Legion and even worked a member of the Commune
itself, the greasy and unpopular Urbain, whose mistress,
the Widow Leroy, he shared. There were also a few quite
honest young bourgeois who had got swept into the Commune's service, could not leave, but were unwilling to work
for it. Obviously, not much is known of them. One was
the director of the powder magazine in the rue Philippe-
Auguste, young Bertin, who had taken the post because
the staff, constituted during the first siege, were not National
Guards and so had not a sou ; he did not make an ounce of
powder, but held the magazine and secured the workers'
pay.

There were, strangely, few attempts to assassinate Communard leaders. A pair of somewhat mysterious individuals
were sent to Mazas, on April 13, on the suspicion, reported
by Jourde, of plotting to murder Delescluze. An even more
obscure report was sent in by Cattelain of the Ex-Prefecture

on May 13 concerning a Russian or Polish artist, one Nicolas Alexandrowicz Schileff, a man of " prodigiously agitated life," possessing a sword-stick and 1,460 francs in cash, who had bought some strychnine, with which he apparently intended to poison Dombrowski.

Thiers wisely pinned most of his faith upon the purchase of an entry into Paris. His chief agent was Georges Veysset. Veysset had been thinking of this plan since the beginning of April and had put it on a regular basis, half commercial, half family. The conspiracy included his mistress Marguerite Forzi, most of his relations, four or five others, with a capital of 20,000 francs and a base at Versailles. He had got into touch with one of Dombrowski's staff, Hutzinger, who seems to have acted as an *agent double* at the least, alternately betraying Veysset and Dombrowski and slandering both. Veysset proposed to sell a gate to the Versaillese and buy Dombrowski too. Hutzinger immediately told Dombrowski and proposed to the Committee of Public Safety that he should lead the Versaillese troops into Paris, when the Communards would fall upon them and take them prisoner. He asked for 20,000 men; but Pyat and Ranvier would not take the risk of denuding the defences and offered no more than 300 or 400. Hutzinger went to Versailles with Veysset, saw the irrepressible Admiral Saisset, still dreaming of a *putsch*, who offered himself as a hostage for the execution of the promises made to Dombrowski. By now, everybody was double-crossing everybody else. Saisset was to go secretly to the Place Vendôme one evening; and the Committee of Public Safety was preparing to arrest him when Barthélemy Saint-Hilaire, Thiers's agent in such affairs, forbade the venture. The Ex-Prefecture had not been informed of the Committee of Public Safety's diplomacy, discovered the plot for itself and arrested Marguerite Forzi. Veysset had to flee to Saint-Denis on May 10, where he continued negotiations with Hutzinger. The result of all this was that ugly rumours attached to Dombrowski, whose Slavic subtlety was not appreciated by Rigault and Ferré.

There had been a definite attempt to buy a gate some

time previously, significantly enough on the night of the Moulin Saquet surprise, May 3-4. The connection has, however, not been proved. Boudard, a corporal in the National Guard, and Laporte, commander of the Passy sector, were to open the Porte Dauphine. MacMahon was dubious about such a venture, but Thiers approved. But Laporte had not warned Lavigne, commander of the reactionary 38th, to be ready. Thiers slept at Sèvres, and the troops waited in the Bois de Boulogne all night in vain. The plot was discovered, Laporte arrested; Boudard escaped to Versailles.

Now Beaufond was to imitate Boudard in the confusion following Rossel's fall. He was to open the Portes Dauphine and d'Auteuil on the night of May 12-13. With the help of Laroque and Lasnier, he had gained a colonel on Dombrowski's staff, Stawinsky. At midnight, Ladmirault came silently down from Courbevoie and massed his troops near the Portes de la Muette and d'Auteuil. Douay left the trenches and came up to the Porte de Passy. In front of them bodies of police and engineers waited to rush in and open other gates. The evening before, several carts loaded with a complete escalading-outfit had been sent from Versailles. Vinoy's whole reserve was on the move. Eighty thousand men were hidden in the Bois. Thiers was there, with Douay and MacMahon. After waiting four hours, Mac-Mahon, fearing a trap, ordered the retreat. The plot had been denounced to the Commune.

Another far wider and more dangerous plot was discovered next day by pure chance. A Madame Legros kept a workshop near the Bastille. She did not pay her sempstresses, and one of them, supposing that she was working for the Commune, came to the Hôtel de Ville to demand her wages. But Madame Legros was emphatically not working for the Commune. She was making tricolour armlets—brassards—to be worn by enemies of the Commune when the Versaillese troops entered Paris; 20,000 had already been sent from Versailles, stamped with the seal of the Ministry of War ; hundreds more were being made in bourgeois homes in Paris. A score of National Guards at once occupied the shop, found a great number of the *brassards* and a list of the conspirators' names. Lasnier was involved and was arrested; Laroque and Beaufond had to go into hiding; Troncin-Dumersan scuttled back to Versailles. Lasnier was released ten days later.

The Committee of Public Safety announced the discovery of the Brassard Conspiracy, tried to connect it with Rossel and the others: "The abandonment of Fort Issy, announced in an impious proclamation by the wretch who handed it over, was only the first act in the drama: a Royalist insurrection at home, coinciding with the surrender of one of our gates, was to follow it and plunge us into the depths of the abyss. But once again victory is with the just cause. All the threads of the sinister plot in which the revolution was to be trapped are in our hands. The majority of the guilty have been arrested." This was nonsense, and the Committee knew it: Lasnier and Marguerite Forzi could hardly be the " majority " of so widespread a conspiracy as was announced. The scare, justified though it was, meant a reinforcement of the Ex-Prefecture's activity.

The Assembly at Versailles was also working to envenom the struggle yet more. On May 10, Thiers had seemed to listen to another proposal by the conciliatory National Union of Syndical Chambers, promising that, if the Communards would cease fire, the gates of Paris would be left open for a week to all save the murderers of Generals Lecomte and Clément Thomas. The proposal was absurd enough for Thiers to continue his usual tactics; but the Assembly was furious at this apparent weakening.

Next day the ultra-reactionary Belcastel raised the question whether the provisions of the Penal Code dealing with religion, the ferocious repression of " sacrilege " decreed by the Restoration fifty years before, would be applied to the Communards. Mortimer-Ternaux, a lifelong Orleanist friend of Thiers, reproached him bitterly with yielding to thoughts of conciliation. Thiers wept, parliamentarily. " I beg the Assembly to excuse the emotion under which I am labouring. I hope that it will be understood when you realise that I am dedicating my life, day and night, to the country's service with a disinterestedness which I think is evident." His resignation was ready. But when the Right shouted that they would be only too glad to accept it, Thiers hastily backed down, cleverly putting them in the wrong and arousing the sympathy of the Left, who saw in him at least some guarantee of some sort of Republic. " If I displease you [*Cries of* " *No ! No !* "], tell me so. . . . We must not take refuge in ambiguity. I say that there are among you people who are in too much of a hurry. They must wait one week more; at the end of that week, the danger will be over and the task will be proportionate to their courage and their capacity." The sneer went home. The Right came to heel. Pyat himself could not have wriggled out more effectively. Thiers finished off the discomfited Right with one of those personal appeals which his vanity never failed to suggest, and which, equally, never failed of their effect: " You choose the very day on which I am proscribed, on which my house is being demolished. That is what I call an unworthy act ! " Poor Mortimer-Ternaux was so crushed that he slunk out, literally to die of shame. Thiers received the vote of confidence he demanded. The Right got little consolation for this rebuff from an open letter published from Goritz by the Pretender, the Comte de Chambord, declaring that " the word is to France and the hour to God."

The Commune printed the report of this session in full, pointing out that it " gave an exact idea of the spirit of dissolution animating the enemy." The Versaillese papers had remarked the same of some of the Commune's sessions.

On May 15 the Commune replied to the " tears and threats of Thiers the Bombarder " by decreeing that the linen from his house should be given to the ambulance service, the art treasures and books, four cart-loads of them, be sent to the national museums and libraries, the furniture sold by auction and the proceeds given to war victims, and that a public square should be laid out on the site of the house.

On May 13 the Assembly voted almost unanimously a proposal by Cazenove de Pradines for a day of prayer in all churches of France, " to beseech God to appease our civil discord and put an end to the evils which afflict us " : this method, together with intensified bombardment, seemed to them preferable to the efforts of the conciliatory bodies. By a coincidence of date, this day of prayer was held while the Commune was pulling down the Vendôme Column, on May 16.

The political struggle had become defined : a Jacobin Paris against a Monarchist Assembly; both the Socialists and the bourgeois Republicans were increasingly forced out of the Commune and the Assembly. It was to be a final struggle between the two elements which, in default of a programme, could rely only on force, the Right Extremists and the Left Extremists.

In the Commune, the Jacobins forced another reshuffle of the executive, consolidating their predominance. Delescluze, ill and overburdened with his work as Delegate for War, resigned from the Committee of Public Safety. The Minority proposed Varlin to replace him; but, after a violent debate which made the cleavage final, the Majority elected Billioray, who had been one of the most enthusiastic in suggesting the Committee's creation.

The Military Commission was completely changed, in order to give the Majority full control and some ground upon which to meet the Central Committee. Johannard, Arnold, Avrial, Tridon and Varlin, the last four being members of the Minority, were replaced by Bergeret, Cournet, Géresme, Ledroit, Lonclas, Sicard and Urbain. This new composition was, to say the least, peculiar. Bergeret and Géresme represented the extremer malcontents of the Central Committee, Ledroit and Lonclas, somehow always paired, were almost unknown, their antecedents somewhat (although unjustly) suspect; Sicard was a violent talker, well fitted for a military executioner; Urbain, under

Barral de Montaud's influence, something near a traitor; and Cournet, from the police service, nothing of a soldier.

Henri, Military Commander at the Ecole Militaire, was removed, the command centralised under Dombrowski in the Ministry of War itself. Dombrowski tightened up the military organisation by forbidding all local councils of war and consultations by groups of officers—an obvious hit at the Legion-Commanders: " Orders emanating from above will be carried out without discussion."

The Committee of Public Safety attempted to placate the Central Committee and revive yet another of the institutions of 1793 by attaching, on May 16, Civil Commissioners representing the Commune to the three generals appointed by it, Dereure to Dombrowski, Johannard to La Cécilia, Melliet to Wroblewski, " considering that, in order to safeguard the interests of the revolution, it is indispensable to associate the civil with the military element and that our fathers perfectly understood that this measure alone could preserve the country from military dictatorship which sooner or later invariably ends in the establishment of a dynasty." It was, of course, perfect nonsense to suggest that the generals had any notion of setting up a dictatorship, although Rossel had given the Committee of Public Safety a bad scare; what was important was that the Committee of Public Safety was putting out feelers towards the Central Committee, casting insinuations upon the generals responsible to the Commune and the Military Commission, not to the Central Committee, and bringing the whole military administration in line with the appointment of Delescluze as Civil Delegate for War. At the same time, the Central Committee's leader, Moreau, was appointed Director of the Intendance, Varlin's old post, which amounted to a seat on the Military Commission.

Next day, the Committee of Public Safety published a proclamation to the National Guard, into which there creeps a certain note of humble appeal for co-operation. It is no longer the social regeneration and the new world for the workers that are promised as the reward of victory, but "the sublime programme traced by our fathers in 1792." The National Guard alone stood between Paris and "a frightful retrogression to all the orgies of monarchism."

In the general shake-up caused by Cournet's transfer from the Ex-Prefecture to the Military Commission, the Police Commission was renewed. Protot, Delegate for Justice, had been fighting Cournet for some time: the perfectly irresponsible behaviour of the police was intolerable, and the police complained that Protot would never back their prosecutions. Through the efforts of Billioray, Ferré was appointed to Cournet's place as Delegate for Police, replaced by an obscure person, Martin. Vermorel resigned from the Commission and was replaced by Emile Clément, until Rigault ferreted out that he had once been an Imperial police spy.

A local police was created. On May 14 every citizen was ordered to procure an identity card from the local police commissioners, in order, the decree announced, that Versaillese conspiracies might be checked; but also to round up those who were unwilling to serve in the National Guard. Any National Guard might compel any citizen he met to produce this card. But there was no time to prepare and distribute them.

Otherwise, the local police did not act politically, but confined themselves to keeping order. Thus in the XIth and XIVth districts they tried to put down drunkenness and prostitution: citizens found drunk would be kept for at least two hours at the local police-station to sober off, and the publican would be fined for the benefit of the poor relief.

The sudden increase of prostitution, which had almost disappeared from the streets in April, is to be traced to the well-meaning, but somewhat hasty, decree, passed by Pottier, closing the *maisons tolérées* and throwing their workers out of regular employment. Regular boulevard professionals, such as those rounded up in a razzia at Noel-Peters in which the Russian Consul and the correspondents of the London *Times* and *Morning Advertiser* were involved, were dealt with by Rigault's regular police and sent to the Saint-Lazare women's prison to sew sacks for the barricades.

Another change was that in the editorship of the Commune's *Journal Officiel*, where Vésinier at last ousted Longuet, introduced a somewhat lighter tone by irresponsible Jacobin articles in place of Longuet's sensible, but dull, expositions of Socialism, sold the paper at five centimes to compete with the rest of the revolutionary Press, and used his position to puff his own works.

The Minority found it increasingly impossible to work with the Jacobins. In the midst of the crisis, they had still not given up all hope of carrying out at least some part of their social programme, of saving something of the Socialist State. They had been deprived of all executive posts. The Commune, by Article Three of the decree constituting the Committee of Public Safety, conferring full powers upon the Committee to appoint and dismiss the members of the commissions, had abdicated. The first sign of the split had appeared when Billioray defeated Varlin for nomination to the Committee of Public Safety; it had become more irreparable when Cournet was replaced by Ferré. Cooperation seemed no longer possible, abstention the only method of protest.

The Minority came to the Hôtel de Ville on Sunday, the 14th, to protest formally, but found no one there. They came again on the Monday, with a protest which they proposed to read to the Communal Assembly, but still found only four or five of the Majority. They then very rashly sent the protest to the papers of the 16th, notably to the *Cri du Peuple*, without warning the Commune. Twenty-one members signed: Arnold, Arnould, Andrieu, Avrial, Beslay, Victor Clément, Courbet, Clémence, Franckel, Eugène Gérardin, Jourde, Lefrançais, Longuet, Ostyn, Pindy, Serrailler, Theisz, Tridon, Vallès, Varlin, Vermorel; Malon adhered next day. Since the voting for the first Committee of Public Safety, the group had been joined by Arnold, thoroughly disgusted by his experience of office, and Franckel and Theisz, both of the International, who joined their fellow Socialists. Babick, Langevin and Rastoul, of no importance, had deserted the first Minority.

The protest declared:

" By a special and precise vote the Commune of Paris has abdicated its power into the hands of a dictatorship to which it has given the name of the Committee of Public Safety. By this vote the Majority in the Commune has declared itself irresponsible and has abandoned to this Committee all the responsibilities of our situation. The Minority to which we belong affirms, on the contrary, the idea that the Commune owes it to the political and social revolutionary movement to accept all responsibilities and decline none, however worthy may be the hands into which it is desired to abandon them. . . . We will not present ourselves again before the Assembly until the day on which it constitutes itself a Court of Justice to judge one of its members. Devoted to our great communal cause for which so many citizens are dying every day, we retire to our districts which have perhaps been too much neglected. . . . There we shall serve our convictions usefully and will avoid creating in the Commune dissensions which we all reprobate; for we are persuaded that, Majority or Minority, despite our political differences, we are pursuing the same end: political liberty, the emancipation of the workers."

The protest made an enormous sensation. It must be remembered that only the most curtailed accounts of the Commune sessions were appearing in the Press. Few in Paris had realised that the Commune was so definitely split; and, because of this ignorance, this rash outburst seemed more serious than it was. The phrase " until the day on which the Commune constitutes itself a Court of Justice " seemed to mean more than the trial of Cluseret and Rossel; the possible arrest of the Minority itself, and then complete anarchy. Versailles was openly jubilant;

used the protest to justify its persuasions that the Commune was " a mere handful of bandits."

Grousset, Delegate for Foreign Affairs, chose this day of all days to make a last appeal to the cities of France. " After two months of hourly fighting, Paris is neither wearied nor impaired. . . . Paris has made a pact with death. Behind her forts she has her walls; behind her walls her barricades; behind her barricades her houses which they will have to tear from her one by one and which she will blow up, if need be, rather than surrender. . . . If Paris falls for the freedom of the world, the vengeance of history will have the right to say that Paris was murdered because you permitted the murder." But behind the forts, the walls, the barricades, the houses there was the Commune; and in the Commune there was a great crack, and behind the Commune there was nothing.

The Minority Protest came most inopportunely upon the great day of the Commune, the 26th Floréal of the Year 79 (May 16): the day of the fall of the Vendôme Column. The *Journal Officiel* came out for the first time dated by the revolutionary calendar.

The Great Revolution had its festivals, the Forty-Eight its banquets: the Commune had its demolitions.

On April 6 the 137th battalion had burnt a guillotine in the Place de la Mairie in the XIth district, beneath the cynical smile of the Voltaire statue. The Commune had approved the gesture: the " seizure of those servile instruments of monarchic domination and their destruction for ever." Rochefort had remarked that there was not much use in destroying the guillotine to replace it by sticking a man up against a wall and firing a dozen or so bullets into him.

Carrying on this symbolism, street names had been changed. The rue de Morny, rue MacMahon after September 4, now became rue de la Commune. Rue Bonaparte was rue du 31 Octobre. The Place d'Italie was named Place Duval, after the commander killed on April 4. Streets named after saints and wards in public hospitals were secularised. The Place Vendôme, originally Place des Conquêtes, then Louis-le-Grand, was called by the Delegation for Justice, situated there, the Place des Piques; Vallès's *Cri du Peuple* made the popular suggestion, Place de la Fraternité; but after the demolition of the Column, it was officially named Place Internationale.

Measures against their enemies' property were more than half symbolical. Thiers was indicted on April 3. On the 6th Rochefort pointed out that Thiers had a Paris house and that the Commune might avenge the bombardment of Courbevoie by demolishing it. There was only one objection: "On hearing that popular justice is pulling down M. Thiers's house which cost two millions, the Versailles Assembly would immediately vote him another costing three; and since the taxpayer would have to foot the bill, we are compelled to advise against this method of expiation."

The suggestion was, however, adopted by the Commune, the house occupied on April 14 and condemned to destruction on May 10.

Melliet, on his appointment to the Committee of Public Safety, proposed the demolition of the chapel commemorating General Bréa, killed by the insurgents in June 1848. Nourry, the man transported for the killing, was to be reprieved and a pension paid to his aged mother.

Quite incidentally, the heated debate about the amount of this pension gave rise to the proposal that the Paris churches should be declared municipal property. This was passed without discussion, as a matter of course. In actual fact, they had already been occupied as clubs. Their organ, the *Bulletin Communal*, describing the occupation of a church in the IIIrd district as a " great revolutionary act," added: " Follow our example, open communal clubs in all the churches. The priests will be able to officiate by day and you can carry on the people's education in the evenings."

On May 6 the Commune voted that the Louis XVI Expiatory Chapel be pulled down, for it was " a permanent insult to the first Revolution and a perpetual protest against the People's justice."

Most important of all was the proposal, first vented in the *Cri du Peuple* of April 4 and passed by the Commune on April 12, to demolish the Vendôme Column, " since the Imperial Column is a monument of barbarism, a symbol of brute force and false glory, an affirmation of militarism, a denial of international law, a permanent insult by the conqueror to the conquered, a perpetual attack upon one of the three great Principles of the French Republic: Fraternity."

The proposal had been made before this; but had usually been confined only to the figure crowning the Column, the alterations in which are an interesting summary of the fluctuations of the Napoleonic Idea.

Napoléon I himself had intended the Column to commemorate the victories of the Grande Armée, but had later decided to annex the glory for himself alone. Chaudet's original statue of 1812 represented the Emperor in toga with a small antique figure of Victory in his hand.

In May 1814 a party of Royalists had tried to haul down this statue, but their ropes broke. Under the Restoration, however, Police-Prefect Pasquier and Alexander of Russia's aide-de-camp, Comte de Rochechouart, had it melted down for Baron Lemot's Henri IV on the Pont Neuf, replacing it by a silken Bourbon banner.

Louis Philippe put up a statue by Seurre in 1831. The forerunner of the Bourgeois Monarchy was now represented in riding coat and cocked hat. Thiers distinguished himself during this ceremony by appearing on a horse especially christened Vendôme for the occasion, which bolted with its unskilful rider, charged a drum-major and upset him with all his drums, Thiers clinging like a monkey to the saddle and saluting the event with meridional cries of " *Vanndomme ! Vandomme !* "

Napoléon III embraced the Cæsarian form of the Legend, and in 1864 a statue by Dumont, closely following Chaudet's original, restored the togated Emperor.

Napoléon III's identification of himself with his Cæsarian uncle raised again the old hatred of the Column. Democrats

cursed it in the cafés. Jules Ferry himself forecast its
overthrow should the Republic ever come, Courbet
enthusiastically demanded its *deboulonnement*, a word of his
own invention, which appears to mean that he wanted to
deflate it like a balloon, as he believed it was hollow.
Actually, it was a thin skin of chased bronze round a stone
core with a hollow shaft containing a spiral staircase.
Courbet's excuse to the courts martial after the Commune
was that he disliked it æsthetically, as a bad copy of the
atrocious Column of Titus, and that it got in the way of
traffic. He proposed to have it melted down together with
all the French and Prussian guns to found a gigantic and
complicated monument to Universal Peace and Republicanism. He did not, however, vote for its demolition by
the Commune, as he was accused of doing, since he was
not a member of the council when the motion was passed.

The pulling down of the Vendôme Column was looked
upon by friend and foe alike as the supreme revolutionary
act of the Commune; and even to-day it is almost the only
fact that is connected with that movement by the historically uninformed. Although Bonapartist sentiment had
almost entirely vanished after September 4, and although
no one could have any serious affection for a monument
of execrable taste which a Bonaparte, cheating the Great
Army, had put up for his own glorification, the official
and defiant destruction of this " great exclamation mark
set at the close of the sonorous phrase of the First Empire,"
as Théophile Gautier had called it, did seem to contemporary observers something more tangible, more menacing
than such measures as the breaking-up of bourgeois State-
forms by the composition of the Commune. To the Communards themselves, it was their first public holiday—
except the funerals.

After the decree for the demolition had been passed, on
April 12, nothing had been done for some time, as the
contracting engineers had held up the negotiations. May 5,
the anniversary of Napoléon I's death, had been originally
proposed; but the engineer who had undertaken the work

" in the name of the Positivist Club of Paris " could not complete his arrangements by then. After a fierce attack by Blanchet, the Commune had imposed a fine of 500 francs for every day's delay. At length, the Commune invited the people of Paris to be present at the Place Vendôme at two o'clock on the afternoon of May 16.

Ferré, warned that hostile demonstrations might take place, had ordered Dombrowski to take energetic steps. For several days, the Invalides pensioners had come to take their last look at their Emperor: strange crippled figures in the odd uniforms of half a century ago; the Parisians greeted them with pity; it was said that they had made fantastic plots to resist by opposing their defenceless bodies to the falling Column.

Everyone had been discussing the event for days. Most of the inhabitants of the streets round had pasted strips of paper over their windows. There was much anxiety in case the Column should fall on the houses. A great pile of sand and shavings had been prepared to receive it as it fell.

The rue de la Paix and all the other neighbouring streets as far as the boulevards were crammed. Three military bands. Only the privileged were allowed inside the great barricades, on presentation of a special card adorned with a Phrygian cap on a pike. The commander of a free corps, dressed from head to foot in scarlet, stood by the pedestal. The Place was brilliant with red shirts, masonic scarves, sabres, gold braid. The photographers were frantically busy. Bergeret was there in full regimentals, smoking cigarette after cigarette; Miot, beard waving in the wind; Tridon, pale, feverish; Ferré, talking briskly to an old Forty-Eighter, Glais-Bizoin, dressed to his period, complete with silk-hat; Félix Pyat in a most romantic black cloak and a pair of revolvers at his belt. Protot entertained a select company on the balcony of the Ministry of Justice. Georges Cavalier, *Pipe-en-Bois*, was fussing round the engineer Iribe and the contractor Abadie.

The crowd was not discussing politics. The Minority Protest was forgotten. The war might not have existed.

What interested them was whether the Column would really fall at last, or whether something would go wrong at the last moment, or if it would smash some windows or a house. Small boys sold drinks and satirical engravings. The usual jests and songs. They repeated with relish a quatrain, by a contributor to Rochefort's *Mot d'Ordre*, which had been hung on the Column a few days before:

> " *Tyran, juché sur cette échasse,*
> *Si le sang que tu fis verser*
> *Pouvait tenir dans cette place*
> *Tu le boirais sans te baisser !* "

It might have been more effective to engrave it on the pedestal than to pull the Column down.

Rochefort himself was driving along the boulevard and bowing to the crowd: almost his last public appearance in Paris for many years.

Of course, the ceremony was late. Only at half past three did one of the bands strike up the " Marseillaise "; an officer of the National Guard, old Simon Meyer, was visible on the platform on top of the Column; he changed the red flag for a tricolour destined to fall with the Column, made some speech, naturally inaudible. Protot made a sign to the engineers. The second band struck up the " Chant du Départ." Glais-Bizoin raised his hat. A trumpet sounded. The workmen bent to the capstan. There was a loud crack.

One of the cables had snapped. There were immediate cries of treachery. Iribe showed that the cable had been sawn through. But Tridon simply threatened to arrest him if it were not replaced within the hour. The crowd whistled and hissed and sang with the greatest good humour: no one really believed that the Column would fall. They were reading the evening papers, which already contained full descriptions of the successful ceremony. It was said that an English milord had paid £20 to climb the Column just before its fall.

Iribe got back by five. After more delay, the Column

began to tremble. The " Marseillaise " once more, and the trumpets. The Column leant over, broke into three sections, and crashed with a loud dull noise into the bed prepared for it.

When the dust cleared away, Glais-Bizoin was waving his hat, Bergeret and several Guards red flags. The statue of the Emperor lay on its back, with one arm and the head broken. The winged Victory disappeared, and may be the one now in the Wallace Collection, London. There were tremendous cheers and music; and above all rose " Hail Columbia," played by an American girl on the first floor of the Hôtel Mirabeau.

Mounted artillery and mounted marines cleared the Place, and the crowd flowed to the Hôtel de Ville, where, to the strains of the " Chant des Girondins," Miot, Champy and Ranvier announced that the Place Vendôme would henceforth be called Place Internationale.

At the Ministry of Justice they were discussing the anonymous threatening letters received by Courbet, who had finally been persuaded out of his fright by Vermesch and Vuillaume of the *Père Duchêne*. Vermorel had just refused the passport offered by a friend: he would stay to the inevitable end. Rossel, hidden at a friend's in the Boulevard Saint-Germain, was waiting for Delescluze, who had been secretly consulting him. Cluseret was writing letters to the papers from jail. People were beginning again to discuss the Minority Protest. And, at Versailles, the Assembly, having refused to consider a proposal from the Left that the Republic should be approved as the Government of France, was giving itself up to prayer to the God of Hosts.

MacMahon reported the Commune's horrid deed to the army: " Soldiers—The Vendôme Column has just fallen. The foreigner respected it, the Commune of Paris has overthrown it. Men calling themselves Frenchmen have dared to destroy that witness of your fathers' victories against the coalition of Europe, *beneath the eyes of the Germans*. Did they hope, those infamous scoundrels, to efface the memory of the military virtues, of which that glorious monument was the symbol, by this attempt upon the national glory ? Soldiers, if the memories recalled to us by the Column are no longer engraved upon bronze, they will at least remain living in our hearts and, taking them as our inspiration, we shall give France a new pledge of bravery, devotion and patriotism."

More than forty years before, Heinrich Heine had written: " Once before, the storms have torn from the summit of the Vendôme Column the Iron Man posed upon its pinnacle, and if ever the Socialists come to power, the same fate might befall him a second time; or else the rage for radical equality might well overthrow the whole Column and utterly wipe out from the earth this symbol of militarist glorification."

# CHAPTER VIII

# LAST DAYS OF THE COMMUNE

" Paris has signed a pact with Death "
PASCHAL GROUSSET, *Appeal to Cities of France, May 16.*

" The insurgents' bravery ? Nonsense. Why, they were standing behind barricades ! "
FLAUBERT, *L'Education Sentimentale*

THE VERSAILLESE LINES were closing rapidly upon the doomed city. The final general attack was scheduled for Tuesday, May 23.

In the south, the troops, supported by the captured Forts Issy and Vanves, were advancing between Petit-Vanves and the Seine to threaten the Porte de Sèvres and the Porte d'Issy. On their left, protected by the great batteries at Mont-Valérien and Montretout, Douay and Clinchant were almost up to the fortifications. On the 17th, fire had opened all along the line from the Porte de la Muette to the Point-du-Jour. On the evening of the 18th, the Versaillese assaulted the barricade at Cachan and were checked only by the desperate resistance of Hautes-Bruyères. An intense bombardment was opened against Fort Montrouge and the surrounding district called La Californie. New batteries at Bécon, the Gennevilliers redoubt and the Grande-Jatte Island fed the bombardment. Shells from Bécon were falling as far within the city as the Montmartre Cemetery and the Place Saint-Pierre; and the Communard battery on the Butte replied so badly that their shot fell only on their own men at Levallois.

The surviving inhabitants of the Point-du-Jour, Auteuil, and Passy existed in their cellars. The fortifications from the

Porte de Clichy to the Porte de Vanves were almost dismantled and deserted. The men had not been relieved for
days, had been killed or had retired. No reinforcements had
come from the Ministry of War. Passy ranked almost as
outpost duty: the few gunners left alive, men from Belleville and Ménilmontant, could not be expected to show
great zeal in defending a wealthy and hostile quarter where
the inhabitants were only waiting for the entry of the
Versaillese troops to don their tricolour brassards. There
was no second line of defence: the chain of scientific
barricades from the Trocadéro to the Panthéon, recommended by Rossel, had not even been attempted. The
Versaillese lines were so close to the walls that Lefrançais,
passing the Porte de Saint-Cloud at noon on May 21, had
heard them talking in the trenches immediately under
the drawbridge. He had immediately sent a warning to
Delescluze, but the message went astray. The Versaillese
had strict orders from Thiers not to attack until the 23rd.
The final bombardment, begun on the afternoon of the
20th, must do its work thoroughly first.

The Commune was making a last desperate attempt to
form a unified resistance. A notice in the *Journal Officiel* of
Wednesday, May 17, summoned the Commune to a sitting
at 2 p.m., very precisely; a call-over would be taken and
published. Much to everyone's surprise, 66 members
appeared, among them 15 of the Minority, despite the
Protest. Of the 14 absentees, one, Beslay, had resigned after
the decree on the destruction of Thiers's house; another
came in late; one had fled; four were in jail; and one,
Emile Clément, was expecting arrest. So large an attendance had not been known since the earliest days.

The Minority had suffered considerable criticism from
their constituents and organisations. The International
had held a consultative meeting on the 17th, summoned
the Minority members who belonged to it—Avrial, Durand,
Franckel, Johannard, Malon, Ostyn, Serrailler, Theisz and
Varlin—to justify themselves, approved their demand for
the publicity of the Commune sessions and the modification

of Article Three subordinating the Commune to the Committee of Public Safety, but invited them to make every effort to maintain the unity of the Commune whilst safeguarding the workers' interests.

The supporters of the Majority wanted, not the return of the Minority, but their arrest. The *Père Duchêne* and Richard's *Salut Public* had been especially violent. Rigault headed a group of the Majority who were for forcibly liquidating all opposition. He arrived at the session, took aside the Delegate for Justice, whispered to him, eyeing the Minority, " The warrants are ready." Protot called Pyat and Delescluze out of the room, asked their opinion. They dared not agree for fear of arousing still greater disorder, and because it was doubtful whether the National Guard, who disliked the Commune sufficiently to approve any opposition to its leaders, would act. The Minority were safe for the moment.

Grousset opened the session with an attack upon the Minority. It was amazing, intolerable that these " latter-day Girondins " should return to their seats after declaring their withdrawal to their districts. It was far better that they should so withdraw than that they should come to the Commune to hinder men of courage and resolution from taking measures demanded by the situation—measures for which the Majority would accept all responsibility. The true motive for the withdrawal was not Article Three, for they had taken part in the election of the second Committee of Public Safety when the article was already in existence, but their failure to obtain representatives on that Committee and on the revised Military Commission. If these members, instead of loyally keeping their word, tried manœuvres that might compromise the Commune, the Majority would know how to treat them.

" If you call us Girondins," replied Franckel, " it is probably because you lie down and get up with the *Moniteur* of '93; that is doubtless the reason which prevents you from seeing the difference between those bourgeois and us, the revolutionary Socialists ! " Vallès maintained that the

Minority had sacrificed its feeling about the election of the second Committee of Public Safety in face of the bombardment of Paris. Arnold and Régère attempted a reconciliation, in vain. Vaillant was sick of these interminable wrangles: he was for neither Majority nor Minority; he blamed the Protest, but was ready to close the incident now that the Minority had returned; and brought in a conciliatory motion. But Grousset, Rigault and Pyat would have no such easy solution: they wanted blood. They carried the Commune, and a motion by Miot that the Majority would forget the conduct of the Minority if they would withdraw their signatures from the Protest was just being carried when Billioray, of the Committee of Public Safety, rushed in, crying: " The powder-magazine in the Avenue Rapp has just been blown up, it's still burning! There is treachery abroad and you go on talking! The traitor who set it on fire has been arrested! " The session broke up in consternation.

The explosion was more terrifying than disastrous. The whole Grenelle quarter suffered, the road strewn with bits of glass and cartridges. A huge column of flame hung in the air. Fragments were carried as far as the Champ de Mars. Half Paris was shaken. Several people had been killed, some 50 hurt; four houses had been smashed. The explosion had threatened the Ministry of War, the Ecole Militaire, the artillery park and bivouacs on the Champ de Mars; but there is little evidence of deliberate arson beyond the alleged discovery in the train between Paris and Versailles of a document incriminating one of the commanders of the magazine, signed Gorbin (possibly Corbin, who had certainly been asked for dynamite by a known conspirator, Charpentier), and another document by one Jarriait, who seems to have tried to take credit for the explosion. It is quite as likely that it was caused by carelessness. But naturally it gave rise to a new conspiracy scare.

This scare increased the demands of the Majority for an intensification of Jacobin revolutionary Terror. At the beginning of the session so rudely interrupted, Urbain had

again brought up the question of the hostages. It was
Urbain who had most strongly supported the sinister
Blanchet, now in jail, when he had raised the question on
April 22. Now, Urbain was under the influence of the *agent-
provocateur*, Barral de Montaud; and a massacre of the hostages would have been extremely useful for Thiers's propaganda, as his whole treatment of the matter amply proves.

At this session, Urbain reported the violation and murder
of an ambulance nurse near Fort Vanves. The report was
signed by a Lieutenant Butin of the 105th Battalion of the
VIIth Legion. The VIIth was Barral de Montaud's and
had already had treacherous dealings with Versailles.
Urbain demanded that five of the hostages should be
solemnly executed inside Paris in the presence of a delegation from all the battalions, and that five more be shot at
the outposts in the presence of the Guards who had wit-
nessed the atrocity. J. B. Clément supported him, in view
of the atrocious treatment of prisoners by the Versaillese.

Rigault, supported by Urbain and Chalain, proposed the
execution of the guilty rather than of hostages chosen at
hazard: he would prefer the guilty to escape rather than
strike down a single innocent. But Rigault's conception of
guilt included not only the accomplices of Versailles, but
also of Bonaparte, retrospectively. Protot disputed the
legality of this. Rigault wished to set up a special revolutionary tribunal like that of Hébert and Chaumette in '93.
But the Commune, brought to its senses by Vaillant, set
aside Urbain's ferocious proposal and simply voted the
immediate execution of the original Law about the Hostages.

Rigault had originally held some idea of exchanging the
hostages for Blanqui as well as to check the Versaillese
shooting of prisoners. Darboy, Archbishop of Paris, his
Grand Vicar, Lagarde, and the magistrate Bonjean,
arrested on April 4, had been held *incommunicado* at Mazas
until the 12th. But Rigault's intimate friend, Gaston da
Costa, had secretly visited Darboy on the 7th to ask him
to use his influence with Thiers to stop the shooting of
prisoners. The real reason for the visit was to sound Darboy

about the exchange, a project upon which the whole Commune did not agree with Rigault. After conversations with Flotte, an old friend of Blanqui, Darboy had approved of the idea and had written to Thiers, adding that " public opinion would perhaps not understand a refusal." But Thiers, even if he wished, could not dare to treat thus openly with the Commune: the Council of Fifteen set by the Assembly to watch him were perfectly willing to sacrifice a Republican magistrate and a cleric who was notoriously Gallican, almost a heretic. A remark of Barthélemy Saint-Hilaire, Thiers's confidant, was reported in Paris: " The hostages ! But we can do nothing about them ! What can we do ? So much the worse for them ! " This alleged remark, however, was reported by Barral de Montaud, the *provocateur* behind Urbain. Thiers simply resorted to his favourite method of dealing with conciliators, and continually put off seeing Lagarde, Darboy's representative.

After April 23, when Urbain had again raised the question in the Commune, various distinguished foreigners took a hand in the negotiations: Washburne, the American Minister; Mgr. Favius Chigi, the Papal Nuncio; Norcott, delegate for the Lord Mayor of London, engaged in distributing a fund raised in London for the relief of the siege victims. A London *Times* correspondent, O'Connel, who was given great facilities by the Commune, was allowed to visit Darboy, and sent back remarkably impartial reports. There was even an attempt to interest the Prussian General von Fabrice. Washburne, the chief foreign negotiator, was curiously lukewarm in his dealings with the Commune, which he still seriously believed to be nothing but a gang of terrorist blackguards.

The whole negotiation was ruined by the curious behaviour of Lagarde. He had promised Darboy faithfully to return to Paris, but, once at Versailles, he stayed on in safety. Darboy at last despaired. But so long as Protot and the Minority had any influence, they were safe enough. In spite of a sensational article in Maroteau's *Montagne* on

April 21—" Dogs will no longer be satisfied with looking at bishops, they will bite them. . . . Not a voice will be raised to curse the day on which Archbishop Darboy is shot. . . . Let the justice of the tribunals begin, said Danton on the day after the September Massacres, and that of the people will end. Ah ! I fear greatly for My Lord Archbishop of Paris ! "—Protot had once more put off Blanchet's insistence by setting up a Jury of Accusation.

When, on April 27, a commission reported upon the Belle Epine massacre, the Commune had merely decreed its publication; but three days later, *Père Duchêne*, most influential of the popular Jacobin papers, had declaimed " his Great Wrath against the citizen members of the Commune who do not avenge the death of National Guards shot at Versailles by applying the Law about the Hostages." After the session of May 17, the Rapp magazine explosion and the increasingly violent Jacobinism within and outside the Commune, carefully manufactured reports of Darboy's execution began to circulate freely at Versailles. Rigault now had plenty of backing in the Commune, Protot almost none; Rigault was now Public Prosecutor, president of the Jury of Accusation, no longer a harmless " tribunal," but representative of " the justice of the people." On May 19 it at last opened its public sessions.

Much has been written about the Commune's reign of terror. It existed in reality only in Rigault's hopes and in the fears of bourgeois who, terrified by the propaganda from Versailles, believed that arrest automatically meant execution. There were, it is true, frequent unjustifiable arrests, but prisoners were often equally unjustifiably released. There were house-searches, requisitions. But the Commune was in a state of war and threatened by conspiracy. Of looting, of beatings such as those inflicted upon Communard prisoners by the citizens of Versailles there is no trace.

Only three persons were executed by the Commune in two months, and these for military offences by local courts martial. On April 13 the Council of War of the XVth

Legion shot a National Guard for murdering his superior officer. Another Council of War, held by Melliet at Bicêtre, shot a Guard, Thibault, for suspected treachery, in the presence of Dereure and Amouroux, officially representing the Commune, which gave its approval at the session of May 12. On May 19, Johannard, Civil Commissioner to General La Cécilia, reported the shooting of a spy. It is possible that Dombrowski shot some peasants on the northern front around April 16, for murdering his men— the evidence is not very clear. But nothing was ever done on the Versaillese scale.

A military arrest on May 19 led to irregular execution. The Dominican Fathers of the Albert-le-Grand school at Arcueil were arrested, not, as usual, for exercising their profession, but on a charge of espionage brought by the military authorities. They had been suspect since the Moulin Saquet disaster, and were now held responsible for a fire in the building occupied by the staff of the 101st Battalion. This arrest had nothing to do with Rigault's police terror.

Towards the end of the Commune's period of power the regime did begin to tighten up. On May 18 the Committee of Public Safety suppressed nine more papers—the *Echo de Paris*, *Indépendance Française*, *Avenir National*, *Patrie*, *Pirate*, *Echo de Ultramar*, *Justice*, *Commune*, even the *Revue de Deux Mondes*. The *Commune* and *Justice* were revolutionary papers, but had gone too far in criticism, and the *Justice* had professional quarrels with Delescluze's *Reveil du Peuple*. The *Commune*, edited by Millière and Rogeard, sympathetic, but not members of the Commune, was staffed by most of Pyat's ex-contributors and had only lately become unsatisfactory. Even the *Père Duchêne* was in danger for a moment, having been too friendly with Rossel. It was decreed that no new paper should appear before the end of the war; chiefly because suppressed papers had a habit of reappearing under a new name. Every article was to be signed by its author. Attacks upon the Republic and the Commune were to be brought before the court martial. The Commune suppressed more than forty papers in all, some of the suppressions not even being notified in the *Journal Officiel*.

Rochefort himself was threatened wtih arrest. Next day, having cut his characteristic hair and beard, he left Paris. But luck was against him: he had fought too long on two fronts. A Versaillese police official picked him up at Meaux, on the German railway. At Saint-Germain, he was handed over to Galliffet; and he arrived in Versailles in a little railway omnibus between two squadrons of cavalry. It was lunch-time. The guests at the Hôtel des Réservoirs thronged into the street, waving their napkins, shouting over and over: " Rochefort ! Rochefort ! "—an ovation of hatred from the same crowd which had so eagerly applauded his sallies against the Empire. The Commune was perhaps Rochefort's final tragic irony, a comedy inverted.

At this last hour, the Commune seems to pull itself together for the final struggle. The demolition of the Vendôme Column was a symbol of common reunion, at once the vindication of the Great Revolution of 1793 and the Social Revolution of 1871. The Jacobin Majority, by the very force of circumstances, by military defeat and the rise of counter-revolution, encouraged by these defeats, moved towards the Central Committee and towards the revolutionary rank and file beneath it: but this movement regarded the National Guards rather as Parisians, heirs of '93, than as workers. The Minority, while continuing to fight this conception, could no longer refuse their loyalty to the founders of the revolution of 1871.

May 18 saw a remarkable number of stern measures in every department, amounting almost to a declaration of a state of emergency. The Committee of Public Safety suppresses nine papers; Vaillant, Delegate for Public Education, orders the complete expulsion of clergy from the schools; Jourde sets up a special supervisory service to check the scandalous maldistribution of the National Guard pay; Parisel threatens the immediate seizure of all inflammable chemicals not voluntarily surrendered; Rigault is preparing the revolutionary tribunal.

Next day the Commune, " whereas in revolutionary days the people, inspired by their instinct for justice and morality, have always proclaimed the maxim, ' Death to thieves ! ' " decreed that all officials and contractors accused of embezzlement should be tried before the court martial, the sole penalty being death. It decreed that no official should draw pay for more than one post at a time. Varlin published a letter, dated May 16, exonerating the Brothers May from all blame with regard to the mismanagement of the Intendance; but Bergeret wrote to Moreau, now at the head of this service, doubting Varlin's qualifications. Delescluze dismissed Combatz, colonel of the VIth Legion, one of the officers Rossel had wanted to shoot, because he had not disarmed the disloyal battalions in his district. The Committee of Public Safety threatened with the court martial any refusal to carry out its orders. The various groups were moving towards each other without surrendering their own authority.

The Central Committee once more reorganised the Federation, chiefly in order that the Military Commission might not attempt to anticipate them, as Rossel had tried to do. On May 19 the Organisation Commission issued its instructions, "Whereas it is in the Federation of the National Guard alone that are to be found the powerful means of revolutionary action and effective control which will give to the decrees of the Commune and the orders of the Delegation for War the sanction which they have hitherto lacked."

The Central Committee was to sit every afternoon at the Ministry of War, and all delegates must attend. But it was important to define the functions of these delegates from the Legion-Councils. The Legion-Councils had been acting almost independently of the Central Committee, especially in their dealings with Rossel. By now, the National Guard was in the absurd position of receiving orders from at least eight different sources, besides those from all sorts of local powers: the Committee of Public Safety, the Delegate for War, the Military Commission, the Civil Commissioners to the Generals; the General Headquarters of the three

Generals; the Central Committee and its specialised branches, often, like the Central Artillery Committee, almost independent; the Legion-Council-Commanders; local commanders.

The Commune had done much by the appointment of a Civil Delegate for War and by various internal agreements to unify the civil and military authorities. It was now essential that the Central Committee be brought into line. The delegates from the Legion-Councils were under no circumstances to issue orders or hinder their execution; their role could be summed up in three words—control, intermediacy, justice. They were to express the desires and complaints of the groups they represented. Chosen for their civic virtues, they were to profit by their moral authority to support the authority of the military commanders. " To see and to report, such are their functions; to be charitable without, however, ceasing to be energetic, such is their duty." They were, therefore, to parallel the Civil Commissioners of the Commune. The whole organisation was thus more centralised, but depended more upon the efficiency of the Central Committee itself, which had now appointed itself as a parallel military Committee of Public Safety.

Both the Federation of the National Guard and the Commune had surrendered their destinies to a directory, and it now remained for the civil and the military directories to unite. It was unfortunately inevitable that this union, the only effective organ for directing the revolution, should not have been worked out at the beginning. But it was only made possible by approaching defeat and the need for united resistance; yet it was the lack of this union which had made that defeat certain. The revolution had been forced upon Paris before the least preparative organisation had been even conceived. When the correct leadership was instituted it was already too late, and it could be correct only by contradicting the character of the revolution, by regressing to an anachronistic imitation. That the combination failed at the test because it had been created too late, being possible only when its usefulness had passed, was due precisely to the fact that it was a mere imitation of an irrelevance. The remorseless logic of revolution had involved it in a contradiction from which there was no issue but self-destruction.

To seal the union of the two directories, the Central Committee made what it called " a sort of public pact " with the Committee of Public Safety, signed by the whole Military Commission and the forty members of the fifteen Administrative Commissions set up at the Ministry of War to parallel the Civil Commissioners to the army. " The Central Committee which has borne the banner of the Communal Revolution has neither changed nor degenerated. It is to-day what it was yesterday: the defender born of the Commune, the force placed in its hands, the armed enemy of civil war, the sentinel set by the People over the rights it has won. In the name, then, of the Commune and the Central Committee who are signing this pact of good faith, let suspicions and irresponsible slanders vanish, let hearts beat high, hands be armed, and let the great social cause for which we are all fighting triumph in union and fraternity ! "

The first result of this new union of civil power and executive was the functioning of revolutionary justice. All three judicial bodies of the Commune began to work almost simultaneously: the Court Martial, the Jury of Accusation, the Commune itself as High Court.

The court martial, of which Cluseret had made Rossel first president, had hitherto done little. The Commune had hindered Rossel, notably in the affair of Mégy and the abandonment of Fort Issy.

Rossel's successor, Emile Gois, was a very different person, a violent and audacious man whose very ape-like appearance perfectly represented the terrified bourgeois's idea of a member of a revolutionary tribunal. One of the earliest Blanquists, he had been deported to Lambessa in 1851, and had returned fiercer than he went. It was at his lodgings that were made the daggers used in the Blanquist attempt on the Villette fire-station in August 1870.

He conducted the trials with a high hand. The first was tumultuous. On May 15 two officers of the 115th Battalion, Daviot and Vanostal, were accused of deserting their post at Issy village and with threatening their superior officers with death in order to force the Paris gates in their flight. There were political implications: the trial was aimed at Brunel—a report by Goullé, one of the judges, accusing him of responsibility by handing over the command to an unworthy officer when he went to Delescluze's Council of War in Paris. This was also to be linked up with Rossel's " treachery " in the matter of Fort Issy. The Court was filled with men of the 115th, who kept interrupting and shouting their sympathy for the accused. At the second sitting, on May 17, Gois threatened to punish any inter-rupter on the spot. One of the Guards who applauded a passage in the evidence was arrested, condemned to a year's imprisonment and carried off without any hearing. Daviot got fifteen years' hard labour, Vanostal ten, and the 115th was dissolved. There had not been much damning evidence.

The Jury of Accusation, set up to decide the fate of the hostages on April 5 and decreed again on April 22, had been chosen by lot only on May 6. It consisted of eighty delegates from the National Guard; and it is noticeable that none came from the bourgeois VIIth and VIIIth districts, one each only from the bourgeois VIth, IXth and XVIth, while twelve came from the revolutionary XXth, ten from the XIth and nine from the Vth. The distribution was justified by the population as shown at the elections of April 16, but it held out poor chances for the hostages.

After the appointment, nothing further was done for ten days. Finally, after the session of May 17, the Commune was forced to act, and to act in such a hurry that serious questions of law and procedure had not been settled before the opening.

The Commission for Justice itself was in chaos. At the Commune session of May 19, Langevin offered his resigna-tion, since, of the five members, Gambon had abandoned it for the Committee of Public Safety, two more members had not appeared to take up their posts, and Clémence refused to go on holding what was practically a sinecure. Urbain was clamorous that sentence be passed by the jury. Protot tried to uphold against Rigault the provision of the decree that " the accused declared guilty will be retained as hostages of the People of Paris," while Rigault demanded their execution. The Commune decided nothing: the fate of the accused was still to depend upon events. It was not at all clear whether the hostages were to be executed as traitorous criminals or in reprisal for Versaillese atrocities. No magistrates were appointed by the Commission for Justice: the Public Prosecutor was Rigault, and the jury soldiers of the revolution. It was to be, not " the justice of the tribunals," but " the justice of the People," as Danton had demanded nearly a century before.

Rigault divided the hostages into two categories: in the first, Darboy and other priests, Bonjean, Chaudey, accused of ordering the shooting on January 22, Chevriaux, commander of the Hôtel de Ville on October 31, Jecker, the Swiss financier of the Mexican expedition of 1864; in the second, police officers, municipal guards, gendarmes, captured on March 18. He decided to take the second lot first to try his strength and influence over the jury.

The sitting opened at eleven o'clock on the morning of Friday, May 19. The trial was semi-public: some journalists had been admitted by special cards from the Committee of Public Safety and the Delegation for Justice. The ushers were unarmed National Guards. The jury wore uniform. Rigault and his colleagues appeared on the Bench dressed in correct black relieved by the broad scarlet scarf. The gloomy room was dominated by a vast crucifix, forgotten in the hurry.

Rigault opened the " grand revolutionary assizes." He was disappointing, lacked the fire and violent legalism of his heroes and predecessors, Chaumette and Fouquier-Tinville. The usual denunciation of Versailles and praise of the Commune's resistance. It was for the jury to help in this great work by wiping out internal treason. " Unfortunately, your work has begun too late, but, as the proverb runs, better late than never." The real criminals, he remarked, were to be tried later; there was no suggestion that these policemen were themselves guilty of treason. It was for the jury to decide merely whether they should be detained as hostages; if so, they would be handed over to " administrative action." The audience were delighted, applauded; and the session was suspended to cries of " Long live the Commune ! "

At the next audience, that afternoon, Rigault had decided, in order to save time, to take simultaneously the gendarmes and Municipal Guards in one court, the constabulary in another. There were 84 accused. Rigault took one court, Breuillé of the Ex-Prefecture the other.

In Rigault's court were chiefly the gendarmes captured on March 18. He took them in three groups, four, five, five. His attack was so vehement that the wretched men were swept off their feet. They had no defender, could make no defence of their own to such purely hypothetical questions as, " Would you have fired on the people on March 18 ? ";
" What would you have done in December 1851 ? "
Rigault was not arraigning the wretches themselves, but the whole system they represented. They were to be demolished, like the Vendôme Column, for the sins of the system. " These men have been part of the Paris Police whom our backs know even better than our minds. . . . It is for this reason that we ask you to declare these men hostages. The facts are evident, established, there is no defence to be heard."

Only one question was put to the jury: " Are these men to be inscribed on the list of the hostages ? " By the decree of April 22, a majority of 8 votes in 12 was required for a verdict of guilty. Of the 14 accused, 12 were convicted, one was convicted by 7 to 5 and was acquitted, one was acquitted outright. The trial had taken just over three hours. It was decided that the crucifix was to be replaced by a bust of the Republic before the next session.

Breuillé took the accused singly, treated them much less severely. All except one were detained. Breuillé ordered the immediate release of the " non-hostage."

The next session, taken by Huguenot, one of Rigault's colleagues, was very dull. The room was almost empty: Rigault was not performing; people had lost interest in these unimportant preliminaries. The session was an hour late in beginning. It was a disorderly and futile business. More gendarmes. Members of the jury kept interrupting. Huguenot seemed to be trying to prove that the accused were Bonapartists—hardly a relevant charge. Of 19 accused, 13 were detained. Huguenot, however, did not release the six " non-hostages," but wrote to the Director of Mazas Prison to hold them for the duration of the war.

The *Journal Officiel* of May 20 summoned the jury again for the following Monday and Tuesday. It was rumoured that Darboy would be taken on the Tuesday or Wednesday. Several eminent lawyers were preparing his defence, hoping that they would be heard. Rigault was making out his case against Chaudey, his particular enemy, alleged murderer of Sapia on January 22. But the Jury of Accusation never had the opportunity to meet officially again.

The Revolutionary Government had from the start put its own members on trial, without reference to any other jurisdiction. The Central Committee had, during its period of office, tried some of its members, acquitting Chouteau and Billioray, condemning Henry, du Bisson, d'Abin and Wilfrid de Fonvielle. The Commune had arrested Assi, on April 2, for giving *Paris Journal* a report of its secret debates, and Bergeret, on April 6, for seditious behaviour at Headquarters. Assi had been easily acquitted by a secret session on April 12, and Bergeret, after an investigation by Protot, Ranvier and Beslay, on April 22.

The arrest of Cluseret, on April 30, raised more complex problems, which were now to be discussed. It had been the occasion for settling a definite mode of procedure. The Majority and Minority were then coming to grips on the question of the Committee of Public Safety. The Minority realised their danger, and even some of the Majority were not too easy. It was essential that they be not handed over to Rigault without some check by the Commune. While Cluseret was waiting outside the room to be taken to Mazas, the Commune had passed one of its few unanimous resolutions: on a motion by Vésinier, whose own conduct was not above suspicion, they voted that members of the Commune could be tried by the Commune alone.

Four members were arrested at various times: Blanchet, alias Pourille, Emile Clément, Allix, Brunel. Blanchet and Clément, accused of being former police agents, were never tried; Brunel, arrested for the Issy village affair, a military charge, at his own request, on Rossel's model, in order to clear himself, was not heard either. Allix, arrested on May 10, by Rigault, for odd antics in the VIIIth district, which he represented, was released by the Commune next day, in Rigault's absence; but, since he continued his irresponsible behaviour, was re-arrested, Rigault accusing him of " rashness, crime or lunacy "; the Commune had adopted the last explanation, had not tried him but interned him in an asylum.

Cluseret had not been heard, although it had been decided that prisoners should be questioned within twenty-four hours. Gambon brought up the case on May 6. Pindy, charged with the investigation, had done nothing. A new commission was appointed: Vermorel, Vallès and Miot, two Minority members and the most energetic member of the Majority.

Cluseret was allowed some liberty. He left Mazas and lived on parole at the Hôtel de Ville. On the day he left, the 9th, he was allowed to visit Issy, with Vésinier, and give Brunel his advice about the military situation; which is perhaps the reason that Brunel afterwards fell under suspicion. It was the moment of Rossel's fall, and, although Rossel himself had intervened in favour of his former chief, it is possible that the Commune was thinking of restoring Cluseret as a move against the Central Committee's intention of making Rossel Dictator. Cluseret himself had made no secret that he was still quite ready to let bygones be bygones. Or it may simply have been that the Commune was looking round in desperation for an efficient military leader. That problem was solved by the appointment of Delescluze and the new *rapprochement* of the Commune and the Central Committee.

The Commune heard the commission's report at its last session, on the 1st Prairial of the Year 79 (May 21). Vermorel and Vallès were in favour of releasing Cluseret, not because they approved of him personally, but because there seemed no adequate case proved against him. But it was Miot, enemy of the whole Military Commission, who drew up the charges, thirteen of them; and a very mixed and irrelevant lot they were. A proposal made to him, in 1848, by Ledru-Rollin, to rally to the House of Orléans, a charge laid by Delescluze, Ledru-Rollin's Commissioner for the North, was shown to have no foundation. Charges about his activities with the Fenians in New York, with the Separatist movement in Savoy, in 1864, at Lyons and Marseilles, in 1870, were all easily answered. An accusation of bribery was probably due to a misunderstanding of the American language: an American had told Cluseret that " he was worth a million," a slang beyond Miot's linguistic capacities. Cluseret just smiled at this charge.

There was really no serious accusation except that of having neglected Fort Issy; and the whole military administration was equally to blame. But Miot, without collecting much tangible evidence or even calling the Military Commission, decided to present his report. Cluseret, too, had written to the Commune demanding to be heard in his own defence: " As a member of the Commune, I have a right to my seat. As a son of Paris, I have the right to defend my native city. As a man, I have a right to justice. Do not refuse me. What use am I here ? And above all, be well persuaded that I am one of those who think that there is as much glory in obeying as in commanding when the people commands."

For the session which was to hear Cluseret a concession

had been made to the Minority. Vallès, one of the commissioners and known to be favourable to Cluseret, was
elected President, with Courbet as Assessor. " Period of
lassitude," says Lissagaray: rather, period of attempted
reconciliation in face of imminent danger. The trial had
collected a packed house. The Minority had come in full
force; of the Majority, Cluseret's fiercest opponent,
Delescluze, was detained at the Ministry of War on Cluseret's own business. Outside, the guns roared unceasingly,
ever closer.

The session got under way slowly. Everyone was tense
with expectation of the great affair. There were the usual
disputes and complaints: about the reports of the sessions,
the Rapp explosion, Brunel's detention. Arnould tactlessly
brought up again the subject of the Minority Protest, and
nearly raised a storm by the contemptuous terms in which
he announced that he had come back to take his seat only
on the orders of his electors in the IVth district. Avrial
pointed out, impatiently, that they had come to try
Cluseret, not to quarrel about trifles.

But there was a serious affair before the great event.
Despite the " public pact " between the Committee of
Public Safety and the Central Committee, one of the
Central Committee's members, Grêlier, an intriguing
little man who had been turned out of office early in its
regime, had inserted a notice in the *Journal Officiel* on his
own initiative, declaring that " the inhabitants of Paris are
invited to return to their residences within 48 hours, after
which period their rent-titles in the *Grand Livre* will be
burnt." Langevin furiously wanted to know if the Committee of Public Safety had given the Central Committee
the right to take the place of the Commune. Jourde,
remarking that expenses were rising—1,800,000 francs the
previous day, 4,500,000 in the last ten days—demanded
immediate repudiation of the note. Billioray believed that
there was an actual conspiracy afoot to damage the
Commune's finances: thus, a few days ago, there had been
an attempt to close the Bourse without orders from the

Commune or Committee of Public Safety. The incident threatened to drag on. Varlin brought them back to the business in hand—Cluseret. Ubiquitous and indispensable in Paris, he had come especially for the trial; it should be taken at once. Again there was a row. Melliet was furious that the Minority should try to impose its wishes upon the Commune. Varlin replied, no less heatedly, that the Minority equally refused to be at the mercy of the Majority. Vallès, as President, closed the incident by putting to the vote the question whether Cluseret was to be heard immediately. It was carried.

Miot simply read out a statement of the questions put to Cluseret and his answers, without drawing any conclusions. Vermorel and Vallès took the opportunity of protesting. Miot could only say that he had had no time to draw conclusions: his report was based only on notes. The Commune was thoroughly dissatisfied. Lefrançais demanded that Cluseret be heard: " It was already quite bad enough that they should have to sit through so incoherent a report."

Pyat introduced a red herring. Unable to accuse Cluseret plausibly, he picked upon the Executive Commission which had arrested him. Five members of the former Commission, Jourde, Vaillant, Grousset, Franckel and Andrieu, defended themselves, asking why Miot had not collected his evidence earlier: Delescluze and the Commune had almost unanimously approved their action, as had the first Committee of Public Safety, including, of course, Pyat. Jourde wondered what personal grudge Pyat had against the Executive Commission: his attack was obviously not inspired by dissatisfaction with Miot's report.

Cluseret was then allowed to defend himself. In a few contemptuous words he disposed of the charges. Then attacked the Commune: the Neuilly armistice had given the Versaillese the chance to concentrate on the southern front; the suppression of the court martial had destroyed all discipline. The Commune listened in silence. Occasionally there was applause. Cluseret retired while the Commune considered their verdict.

It was left to Vermorel to sum up in his favour: " Let him come back to us, either in the Commune or in the defence. Perhaps he is a bad Delegate for War, but undoubtedly he is a good general, a man of really remarkable energy and coolness." The ease with which the Commune arrested a military leader when he seemed harmful was one of the best signs of its strength.

He was going on to describe Cluseret's conduct at Issy, when Billioray, the only member of the Committee of Public Safety permanently sitting, came in, very pale. He sat down, listened to Vermorel for a moment. Suddenly, he sprang up: " Finish ! Finish ! I have a communication of the greatest importance, for which I demand a secret session ! "

The doors were shut. Billioray read from a paper that trembled slightly in his hand: " Dombrowski to Ministry of War and Committee of Public Safety. The Versaillese have entered by the Saint-Cloud Gate. I am taking steps to repulse them. If you can, send me reinforcements. I answer for everything." It was just seven o'clock.

There was a clamour of pell-mell questions. Billioray answered that the Committee of Public Safety was on the watch. They returned to the session, hurried through the rest of the debate. Were eager to finish, to get to the work which awaited them, some to die. Twenty-eight favoured Cluseret's immediate release. Seven were against it: Vaillant, Arnold, Trinquet, Clovis Dupont, who wanted " the detention of the accused until the finish of the present military events," two members of the second Executive Commission and Miot. Cluseret made the usual little speech of thanks, declaring that he bore no malice. It all ended with the reading of an appropriate enough letter from Melliet: " Since Cluseret has not been shot already, it is useless to keep him in prison, for imprisonment has been nothing but a precautionary measure."

The last session of the Commune broke up at eight o'clock on this 1st of Prairial of the Year 79. It left nothing behind at the Hôtel de Ville, no permanent committee, no central direction for the coming struggle. Paris was abandoned to its sections, its barricades. The Commune, as Commune, was over: but Paris remained.

Delescluze sat in the Ministry of War. The Central Committee had brought Dombrowski's despatch to him. The old Jacobin was calm. He believed in the barricades. But there were no barricades. Rossel's strategic line had not even been begun. A few at the Bineau and Asnières Gates and on the Boulevard d'Italie, two redoubts on the Place de la Concorde and in the rue Castiglione, a trench in the rue Royale and another at the Trocadéro, a useless ditch on the Tuileries Terrace: that was all. But Delescluze, sure of his own death, was sure of Paris.

The commander of the Point-du-Jour sector came to deny Dombrowski's report. Delescluze believed what he wanted to believe, without corroboration. As the Commune was breaking up at the Hôtel de Ville, Delescluze published a notice, full of reticences: " The observation-post on the Arc de Triomphe denies the entry of the Versaillese, at least it sees nothing resembling it. Commander Renaud of that section has just left my office, and declares that there has only been a panic and that the Auteuil Gate has not been forced; that if some of the Versaillese have presented themselves, they have been repulsed."

Officers began to flock in for orders. The General Staff refused to allow the tocsin to be rung for fear of alarming the people. But, spontaneously, drums began to beat in the streets, trumpets sounded. At the Ministry of War, members of the Commune straddled chairs, poring over a great map of Paris. Delescluze shut himself up in the next room to compose a proclamation. There could be no further doubt: the Versaillese were really in Paris.

In the streets outside, life went on as usual. The Parisians cared nothing for the approaching end, for they felt that they could do nothing now to prevent it. This Sunday, the theatres were more packed than ever. At the Gymnase, it was gala night, the *première* of Dumanoir's *Les Femmes Terribles*, with Desclée; the box-office took 2,355 francs.

Assi sat with other members of the Commune in the Imperial box. A pallid messenger whispered to them during the second interval. They hurried out.

That afternoon, the Parisians had attended a grand concert in the Tuileries Gardens. It was brilliant with staff uniforms and spring dresses. Three hundred yards away, Versaillese shells burst unheeded at the bottom of the Champs-Elysées. The Communard gunboats, driven from the Point-du-Jour, lay, much admired, beside the Place de la Concorde. The Commune had opened the fishing season, and the quays were dotted with anglers. That was far more important than the war. Even on May 27, there were a dozen between the Pont Royal and the Pont de la Concorde, with all Paris burning at their backs; and the Communard Director of the Hôtel-Dieu Hospital, with the Versaillese hot on his trail, was found by his friends calmly fishing opposite the blazing Hôtel de Ville.

At the end of the concert, a staff officer mounted the stage: " Citizens," he cried, " M. Thiers promised to enter Paris yesterday. M. Thiers has not entered. He will not enter. I invite you to our second concert on behalf of the widows and orphans at this same place next Sunday."

The Versaillese had been in Paris for an hour.

# CHAPTER IX

# THE BATTLE OF PARIS

" Enough of militarism ! . . . Make way for the People, the fighters, the bare arms ! The hour of revolutionary warfare has struck ! "

CHARLES DELESCLUZE : *Proclamation, May 21, 1871*

WHILE THE COMMUNE MET for the last time at the Hôtel de Ville, and Paris listened to the drums and trumpets of the Commune's last concert, the spies Veysset and Hutzinger, in the neutral zone at Saint-Ouen, discussed opening a gate before the great offensive planned for the 23rd. Veysset accompanied Hutzinger back to the outposts. But for once he had overreached himself. Both were arrested : Hutzinger, jailed at Cherche-Midi, managed to escape ; but Veysset, compromised by papers and a sum of 20,000 francs found upon him, was taken to the Dépôt, confessed, and was kept for the special attentions of Ferré.

Meanwhile, an amateur traitor was at work. The Versaillese troops, still protected by the intense bombardment, were resting in their trenches. Suddenly, at three o'clock, a man was seen to wave a handkerchief from a bastion near the Porte de Saint-Cloud. He was shouting ; but all that they could make out was the one word : " Come ! " They hesitated : twice they had been deceived. At last a naval officer went forward, investigated, found the invitation genuine : a whole section of the walls was abandoned. The traitor, working entirely on his own, was one Ducatel, a civil engineer. The officer returned, reported to Douay, who ordered the batteries to cease fire. In small detachments, the Versaillese troops filed into Paris.

Thiers was watching, with MacMahon and Ladmirault,

from Mont-Valérien. He had summoned Douay to a Council of War. A staff officer rode up, carrying Douay's apologies for his absence: he was just entering Paris. In confirmation, Montretout suddenly ceased fire. MacMahon bent over the telescope; suddenly cried out: " We are repulsed ! " But Krantz, Thiers's military secretary, turning his glass upon Paris, reassured them: the troops were not fleeing, but simply carrying out a manœuvre inexplicable at that distance. A detachment had entered the Porte de Saint-Cloud, moved along inside the walls, and opened the other gates to the main body.

Thiers hastily ordered MacMahon to take over Douay's and Ladmirault's divisions and push on cautiously. Then he hurried back to Versailles to send on Clinchant and Vinoy's reserve and to order Cissey to occupy the Left Bank of the Seine. With Krantz and Ranson, the Military Quartermaster, he spent the evening supervising the provision supply and in drawing up a deliberately false proclamation for the provincial prefects: " The Porte de Saint-Cloud has just fallen under the fire of our guns. General Douay has thrown his troops into Paris." A short and frugal dinner with his family and some intimate friends, a shorter sleep, and, at two in the morning, Thiers was up again, and in Paris by three.

The Communards at Passy had been taken completely by surprise. Dombrowski had been away from his headquarters at the Château de la Muette for some hours, and got back only about four o'clock. He heard the news with his habitual calm, wrote to the Ministry of War and Committee of Public Safety, sent a battalion of volunteers to hold the Porte d'Auteuil.

The volunteers, fighting desperately, checked the Versaillese for a moment, held the line of the Ceinture railway, raised barricades. The National Guard was rousing all over Passy, running to and fro in the shattered streets, without aim or order. The quarter was in an uproar; but so confused were the Guards that the Versaillese had little trouble in dispersing them.

By nightfall, 70,000 men were moving in Paris, unknown to the bulk of the population. By nine o'clock, there were two columns inside the walls, one making slowly to the right, between the walls and the Ceinture railway, invading the south-west of Auteuil, and, at one in the morning, capturing the Trocadéro with hardly a struggle. The other column, turning left, lodged itself right in the centre of Passy. All this without any attempt at resistance, almost in silence.

Assi came cantering down to seek confirmation of the news whispered to him as he sat in the Imperial box. At eleven o'clock, he was riding down the unlit and apparently deserted rue Beethoven. He noticed a number of figures huddled along the walls in curious postures, and more than once his horse slipped in pools of what seemed to be blood. Suddenly, figures rushed from the shadows, surrounded and seized him: they were Versaillese. The other shapes had been dead National Guards.

The volunteers held out on the railway line until midnight. Then were forced back to La Muette. Clinchant followed them, occupied the Auteuil and Passy gates and the Château de la Muette, Dombrowski's headquarters, after a brief tussle. By half past one, the survivors, threatened from the Trocadéro, had retreated to the Champs-Elysées.

On the Left Bank of the Seine, Cissey advanced to the walls outside the Sèvres and Versailles gates, neglecting for the moment the uncaptured Communard forts outside the walls, built bridges across the moat and entered without opposition.

By three o'clock in the morning of May 22, the Passy, Auteuil, Saint-Cloud, Sèvres and Versailles gates had been opened; almost the whole of the XVth and XVIth districts were in Versaillese hands; some 1,500 National Guards had surrendered without striking a blow, taken utterly by surprise.

MacMahon came to the Trocadéro, established his headquarters there. Shortly afterwards, Thiers arrived, beaming. They held a Council of War while the troops rested on their arms, eating their iron ration: there had been no time to bring more.

The invasion had proceeded with suspicious ease: with one audacious thrust they could have reached the heart of Paris. But they were afraid of the fortresses in the rue de Rivoli and the Place Vendôme; it was rumoured that the sewers, the catacombs and the vaults beneath the Panthéon had been mined; it was essential not to fatigue the troops, to allow supplies to come up; and even the embittered veterans returned from the Prussian prisons could not yet be entirely depended upon to resist the contagion of Paris disorder. Thiers therefore decided to go slowly, to take the barricades by turning movements rather than by direct assault.

Delescluze sat writing all night at the Hôtel de Ville. The Committee of Public Safety, except Billioray, met and discussed and discussed; on the whole, they were optimistic. But at two o'clock in the morning, Dombrowski arrived, badly shaken by a blow in the chest from a spent bullet, and confirmed the terrible news. The Committee, recalling the Veysset incident, were insultingly surprised at the ease of the invasion. Dombrowski, taking the suggestion as a direct accusation, was horrified: " What ! The Committee of Public Safety takes me for a traitor ! My life belongs to the Commune ! "

Delescluze came out of his room, gaunt and haggard, with his proclamation—a fatal proclamation which was soon to be on the walls, on too many walls, says Lissagaray. It was the abdication of all discipline, an ill-timed declaration of faith in Jacobin " spontaneity ":

" Enough of militarism, no more staff officers bespangled and gilded ! Make way for the people, the fighters, the bare arms ! The hour of revolutionary warfare has struck ! The people knows nothing of scientific manœuvres, but when it has a musket in its hand, paving-stones under its feet, it fears not all the strategists of the monarchist schools. To arms ! Citizens, to arms ! It is a choice now, as you know, between conquering and falling into the merciless hands of the reactionaries and clericals of Versailles, of those scoundrels who deliberately delivered up France to the Prussians and are making us pay the ransom of their treachery ! If you wish that the generous blood which has flowed like water this last week be not infertile, if you wish to live in a free and equal France, if you wish to spare your children your sufferings and your misery, you will rise as one man and, faced with your formidable resistance, the enemy who flatters himself that he may once more submit you to his yoke will win no more than the shame of the vain crimes with which he has befouled himself for the past two months. Citizens, your representatives will fight beside you and die beside you if need be. But in the name of this glorious France, mother of all popular revolutions, eternal home of those ideals of justice and solidarity which must and will be the laws of the world, march against the enemy ; and let your revolutionary energy show them that Paris may be sold but Paris cannot yield nor be conquered. The Commune trusts in you, trust in the Commune ! "

The proclamation, finally demolishing the military conceptions of Cluseret and Rossel, was inevitable ; but it was inevitably ruinous. When the military executive itself proclaimed the necessity of disobeying officers, it was impossible that its orders should be carried out. The union between the civil and military authorities became illusory.

Dawn broke warm and sparkling. Three or four thousand National Guards were afoot in response to the tocsin and drums. But hundreds were evacuating Passy and Grenelle. The fall of the Trocadéro had started a panic.

In spite of the efforts of the VIIIth Legion, the fugitives broke through back to the centre of Paris. Here, however, they pulled themselves together, and set to building barricades in the Faubourg Saint-Honoré opposite the British Embassy, in the Place Saint-Augustin at the corners of the converging streets, and all over the VIIIth district. Brunel, released from Mazas the night before, fortified the Tuileries, bringing up artillery. More guns were brought to the great barricades in the rue Saint-Florentin and the rue Royale. At five in the morning, the General Staff evacuated the Ministry of War, now too close to the fighting area, but neglected to take with them the compromising papers deposited there. The Military Commission came to sit at the Hôtel de Ville.

The Versaillese advance got under way again at dawn. All morning the troops flowed eastward, occupying a district which had never been loyal to the Commune. Paris was held in two great tentacles gradually closing upon the centre, the Hôtel de Ville with its two great outworks at the Tuileries and the Place Vendôme. Douay and Vinoy, the right tentacle, pushed straight forward upon the Etoile, surrounding the gunners of the Porte Maillot, who fled precipitately north-east into the Batignolles, almost capturing the guns which were to have been hoisted up to the battery on the Arc de Triomphe, and moving on down the Champs-Elysées to the Palace of Industry, occupying it, the Elysée Palace and the Pépinière barracks with ease, and spreading out on the deserted Place de la Concorde. Suddenly, a withering fire from the Tuileries Terrace checked them, and they scuttled back to the Palace of Industry with heavy losses. It was the first real engagement.

Simultaneously, Clinchant and Ladmirault, working round the walls to the north from the Asnières gate to the Saint-Lazare railway-station, occupied the Ternes and took in the rear the Federals at Neuilly, Levallois and Saint-Ouen. Many were captured; the survivors, escaping into the Batignolles with the first news of the enemy invasion, filled the quarter with panic rumours of treachery.

The Parc Monceau was lost by a costly mistake: a battalion of engineers from the Batignolles, in their red trousers, were engaging Clinchant's advance guard when the local National Guards, mistaking their uniform, opened a devastating fire and drove them from the park.

The Versaillese pushed on towards the Batignolles, the advance post of the great Montmartre fortress. But Montmartre had not fired a shot. The battery, neglected since March 18, and entrusted for some time to the treacherous Raoul du Bisson, had been utterly disorganised. La Cécilia, arriving there at nine that morning, sent in a gloomy report to the Hôtel de Ville, asking for reinforcements and munitions; but nothing came. The Guards were busy fortifying their own quarters, supposing that the other quarters would do the same sufficiently well. In vain Malon and Jaclard in the Batignolles and La Cécilia, joined now by Cluseret, at Montmartre, begged each other for support. The Guards would not leave their districts, wandered about the streets, chatting in groups, cleaning their rifles, building amateurish barricades, waiting stolidly for " them " to come.

In the south, the other tentacle was gradually closing towards the right. At dawn, Langourian advanced upon the Champ de Mars, set the huts on fire and captured their few defenders. Working parallel to Vinoy on the other bank of the Seine, he captured the Ecole Militaire, the Invalides, the Ministry of Foreign Affairs, the Corps Législatif.

But now he had to fight. The VIIth rose. Barricades sprang up in all the streets around. The quiet ways of the Faubourg Saint-Germain rang with the clatter of arms, shots, shouts, with the " Lend a hand for the Republic, Citizen," of the barricaders.

On Langourian's right, Cissey marched down the rue de Vaugirard and occupied the Montparnasse railway station. Here the fighting was hot. A worker sat calmly in a newspaper-kiosk long after his comrades had retreated, deliberately loading and firing into the station, walking as deliberately away after he ran out of ammunition. The defenders of the station fell back and put up a barricade in the rue de Rennes, under heavy fire. On the extreme right, the Versaillese took the Vanves gate and cleared the line of the Ouest railway.

It was noon. The Versaillese army halted for the day. It

was necessary to consolidate their immense, their too-easy advance. But they were safe enough: the districts were almost entirely bourgeois, hostile or lukewarm to the Commune. Few Parisians outside the National Guard had yet taken up arms: they were barricading their own districts. The " hour of revolutionary warfare " had not yet sounded. But already the Versaillese had begun shooting prisoners: in the rue de Ranelagh, at La Muette, the Parc Monceau, the Ecole Militaire, the Champs-Elysées, the Montparnasse station. These were, however, all National Guards.

At the end of this preparatory offensive phase of the battle, the Versaillese held the whole western section of Paris. The Communard line of defence now ran through the Batignolles, from La Fourche to the Place de Clinchy and the rue Lévis, with two main fortified positions at La Fourche and the Place de Clinchy defending Montmartre. It continued down the Boulevard Malesherbes, with a strong barricade at the rue Bossy d'Anglas, then along the western façade of the Tuileries and across the Seine, with a chain of barricades blocking all the streets leading to the Invalides as far as the rue de Varennes; then bent back eastwards to the Croix-Rouge square, continued up the rue du Vieux-Colombier to the rue de Rennes and ended in a tangle of small barricades cutting off the lost Montparnasse station. The Place Saint-Pierre de Montrouge was fortified very strongly against attack from outside the walls through the Porte d'Orléans and from the north-east through Montparnasse Cemetery. But, beyond the great fortresses in the centre and another which was hastily building farther east in the Place du Château d'Eau (now de la République), the key to Belleville and Ménilmontant, there was no regular military line of defence. And, after Delescluze's proclamation, there was no more hope of military organisation.

The Commune as an official body had dissolved. On Monday morning, however, twenty members met at the Hôtel de Ville. Pyat was there, more Pyatesque than ever:

" Well, my friends, our last hour has come. Oh, as for me, what does it matter ? My hair is white, my career is over. What ending more glorious could I hope than on the barricades ? But when I see around me so many fair young heads, I tremble for the future of the Revolution ! " He insisted on a roll-call of those present; then, having assured his little place in history, vanished, was seen on no barricade, and reappeared only in exile.

The previous evening, some fifteen of the extremer Majority, mostly Blanquists, had met at the Ex-Prefecture. Rigault, Ferré and Trinquet had proposed to blow up all the bridges and hold out on the Cité island till the last gasp. The hostages should be transferred with them and die with the revolution. Trinquet now brought this scheme forward; but this last session of the Commune preferred to decide that the people's representatives should retire to their districts and direct the fighting there. If compelled, the Commune would retreat eastwards, making a stand first at the *mairie* of the XIth, then at that of the XXth.

In the next room, Rigault sat with two documents he had long desired. One, signed by Ranvier, Eudes and Gambon, ordered the immediate transfer of all the important hostages, including Darboy, Bonjean and the priests, to the condemned cells at the Roquette prison. The other, signed by Delescluze and Billioray, charged Citizen Rigault and Citizen Ranvier to carry out the Commune's Decree about the hostages. Rigault went off immediately to find what hostages there were in the other prisons besides the fifty-four at Mazas. The transfer from Mazas he entrusted to his young assistant, Gaston da Costa.

At a meeting in the afternoon the Central Committee once more tried to assert its superiority and independence. The Committee of Public Safety had just issued another proclamation to stir up an enthusiasm which had no need of big words to excite it: " To ARMS ! Let every street be unpaved; firstly, because the enemy's shells, falling on earth, are less dangerous; secondly, because these paving-stones, a new means of defence, should be piled up on the balconies of the upper floors of the houses." It was not very inspiring: but the Central Committee could do no better. And Delescluze sat alone, signing order after order that were never delivered, orders obedience to which he himself had forbidden.

A delegation from the Liberal-Democratic Congress of Lyons came in to offer to try to avert the sack of Paris. The Commune was sceptical, cold. The evening before, the delegation had been politely ushered out by Thiers, who had then telegraphed to Favre: " I have just returned from Paris, where I have seen some very terrible sights; come, my friend, and share our satisfaction." At this moment, he was addressing the Assembly amid frantic applause. The cause of Justice, Order, Humanity, Civilisation had triumphed. The expiation would be complete; but in the name of the Law, by law, lawfully. The Assembly cheered him to the echo, unanimously voted that this new Cavaignac " had deserved well of his country," and went off to watch the agony of Paris from the Terrace at Saint-Germain.

In the midday pause, the shootings had begun again, on both sides. Sixteen National Guards, captured in the rue du Bac, had been summarily shot in the Babylone barracks. There had been a shifty affair in this same rue du Bac before it fell. A party of National Guards, wearing the conspiratorial tricolour armlet and headed by the conspirators Vrignault and Durouchoux, had run into Sicard and some of his men. There was a scuffle, Durouchoux fell dead, the others vanished. Treachery was already afoot, suspicion commoner than the fact. Early in the afternoon, a furious crowd brought to the Tuileries, where Bergeret, driven from the Corps Législatif, had installed himself, a chemist called Koch: he had, it seemed, protested against some urchins taking away the supports of a scaffolding to make a barricade; consequently, he had traitorously hindered the work. The charge was absurd, and Delescluze, informed of it, had actually signed an order for his release; but it came too late. Three other persons, brought to the

Tuileries on similar charges, were taken to the Hôtel de Ville, questioned by Ranvier, sent back without a decision, and, after a show of court martial, taken out and shot. Bergeret watched from a balcony, waving his *képi* and shouting, " So perish our Versaillese foes ! " It was senseless enough.

In the afternoon, Cissey pushed on from the Invalides, but was driven back again by the explosion of the stables at the Staff School. Two Communard guns enfiladed the rue de l'Université. Four gunboats bombarded the Trocadéro from beneath the Pont-Royal. The fighting in the VIIIth district and the Batignolles had quieted to desultory sniping. The Faubourg Saint-Germain was holding out well. The Montparnasse station was swept by the Communard artillery. In the VIIIth, the Versaillese turned the barricade in the Faubourg Saint-Honoré by way of the garden of the British Embassy, but that was their only advance.

But the great fires had begun. The Ministry of Finance had been set alight by Versaillese incendiary shells intended for the Tuileries Terrace. The masses of documents caught fire, and soon the rue de Rivoli was covered with charred fragments. Scraps of burnt paper were carried by the wind as far as the Terrace at Saint-Germain, ten miles away. The Communard firemen put out the fire once, since it threatened to render the rue Saint-Florentin barricade untenable. But the flames burst out once more and could not be extinguished.

" Now began those tragic nights which were to strike seven times. . . . There were nights that were louder, riven by more awful lightnings, of a more awful grandeur, when the flames and the cannonade enveloped all Paris; but none left a more funereal impress upon the imagination " (Lissagaray). A night of preparation. All was not yet lost. The Versaillese had not yet encountered the real Paris. The city was lighted as usual except in the invaded quarters: west from the Faubourg Montmartre stretched a great blackness in which there moved seventy thousand armed men. In the dark, the outpost sentinels called from time to time their " *Passez au large !* "

Paris had recovered the revolutionary enthusiasm of March 18. Battalion after battalion marched to the Hôtel de Ville to receive instructions, reaffirm their loyalty. The streets resounded with the tramp of armed men, the clang of bugles, the roll of drums. National Guards slept the last sleep they were to know for five days, many for ever, huddled along the pavements. Yet life went on as usual. Those who wished to sleep safe at home were not disturbed. But in many bourgeois homes, women sat all night sewing the tricolour armlets for those who were to turn upon their fellow-citizens on the morrow.

Barricades rose everywhere, the barricades of 1871, spontaneous, improvised from a few paving-stones, breast-high, red flag planted above. Some with a gun or two, most defended by a score of desperate muskets. All over the IXth district they rose. There were barricades at La Chapelle, the Buttes-Chaumont, Belleville, Ménilmontant, the Bas-tille, the Place du Château d'Eau, the Grands Boulevards, especially east of the Porte Saint Denis; all the way down the Boulevard Saint-Michel, at the Panthéon, the rue Saint-Jacques, the Gobelins. Fifty skilled masons worked at a huge barricade at the corner of the rue Saint-Denis and the Square Saint-Jacques: finished in a few hours, it was as strong as that built in several weeks by Napoléon Gaillard in the rue Saint-Florentin. Women and children helped. The Place Blanche was barricaded and defended by a battalion of a hundred women. Every passer was forced to help. Those who were not for the revolution were against it. "Lend a hand for the Republic, Citizen ! "

La Cécilia was in command at Montmartre ; Brunel, quartered at the Ministry of Marine in the rue Royale, was defending the Place de la Concorde, the Madeleine and the Place Vendôme from the rear. The Place Vendôme itself was occupied by three battalions under Legion-Com-mander Spinoy. Bergeret was at the Tuileries. The

Commune, forgetting political differences, had called upon its most energetic commanders.

At the Hôtel de Ville, reports were coming in from all quarters. Officers sat at the long tables studying maps, despatching orders. The courtyards were full of armed men, wagons, gun-carriages, horses. The Central Committee, the Committee of Public Safety, Delescluze sat writing orders, proclamations. The Committee of Public Safety and the Commune appealed forlornly to the Versaillese soldiers: " Do not abandon the cause of the Workers ! . . . Leave the aristocrats, the privileged, the hangmen of humanity to defend themselves, and the reign of justice will be easily established. Quit your ranks. Enter our homes. . . . You will be welcomed fraternally and gladly." And again: " What you did on March 18 you will do again, and the people will not have the sorrow of fighting men whom it looks upon as brothers, whom it would wish to see sitting down with it to the civic banquet of Liberty and Equality."

Ranvier, more practical, published in the name of the Committee of Public Safety an order authorising the barricade-commanders to demand the opening of all doors and the requisition of all necessary materials, and another decreeing that all window-shutters should be left open and that any house from which came a single shot or act of aggression against the National Guard should be immediately burnt down.

About ten o'clock, a crowd of angry National Guards brought in Dombrowski. Badly hurt the previous day, he had attempted to get into touch with the Prussian commander at Saint-Ouen to obtain a pass for himself and his staff through Saint-Denis to the Belgian frontier. The Prussians had refused. Already, terrified Parisians were attempting to pass the Prussian lines, but the passage had now, by arrangement with Versailles, been rigorously closed. Dombrowski shared their fate. He was inconsolable at this suspicion of treachery. His role as commander was over, he was no Parisian, but a soldier of the Revolution, that Revolution which would live on and need skilled fighters long after the Commune had perished. Curiously enough, it had been a commander called Vaillant (no relation to the member of the Commune) who had had Dombrowski arrested, and Vaillant was shot next day by the Communards as a traitor. The Committee of Public Safety, involved with him in the Veysset affair, tried to console Dombrowski; but when he rose from supper, he shook hands with his brother officers in a way which made them realise that he was taking his leave of them for ever.

Dawn of the 23rd broke early. At three, the cannonade began again all along the line. An hour later, the Versaillese, refreshed and reinforced, moved forward. The aim of that day's operations was the formidable Butte Montmartre. Montmartre was utterly unprepared. La Cécilia, Lefrançais, Vermorel and Johannard had managed to send a hundred men to Malon in the Batignolles during the night: it was all they could raise. But Montmartre's safety depended entirely upon that of the Batignolles, and that of the whole Right Bank upon Montmartre. The Montmartrois would obey only their own legion-commander, Millière (no connection with the Paris Deputy), and he was quite incompetent. Cluseret had vanished. La Cécilia could get no help from the Hôtel de Ville. Vermorel, going himself to get munitions, returned too late.

Ladmirault moved along inside the walls, taking all the gates in the rear, and occupying the Porte de Clignancourt on the north-east of the Butte isolated it from La Villette. He went on down the Boulevard Ornano and threatened the Gare du Nord, cutting the Butte's communications eastward. On his right, Clinchant was sweeping away all the small barricades in the Batignolles. Malon, almost surrounded in the *mairie*, broke out to the Place Clichy with a detachment of twenty-five women headed by Louise Michel and Dmitrieva. The Butte was now cut off from the west. Suddenly, a new column burst in through the Porte Saint-Ouen from outside the city: it was Montaudon's Division, allowed through the neutral zone by the Prussians.

Fifty men still held out in the Place Clichy, loading their

guns with stones and asphalt when their bullets gave out. But Ladmirault turned their flank, joined Clinchant, who was attacking from in front. Twenty Guards who refused to surrender were shot on the spot. By nine o'clock, the Batignolles was occupied, and it needed only a brief vigorous assault to take the Butte.

But its reputation was formidable. Huge forces advanced very slowly, resisted by a handful of desperate men. It was not until two in the afternoon that Montmartre was finally occupied. The great battery had hardly fired. It was as much a moral as a tactical disaster.

The women's battalion in the Place Blanche held out bravely. Driven back, they joined the Place Pigalle barricade and fought on till two o'clock. At last, they were surrounded, forced to surrender. Their commander, Lévêque, member of the Central Committee, bricklayer, was shot in cold blood by the Versaillese officer, who exclaimed as he fired: " Oh, so bricklayers are to be commanders now ! "

Clinchant went on through the IXth district, but now he had to fight every foot of his way. The Collège Rollin and the rue Trudaine held out all day. Douay, protected by a barrage from the captured Butte, smashed his way down the Boulevard Haussmann, through a great barricade outside the Printemps store, bore down upon the Madeleine and Opéra from two directions. In the Faubourg Montmartre a three-foot barricade, defended by thirty men, held out till nightfall. The Versaillese right wing could make no head against Brunel in the rue Royale. Shells from Montmartre and from smaller field artillery devastated the Boulevard Malesherbes. Versaillese snipers nested in the houses on the left of the Boulevard murderously enfiladed the barricade across it.

Brunel's headquarters, the Ministry of Marine, became untenable. He decided to evacuate. Already known as " Brunel the Burner," from an incident during the Prussian Siege when he had burnt down a house obstructing his line of fire, he carried out Ranvier's published order to burn down all hostile houses. The block between Number 13 of

the Boulevard Malesherbes and the corner of the Faubourg
Saint-Honoré was set alight. Brunel prepared to burn the
Ministry of Marine also, but the arrangements did not
succeed. The Versaillese were effectually halted by a wall
of flame. When Brunel finally retreated, at midnight, the
whole of the rue Royale was ablaze.

On Brunel's left, the Tuileries terrace and the rue Saint-
Florentin held out magnificently under the fire from sixty
guns from the Quai d'Orsay, Passy, the Champ de Mars,
the Etoile. The Place de la Concorde, caught by the fire
from three sides, was a mass of twisted wreckage. Our Lady
of Lille had lost her head, Strasbourg was riddled. The
Versaillese could not advance frontally at all.

On the Left Bank, the Versaillese objective was the fortress formed by the Panthéon and the Luxembourg. But
here they met with fierce and organised resistance. The
Vth under the brave and dashing Lisbonne, the VIth under
the calm, efficient Varlin, the XIIth and XIVth under the
Commune's best strategist, Wroblewski, worked well
together. The plan of Versaillese attack aided them, for
all four districts had to resist almost simultaneously, and
so were able to defend themselves and each other at the
same time. Wroblewski, too, did not spend his time protesting and sulking when he heard that Lisbonne had been
appointed by the Hôtel de Ville to the command of the
Panthéon without any notice to him, the nominal
Commander-in-Chief, but, accepting it, at once fortified
the positions still left in his charge, placing batteries on
the Butte-aux-Cailles, a hill protecting the line between the
Panthéon and the Forts, barricading the Outer Boulevards,
establishing strong reserves in the Place d'Italie, the Place
Jeanne d'Arc and at Bercy, fixing his headquarters at the
Gobelins *mairie*.

Wroblewski had the good fortune to be seconded by men
who cared as little for commands from the Hôtel de Ville
as he did. The initiative should obviously lie with the commanders on the spot, who should then report back. This
was the opinion of Léo Melliet, member of the Committee

of Public Safety, now Civil Commissioner at Bicêtre. On the 21st, Delescluze had sent an order that the garrisons of the Forts should fall back into the city. Melliet, deliberately defying the proclaimed orders of the Commune, had immediately called a Council of War. Present: Wroblewski, Bougault from Hautes-Bruyères, Landy from Villejuif, Kamieniecki from Moulin Saquet, and six other local commanders. It was unanimously decided that they should not abandon their positions and that the commanders should " consult only their patriotism and their energy to face the necessities of the situation." Wroblewski had immediately gone to Delescluze to persuade him to transfer the whole struggle to the Left Bank. He realised that the Versaillese attack here was planned as a turning movement by way of the southern Outer Boulevards and through the XIIIth and XIIth districts to strike at the XIth and eventually the XXth in a semicircle from the south. The Seine, the forts, the Panthéon and the Bièvre river formed a sure line of defence beyond which lay a line of retreat across open country. But Wroblewski was not a Parisian but a strategist, and did not take into account what Delescluze realised that, as Lissagaray puts it, " the heart of a revolution cannot be displaced for military purposes."

Wroblewski's view of the Versaillese strategy was proved correct. The right wing continued its flanking movement. Outside Paris, Cissey was preparing to reduce the forts in order to join up with Lacretelle, attacking the Luxembourg through the Faubourg Saint-Germain, and Levassor-Sorval, creeping round by the south.

There were still some 400 Communards in Little Montrouge. On the 23rd the Versaillese cut the telegraph between Montrouge and Paris, expected their surrender. Cissey wired to his Chief of Staff, Leperche: " Continue to see that no one leaves Paris. We have just intercepted a despatch from the commander of Fort Montrouge, who finds his position untenable. Continue an active bombardment of the Fort and try to find a native to tell the commander that our army is occupying half Paris and that the insurrection is completely demoralised. Give him a forged letter signed by some member of the Commune, General La Cécilia for instance, ordering him to retire upon Bicêtre." But Cissey reckoned without local insubordination. Montrouge held out until the 25th.

Levassor-Sorval inside the walls captured the Montparnasse Cemetery after a brief but hot struggle; but fell into bad trouble at the Place Saint-Pierre-de-Montrouge, the key to the southern second-line defence. The great barricade in the Chaussée de Maine held out for hours under repeated attacks by overwhelming numbers. Snipers in the belfry of Saint-Pierre kept up a dangerous fusillade. But ammunition ran short behind the barricade. The church was mercilessly bombarded. As the tricolour was run up on the Montmartre *mairie*, the Place Saint-Pierre had to be evacuated, and the flag mounted on the Montrouge *mairie* on the other flank of the battle.

The way was open to the Place d'Enfer (now Denfert-Rochereau). The Luxembourg and the Panthéon were now defended on the south only by the barricades in the rue Vavin, at the Observatoire, on the Boulevard Saint-Michel. Lacretelle was advancing through the Faubourg Saint-Germain to meet Levassor-Sorval.

But Lacretelle could advance no further. At the Croix-Rouge, junction of five barricaded narrow streets, defended by nests of snipers in every house, and commanded by Eugène Varlin, they met a desperate resistance. It was not so much that the Croix-Rouge was of supreme strategic importance as that here there were gathered a large number of desperate and well-equipped men under superb leadership.

The action was begun by some disloyal National Guards wearing the tricolour armlet, from the 15th, 16th, 17th and 106th bourgeois battalions. In spite of the death of their leader, Durouchoux, the previous day, they raised barricades in the rue du Bac and the rue de Babylone and appealed to the Versaillese troops near the Observatoire for support.

Between the Croix-Rouge and the Seine, the National
Guard of the district, the Tirailleurs and the Enfants Perdus
fought desperately along the quiet aristocratic streets, the
rues de Lille, de l'Université, Saint-Dominique, de Grenelle.
The fighting went on all day without pause. Varlin was
everywhere, cool, conscientious, organising and encourag-
ing. The battle went on far into the night.

The XIXth and XXth districts, true home of the revolution, began to prepare for the inevitable defence. They
were to protect the last retreat of the Commune. Raoul
du Bisson, ubiquitously treacherous, had attempted to get
himself recognised commander at La Villette, but was
shown up and replaced by the brave and popular Passedouet, member of the Central Committee. Passedouet
immediately set about raising five lines of defensive barricades, the flanks protected by the walls and the huge
fortresses on the Grands Boulevards at the Porte Saint-
Denis and the Porte Saint-Martin. Artillery, posted on
every height, fired across Paris to the Place de la Concorde
and the Butte Montmartre.

The city, streets deserted, shops closed, cowered under
the shells. But in the invaded quarters the bourgeois began
to creep out. The day was hot, and the gaily-dressed women
who had come out to greet their gallant deliverers carried
parasols. The soldiers, with some feeling of military decency,
had covered the dead Communards' faces with their caps.
It was no uncommon sight to see one of these charming
ladies delicately tilt back the cap from the dead face with
the tip of her parasol; some went rather further. The
London *Times* recalled to its sober readers a remark of
Voltaire's, " A Parisienne is half monkey, half tiger." The
soldiers were no more enthusiastic about their reception by
the bourgeois of Paris than they had been about those of
Versailles.

But the military, too, had their orgy that afternoon, after
the capture of Montmartre. Lecomte and Clément Thomas
were to be avenged. Forty-two men, three women and four
children, picked out haphazard, were dragged to Number 6

rue des Rosiers, forced to kneel bareheaded by the wall against which the two generals had been shot; then they were massacred. This pilgrimage to the wall went on all through the battle.

These were not the only shootings of the day. Firing-squads worked hard at the Square des Batignolles, the Porte de Clichy, the Elysée, the Parc Monceau. It made little difference whether the Communards had surrendered or had been captured.

Meanwhile, a tragi-comic scene was taking place at the Hôtel de Ville. Conducted by ex-Mayor Bonvalet, the League for the Rights of Paris came to the Committee of Public Safety to propose a new plan of conciliation, worked out together with the Lyons Congress delegation. The Committee rather doubted the practical effect. The League then put itself at the Commune's disposal. " Very well," they were told, " get a gun and go and fight on the barricades ! "

Terribly shocked, the League went to the Central Committee and worked on them so strongly that these honest men drew up, in the midst of the worst street-fighting Paris had ever seen, a poster declaring themselves the enemies only of civil war and proposing the dissolution of both the Assembly and the Commune, the withdrawal of the army " called regular " 25 kilometres from Paris, the appointment of a provisional authority composed of dele-gates from towns of over 50,000 inhabitants to elect a pro-visional government from among its members, this govern-ment to proceed to the election of a Constituent Assembly and the Commune of Paris, and no reprisals to be taken against the members of either the Assembly or the Com-mune for acts committed after March 26. These Rip van Winkle conditions were to be accepted in full or not at all.

In the same tone was another proclamation to the soldiers who were shooting men of the Central Committee in cold blood: " We are the fathers of families. We are fighting to prevent our children from being one day subjugated, like you, to military despotism. You too will one day be the fathers of families. . . . When the order is vile, disobedience is a duty."

The Committee of Public Safety did not share these ingenuous illusions. Remembering that " the Revolution means paying the army," they sent to the Bank of France for another half-million francs. The trembling de Ploeuc paid up promptly; and Jourde went off to see personally to its distribution. At the Mint, the Delegate-Director, the bronze-worker Camélinat, was founding his first 153,000 francs in gold five-franc pieces from the inartistic plate from the Tuileries. Active preparations were going forward to transfer the Commune to the *mairie* of the XIth district, according to plan.

In the evening a solemn procession filed into the doomed building. Dombrowski, suspect and despairing, had fallen beside that other innocent suspect, Vermorel, at the barricade in the rue Myrrha. As he was carried to the Lariboisière hospital, the defenders of the barricades presented arms. Two hours later, he was dead, silent upon his mystery. The body was brought in state to the Hôtel de Ville. He lay on the blue satin quilt of Valentine Haussmann's bed. From time to time, armed mourners filed past, bareheaded.

The battle grew fiercer towards nightfall. At six o'clock Douay turned the barricade in the Chaussée d'Antin, then advanced upon the Opéra, capturing it after a sharp struggle. His right wing, fighting its way from house to house, carried the rue Royale and the Madeleine amid the flames. They were almost upon the Place Vendôme.

On the Left Bank the battle raged more furiously. Every house nested its snipers, Versaillese and Communard. Lacretelle took the Babylone barracks, the Abbaye-aux-Bois, pressed hard upon the Croix-Rouge. Bruat's marines, doubling along the rues de l'Université and Grenelle, occupied the Ministry of War and the Central Telegraph Office, bayoneting the whole garrison, including its *cantinière*. In spite of orders not to push on beyond the Boulevard Saint-Germain, they rushed a barricade in the rue du

Bac with heavy losses. Later in the evening, Levassor-
Sorval swept down from the Gare Montparnasse, assaulted
the barricades in the rue de Rennes, and after a desperate
struggle almost cleared the rue Vavin. The Versaillese
almost reached the Luxembourg. The artillery battle
crashed on far into the night. The incendiary shells of the
Versaillese guns completed the deliberate fire-tactics of the
Communards.

Huge flames made daylight in the lampless streets. From
the Madeleine to the rue de Rennes, a wall of flame
separated the armies. The rue Royale and the rue de
Castiglione, the Ministry of Finance, the Tuileries, the
Louvre Library, the Legion of Honour, the Council of
State, the Court of Accounts, the Orsay barracks. The guns
still crashed amid the flames at the Croix-Rouge. Buildings
fell down with dull thuds, explosions burst from the flaming
streets, windows cracked like rifle-shots, clattered down.
The heat was suffocating, the ground roared and trembled.
Masses of scorched papers fluttered from the Ministry of
Finance.

This burning of Paris infuriated the bourgeois and
officers against the Commune in the same way as the
demolition of the Vendôme Column. Yet little of it was due
to wanton incendiarism on this first night. The rue Royale,
the Croix-Rouge, the Legion of Honour and the neighbouring streets were fired by Brunel, Varlin, Eudes, for purely
tactical reasons, in accordance with the proclamation of
the Committee of Public Safety. Whatever their public or
historic associations, these buildings had become simply
military positions; and the Versaillese themselves had
bombarded them. The Ministry of Finance, indeed, had
actually been set alight by Versaillese shells, in spite of the
Communards' efforts to extinguish it.

There can be no doubt that a similar reason would have
justified the burning of the Tuileries: but there is evidence
that Bergeret had it set on fire deliberately to take a sort of
symbolical revenge, in the same way as the Commune had
decreed the demolition of the Bréa and Expiatory Chapels.

But even so, the exact responsibility has never been cleared up. There is a curious story of an individual coming to the Hôtel de Ville that evening to get written confirmation of the Commune's alleged verbal instructions to fire the Tuileries, saying that he came from Bergeret. This seemed suspicious, and it turned out that this messenger did not know Bergeret at all. Bergeret's assistants, Bénot and Boudin, were implicated by the Versaillese Councils of War in all sorts of " crimes " in which they obviously took no part. Deliberate forgery was used to fix the blame on " star " criminals, such as a forged letter of Ferré, *Flambez Finances*, which could, if genuine, have been sent only after the Ministry of Finance had been already set on fire by the Versaillese shells.

Bergeret, whose own conduct had been more than once suspect, certainly took full responsibility. Barrels of powder had been brought in that morning, exactly at the same time, as it happened, as Thiers's valuables had been carried from the Garde Meuble, threatened by the battle, to the Cour du Carrousel. Bergeret came from the Hôtel de Ville to supervise the arrangements. At this time, the burning was certainly part of Brunel's tactical plan. The hangings, doors and furniture were soaked in petrol, covered with tar. The bulk of the gunpowder was heaped in the famous Hall of the Marshals, under the cupola. At ten that night the trains were fired.

Bergeret watched from the Tuileries Terrace. It was a fantastic and magnificent spectacle. The flames raced along the 1,200 feet of the façade, swept towards the cupola, which blew up like a volley of rockets at exactly a quarter past one. Bergeret pencilled hastily: " The last vestiges of Royalty have just vanished," and handed the note to a young National Guard, Victor Thomas, a nephew of General Clément Thomas, to take to the Hôtel de Ville.

Rigault watched the burning of the Tuileries from a window in the rue de Rivoli. He had just come back from the Saint-Pélagie prison. With his secretary, the carica-turist Slom, he had gone there about eleven that evening.

For weeks, Rigault, backed by Delescluze, had been nursing his vengeance against Chaudey, who, he believed, had given the order to fire that January 22 when Sapia fell. Now, deprived of the chance of a spectacular indictment before the Jury of Accusation, Rigault had determined to make sure at least of his revenge. Without any order from the Hôtel de Ville, he went to get his man.

Chaudey was sitting in his dressing-gown in the cell once occupied by Rochefort, correcting an " Ode to Liberty," submitted to him by Préau de Vedel, the prison librarian. Rigault summoned him. Rigault's assistants—Slom, Clermont, Augustin Ranvier, director of the prison and brother to the member of the Commune—his staff—Benn, Clément, Gentil, Berthier, Préau de Vedel—waited in the dim hall. Rigault in full dress of a commander of the National Guard, sabre in belt, revolver in red sash. The examination brief and tragic. " Was it you who from the Hotel de Ville asked for troops to clear the square ? " Chaudey: " I was doing my duty." Question and answer solemnly three times repeated. Rigault: " So it was your duty to kill women and children. You killed my friend Sapia. My duty is to tell you that you have three minutes to live." Chaudey: " But I am a Republican——". Rigault: " Like your friends from Versailles who will be murdering us to-morrow. . . . Come along, march." Chaudey: " But, Rigault, I have a wife, a child. . . . " Rigault: " The Commune will take care of them better than you can. Come along, march."

The procession filed along the dark corridors in dead silence. Berthier in front, with a lantern, then Chaudey and the others, Rigault last.

At a turn in the passage, a dozen men of the 248th, Longuet's, afterwards Régère's, Battalion. A firing squad. They stood there. The single figure in the light of the single lantern, the silence, the night of terror got on their nerves. Suddenly, Rigault raised his sabre. " Long live the Republic ! " cried Chaudey, three times. " Fire ! Fire ! " Rigault shouted to the wavering squad. Chaudey, wounded only in one arm, waved the other, still shouting, " Long live the Republic!" The prison staff, seeing that the National Guards had had enough, rushed upon Chaudey, finished him off with revolvers and a *chassepot*, savage with terror.

Rigault went back to the hall, chose three constables, ordinary hostages. The firing-squad had little taste for more such work. Only one gendarme fell dead; another was finished off at close quarters; the third escaped into the dark. Clermont ran after him with Slom's revolver—it was not loaded. " Don't kill him; bring him back!" Rigault shouted after him. A brief, grim chase in the dark, and the wretched man was brought back to the wall, shot down beside his comrades.

Rigault dictated to Slom a summary accusation covering Chaudey as well: " Whereas the Versaillese have entered Paris; whereas their friends are firing upon us from the windows; whereas it is time to put an end to these activities," the prisoners were to be shot immediately. As they were leaving the prison, Berthier suggested, " Citizen Raoul Rigault, now that all is over, let us cry together, " Long live the Commune!" His voice rose single as his lantern. Two days later, Augustin Ranvier hanged himself.

At the Ex-Prefecture, the evacuation and burning of which had been decided two days before, Ferré, commanding in Rigault's absence, and bully Pilotell slept on camp-beds. " They're not sheets we're sleeping in," said Pilotell, " but winding-sheets." " What of it?" Ferré replied coldly.

At the Hôtel de Ville a tremendous activity. The building was to be fired next morning as soon as the Commune had made good its retreat. Wounded lay groaning in the great halls. Two officers kept vigil over Dombrowski, while another rapidly sketched the fine head. Delescluze, exhausted, dying, but indomitable, sat in his room, writing, writing. His voice was almost gone. Strange faces appeared: members of the Commune who had shaved off their revolutionary beards, officers who had changed their uniform for a private's tunic or a worker's overalls, shadier figures come to " plant " incriminating documents to serve the inevitable prosecutions. Ranvier, meeting two of his colleagues thus disguised, threatened to have them shot if they did not return to their duties at once. Pindy, Military Governor of the Hôtel de Ville, paced up and down, impatient to get clear. Delescluze was still for holding out in the old centre of Parisian popular revolution. But he was overborne.

The Versaillese advanced amid the flames of the rue Royale. Brunel finally obeyed the Committee of Public Safety's orders and fell back on the rue Saint-Florentin. But meanwhile the Versaillese had walked into the Place Vendôme. It had been strategically evacuated earlier in the evening. Now that the Hôtel de Ville was to be abandoned, there was no sense in holding these advanced posts. An urchin planted the tricolour on the pedestal of the fallen Column. As he climbed down, a shot whistled past his ear. A National Guard had fired from one of the houses. Arrested, he was shot on the spot. A few minutes later, a woman caught musket in hand was also summarily shot. A Versaillese gunner, finding some difficulty in hoisting his gun over a hole in the paving, turned to a comrade, and, pointing to the corpse of a Federal, " Take the old Forty-Eighter and make a step of him," he said.

The Versaillese followed Brunel down the rue de Castiglione, turning the barricade by passing through the back entrance of the Hôtel du Rhin, but did not venture to push on to the Hôtel de Ville. On the Left Bank, Varlin evacuated the Croix-Rouge and the rue de Rennes amid the flames, after forty-eight hours' incessant fighting. There were only thirty men left at the rue de Rennes. The Versaillese were now able to clear the rues d'Assas and Notre-Dame-des-Champs and move right on to the Luxembourg. On the extreme right, by capturing the Val-de-Grace military hospital, they threatened the Panthéon.

The next day's objective was the clearing of the Left Bank, the fortress of the Luxembourg and the Panthéon, as this day had cleared Montmartre and the Right. The tentacles were closing on the Hôtel de Ville, slowly, methodically, irresistibly. The battle was moving east in a series of great zigzags.

Early in the morning the guns rested. Only a few isolated shots: a sniper or a murdered prisoner. Over all, the steady roar of the huge flames.

# CHAPTER X

# THE END

*" Quelle guerre ! Quelle guerre ! "*
CHARLES DELESCLUZE : *May 25, 1871*

THE DAWN of the 25th broke stifling. Central Paris was a brazier. The Commune was no longer resisting, it was lashing out in its death-agony. Huge crowds from Versailles, the Prussians at Saint-Denis, English and American tourists watched the burning of the modern Nineveh.

Lord Lyons, the British Ambassador, returned from Versailles to visit the scene. " The state of Paris," he wrote to the Foreign Office, " is heart-breaking. The night I spent there was calculated to give one an idea of the infernal regions. Fires in all directions, the air oppressive with smoke and unpleasant odours, the incessant roar of cannon and musketry and all kinds of strange sounds. . . . I hope it will really all be over by to-night." His hopes were not to be granted so soon.

In the quarters now occupied by the Versaillese, normal life began again, and the inhabitants vied with one another to make much of the troops, some of whom, Bretons, could not even speak French.

They did more than pet the soldiery. Infuriated by the destruction of public, and even more of private, property— some four hundred private houses were burning—they turned upon captured and fleeing Communards with the fury that their fellows had already used against the prisoners at Versailles. They denounced all against whom they had any grudge; the concièrges especially were zealous in informing against lodgers who had somehow displeased them. The most innocent remark, or even gesture, might lead to instant execution.

The diary of a typical " bourgeois of Paris " in these days, one J. Audéoud, has been preserved in manuscript. It gives an excellent idea of the mentality which reigned amid the massacre. " What hovels," he exclaims, describing the shooting of eight Communards on May 21, " what sewers, what jails could have spewed forth these ferocious brutes ? How the honest man's heart delights to see them lying there, riddled with bullets, befouled and rotting ! The stink of their corpses is an odour of peace, and if the all-too-sensitive nostril revolts, the soul rejoices. There they lie, the masters of Paris who fired point-blank upon the unarmed crowd ! There they lie, the monsters who recoiled before no atrocity ! What joy to see them lying there, their flesh in rags ! We too, to use those fine words of Bossuet's, we too have become cruel and pitiless, and we should find it a pleasure to bathe and wash our hands in their blood ! "

The terrible legend of the *Pétroleuses*, started by Versaillese columnists who had long exercised their imaginations in popular romances, was spreading panic. It was said that bands of women had been organised especially to set fire to the city. The *Gaulois* (May 29) " discovered " that these women were paid ten francs a day and, " armed with tin cans about the size of a sardine-tin containing a composition of petrol, tallow and sulphur, slip into houses, and, after lighting a fire, escape." " Not only do these furies attempt to burn the public monuments," said *Paris-Journal* (May 28), " but in the quarters occupied by our army they burrow, looking for a favourable opportunity to burn those houses which the *mitrailleuse* has spared." It was, of course, a pure legend: not the slightest evidence for the existence of the *Pétroleuse* has ever appeared, even if it were possible to fire a house with a sardine-tin full of combustibles.

None of the English correspondents at the time took it at all seriously. But the Audéouds drank it in, were panic-stricken. Every coal-chute, every crevice was tightly stopped. Worse, innocent women were denounced and murdered. Audéoud himself tells complacently how he saw a well-dressed woman in the rue Blanche carrying two "phials," quite probably milk-bottles. He at once denounced her to a soldier to whom he had just been giving wine. The drunken soldier grabbed at her, she flung him off disdainfully and passed on. Raising his gun, the soldier deliberately shot her in the back.

No one was safe. Audéoud was watching the burial of a Communard corpse. " I remark that not one but twenty thousand would have to be shot down to let us breathe at all easily. Two women of abominable appearance look at us angrily and seem to defy us. They obviously want to say something but prudence restrains them. Luckily for them; otherwise, we should have them arrested. Perhaps we were wrong to let them go ? What if they were *pétro-leuses* ? At such a time, everything is of importance. One must not only listen to words but study faces. Whoever is not absolutely for us is entirely against us."

This motto applied no less to the extreme reactionaries who did not share Audéoud's grovel before Thiers. An old gentleman wearing the rosette of the Legion of Honour indignantly wrote on a Governmental proclamation to the troops recommending moderation: " So it's conciliation, is it ? Sheep in wolf's clothing ! " Audéoud immediately denounced him for anti-Governmental propaganda, and the poor old reactionary was carried off to the local court martial. Once there, there was small hope.

The Communards were too busy for atrocities. A couple of spies were shot outside the Hôtel de Ville during the night; and there were Rigault's four: that was all.

The Communards gathered at the Panthéon to await attack. Lisbonne had come from the rue Vavin, Varlin from the Croix-Rouge, Vallès from the Hôtel de Ville, his red sash rolled up in newspaper under his arm " like a lobster," since the Guards showed clearly that they had no use for the " talkers " of the Commune. Three great barricades defended the square: one at the top of the rue Soufflot, another across the middle of the square, a third running from the *mairie* of the Vth to the Ecole de Droit.

The Versaillese came on again at dawn. Two battalions rushed the abandoned Croix-Rouge amid the flames. Fighting their way down every street, shooting every man who fell into their hands, Lacretelle's men swept through the Faubourg Saint-Germain, capturing the Beaux-Arts, the Institute, the Mint and the barricades in the rue Taranne. Bruat's marines ran on towards the Luxembourg.

Meanwhile, Cissey was creeping round west and south by way of the rues d'Assas and Notre-Dame-des-Champs. The Communards fought back, desperately, from the barricade in the rue Soufflot.

Levassor-Sorval was moving round upon the Panthéon from the east, advancing from Val-de-Gràce and the Parc Montsouris down the rue Mouffetard without much difficulty.

Lacretelle, coming from the north, crossed the Place Saint-Sulpice and pushed on as far as the west side of the Boulevard Saint-Michel. Another column moved round to the north of the Luxembourg Gardens by way of the rue de Vaugirard. The rue Vavin, which had held out for two days, was isolated, and its defenders had to retreat, after blowing up the powder-magazine, leaving the houses round in flames.

At the Panthéon the explosion created a panic. Everyone believed that the vaults below were full of explosives and that the whole quarter might blow up any minute. Some of the Guards, intoxicated by the burning of the Right Bank, were eager enough to blow everything into the air, but Vallès and others over-persuaded them: it would have been mere massacre of their own men. The last defenders hastily evacuated the Luxembourg. Cissey's columns rushed forward, smashed in the Gardens' palings, and occupied the building without further trouble.

To consolidate this position the Versaillese rushed the rues Cujas and Malebranche and the first barricade in the rue Soufflot, with heavy losses. A Communard battery on the Pont Saint-Michel kept the Boulevard clear all day, but finally ran out of ammunition. The Versaillese were able to reach the Place Maubert. Levassor-Sorval rushed at the Panthéon from the rear, closing the ring. The thirty defenders left were surrounded; only a few escaped.

The massacres began at once. Forty prisoners were shot, one after another, in the rue Saint-Jacques; and single shootings went on in the neighbouring streets all afternoon.

After twelve hours' heavy fighting, the Versaillese were now masters of the whole centre of the Left Bank. Nothing was left to the Revolution except its true centre, the workers' quarters: the XIth, XIIth, XIIIth, XIXth and XXth districts.

The Prefecture and the Palais de Justice had been fired that morning. Mégy had appeared for a moment to arrange the materials, smashing furniture, pictures, mirrors with great swings of his sabre. Then Ferré, having released the common-law prisoners in the cells to fight for the Commune, and having made certain arrangements regarding the political spies and hostages, had given the order to light up. Rigault had not returned.

Like most of the other Blanquists, he had made for the Latin Quarter, their old battle-ground. With the burning of the Ex-Prefecture, his official duties were over. He wanted to fight, to forget Chaudey. About noon, he met Vuillaume on the Boulevard Saint-Michel. They forced their way into the closed Café de Harcourt. Rigault was still in full regimentals. Unusually laconic. " You know. . . . Last night. . . . I had him shot. . . ." " Shot ? Whom ? " " Chaudey." They drank their coffee in silence.

Rigault went along to the Panthéon. He was there till the end, directing the barricades in the adjoining streets. At three o'clock he went towards the rue Gay-Lussac where he had hired a room under an assumed name. The Versaillese had just broken through to the street. They were running in from both ends just as Rigault reached his hotel. One of them noticed his uniform. Rigault slipped in, slammed the door. The soldiers broke in after him. Rigault found Slom sitting in his room. The Versaillese were in the hall. " Stay here," said Rigault, " no need to get your-self shot with me." Came downstairs, surrendered. They had not recognised him.

They took him a short way up the Boulevard Saint-Michel towards the court martial just set up at the Luxembourg. There was a scuffle. Rigault shouted " Long live the Com-mune ! " A sergeant emptied his revolver into his head. Two more shots were fired into his body. " Shot while attempting to escape."

They left the body in the gutter, just below the window of his old mathematics professor. The women of the quarter fell on it, insulted it, tore off the boots. It lay there horribly naked for two days. Rigolette, *patronne* of the " Cochon Fidèle," one of Rigault's favourite haunts, dared to fling an old coat over the body, another hand scribbled a notice : " Respect the dead ! Pity his unfortunate father ! " Pilotell, passing that evening, stopped to make a swift and bitter drawing of the Public Prosecutor of the Commune lying in the gutter, arms crossed, barefoot. He had been Rigault's friend.

Ferré was left to carry on Rigault's work. He had begun at once. An hour before the burning of the Ex-Prefecture, he wrote out an order, handed it to Pilotell, who had just returned from distributing the last of the money from the police cash-box. A few minutes later he left the room, went up to a platoon of Vengeurs de Flourens, explained what he wanted. Some gendarmes, former Bonapartist agents, were to be shot; he would force no one against his will. Two boys and an old man left the ranks and went to fight on the barricades. The rest followed Ferré to the Dépôt.

Pilotell had already demanded the spy Veysset. Veysset paled : " Citizen Ferré, you promised to spare my life." " We are not murderers, but you have conspired against us. You took money from Versailles to corrupt Dombrow-ski." " That is true." The Vengeurs, one of them so nervous that Ferré had to shake him roughly, took the spy out on to the Pont-Neuf, shot him, tipped the body into the Seine. Pilotell watched his hat float downstream for a long time.

Ferré, icily smiling now that the thing was done, walked away. The Ex-Prefecture was burning furiously.

The Hôtel de Ville, too, had been fired. And now there was a solid wall of flame all down the rue de Rivoli, from the Tuileries to the Place Lobau. Forty men broke into the Théâtre Lyrique (now Sarah Bernhardt) and set it on fire. The Théâtre Châtelet was just saved. The staff of the Hôtel-Dieu Hospital opposite Notre-Dame got permission from the Committee of Public Safety to stop the burning of the Cathedral in order to save their 800 wounded and sick. The Ex-Prefecture and the Palais de Justice were blazing. The whole Cité island was a stifling hell. The commander of the Palais-Royal, in spite of repeated protests that he could hold out, at last obeyed orders, evacuated, fired his position. The galleries and the Théâtre Français were, however, saved by the advancing Versaillese and by citizens pressed into service.

Ferré went on to the *mairie* of the XIth district, the seat of the Commune. Hardly had he arrived when he was called upon to sign another death-warrant. A crowd of Guards of the 66th, headed by their *cantinière*, Lachaise, brought in the dashing young Captain de Beaufort, accused of treachery. As a matter of fact, it is probable that this young gallant, cousin of Edouard Moreau of the Central Committee, had been involved in counter-revolutionary conspiracy more through impatient folly than actual disloyalty; but his men could not know that. A hastily improvised court martial could find no evidence. But there was no holding the crowd. Ferré bowed to the inevitable, and, calm as ever, signed the death-warrant. They pelted de Beaufort for quite a long time before they shot him.

Not a mile away, they were burying Dombrowski. They had carried him to Père-Lachaise during the night. The defenders of the barricades in the Place de la Bastille had halted the procession; had laid the body of their general at the foot of the July Column, standing around with solemn torches. Man after man had filed past to touch with his lips the leader's forehead. At Père-Lachaise, Vermorel, slandered as Dombrowski had been slandered, made his last great speech, a defence of his whole life and the lives of all the Commune. " This is he whom they accused of treachery ! He has been one of the first to give his life to the Commune. And we, what are we doing to follow him ? Let us swear to leave this place only to die ! " There were not many there who did not weep. There were not many there who did not follow Dombrowski and Vermorel, tortured and self-torturer, to death for the Commune. The slanderer, he who on May 22 had greeted the glorious prospect of death on the barricades, had gone away into the shadows.

In the hot room at the *mairie* members of the Commune and the Central Committee sat silent while Delescluze spoke. They had lost much of their desperate energy. For forty-eight hours they had been fighting, or attempting to control the fighting—forty-eight hours without sleep, with snatched food, tortured with anxiety, the terrible responsibility, the intolerable heat.

The dying Delescluze rallied them for a last effort. " I propose that the members of the Commune, girded with their official sashes, hold a review on the Boulevard Voltaire of all the battalions that can be assembled. We will then place ourselves at their head and lead them against the positions we have to recover." They listened in silence, straining to catch the failing voice, magnificent now when magnificences were over.

Outside, the battle roared nearer. Closer beneath the windows, the murmur and rattle of the men preparing for a last stand. The voice died away. Applause. Discussion. A box of dynamite stood open on the table. They were, as ever, at the mercy of one careless gesture.

The Central Committee, phantom military command, agreed to take the orders of the Committee of Public Safety, phantom political command. No one had heard from the Committee of Public Safety for hours. The Commander of the XIth Legion was to collect and organise all the Guards who had flocked for refuge into the district. The barricade-system, still merely improvised, was to be strengthened for the last resistance.

It was time. The Versaillese forces on the Right Bank had made huge advances. Douay had passed on beyond the Place Vendôme to the Bourse district, where the Brassardier conspirators crept out of their houses to help in the round up. One after the other, fighting desperately, the Louvre, the Palais-Royal, the Square Montholon, the Boulevard Ornano, the Gare du Nord had fallen. The counter-revolutionary staff organised for the " defence " of the Bank of France had joyfully opened its doors. But the Versaillese had to struggle furiously for every foot of the IXth district. The IIIrd, defended by barricades on the Boulevard Sébastopol and the rue Turbigo, held out all day, remembering the Forty-Eight. The fighters in the Avenue Victoria and on the Quai de Gesvres, tormented by the frightful heat from the Hôtel de Ville, snatching the scantiest food and rest, hung on till nightfall covered their retreat. It was not until nine in the evening that the Versaillese dared move on the flaming wreck of the Hôtel de Ville.

Leaving piles of dead in their wake, they moved steadily upon the Place du Château d'Eau. It was the Commune's last great stronghold, the Panthéon and Montmartre of the east, the way into Belleville, the protection of the north of the XIth district.

On the Left Bank, Wroblewski held out heroically on the Butte-aux-Cailles in the XIIIth. But he was terribly isolated. Leperche was bombarding Fort Bicêtre, sending them summonses to surrender, which they repeatedly ignored. After the fall of the Panthéon, communications northwards were cut, so that retreat to the XXth by the Boulevard de la Gare and the Pont de Bercy would take the fugitives very far south of the protected XIth district and the Bastille. The Butte-aux-Cailles was almost the only important position on the Left Bank remaining to the Communards at the end of the day.

By eight in the evening, the Versaillese had taken the great barricade at the Porte Saint-Denis on the Grands Boulevards after one of the hottest battles of the day. Under the incessant bombardment, the Porte Saint-Martin had become untenable. The theatre was set on fire by the shells, the heat was intolerable, the barricade at length evacuated. Another column of the Versaillese was close upon the Château d'Eau.

The Versaillese forces now spread across Paris in a great fan with the Pont-au-Change as its axis, the wings extending along the rues du Faubourg Saint-Martin and de Flandre on the left and the streets east of the Boulevard Saint-Michel on the right. MacMahon, with headquarters now at the Ministry of Foreign Affairs on the Quai d'Orsay, had decided to close the fan on the morrow, sweeping away the Bastille and the Château d'Eau on the left and the Butte-aux-Cailles on the right and crushing the Communards together and back into Belleville and Ménilmontant.

At the Château d'Eau, Delescluze reviewed the defences. On the south the Place de la Bastille was solidly defended by a barricade with three guns at the end of the rue Saint-Antoine and another covering the rues de Charenton and la Roquette. In the centre, protecting the *mairie* of the XIth from attack through the Temple quarter, a huge rough barricade of barrels, paving-stones and bales of paper at the junction of the Boulevards Voltaire and Richard-Lenoir. Strong barricades at either end of the Place du Château d'Eau, supported by smaller barricades in the adjoining streets.

The outer defences extended into the Xth district, where Brunel, hot from the rue Saint-Florentin, barricaded the corner of the Boulevards de Strasbourg and Magenta and the rue du Château d'Eau. North, the Communards holding firm in the Gare de l'Est kept up a heavy bombardment of the Gare du Nord. In the XIXth, Ranvier commanded the artillery on the Buttes-Chaumont, three mortars and four sevens. Five more guns covered the rue Puebla. Six more on the Carrières d'Amérique. Another

battery at Père-Lachaise. The artillery had kept up a heavy
fire all day upon the invaded quarters, especially round the
Bourse, where the Brassardiers had prevented the retreating
Communards from firing the district.

During that night of flames the Versaillese were shooting
everywhere. The military provosts shot down groups of
prisoners in every *mairie*, in every public building. Individual officers, individual troopers shot against the walls
and the captured barricades in every street. No one knows
how many perished that night. It was not uncommon to
find a pile of bodies six-feet high behind an abandoned
barricade. Not all of these bodies were quite dead. Wagon-
loads of dripping corpses rolled horribly through the
streets.

The massacres were infectious. So far, the Communards
had hardly shot a man. They had not acquired the military
attitude even to open traitors. But, about seven o'clock,
there was a great clamour outside the Roquette prison, to
which some three hundred hostages had been transferred
from Mazas. There was one continuous howl for blood :
" The hostages ! We want the hostages ! " A delegation
went off to the *mairie* of the XIth, was received by Ferré,
Delescluze, Investigating Magistrate Genton, and Fortin,
Ferré's secretary. A brief conversation. " The hostages. . . . "
It was an order. Ferré, shrugging, obeyed. He wrote out an
order to execute six hostages to avenge six National Guards
shot earlier in the rue Caumartin. He mentioned no names.
Henceforth, Genton and Fortin saw to the whole business.

Genton went out to recruit men. " Six hostages to be shot.
What volunteers ? " " I ! I ! I ! " cried a hundred voices.
" They have shot my father, brother, son ! " They had to
turn volunteers away. Genton picked up Mégy, whose
natural violence had been redoubled by his humiliation at
Issy. The rest were mostly Guards of the 66th, those who
had shot de Beaufort. Their officers' protests were vain.
" Officers don't give us orders now," they were told ; " We
give the orders. And don't shout too loud, or you go with
them ! " On the way to the prison they met Sicard. His

officer's uniform would be useful to impose some order on the proceedings. Sicard, a hard-bitten revolutionary, was nothing loth.

François, the director of the prison, trembled. They held him up at the point of the revolver. Finally, he made out a list: Deguerry, Bonjean, Allard, Clerc, Ducoudray and another whose name has been lost. One of the Guards suddenly remembered: " And the Archbishop ? " Fortin told François to substitute the name; but François, in the absence of definite orders, refused. Fortin went back to Ferré, explained. Ferré, without a word, took the slip, wrote at the bottom: " And particularly the Archbishop," handed it back.

The Guards were stamping with impatience. At last the prisoners were brought down. Bonjean was moaning, " Oh my beloved wife ! Oh my dear children ! " The Archbishop, wearing the cross of Mgr. Affre, killed in 1848, the ring of Mgr. Sibour, murdered in 1857—it was no safe place, the Archbishopric of Paris—stopped for a moment to say: " But I wrote to Versailles. . . ." That was all. Sicard raised his arm. " Fire ! " " Long live liberty ! " shouted Allard, opening his soutane. The Archbishop still stood. " Is he armoured ? " cried a Guard, firing again. This time the Archbishop fell.

There was no sudden gloom, as after the shooting of the generals on March 18. Mégy has described the scene: " When the last of the bandits had fallen, the picture was magnificent. The oncoming night rendered it sublime. The traitors stretched on the ground, we felt our revolutionary strength, we felt that we were already lost, we wanted to die too, but to revenge ourselves first, and we looked at our dead foes and we breathed deep."

Three hours later, two officers came to the *mairie* to report. " They died bravely," said one. " They died as we will die," Ferré snapped back. They went in to Delescluze. He was writing, writing. He did not look up: " How did they die ? " When the officers had gone, he covered his face with his hands: " What a war ! What a war ! "

The night was terrible with fire and cannonade. The whole centre of Paris was a great brazier, with fantastic shapes of smoke and flame, fantastic firework displays when some building blew up. More than two hundred houses, ten palaces, two theatres were burning. And over it all, the batteries on the Buttes-Chaumont and at Père-Lachaise replied to the Trocadéro, the Panthéon, Montmartre.

There were still sixteen of them left with Delescluze in the *mairie*, the last centre of the Commune, sixteen bombarded with demands for instructions, for men, munitions, guns. Sixteen who still seemed to represent some central authority, although they had neither men, munitions nor guns to send, although their orders meant nothing. And around them a great camp of tired men, women and children snatching a mouthful of food, a moment of sleep, under the cynical smile of the stone Voltaire.

The Versaillese advanced irresistibly. Under cover of darkness, the Communards had evacuated almost all the Xth district. Brunel and the lads' battalion, the Pupils of the Commune, held out bravely in the rue Magnan and on the quai Jemappes. Under terrible bombardment, Wroblewski clung to the Butte-aux-Cailles with the legendary 101st, that shock-troop of the Commune, commanded by Serizier; a battalion that had been everywhere, fought everywhere since the beginning of the Prussian Siege, indisciplinable and ferocious, counter-attacking as often as it was attacked, the very spirit of the revolution. With these men, Wroblewski was holding off a whole division. Cissey could do nothing but bombard.

But at last the forts had fallen. Bicêtre had been silent since the 22nd, but there were still some men there who refused to answer every summons to surrender: 35 men of the 77th, 15 under twenty-one years of age. Leperche had tried a summons for the last time on the evening of the 24th; they took no notice. At last an infantry detachment dared to march in, found the fort abandoned. The cavalry got the credit in the official report.

A brigade slipped along the fortifications to the Seine;

took the Pont Napoléon, the Orléans goods depot. Two other brigades attacked the Butte-aux-Cailles from front and flank, capturing the Gobelins, which the Communards fired as they fled. Wroblewski, abandoning twenty guns and hundreds of prisoners, retreated to the Place Jeanne-d'Arc. Here he still held out under murderous fire; finally got back in good order to the strongly barricaded Pont d'Austerlitz. Lacretelle had managed to advance through the Jardin des Plantes, take the Halle-aux-Vins. Bruat's three brigades had already taken the Gare d'Orléans. But here they were checked. The quai de l'Arsenal, swept by the artillery from the Pont d'Austerlitz and the Bastille, was impassable. On the other bank, La Mariouse managed to occupy the great warehouse known as the Grenier d'Abondance. The Communards set it on fire to smoke him out. The vast building made the biggest blaze of all the great fires lighted in Paris.

In the centre the Versaillese moved from the occupied Hôtel de Ville along the rue Saint-Antoine and the quais to take the Bastille in the flank. They assaulted the Gare de Lyon and the Mazas prison, where the prisoners, after mutinying to prevent the director firing the building, were released. More divisions fought their way down the Boulevard Saint-Martin and the Boulevard Magenta to attack the Place du Château d'Eau. After the fall of the Butte-aux-Cailles, the Château d'Eau and the Bastille remained the Commune's last two strongholds.

Between them, the streets fell, one by one, after desperate struggles, often of one man against thirty. Protot especially was fighting like a demon, and Lisbonne, Varlin, Vermorel. And after every barricade fell, the inevitable shootings. Seventeen Guards, summoned time after time to surrender at Saint-Lazare, shouted their invariable reply: "Long live the Commune!" As they fell, the Versaillese officer turned to the bystanders: "It's their own fault; it's their own fault! Why wouldn't they surrender?" Why? Because now it was equally fatal to surrender or not to surrender. They knew that.

At the *mairie* they still hoped that they represented something. The carnage was still a battle, not yet a man-hunt. That morning Arnold suggested a last attempt to put an end to the horrors by asking the Prussians to mediate. There is considerable uncertainty about this plan which itself was extremely uncertain.

As early as May 23 Robert Reid, an ex-correspondent of the London *Daily Telegraph*, had suggested to Washburne, the American Minister in Paris, who was charged with the care of Prussian citizens' interests, to negotiate. Washburne refused; he said that " all who belong to the Commune and those that sympathise with them will be shot." Washburne hated the Commune, for he had had to move his quarters owing to the Versaillese bombardment; and he had already done a good deal to sabotage the negotiations for the liberation of the Archbishop. However, a relative of Arnold's, Berthier, got into touch with an attaché at the American Embassy, one Steinwerk, and suggested the negotiation with the German quarters at Vincennes in order to save his relative. At the same time Washburne's secretary, McKean, offered, on the part of the Prussians, an intervention on the following conditions: suspension of hostilities; simultaneous re-election of the Commune and the Assembly; the Versaillese troops to leave Paris and take up their quarters on and around the fortifications; the National Guard to continue as the Paris police; no punishment for service in the National Guard. These conditions were much the same as those proposed by the League for the Rights of Paris to the Central Committee three days before. There was about as much chance of success.

The whole affair is as mysterious as it is important. Lefrançais says it was Arthur Reeves, not Reid, McKean not Steinwerk. An unpublished account by Serrailler also mentions McKean. Since Washburne's whole policy towards the Commune was one of, to say the least, diplomatic incorrection, it raises some suspicion of deliberate provocation. As Serrailler says, the evil effect of this inter-vention was to make the Communards believe in the neutrality of the Prussians and so to paralyse the defence. Although the Commune tried to keep the negotiations secret, they leaked out, and the National Guards who gave themselves up to the Prussians, trusting in their neutrality, were handed over to Versailles.

Arnold explained his idea to a special session of the Commune. It seemed a last hope. Delescluze and Vaillant opposed such an indignity as going hat in hand to the Prussians. But the others over-persuaded Delescluze, and, with a heavy heart, he consented to go. Vaillant, too, was to go with Arnold, since he was the only one that spoke fluent German.

Before they went Delescluze asked to be relieved of his functions as Delegate for War. He proposed Pindy, lately Military Governor of the Hôtel de Ville; but Pindy, refusing, proposed Eudes, who replied, according to Pindy, " with an enormous obscenity." Finally Delescluze signed Pindy's appointment; and the delegation started for Versailles.

But at the Porte de Vincennes they were held up by the Guard. " Where are you going ? " " To Vincennes." " No, you don't; you stay here; we're all in this together ! " Delescluze told them his name; but even that did not shake them. Finally, Vaillant went back to the *mairie* to get a pass from Ferré. Delescluze and Arnold were escorted into a little wine-shop. Delescluze sat with his head in his hands: " I no longer wish to live. All is over for me." Vaillant returned, showed the pass, but still could make no impression. Without insisting, Delescluze and the others walked back to the *mairie*. On the way Delescluze said heavily: " I have seen two reactions triumphant. I shall not see another." They returned about six o'clock. The sun was going down in a perfect sky stained with smoke.

When they got back, they found Pindy furious. He had no desire to sit signing orders. He went off with thirty cavalry, " riding like a philosopher," leaving Varlin nominally commander of the Commune's forces.

Delescluze sat for a moment to write a moving letter to

his sister. A crowd was cheering a parade of some eagle standards which they supposed had been captured from the Versaillese; a rather childish bluff. Dmitrieva, herself wounded, brilliantly blonde in a black velvet dress, came in supporting Franckel, wounded on a barricade in the Faubourg Saint-Antoine. Wroblewski came from the Butte-aux-Cailles. Delescluze offered him the command. " Have you got a few thousand determined men ? " asked Wroblewski. There were hardly a few hundred. Wroblewski could not take the responsibility; picked up a gun, and went off to fight as a common soldier.

At a quarter to seven Delescluze, Jourde, Lissagaray and some two score National Guards went towards the Château d'Eau. Delescluze, dressed as always in the uniform of Forty-Eight, top-hat, frock-coat, black trousers, the red sash round his waist almost concealed by the coat, leant on his cane. They met Lisbonne, wounded, supported by Vermorel, Theisz and Jaclard. Vermorel, too, fell, his legs broken. Theisz and Jaclard put him on a stretcher, Delescluze pressed his hand, said a few words of farewell in his ear. Fifty yards from the barricade, Delescluze's companions stopped. It was certain death to go further.

Delescluze walked on, without noticing whether anyone were following. He walked quite steadily among the bullets, the only living thing on that street. Steadily climbed the barricade, stood there a moment. The setting sun silhouetted his tall Jacobin figure. Suddenly, he pitched forward into the Place du Château d'Eau. He had been killed on the spot by three bullets. His body could not be recovered until three days later.

The Place du Château d'Eau was no longer habitable. A continuous wave of fire beat over it. The Versaillese did not yet dare attack, but at least they could prevent its defence. The whole great square was a mass of twisted metal, shattered stone, ravaged trees. Two flaming houses at the entry of the Boulevard Voltaire were all that protected the square from direct assault. Down by the Bastille, the Versaillese could not advance. They had forced the

rue Magnan, where Brunel had fallen, desperately wounded
after four days of continuous fighting. On the right,
Ranvier's admirably commanded batteries on the Buttes-
Chaumont held the line of the East Railway. By the
evening of the 25th, the Versaillese held an irregular line
from the Gare de l'Est along the Château d'Eau to the
Gare de Lyon. The Commune still held the XIXth and
XXth districts and part of the XIth and XIIth.

That Thursday night was another night of flame and
massacre. The bourgeois denounced right and left. Even
in the districts long occupied by the Versaillese troops the
carnage went on. It was dangerous to go into the streets;
and the shopkeepers speculated on the general panic. A
salad cost two francs, a cheap cut of beef or veal 2 francs 50
a pound. Audéoud once again gives the general feeling;
it was supposed that 3,000 insurgents were being stifled in
the cellars of the Hôtel de Ville: " the idea of the fate
which awaits them does not excite people's pity; far from it.
All of us wish to see them die in torment. We should like
to appease our hatred with the sight of their torture, for we
are no longer men but savage beasts. To-day no one dare
ask pity for these monsters, no one dare say that the repression is going too far. Anyone who risked preaching this
idiotically philanthropic idea would get a good hiding at
the very least."

The Communards could not escape contagion. That
afternoon the 101st, retreating from Arcueil, had driven
along with them the Dominicans, suspected of treachery
but cleared by Melliet. Nevertheless, they were hated
priests. In the Avenue des Gobelins, they were shut in a
house, temporary headquarters of the Battalion. They were
given the choice of working at the barricades. They refused,
offering to tend the wounded. The 101st outside were
clamouring for their blood, despite Serizier's desperate
efforts. An officer opened the door, told them to run for it.
They walked out, in holy simplicity, practically in a
crocodile. The 101st bowled them over like rabbits as they
came out.

The Versaillese continued to advance in little rushes under cover of night. An officer who had pushed too far forward at the Bastille was caught and shot, "without respect for the laws of war," Thiers said next day. But the Versaillese line drew ever nearer. The Château d'Eau was seriously threatened. The few members of the Commune still at the *mairie* debated anxiously. Delescluze was no longer there to steady them with his indomitable pessimism, Jourde sat calmly adding up figures, making at least a clean balance for these looters and bandits. Vermorel lay there in agony. Ferré, talking to him, seemed, for the first time, moved. At midnight it was decided to evacuate the *mairie* and fall back on Belleville.

The Boulevard Voltaire was not yet lost. And in the unconquerable Bastille, in the midst of a carpet of broken glass from the great department-store on the corner, desperate men still stood around the July Column which, riddled with bullets and blazing all the way up the inside from a couple of barges of petrol accidentally set on fire on the canal beneath, shot great streamers of flame through the holes all up its shaft and a great red banner of flame waving from its summit.

The dawn of Friday the 26th broke drizzling and foggy. Then came the rain brought down by the great guns. Flies no longer clustered on the corpses sprawling in the gutters. Men parched and thirsty at first welcomed the rain, then fought cursing the invisible enemy, drenched to the skin. The smoke hung low and into the eyes in great greasy coils. The pavements became slippery with blood and slime and sodden charrings. The battle lost its spectacular grandeur, became a last bitter, gloomy struggle in the murk. Yet the Communards still knew how to die. The Bastille, almost surrounded, beat off attack after attack, held out for another six hours of hand-to-hand fighting. A hundred bodies lay behind the barricades when the Versaillese at last entered the riven square that afternoon. The men of 1871 were defending what their fathers had defended in 1848. It was worth defending, and worthily defended.

As for dying, there were many who died well although they had not fought at all. Millière, the Deputy, who had not only not been a member of the Commune, but had severely criticised it from a Liberal humanitarian standpoint, was arrested that morning. Garcin, the savage military provost, was lunching at Foyot's with de Cissey. Millière was brought in, " in order that the crowd might not give him his deserts itself." Garcin told Millière that he would be shot. " Why ? " asked Millière. Garcin replied that he had read articles by Millière which had revolted him : " You detest society." " Yes," replied Millière, " I hate *this* society." Garcin ordered that he be shot on the steps of the Panthéon ; on his knees, to beg society's pardon for the wrong he had done it. Millière firmly refused. They forced him down on one knee. " Long live the people ! Long live Humanity ! " he shouted, and it was over. No Communard while he lived, he died like a Communard.

About the same time, Clavier, Commissioner for the Commune at Bel-Air, went to La Roquette, held up François at the point of the revolver, and made him bring out Jecker, the financier of the Mexico expedition. It was a curious business. Jecker was perfectly calm. He walked with his executioners half across what was left of revolutionary Paris, till they came to a ditch in the rue de la Chine. Jecker chatted amiably all the way about how he had been swindled by Morny. When he came to the ditch, he asked : " Here ? Will that do ? " crossed his arms, and died with an enigmatic smile. Clavier put his hat over the face and left a slip of paper with the scribbled name.

The Commune's magistrate, Colonel Gois, was walking near by when he heard the shots. Furious that an execution had been undertaken without him, he collected ten of his men, borrowed a score of Enfants Perdus from Eudes, and, joined by Clavier and his four men, arrived at La Roquette about two in the afternoon.

Belleville was now the centre of resistance. A thousand men, mostly those " sedentary Guards " whom Rossel had so despised, had reserved for their own quarter the fighting fury they would not take to the defence of wealthy Passy. The Communards concentrated along the line of the canal, barricading the rue de Crimée, the quai de la Loire, the Rotonde. The supplies service was centred at the *mairie* of the XXth; the military headquarters in the rue Haxo, in a complex of buildings and gardens known as the Cité Vincennes.

At the rue Haxo, all traces of central command had disappeared. Officers strayed about haphazard, looking for news. Traitors arrived: Raoul du Bisson, unmasked at La Villette as he had been at Montmartre. There were still a dozen members of the Commune trying to establish some sort of order. The Central Committee arrived, demanded the supreme command. The Commune yielded it gladly. Varlin, an old colleague of the Committee, was co-opted. The Committee of Public Safety had not been heard of for days.

Once more, Ranvier, popular ex-mayor of Belleville, took the lead. His dispositions, worked out with Passedouet, member of the Central Committee in the XIXth, had been excellent, especially the artillery.

Ranvier printed and posted the Commune's last proclamation—the 395th in two months !—" Citizens of the XXth district, if we yield you know what fate is in store for us ! To arms ! Vigilance, especially at night. I ask you to carry out orders loyally. Lend your aid to the XIXth district; help it to repulse the enemy. There lies your own safety. Do not wait for Belleville itself to be attacked, and Belleville will triumph yet once more. Forward ! Long live the Republic ! "

The battle was drawing nearer. The last positions of the Commune were being surrounded. Ladmirault had captured the jetties and stockyards of La Villette. At midday, the bombardment set on fire the western part of the Villette warehouses, an immense depository of oils and petrols. The enormous heat drove the Communards from the rues de Flandre and Ricquet; but the Versaillese, when they tried

to cross the canal by boat, were driven back by the guns at
the Rotonde and the rue de Crimée. On the right, Vinoy
had carried the Faubourg Saint-Antoine, the Bastille, the
Trône, the Gare de Vincennes. But the centre, advancing
more slowly in order to let the wings encircle the Communards' position, met with a furious resistance in the
Faubourg du Temple. Protot defended a barricade almost
alone in the rue Fontaine-au-Roi; finally fell, terribly
wounded in the face. A woman had seen him fall, took him
in, and when the Versaillese broke into the house they were
confronted by a strange bandaged figure, suffering, they
were told, from a frightful erysipelas.

-From the Buttes-Chaumont they could see the Prussians
clearly. By a convention agreed on with Versailles, the
Prussians had been blocking Paris on the north and east
since the Monday. On Thursday evening five thousand
Bavarians came down from Fontenay, Nogent, Charenton
and formed a cordon from the Marne to Montreuil. Another five thousand, with eighty guns, occupied Vincennes,
disarmed the fort and the Communards who were trying
to return to Paris. They arrested many of them, handed
them over to Versailles. There could be no doubt now that
the Versaillese Government would be able to guarantee
the payment of the five-milliard reparations.

There was a last surge of fury in the drizzling twilight.
News began to filter through into Belleville, news of huge
massacres, of cruel tortures, of the lie about the *Pétroleuses*.
The battle was coming closer. Nerves were on edge.

At six o'clock, a column of priests, gendarmes and
National Guards, surrounded by a yelling mob, came to the
*mairie* of the XXth. It was Gois and his men escorting 50
hostages: 36 gendarmes, 10 priests, 4 Imperial police spies.
Gois had got them by the usual method—the point of the
revolver. The gendarmes had marched correctly in file and
step, the priests trotting along behind in their soutanes. The
escort was so weak that the inhabitants of the streets round
the prison shouted to the hostages to escape. These martyrs
to correctitude never listened. Others howled: " The

hostages ! Kill them, kill them ! " and this cry had swelled all the way to the *mairie*.

At the *mairie*, Ranvier would have nothing to do with them, sent them away without taking any decision. The column, drums and trumpets in front, went on to Head-quarters in the rue Haxo. There it happened, in the great black shadows of the Cité Vincennes. Eudes, Alavoine, Varlin tried in vain to stop the massacre. They were hooted, themselves threatened. It was an outburst of horrible fury. They shot them down " like rabbits." When they counted the corpses afterwards, there were fifty-one. "Decidedly one too many," remarked Gois. One corpse had received sixty-nine bullets, another seventy-two bayonet-thrusts. Several National Guards had been wounded in the confusion.

On the other side of the barricades, too, the shootings went on far into the night. At the Parc Monceau, the Luxembourg, the Ecole Militaire, on the road to Versailles : men, women and children. And Paris burned.

Silent processions, or processions with one drum, marched down the main street of Belleville carrying biers on crossed rifles. The men marching on either side held torches.

Saturday broke wet and foggy. There was not much more to be done. The Versaillese advanced along the military road to the Montreuil and Bagnolet Gates, occupied the Place du Trône. In the north, Ladmirault threatened the Buttes-Chaumont, whose artillery had almost run out of munitions. The circle was closing.

At eleven that morning, the Commune met for the last time; some nine or ten members. Allix had arrived from somewhere and was exposing a bright plan to fall on the abandoned quarters and take the Versaillese in the flank. They were still talking when Ranvier broke in to collect men for the Buttes-Chaumont. " Go and fight instead of sitting here talking ! " he cried, and broke up the last sitting of the Commune's rump as Billioray had broken up that last full session nearly a week ago, a week that seemed a century.

There was a last attempt to interest the Prussians. Arnold, still accompanied by the mysterious Mr. Steinwerk, went to their outposts and asked to take a letter to Mr. Washburne. He was turned back roughly, with a vague promise that the note would be delivered. Another desperate attempt was made at the Romainville Gate. The Romainville gendarmes shouted to the Prussians to shoot down a crowd of fugitives. One woman was wounded by a German shot. The rest were thrust back into the massacre.

Ferré was not yet at the end of his functions. It was three o'clock, and the Versaillese were close, when he went for the last time to La Roquette, where there were still 315 hostages. But they had barricaded themselves in to wait for the Versaillese. Ferré only had time to scribble an order to release them, did release the common-law prisoners to fight on the barricades, and was off to the prison opposite, the Jeunes-Détenus, where there were 1,333 soldiers who had been shut up in the Prince-Eugène barracks all the time of the Commune, and whom Ferré himself had had transferred when the Commune retreated. He took them in three columns to the Belleville church and shut them in. On the way, the people greeted them with cheers, thinking that they were Versaillese who had come over. They were freed by the Versaillese advance some hours later. Four prisoners, including the Bishop of Surat, who ventured out of La Roquette too soon, were stood against a wall and shot by Communard bystanders.

Ferré's procession had the unfortunate effect of drawing off the incurably curious defenders of the Place des Fêtes; and the Versaillese easily carried the position. The last defenders of the hill had to retire on the Faubourg du Temple and the rue de Paris.

And now it was almost the end. The Versaillese stormed the Buttes-Chaumont at the point of the bayonet. The last great stronghold, the Cemetery of Père-Lachaise, was manned by some two hundred Communards, without cohesion, with very little ammunition. The wall had not even been loop-holed. At six o'clock, the Versaillese, not daring to take the place by assault, bombarded and smashed the main gate. Then there was a long series of desperate hand-to-hand struggles among the graves. The last defenders, massed against a monument, held out for half an hour. Turning as they left, they recognised the tomb of Morny.

That black Saturday night, the Communards had nothing left save two fragments of the XIth and XXth districts. The Versaillese were bivouacking in the Place des Fêtes, the rue Fessart, the rue Pradier. They were held only by the rectangle composed by the rue du Faubourg-du-Temple, the rue de la Folie-Méricourt, the rue de la Roquette and the Outer Boulevard.

All was confusion at the *mairie* of the XXth. Wounded lay everywhere, and there were no mattresses, no doctors, no bandages. Delirious men, men drunk with fatigue, hysterical women, frightened children, wagons, guns, detritus of all sorts everywhere. Only six or seven members of the Commune: Trinquet, Ferré, Varlin, Ranvier, Jourde, the best of them. But they too were utterly worn out. Some had not slept for four days. And it rained. And Paris burned.

In the smoky, rainy dawn of Whit Sunday 1871, the Versaillese moved forward to finish off the Commune. Rapidly they passed along the undefended fortifications, attacked the last barricades in the rue de Paris from behind. At nine o'clock, a column, starting from the Boulevard Philippe-Auguste, released the prisoners at La Roquette. By ten, the resistance was reduced to a little square within the rues du Faubourg-du-Temple, des Trois-Bornes, des Trois-Couronnes and the Boulevard de Belleville. The *mairie* had fallen two hours before. A few isolated streets still held out, notably the rue Ramponneau. Gambon, Varlin, Ferré, Géresme, Jean-Baptiste Clément still fought.

A little column headed by Varlin, Gambon and Ferré, now the perfect little armed bourgeois in appearance, went to defend the barricade at the corner of the rues du Faubourg-du-Temple and Fontaine-au-Roi, not far from where Protot had fallen. A gigantic Garibaldian, carrying an enormous red flag, quite dwarfed Varlin and Ferré. But this barricade, too, the Versaillese turned by the flank, and the defenders had hard work to get away.

Almost shut in, but with their backs to the wall and defended on all sides, they tried to hold out a little longer in the rues du Faubourg-du-Temple, Oberkampf, Saint-Maur, Parmentier. The Versaillese bombarded until the Communards' ammunition gave out.

The shooting became sparser, with longer intervals. The Communards had hardly any more ammunition. At noon, the last gun, double-shotted, roared from the rue de Paris.

The last barricade, that in the rue Ramponneau, held out for a quarter of an hour, defended by a single man. Again and again this dead shot broke the staff of the Versaillese flag on the barricade in the rue de Paris. Then, his ammunition having failed, the last soldier of the Commune walked away. It was quite possibly Lissagaray, its best historian.

The battle was over. Next day, the Fortress of Vincennes, which had taken no part in the fighting, but was still held by 350 National Guards and 24 officers commanded by Faltot, who had done great things for the Central Committee on March 18, surrendered, after some dubious negotiations with the Prussians. When the Versaillese entered, having promised to spare the lives of all, nine officers were taken aside. That night, the nine officers were lined up against the wall not a hundred yards from the spot where the duc d'Enghien had been executed, and shot.

On Sunday morning, one hundred and forty-seven Communards had been lined up against a wall in Père-Lachaise. The corpses were left lying barefoot. The " restoration of order " had begun.

# CHAPTER XI

# THE RESTORATION OF ORDER

" There were nine hundred of them there, heaped pell-mell in the filth, black with powder and caked blood, shivering with fever, howling with rage; and those that died were left there with the rest. Sometimes, when a sudden report rang out, they believed that they were all going to be shot. They would fling themselves against the walls, then fall back, so numbed by suffering that they felt they were living in a nightmare, in some ghastly delusion. The lamp which hung from the vault looked like a great bloodstain. Little green-and-yellow flames from the cellar-gases flitted around. A Commission was appointed, for an epidemic was feared. When its President came down the stairs, he recoiled, horrified by the stench of excrements and corpses. When the prisoners thronged to a vent-hole, the sentries thrust their bayonets into them haphazard.

" Their enemies were all of them without mercy. Those who had not fought wished to distinguish themselves now. It was the backwash of their terror. They were revenging themselves upon the papers, clubs, demonstrations, doctrines, upon all that had infuriated them for the past three months; and in spite of their victory, equality carried the day (as if in punishing its defenders it mocked at its adversaries), the equality of brute bestiality, a single level of bloody vileness. For the fanaticism of vested interest balanced the delirium of destitution, aristocracy raged in the lowest plebeian fury, and the nightcap showed itself no less hideous than the cap of Liberty. Public reason was perturbed as if after a great natural upheaval. Men of sense were driven to idiocy and remained idiots after it for the rest of their lives."

FLAUBERT: " *Education Sentimentale* " (1869)

WHEN THE LAST GUN HAD FIRED from the last barricade, Paris was like a city stricken by some natural catastrophe. Great greasy coils of smoke hung over the smouldering houses, foul with rain-caked soot. Pools of blood,
smashed streets, littered corpses, ruined barricades, ordures.
Whole streets in Belleville were deserted. The order to give
up all arms had been posted, and in the morning piles of
rifles appeared on the pavements, no one knew whence.

The east of the city was dark and tight-shut. In the silence prowled armed patrols who shot at sight.

But in the west " normal " life was flowing back. The streets were brightly lit once more. By June 3, a hysterical " normality " filled the Boulevard cafés with the shrill laughter of relief, a gaiety which sickened decent men almost as much as the slaughter.

Paris remained under martial law, divided into four military districts. Summary execution was still legal. Ladmirault ordered the immediate search of any house from which a shot was fired and the immediate execution of all its inmates. All public places were closed at eleven. Gatherings on the street were forbidden. The sale of petrol was banned. Only certain authorised newspapers were permitted to be sold on the streets. Women found wandering in the Bois de Boulogne were automatically registered as prostitutes and kept under police supervision.

No one was safe from informers. Old scores were paid off, new favours solicited. Between May 24 and June 13, the police received no less than 399,823 denunciations, of which not one-twentieth were signed. So haphazard were the arrests on the slightest of suspicions that 1,090 persons were claimed by their distracted relatives; while it is quite impossible to estimate how many people who had taken absolutely no part in the Commune perished in the wholesale massacre.

The " legal " shootings by the military authorities were even more frightful than the uncontrolled slaughter during the battle. Day and night, the rifles crashed at the provosts' courts at the Luxembourg, the Châtelet, the barracks. The Lobau barracks were perhaps the most terrible. Passers listened to the incessant volleys behind the great iron gates, from under which a broad red stream coiled sickeningly down into the Seine, fouling the water for weeks afterwards. At La Roquette, they shot 1,900 in two days. At Mazas another 400. All sorts of people were swept into these hells haphazard, just as they happened to be picked up by a passing patrol. There were hardly any escapes. There were only two judgments: either immediate execution or sent to Versailles for examination. And one was lucky if one even got as far as Versailles.

For Galliffet was waiting at La Muette. This elegant officer, slim and dandified in his neat uniform as Steinlen has pictured him, rather the air of a highly paid lion-tamer, preferred to do his work outside the mass-massacre. At La Muette he had more scope for the refinements of cruelty. The column of ragged, beaten, terrified prisoners would be halted in front of him. He passed along the ranks. A correspondent of the *Daily News* was present at one of these examinations: " I saw that it was not a good thing to be noticeably, taller or smaller, dirtier or cleaner, older or uglier than one's neighbour." The general picked out any who had the ill fortune to attract his notice. The others passed on. A few minutes later they heard the firing.

The survivors' torments were by no means over. They walked between the dragoons, a terrible crowd, filthy, staggering, some whining with fear, pain and fatigue, many, and especially the women, proud and defiant. At Versailles, the elegant crowd came out to see the sport. With the fury of a lynch-mad mob, they fell upon the prisoners, beating them, spitting on them, howling the foulest abuse. Quite literally, all conception of humanity had vanished. The captors now pandered to this swell mob. Columns of prisoners were paraded around the town. Others were left for hours on the torrid squares, only a couple of yards from the shade they were denied. It is impossible to say how many died before they reached their prison. The limits of human endurance seem equal to those of inhuman cruelty.

There were four hells called prisons: the cellars of the Grandes Ecuries, the Orangerie, the Satory depot and the stables of the Saint-Cyr military school. " Particularly dangerous criminals " were thrown into the " Lions' Den " below the beautiful rose marble steps of the Château Terrace. The horrors of these prisons surpassed anything yet seen in western, civilised, Europe. Many prisoners went mad; none were quite normal when they emerged to the daylight. Crammed together, half-starved, without doctors, clean clothes, water, almost without light. But they were better off than those in the " Lions' Den." These were in utter darkness, stifled, starved. Of those imprisoned there, very few indeed kept their reason.

Satory was hell in the open air; and a favourite spectacle for the good burghers of Versailles during the early days. It was a vast plateau of clay, surrounded by high walls. Thirteen hundred prisoners crammed the buildings; the rest, chiefly women, had to live in the open. It rained hard on the Friday night, the day after the bulk of the prisoners arrived. They had to sleep in the mud. A score died. Shooting went on incessantly near them. Often they thought they were to be shot in mass. One day a breach appeared in the walls, and the ugly muzzles of machine guns covered them.

It was no wonder that these prisoners soon seemed to belong to some sub-human species and became the prey of elegant persons in search of material for social studies. Respectable women who had been swept into the mass, although in fact utterly hostile to the Commune, soon merged their identity in the common squalor. In the end, Versailles began to have serious fears of infection. " There are several thousand of them there," said the *Indépendance Française*, " poisonous with filth and vermin, infecting the air for a mile around. Guns are trained on these wretches, stalled there like wild beasts. The inhabitants of Paris fear an epidemic from the insurgents' corpses buried in the city; those whom the Paris *Officiel* called ' Backwoodsmen ' are even more afraid of an epidemic, the result of the presence of the insurgents living at Satory."

A letter written from prison by Ferrat, an obscure non-commissioned officer in the National Guard, once arrested by the Commune on a vague suspicion of complicity with Versailles, describes these prisons and the prisoners' state of mind even better than such famous accounts as that of the famous geographer, Elisée Reclus; it is dated May 29 and addressed to his mother: " On Sunday morning, I was hurrying to clasp you in my arms and hear about the

dangers you must have run during the battle in your
district, when I was arrested by the soldiers opposite the
Magasins Réunis and taken to the Nouvelle France
Barracks, where I passed the night in a cellar, the floor of
which shone with mud several inches deep; it is true that
to remedy this slight inconvenience the number of prisoners
was so large that there was hardly room enough for us to
stand upright, and then only if the fat ones pressed close
against the thin. The next day, we were taken to Versailles
surrounded by an escort which left nothing to be desired in
the way of keeping us secure. It is quite impossible to tell
you, my dear Mother, of the enthusiastic welcome the
Versaillese gave us. Let it suffice you to know that the words
' brigands ' and ' thieves ' mingled pretty comfortably with
' murderers ' and ' incendiaries.' ' Shoot them ! Shoot
them ! '—such seemed to be the conclusion held by the
Versaillese who had gathered in thick groups on our path.
Strengthened by our good consciences, we remained calm
and dignified in face of this flood of undeserved insults.
Yet for my part, my heart was bitter. What ! said I to
myself, I, whose whole life has been nothing but self-
denial and sacrifice for others, I am to be treated like this !
I a thief ! I, who have had in my hands enough to make me
rich and left my post as poor as when I took it up ? I a
murderer ! I who have had in my hands the lives of a score
of prisoners and set them free ? Incendiary ! Brigand !
Poor people, they little know me who can dress me out in
this character. Let us pass over this chapter of human
error."

The prisons at Versailles were soon crammed even
beyond the limits which this human cattle could bear.
Thiers revived the English system of hulks. Between June
and September, 20,000 prisoners were loaded into 25 aged
ships. 7,837 more were transferred to the coastal fortresses.
Of these, 1,179 died. Even so, there remained 36,300 to be
tried.

Meanwhile, the massacre went on in Paris. All sorts of
persons were picked up by the roving patrols. Edouard

Moreau, of the Central Committee, disappeared into the Lobau barracks before his wife's eyes. Lacretelle gave orders to shoot Cernuschi, the philanthropist: he had subscribed largely to the fund against Napoléon's 1870 plebiscite, and the General of the Republic could not forgive this republican. Dr. Tony Moilin, a genial Utopian and popular poor-doctor, was shot, not because he had committed any crime, but because he was, as the provost said, " one of the people one must get rid of." A slight resemblance to a Communard leader meant death: they shot supposed Billiorays, Brunels, Vallès, Lefrançais, Vaillants, Longuets, Cluserets, Dereures, Gambons, Courbets and Amouroux.

They found Varlin. He was recognised in the rue Lafayette, on the Sunday afternoon, by a priest in plain-clothes. They took him to Montmartre, hands tied behind his back. Here the torture began. It was the same crowd which had hooted Lecomte to death, that battered in Varlin's head with stones. The soldiers made him run the gauntlet all over the Butte for a long hour. At last he reached a court martial at that same little house in the rue des Rosiers where Lecomte and Clément Thomas and so many Communards had met their end. They thought of shooting him in the garden, but the local commander had his quarters there and hated to see his victims in his own house. So they took him out, paraded him about until the crowd had smashed his face to a jelly, and shot him at the corner of the street. An officer stole the watch which the Bookbinders' Union had presented to him, and of which he had been boyishly proud. The workers' movement had had no better leader than Eugène Varlin.

Thiers telegraphed to his prefects: " the ground is paved with their corpses; this terrible spectacle will be a lesson to them." But soon the corpses began to take their revenge. They stank and they stank. Millions of pestilential flies swarmed through Paris. Birds fell dead in the streets. There was grave danger of a plague more terrible than the battle.

Hundreds of corpses had been thrust out of sight; but they returned. The heat swelled the bodies; and some, perhaps, were not quite dead. Passers by the great charnel in the Place Saint-Jacques heard strange noises from under the ground, and limbs forced themselves up through the thin covering, curling horribly. Three hundred had been flung into the lakes at the Buttes-Chaumont and now rose with ghastly noises, bloated, to the surface. Hundreds of corpses lay in the streets—at the Polytechnic School there was a pile a hundred yards long and three yards high—covered only with a sprinkling of chlorate of lime. All the bodies were barefoot.

So the clean-up began. Buses, chars-à-banc, any vehicle which would hold the bodies, many of them far gone in decomposition, were requisitioned. The cemeteries were crammed. Great ditches were filled. The trenches dug during the war at Charonne, Bagnolet, Bicêtre, Bercy, outside the walls, were crammed too. But still there were too many. On the Buttes-Chaumont, once the gallows of Montfaucon, then the municipal dung-heap, then the idyllic pseudo-classical gardens laid out by Haussmann to tame the savage breasts of the Bellevillois, they built a huge pyre. For days and days, a cloud of stinking smoke hung low over eastern Paris.

It is not possible to distinguish the number of those killed by the military justice from those that fell in battle. The total, too, is still disputed, for no account was kept of the radical purification. The reactionary historian Maxime du Camp estimates " 6,500 at the most," which is precisely as accurate as his other statements. General Appert admitted privately that he reckoned 17,000. MacMahon said " only " 14,000. According to the latest unbiased authorities, the number is somewhere between 20 and 30,000 men, women and children in ten days.

The losses of the Versaillese army for the whole operation since April 2 amounted to 83 officers and 794 men killed, 430 officers and 6,024 men wounded, 183 men missing: total casualties of all ranks, 7,514.

The French Revolution has left a bloodier name; yet, between April 6, 1793, and July 27, 1794, the period of the Jacobin Terror, only 2,596 heads fell in Paris. If the September Massacres, the seven Noyades in the provinces, the killings at Lyons, Toulon, Arras and Orange are added, the Revolution accounted in two years for only 10 to 12,000 deaths throughout the whole of France.

Paris appeared an antique city overthrown by some eruption. Expeditions to view the ruins by moonlight were enormously popular. Cooks' ran special excursions after May 25, and splenetic English tourists irritated their hosts by complaining that the city was not still smoking. The Prussian soldiers at Saint-Denis were pleased to lend their glasses to the open-handed strangers who shared their Nordic intuition that this destruction had in it something of God's wrath upon Nineveh, the delicate city. Lieutenant Hindenburg was among them.

A great part of Paris had been burnt down. The more important public buildings included: the Ministry of Finance, the Tuileries, the Louvre Library, half the Palais-Royal, the Hôtel de Ville, the July Column, the Arsenal, the Palace of Justice, the Prefecture of Police, the Ministry of Foreign Affairs, the Legion of Honour Palace, the Council of State and Court of Accounts buildings, the Gobelins, the Mining schools, the Lyrique and the Porte Saint-Martin theatres, the Bonaparte and Prince-Eugène barracks, the Grenier d'Abondance and the La Villette warehouses; the stations at Auteil, Passy and Porte-Maillot on the Loop Railway and the termini Orléans and Montparnasse. Private buildings, like the Hôtel Continental and several large department-stores, and whole blocks of houses in the rues Royale, Saint-Honoré, de Rivoli, Saint-Martin, Saint-Antoine, du Bac, de Lille, Vavin, the Places de la Concorde, du Louvre, de l'Hôtel de Ville, de la Bastille, du Chateau d'Eau, to mention only a few, had been wholly or partially ruined. The suburbs, especially Neuilly,

Meudon, Saint-Cloud, Issy, Vanves and Clamart, had suffered terribly.

It is difficult to estimate exactly the monetary losses caused by the Commune. The costs of reconstruction have to be added to the indemnities granted to private persons and the railway companies; the cost of replacing the burnt documents; the costs of the prosecutions and transportations; etc. Without counting the pensions granted to the widows and orphans of those who fell in the battle, it has been computed that the total cost of the Commune was 231,794,626 francs (£9,658,108).

Another estimate, drawn up by the technical journal *Assurances*, gives a rough total of 229,200,000 francs, with a further loss of merchandise amounting to 270,000,000 francs. But this estimate covers only the supposed insured value of the buildings destroyed, and does not take into account such items as the sums requisitioned by the Commune from the Bank of France. Neither reckon in the 17,000 burials paid for by the City of Paris. The total cost of the Commune must therefore be reckoned at nearly £20,000,000.

The artistic loss was more serious. Not that the Commune destroyed any works of art; but the buildings were reconstructed during the worst period of European architecture. The builders contented themselves with a dead reproduction of the buildings destroyed. When they did not do so, edifices like the new Palace of Justice suggest that their general lack of artistic initiative was justified. The Tuileries, the skeleton of which stood for many years behind a great hoarding which compared not unfavourably with its original façade, was never rebuilt. In spite of the ravages of the Bloody Week, the outward form of most of the principal buildings of central Paris is much as it was in the time of Haussmann: only the spirit of the old genuine architecture perished with the last attempt of Paris to assert and safeguard its individuality.

Meanwhile, Thiers had been celebrating his triumph. On June 29, he held a review of the victorious army at

Longchamps. It is true that this was part of his plan for the national revival, a show of strength in the face of the Prussians. Nevertheless, it was also a celebration of his victory; and he was so moved that he and MacMahon wept with joy on each other's bosoms. " It was the joy," he wrote proudly, " of a happy convalescence on a spring day, and at that moment, I found the burden I had to bear less heavy. . . . Back at Versailles, I gathered at a great dinner all the military leaders; to the reception afterwards there came the greater part of the Assembly, without distinction of Right and Left. So all went off for the best on this day, which was a good day for France."

" Without distinction of Right and Left ": Louis Blanc, Arago, Henri Martin joined in execrating the Communards. It was a " good day " for Thiers's France.

Since Paris was still under martial law, the military authorities were charged with the trials. The prisoners, therefore, were to be judged by those against whom they had fought. Dufaure had been cunning enough to deny the political nature of the charges and reduce the accusation, and the procedure, to simple common-law trials. The death penalty for political crimes had been abolished in 1848; so that the criminal procedure would permit the judges to satisfy their hatred by methods incontestably legal. It also gave the judges the right to cut short any uncomfortable defence.

The Third Council of War was the most important. It was presided over by Merlin, one of Bazaine's officers, and Gaveau, who had recently been released from an asylum. The defenders given to the prisoners were little better than useless. More than one begged the Court not to suppose that he personally had any sympathy for his client. Many did not trouble to arrive in court at all. At best, they attempted to disculpate their own client at the expense of another accused, out of professional jealousy.

The first trial before the Third Council of War was set as a sort of experiment and model. Fifteen members of the Commune and two of the Central Committee: Ferré, Assi,

Jourde, Grousset, Régère, Billioray, Courbet, Urbain, Victor Clément, Trinquet, Champy, Rastoul, Decamps, Ulysse Parent, and Ferrat and Lullier. In them, the Court intended to arraign the whole Commune. The dossiers were submitted generally in inaccurate copies; the most suspect documents were used without question; and Merlin had not the slightest hesitation in enforcing his own views.

The trial took place in a huge hall with 2,000 seats, reserved for all the eminent personalities of the day. A great crucifix hung on the wall. It was a brilliant scene, very different from Rigault's Jury of Accusation.

Except Ferré, Jourde and Trinquet, the accused made a poor showing. That must be admitted. But the reasons why they did not make a splendid revolutionary defence are not hard to find. The open hostility of the audience and the judges, the oppression of the great hall do not explain everything; but add to this two months of the hell of the Versailles prisons, the tortures of the " Lions' Den "; above all, a strong revolutionary defence was not in their character. The general state of mind among the prisoners was that of Ferrat's letter, already quoted: they simply could not understand this attack upon their respectability. In this they were perfectly consistent with their behaviour throughout the Commune, as were those who spoke up boldly in their own defence—Trinquet, Jourde and Ferré.

Trinquet, the Belleville cobbler, was as forthright as he had always been. " I was sent to the Commune," he said, " by my fellow-citizens; I suffered for it; I was on the barricades and I am sorry I was not killed there; I should not then be watching the sad spectacle of my colleagues who shared in the action refusing to share in the responsibility. I am an insurgent, and I don't mind saying so." They gave the square little cobbler hard labour for life.

Jourde's defence was equally typical. He was furious that he should be accused of theft. By a tremendous effort of memory, he reconstituted, without documents, the whole accounts of the Commune, proving that his work was not only not felonious, but even admirable. Beslay had been given a passport to Switzerland by the grateful Bank of France. Jourde did not see why he should not have one too. They sentenced him to transportation.

Ferré was the hero of the trial. Nothing could ever intimidate that terrorist. He had refused to make any statement to the examining magistrate. He had addressed a letter in his neat firm hand that morning to the Council of War:

" Whereas I have had the honour of being appointed member of the Commune of Paris by 13,700 electors of the XVIIIth district, whereas I accepted that mandate and it was my duty to carry it out loyally,

" Whereas, the Commune of Paris having fallen, its defenders are to suffer the usual fate of vanquished popular parties; and whereas their characters, their doctrines, their actions and even their intentions are twisted by partiality and misinterpreted in the most odious way,

" Whereas, the partisans of the Commune being killed, imprisoned or driven into hiding, cannot at present re-establish the truth and brand their slanderers,

" Whereas the judges, military or civil, cannot form a properly impartial opinion of a cause against which they have taken up arms,

" Whereas, too, as far as I am concerned, the unspeakable treatment of which I have been the object and the cruel persecutions exercised against members of my family deprive me of all means of defence,

" Whereas, finally, in order to safeguard his principles and dignity, these circumstances dictate to the true Republican the conduct which he must follow:

" For these motives,

" I declare that, excepting questions concerning my identity, I refuse formally to answer every other question which may be put to me, and that I intend to take no active part whatsoever in the trial that is about to begin."

Nevertheless, when Gaveau, after a prosecuting speech
which was a tissue of the more grotesque accusations flung
at the Commune by the hysterical Versaillese press, called
upon Ferré's lawyer to defend him, Ferré refused this
dubious advocacy and asked permission to read his own
defence. Merlin, the President, interrupted him at every
line. Ferré, true to the attitude he had taken at Blois in
1870, simply attacked. The audience listened, breathless,
admiring in spite of itself. Ferré was permitted to read the
end of his speech, after Merlin had silenced him time after
time. " Member of the Commune," Ferré read steadily,
" I am in the hands of its victors. They want my head. Let
them take it ! Never will I save my life by cowardice. I
have lived a free man; I intend to die no less. I have but
one word to add : Fortune is capricious; I entrust to the
future the care for my memory and my vengeance."
Merlin : " A murderer's memory ! " Then tumult broke
loose, and the hall had to be cleared. Naturally, they
sentenced Ferré to death.

Lullier, too, was sentenced to death, but, in view of his
services to Versailles, afterwards reprieved; Urbain,
curiously, to hard labour for life; Assi, Champy, Billioray,
Grousset, Régère, Verdure and Ferrat to transportation to
a fortified place; Rastoul, like Jourde, to simple transportation; Victor Clément to three months; Courbet to six
months and the reconstruction of the Vendôme Column at
his own expense. Descamps and Parent were, miraculously,
acquitted.

At the next trial, on September 4 and 5, five women appeared before the Fourth Council of War, presided over by
Boisdenemetz, a contributor to the *Figaro*, that paper which
had once employed Rochefort and now vented a lubricious
fury upon Rochefort's allies. It was the famous *Pétroleuses*
trial. Nothing whatever could be proved against these
women, except that they had not been married to the men
with whom they lived, at all times a common practice
among the Paris workers. In the wild fury against the
Commune's alleged subversiveness, this alone was sufficient

to expose them to the foulest insults from the Court. Three of their five defenders did not appear—" they have asked permission to go down into the country," the Clerk of the Court reported. Three of these women, Suétens, Marchais, Rétiffe—who had said in court that she would have picked up a Versaillese soldier as willingly as a Communard when she was working with the ambulance-service—were condemned to death; Papavoine to transportation to a fortified place; Bocquin to ten years' imprisonment. A few days later, Boisdenemetz was equally savage with fifteen children, the oldest of whom was only sixteen.

The trials were perfect farces. The hideous pretence of legality did not hide the continuation of the methods which had slaughtered so mercilessly in the last days of May. Sometimes the absurdity was open. On June 29, 1872, Rigault was condemned to death in absence, after the police had long sought him in vain. On February 4, 1873, they condemned Duval—whose death had been officially reported at Versailles on April 4, 1871—to transportation to a fortified place !

Another big trial, that of the alleged murderers of Generals Lecomte and Clément Thomas, was horrifying. It will be recalled that Lagrange, Simon Mayer, Herpin-Lacroix and Kadanski had done everything humanly possible to prevent the shootings. All except Kadanski were sentenced to death; Kadanski to transportation.

Rossel's trial was more exciting. The bourgeoisie recognised in him one of themselves. His motives were comprehensible, a disappointed patriotism and a hatred of Napoleonic decadence. Nevertheless, he was sentenced to death, on September 8. The prosecutor demanded the death penalty with tears in his eyes: " It is a painful task that I have to carry out, for I am addressing judges whose mission it is to safeguard military honour ! " An influential campaign was set on foot to save Rossel; and the sentence was quashed on September 22. However, a retrial, before the Fourth Council, on October 7, reimposed the death penalty.

Then came the journalists. Rochefort, once the darling of the swell audience, received sentence of transportation to a fortified place; Maroteau, of the *Salut Public*, was condemned to death for a couple of articles; Humbert, of the *Père Duchêne*, to imprisonment for an article demanding Chaudey's arrest which he had not written. And many more.

For months, twenty-six Councils of War, in Paris, Versailles, Vincennes and all over the district as far as Chartres, 1,509 soldiers, including 14 generals, 266 colonels and 284 commanders, applied the law to the men against whom they had fought. The excuse was that these men were not political opponents but felons. Yet felony was rarely proved. The official figures demonstrate the inaccuracy of the accusation that the Commune was the work of criminals and foreigners. Of the 10,137 persons sentenced and the 3,313 more condemned in absence, 9,285 could be proved guilty of nothing worse than carrying arms or usurping public functions; 276 more only for illegal arrests; 171 for street-fighting; 132 for illegal requisitions; and no more than 766 for what even those Courts could term felonies. Of these " jail-birds " 7,119 had no previous convictions; 524 had been punished for political offences; 2,381 had been previously convicted, but upon what charges it was not specified. The foreigners amounted to no more than 396, mostly Poles.

On November 28, Thiers evaded further responsibility by making the Assembly set up a Commission for Pardons, composed of fifteen of its most reactionary members. " Commission of murderers ! " shouted a Deputy of the Left. Of the 6,501 appeals which came before them they granted 2,502, mostly cases of mistaken identity. It is fair to record, however, that the Commission, sitting until 1875, when passions had long cooled and political conditions had changed, commuted 84 out of 110 death sentences and 346 out of 739 transportations to a fortified place. But the Merlins and Gaveaus had already done their worst, sitting from August 7, 1871, until January 22, 1873. A soldier accused of throwing the police spy Vincenzoni into the Seine on February 26, 1871, was shot in 1875.

In that year, the complete list of the legal condemnations was at last published: 270 persons, including 8 women, had been sentenced to death; 410, including 29 women, to hard labour; 3,989, including 20 women, to transportation to a fortified place; 3,507, including 16 women and one child, to transportation. These were only the heavier sentences.

Of these, 29 were members of the Commune, 49 of the Central Committee: which demolishes the legend that the " talkers " did not also fight. There were 225 superior officers, 1,942 lesser ranks, 7,418 non-commissioned officers and National Guards. The figures do not include the repression in the provinces.

The shootings began on the day upon which Thiers set up his Commission for Pardons. To the three posts planted in the vast gloomy plain of Satory came Ferré, Rossel and a Sergeant Bourgeois of the 45th—the regiment of the Four Sergeants of La Rochelle. Ferré was as calm as ever. Rossel made patriotic gestures, babbling. The officer commanding the firing-squad had to warn him that he was prolonging the others' agony. Ferré stood with a cigar clenched firmly between his teeth. His mother had died lunatic; his brother was shut up in a cell at Versailles, his father prisoner at Fouras; his sister, a silent girl of nineteen, worked all night to make the 20 francs she sent the prisoners every week. Ferré had little left to live for; and perhaps this cold death suited him better than the ostentation of the barricades.

Louise Michel, from her cell, wrote to General Appert three days later: " Monster, I am beginning to believe in the triple murder on Tuesday morning. If you do not want to judge me, you know enough about me; I am ready and Satory Plain is not far. You know well enough that if I came out of this alive, I should avenge our martyrs. Long live the Commune ! "

Louise Michel was one of the few who stood up for themselves at their trial. " You must cut me off," she cried, " from society ! You have been told to do so; well, the

Public Prosecutor is right ! Since it seems that every heart that beats for liberty has the right only to a lump of lead, I demand my share ! If you let me live, I shall not cease calling for vengeance, and I shall denounce to the vengeance of my brothers the murderers of the Commission for Pardons ! . . . If you are not cowards kill me ! " They did not kill her, but sent her to the slower death of New Caledonia.

The voyage to New Caledonia was a new hell. The convoys set out on May 3, 1872, after the prisoners had been left in illusory hopes in the coastal fortresses for nearly a year. The only consolation was the welcome at the larger ports, where the people, now firmly Republican, openly demonstrated their hatred of the Assembly by their sympathy for the condemned.

The journey took five months. The prisoners were packed in great cages, covered by machine guns. It was a sharks' banquet. Of the 650 prisoners on board the *Semiramis*, 34 were dead and 60 were seriously ill when the ship reached New Caledonia.

When the *Orne* put in at Melbourne, 300 of the 588 prisoners were down with scurvy. The inhabitants, who had collected £1,500 in a few hours to relieve them, were not permitted to help.

In 1848, the transported insurgents had at least been employed on productive works in Algeria. But an insurrection had broken out there just before the Commune, and, also, it was too close to France for the Assembly's peace of mind. Consequently, the Communards were sent as far away as possible, to a place where their work could be of no use to themselves nor to anyone else. England, it is worth noting, had abolished transportation in 1867; and even in the worst times Australia had offered some chance of gaining a decent livelihood. In New Caledonia, torrid, rocky, inhabited by savage Kanakas still engaged in head-hunting, life was a torment. Those sentenced to transportation to a fortified place shared the hovels of the vilest scum of the jails. Among them were men whose very honesty and respectability had brought them here: Trinquet, Amour-roux, da Costa, Lisbonne, Humbert. Here they suffered, save those released by death, for nine years.

Few escaped. On March 20, 1874, however, Rochefort, Paschal Grousset and three others succeeded in an attempt managed by the ever-ingenious Jourde. They reached Australia, and, after Gambetta had raised a private subscription of 25,000 francs for them, London, where their revelations of New Caledonian conditions caused a great sensation. But the new Governor sent out in consequence merely redoubled the severities.

By this savage repression, mercantile Paris had cut its own throat. Key industries were ruined for ten years. Among those convicted there were no less than 10,000 skilled artisans, including some 2,000 engaged in the furniture industries, several thousand garment-workers and 1,500 cobblers —it was curiously a cobbler's revolution. Many thousands of others emigrated, taking with them their craft-skill and craft-secrets, with which they built up rival industries abroad. Paris fashion artists and workers made the fortunes of English houses. Two Communards introduced the manufacture of Gobelin tapestries at Windsor. Serrailler, of the International and Commune, made French boot-trees at Northampton. Other Communards brought the skill they had learnt in Haussmann's improvements of Paris to the rebuilding of Brussels.

With those killed in the street-fighting and massacres, those who died in prison, on the transports, in New Caledonia and in exile, those imprisoned on long sentences and those deported, it may be reckoned that Paris lost more than 50,000 workers. To these must be added the workers who fled, the dependants of the dead and proscribed, deprived of their means of livelihood: about 70,000 more. One hundred and twenty thousand victims! Few repressions can boast so radical a " purification."

The lives of the Communard exiles were those of all

political exiles. The main groups went to Belgium, Switzerland and London. In Brussels, their welcome was unpleasant. Victor Hugo had written a noble, but tactless, letter to the Press, greeting them, and a mob had stoned his house. However, many Communards settled down there later, and Brussels was less plagued by police spies than was London.

The greater number went to Switzerland; and lost their illusions about the liberties of Swiss democracy. Swiss puritanism tended, too, to isolate them. But they gradually settled down, and several opened prosperous businesses.

Little is known of the London exiles. They settled into dingy lodgings off the Tottenham Court Road. They met at the Cercle d'Etudes Sociales in Francis Street, at the Duke of York near Gray's Inn Road, and sometimes at a pub at 6 Old Compton Street, or the Café de la Sablonière et de Provence off Leicester Square, where Verlaine and Rimbaud saw Vermesch, Vallès and others in September 1872. Vermesch himself lived in Charlotte Street, published a little paper and a few poems, and died of the disease which killed his master Baudelaire. Longuet, Lafargue and Vaillant became intimate with Marx and his circle, Longuet and Lafargue marrying his daughters. Vaillant was given a lectureship at London University, where his mortar-board amused Clémenceau by its exact resemblance to the French lancer's *czapka*. Brunel taught at Dartmouth that Prince of Wales who, as Edward VII, was to become the intimate of the Marquis de Galliffet. Lhéman and Privé decorated and arranged the art collections of Sir Richard Wallace.

But the lot of most of the London exiles was wretched. Unemployment was naturally their curse. As late as 1873, Charles da Costa wrote that he had absolutely not a penny: " I go to the dogs." The majority were the poorer and less distinguished participants in the Commune, semi-skilled labourers. Consequently, far less is known of them than of the relatively important Communards in Switzerland.

Police espionage was worse in London. An attempt made

by Jules Favre to obtain the extradition of Razoua and Franckel from Switzerland failed because he could not prove them to be felons. After this, the exiles were fairly secure. Close co-operation, however, between the English and French police subjected them to irritating surveillance.

Even those acquitted by the courts martial were spied upon perpetually. They were allowed to live where they pleased, except anywhere where they could carry on the trades to which they had been bred: Aix, Marseilles, Brest, Lambezelles, Bordeaux, Nantes, Lille, Lyons, Toulon, Limoges and the whole departments of the Seine, Seine-et-Marne and Seine-et-Oise (Paris and region) were forbidden them. Others suspected by the police but not actually inculpated were given passports with a special mark, " C," as late as May 1873, and were permitted to return to Paris only if they already had certain means of support, if their conduct before the Commune had been " irreproachable " and if they were of " habitual good relations and honourable family." Anyone who had been noticed at all during the Commune—that is to say, even the victim of an anonymous denunciation—could not get this permission. These people, said the police report, were not dangerous, but weak, and might be led astray once more; permission was therefore to be refused " for their own good and the still higher consideration of public security."

The struggle for the amnesty, carried on by the Left with a vigour increasing in proportion as their own position grew more secure, lasted nine years, and became in some sort a political barometer. The Assembly dissolved at last on December 31, 1875, after having thrown out every proposal for an amnesty. The elections of February 1876, which returned 350 Republicans out of 530 seats, brought back at least those who had resigned from the Assembly in 1871: Floquet, Lockroy, Clémenceau. After MacMahon's attempted reactionary *coup d'état*, on May 16, 1877, the Republican forces rallied once more in October, and returned with a majority of 117. But the amnesty these lawyers and petty-bourgeois, Gambetta's famous *nouvelles couches*, brought in concerned only their friends victimised after May 16. MacMahon resigned on January 30, 1879, and was succeeded with suspicious promptness by Grévy, the first Republican President of the Republic. The secretary of Waddington, head of the Cabinet, was a Communard condemned to death by the Councils of War. The Communards were beginning to return; but there were still eleven hundred in New Caledonia and five or six hundred in exile, condemned in absence and not yet pardoned.

In spite of Waddington's refusal to grant a full amnesty, the workers were calling back their old representatives. In April 1879, a 4,000 majority in Bordeaux elected Blanqui. The Chamber annulled the election, but was forced to extend the amnesty. Louis Blanc, who " happened " to be electioneering in the south, had the impertinence to welcome the returning proscripts at Port-Vendres.

The amnesty now became a popular demand, a weapon against the bourgeois Opportunist Party. Humbert, once editor of the *Père Duchêne*, was elected municipal councillor in Paris; another Communard in Lille. The newly formed Socialist Parti Ouvrier agitated strongly for the total amnesty. In 1880, the anniversary of March 18 was celebrated for the first time openly in many quarters in Paris and in the provinces. On May 23, a great crowd carried wreaths to Père-Lachaise in memory of Bloody Week, in spite of fierce police charges. A month later, Belleville elected Trinquet municipal councillor despite the efforts of their Deputy, Gambetta, to dissuade them. Gambetta took this hint, forced the amnesty through the Chamber. On July 10, 1880, the torments of the Communard proscripts were at last ended.

They settled down into political and social activity. Some, like Camélinat, the Commune's Director of the Mint, continued to defend the workers, moving towards Marxism in Guesde's Parti Ouvrier and joining the Communist Party of France on its foundation in 1921. Vaillant led a fraction of the Blanquists, successors of those who had joined the International against Blanqui's instructions in

1868, into Guesde's workers' party, while Jourde and another fraction worked in the reformist Socialist Party of Jules Joffrin, and, later, Jaurès.

The Boulangist agitation (1887–9) was the last occasion on which Communards worked together as a solid group. In this period of tactical confusion, Rochefort, then editor of the *Intransigeant*, made a bad blunder in his attempt to use Boulanger as an instrument to smash Jules Ferry and the Opportunists. A group of Blanquists, headed by Granger, followed him in the old tactic of " penetrating " any mass movement to influence it in the direction they wished. Hence, they found themselves uneasily allied with Maurras, Barrès, Léon Daudet and the Duchesse d'Uzès, under the hidden directions of Ranc and the more openly destructive efforts of his best pupil, Clémenceau.

Vaillant and Camélinat, however, remained with Guesde to carry on the fight against both Boulanger and Ferry on the basis of the class-struggle. The two tendencies implicit in the Commune itself diverged here for the last time.

In the midst of Boulangism, April 1888, a figure who incorporated all that was most fatally romantic in the Commune reappeared in public for a final gesture. H.B.M. Ambassador in Paris, Lord Lytton, wrote to London : " The most interesting thing I have yet seen in the French Chamber I saw the other day. It was Félix Pyat, the old Anarchist, seated at the very top of the ' Mountain,' with a flowing white beard, the image of all that is venerable. In the course of the debate, however, he descended from his perch, mounted the tribune and, addressing the Chamber as ' Citoyens,' delivered with great seriousness and vehemence a speech which was greeted with convulsions of laughter. France on her revolutionary course wears out her politicians as fast as an army wears out its boots, and already this grim old creature is an anachronism."

Forty-four years later, the Socialist and Communist workers of Paris gave Camélinat such a funeral as the Commune had given its fighters two generations before.

With Camélinat died the last of the Commune's leaders, but not the Commune.

" After Whit-Sunday, 1871," wrote Marx, " there can be neither peace nor truce possible between the working men of France and the appropriators of their produce. The iron hand of a mercenary soldiery may keep for a time both classes tied down in common oppression. But the battle must break out again and again in ever-growing dimensions, and there can be no doubt as to who will be the victor in the end—the appropriating few, or the immense working majority. And the French working class is only the advanced guard of the modern proletariat."

# CHAPTER XII

# THE COMMUNE AT WORK

" It is in the Commune that the strength of free peoples resides. Communal institutions are to liberty what elementary schools are to knowledge: they place it within the people's reach; they give it the taste for peaceful manners and accustom it to their use. Without communal institutions, a nation may give itself a free government, but it does not possess the sentiment of freedom. Transient passions, the interests of the moment, the hazard of circumstances may give it the external forms of independence, but the repulsed despotism will always re-emerge to the surface."

DE TOCQUEVILLE

" The last preface to a new German edition of the *Communist Manifesto* signed by both its authors, Karl Marx and Friederich Engels, is dated June 24, 1872. In this preface the authors say that the programme of the ' Communist Manifesto ' ' is now in places out of date.' . . . ' In particular,' they continue, ' the Commune has demonstrated that the working class cannot simply lay hold of the ready-made State machinery and wield it for its own purposes.' . . . As a matter of fact, *exactly the opposite is the case*. Marx's idea is that the working class must *break up*, *shatter* the ' ready-made State machinery,' and not confine itself merely to taking possession of it."

V. I. LENIN: State and Revolution

THE COMMUNARDS have been and are still called Communists, both in praise and in hatred: Is this true? The answer is: Yes and no. Quite obviously, the Commune was not Communist in the modern sense—that is, consciously and determinedly carrying out the methods and aims of collectivist Communism, as explained by Karl Marx, by means of the abolition of classes.

Marx's work was unknown to almost all the Communards; and the few who did know him personally looked upon him simply as the organiser of the International Working-Men's Association. There was, indeed, no party in France at that time which had any full conception of even the fundamentals of modern scientific Communism. The Blanquists used the phrase " dictatorship of the proletariat," but were unable to visualise the State-form and social organisation to which the conquest of power would lead. The Proudhonists were interested only in local federation and economic co-operation, attempting to set up in Communard Paris a form which they hoped to see extended over the whole of France. The manifesto to this effect, drawn up by Proudhon's secretary, Pierre Denis, and published by him in the Commune's *Journal Officiel*, has been taken by some as representative of the Commune's own conception of its aims. But the article was not approved by the Communal Council and expressed ideas which not only were held by almost no one except old Beslay, but which had been antiquated in Paris for more than a decade.

The personal character of the neo-Jacobin petty-bourgeois majority in the Commune (not, be it noted, necessarily the majority of the rank and file) was well summed up by Bakunin, drawing his conclusions from information supplied by the Communard Elisée Reclus: " These generous Jacobins . . . desired above all the triumph of the revolution; and since there can be no revolution without the masses, and since the masses to-day are filled with the socialist instinct and can make no revolution other than one economic and social, the Jacobins, permitting themselves in all good faith to be carried along by the logic of the revolutionary movement, ended by becoming socialists in spite of themselves." This amounts to a typically Bakuninist way of saying that the Jacobins were forced to yield to, and express the pressure of, the rank and file in order to preserve their own position at the head of the revolution.

It is for this reason that the fundamentally revolutionary decrees of the Commune were proposed by the most antiquated Jacobins: the abolition of the standing army, the separation of Church and State, the reconstruction of police and army as a citizen militia with elective commanders, and so on. But Bakunin's description depends entirely upon his major premise: that " the masses to-day are filled with the socialist instinct."

That the " instinct " (another typical Bakuninism !) was widespread there is every evidence; that the instinct for Socialism alone was sufficient to make the Commune socialistic, if not communistic, is a more difficult proposition. Both the Marxist and the Bakuninist " interpretations " might seem to be merely examples of " wish-thinking " if the social and legislative decrees of the Commune are not analysed in all their consequences.

For convenience, it is useful to make a somewhat arbitrary distinction between *subjective* and *objective* Socialism when dealing with the Commune. The *subjective* measures would be those consciously taken in favour of the producing and against the possessing classes. The *objective* would then be those which later analysis shows to be part of what Lenin calls " the first stage in the development of proletarian dictatorship, in which soviet-power is the second." It is of these *objective* measures that Bakunin, himself only very vaguely conscious of their significance, " instinctively " spoke.

These *objective* measures were the substance of Marx's interpretation of *The Civil War in France*. The Commune seemed to him the crowning of his life-work in the sphere of political analysis. The general deductions which he had drawn from the history of the class-struggle, especially from 1848 and 1851, seemed to be proved correct. The Communards, although they did not know it, were his disciples. Naturally, any observer could see in a movement so vast and vague whatever he wished, from Earl Russell's " effects of horrid atheism " to Bakunin's " audacious negation of the State." While it is perfectly correct that the Communards were atheists and that, to some extent at least, they negated the State, chiefly by being impotent technically to reorganise it had they wished, such statements do not cover nearly enough of the Commune's activities to be wholly explanatory. Marx's analysis does fit a larger proportion of the facts than any other, and does so more convincingly. If one analyses inductively, it will be found that his is the most correct view of the Commune's *objective* Socialism.

The chief source for such induction is the way in which Marx's perception of the fundamentals of the Commune bore fruit. When Lenin went into hiding in Finland after the July Revolution in 1917, he took with him two books—Clausewitz's *Art of War* and Marx's *Civil War in France*. When he returned, he had jettisoned Clausewitz, but had substituted for him the manuscript of his own *State and Revolution*, the classic revolutionist's handbook.

In it he noted the fundamental characteristics of proletarian democracy: "(1) The source of power is not law previously discussed and enacted by parliament but the initiative springing straight from the underlying mass of the people, on the spot, a straight 'seizure,' according to the current phrase; (2) it involves the replacement of the police and army, which are separated from the people and opposed to it, by the direct arming of the whole nation; peace and order are maintained under such a government by the armed workers themselves, by the armed nation; (3) the bureaucracy is either cashiered in favour of representatives of the people or held strictly under popular control." All the elements of these three propositions were actually provided by the Commune; and many of the provisions in the constitution of the Union of Socialist Soviet Republics drawn up by Lenin himself in 1920 are to be found already present in the Commune.

The opinion of Marx upon the real *objective* meaning of the Commune, an opinion which led to a very important change in the 1872 German edition of the *Communist Manifesto*, is first expressed in a letter to Kugelmann on April 12, 1871: "If you look at the last chapter of my *Eighteenth Brumaire*, you will see that I declare the next attempt of the French Revolution to be: not merely to transfer the bureaucratic and military machinery from one set of hands to another—as has occurred hitherto—but to *break it up* (' *zerbrechen* '); and this is the preliminary condition of any real people's revolution. . . . This is exactly what the attempt of our heroic Parisian comrades implies." This is why Marx praised the Communards for " storming Heaven."

The measures which in actual fact meant the " breaking-up " of the bourgeois State must be called *objective* Socialism simply because the Commune was driven to take them by the logic of objective conditions, not with any deliberate idea of smashing the State, which, indeed, they had never scientifically analysed nor even conceived. A striking example of this is the abolition of the standing army simply because the National Guard was a citizen militia, consti-tuted far more by the Empress Eugènie's decree than by Lafayette, and because Rossel's attempt to reorganise some-thing like a regular army appeared to be a move towards establishing his personal dictatorship. On the other hand, such measures would not have taken the particular form they did had not " the masses been filled with the instinct for Socialism."

Another incidental measure to which both Marx and Lenin give great attention, as showing the Commune's Socialism, is the fixing of its representatives' salary at 6,000 francs a year, " the ordinary wages of a skilled workman," thus automatically removing the professional politician, abolishing both the prestige and the fruits of office, and, as Marx points out, " fulfilling the bourgeois ideal of ' cheap government.' " In actual fact, 6,000 francs (about £250) was high pay at the time, since the average skilled artisan in Paris received about 1,560 francs per year (about £65) ; and, under the Commune, the Director of its Arsenal at the Louvre only 3,000 (£125), a bench foreman only 2,620 (£117 5s.). Compared, however, with the pay of an English M.P. (10,000 francs at the contemporary rate), or even more with that of the Prime Minister (125,000 francs), the salary of a member of the Commune was infinitesimal.

The *subjective* Socialism of the Commune, the measures taken in favour of the producing class against the possessing, may be studied in detail in the work of the various Commissions set up to deal with the different branches of administration. Although the proposals of the special delegates were discussed by the Commune as a whole and had usually to be decreed by the Commune, not the Commission, the delegates were given a relatively free hand in all matters which did not encroach upon the activities of the military and police. On the whole, too, the police saw to the execution of the decrees with considerable zeal.

The Commune was a body both legislative and executive, at least in intention; and it was chiefly due to the perpetual state of war, as well as to the personal ambitions of Cluseret, Rossel and Rigault, that more social legislation was not carried through. It was the state of war, too, that forced Jourde to starve the Commissions of funds.

The chief complaint, however, was far more of lack of time than of money. While the extreme revolutionary backwardness of the Commune was shown in its refusal to expropriate the millions in the vaults of the Bank of France, it must be remembered that any kind of social legislation seemed to respectable persons in the early 'seventies in France little short of " horrid excesses "; while the very idea of such power being wielded by men " with the faces seen only on the days of revolutions " was itself so frightful that their most harmless legislation seemed the reddest of terrors. It was a legacy from Napoléon III's labour policy: for it appeared that his pandering to the workers' demands had encouraged them directly to seize the supreme power; and his fits of apprehension that the workers, having been offered an inch, would take an ell, had led him simultaneously to exaggerate the conception of the Red Terror from which only the Man of Order could save France. In this, Thiers's propaganda was in no way inferior to that of Louis Napoléon Bonaparte.

The Commune's budget, carefully managed by Jourde, was naturally burdened by police and military expenses. Figures exist only for the period March 20–April 30; but there is evidence that the military expenditure increased enormously in May;

| | |
|---|---|
| Delegation for War | 20,056,573 fr. 15 c. |
| Intendance | 1,813,318 fr. 25 c. |
| Central Committee | 15,651 fr. 20 c. |
| Barricades Commission | 44,500 fr. 00 c. |
| Navy (gunboats) | 29,259 fr. 34 c. |
| | 21,959,301 fr. 94 c. |
| Police Commission | 235,039 fr. 40 c. |
| Justice      „ | 5,500 fr. 00 c. |
| | 240,539 fr. 40 c. |
| Total executive | 22,199,841 fr. 34 c. |

The total sums allotted to all the other commissions were only 266,859 fr. 96 c. Thus:

| | |
|---|---|
| Interior | 103,730 fr. 00 c. |
| Exterior | 112,129 fr. 96 c. |
| Commerce | 50,000 fr. 00 c. |
| Education | 1,000 fr. 00 c. |
| Labour | nil |
| Total | 266,859 fr. 96 c. |

In addition, the municipalities received 1,445,645 fr. 64 c. It is notable that the bourgeois, wealthy and thinly populated IInd got only 5,000 fr. and the VIIIth only 4,000 fr., while the populous working-class XXth received 228,000.

The rest of the budget, some 1,250,000 francs, was devoted to various municipal and administrative expenses, notable being 5,000 fr. to the Metallurgic Union, 20,000 fr. to the Tailors' Union and 4,662 frs. to the Cobblers'.

Jourde managed remarkably well. The whole cost of the

Commune from March 20th to May 21st was only about 46,300,000 francs (about £1,852,000). It was levied thus:

| | |
|---|---|
| Octroi | 13,217,526 fr. 88 c. |
| Direct taxes | 373,813 fr. 00 c. |
| Indirect taxes (tobacco) | 2,629,123 fr. 15 c. |
| Stamp and registration tax | 800,000 fr. 00 c. |
| Municipal markets | 814,323 fr. 82 c. |
| Reimbursements from Nat. Guard | 1,000,000 fr. 00 c. |
| Railway levy | 2,000,000 fr. 00 c. |
| Customs | 55,000 fr. 00 c. |
| Sums seized at Hôtel de Ville | 6,008,608 fr. 91 c. |
| Bank of France | 15,040,000 fr. 00 c. |
| Total | 41,988,395 fr. 76 c. |

Jourde, indeed, was so scrupulous that he insisted on formally handing over to the authorities the last 9,770 francs of the Commune's finances he was carrying upon him when he was arrested on May 30 after wandering for hours amid the massacre, except 120 francs belonging to him personally. All the time he was at the Ministry of Finance, his wife continued to wash her own laundry. Almost all his financing could, unfortunately from the revolutionary point of view, be called regular. There were securities and cash in the Bank of France, worth 2 milliards 980 millions, which were never touched; nor were the 214 million francs' worth of bonds which he found at the Ministry of Finance. Of the 15 millions taken from the Bank of France, 9,400,000 francs were already there to the credit of the City of Paris. The levy on the railways was a tax of 10 per cent on the gross receipts levied by the Commune in place of the former system. It needed Rigault's police to make the companies pay up. But when a battalion of the National Guard seized 183,000 francs from the municipal gas offices, on April 21, the Commune made them restore it and apologise.

The Commune produced some coins of its own—five-franc gold pieces from the 1848 moulds, some 2,400,000 francs' worth. The Mint was very ably directed by the founder of the Metal Workers' Union, Camélinat, one of the most active members of the International. The Bank of France would allow him only two millions' worth of bullion; the rest came from plate and reliquaries from the Tuileries. Officious persons were continually finding valuable objects in the churches, but these usually turned out to be the most hideous silver-gilt: it tended rather to demolish the pretensions of ecclesiastical magnificence. No piece of any artistic value was melted down. Only 153,000 francs were ever issued—to the last fighters on the barricades on May 24.

With the small moneys and less time at their disposal, the Commissions could do very little in the way of social legislation. The members of these Commissions, too, were not always qualified for their posts, some being included merely for their general reputation or to give them some post of honour. The Commissions worked more or less independently, but there are few instances of the Commune vetoing any of their specialised proposals.

These measures fall into two categories: those discussed by the Commune as a whole and those taken on the initiative of the appointed delegates and their commissions. Even when the question arose from immediate necessity, and even when little was done in actual solution, the discussions do bring out the Commune's socialistic intentions. Typical of such emergency measures was the Commune's treatment of the two burning questions: the rents and the maturities. The Assembly's provocative action had been one of the chief causes of bourgeois and petit-bourgeois support of the revolution of March 18.

The rent question was one of the very first treated by the Commune, on March 29. A general moratorium was decreed, expressly considering " that labour, industry and commerce have borne all the burdens of the war and it is only fair that property should make to the country its part

of the sacrifice." Even wealthy persons took advantage of
this decree, a tenant in the rue Tronchet who owed no less
than 10,000 francs to his landlord being not untypical.

The maturities question was far more complicated and
interesting. There were three main schemes, proposed by
Beslay, Jourde and Tridon, representing rather well the
Proudhonist, practical and Blanquist solutions respectively.
Beslay, after consulting the labour and employers' organisations, thought that the interests of all might be harmonised :
by creating an accounting bank issuing circulation notes
on the security of commercial bills as yet unpaid, he would
secure the eventual repayment of existing debts and the
immediate liquidation of frozen assets ; payment would be
distributed over three years in eighteen bi-monthly settle-
ments. At the same time, a " Commercial Liquidation
Bank " would be formed, issuing notes of 20 to 1,000 francs
secured by depositing the bills drawn between July 1,
1870, and June 15, 1871. The Commune would assist the
bank by opening in its favour a credit of one-fiftieth of the
unpaid obligations. All that was necessary to secure the
circulation of these notes on a par with those of the Bank of
France was to declare them redeemable on August 1, 1874 ;
by that time the currency needed for redemption purposes
would have been collected from the debtors. The great
flaw in this proposal was that it presupposed a Proudhonian neighbour-love on the part of the debtors.

Jourde was in favour of suspending payment for two
years, the debts being reduced gradually by the payment
of one-eighth every three months, beginning July 15,
1871. Any debtor who refused to pay would be liable to
prosecution for the eighth due.

Tridon proposed a moratorium for three years and the
imposition of 2 per cent interest ; but this gave no
guarantee whatever of a final settlement. After hearing
Beslay's scheme, Tridon modified his proposal by providing
for an accounting bank " to serve as intermediary between
the opposing interests " ; but this bank was not clearly
worked out. Nevertheless, the scheme was supported by

the extremer Jacobins on the grounds that it was the most socialistic of the schemes (which it was not) and because it was the most clear-cut and radical (which was possibly true, but hardly a practical recommendation).

The Commune, after several debates, adopted Jourde's sensible and non-doctrinal solution in principle. The decree of April 16 provided for the repayment of debts of all kinds within three years in quarterly payments of one-twelfth, without interest, beginning July 15, 1871. This solution was definitely favourable to the poorer classes, although it did nothing to attack the principle of finance-capitalism.

Another such decree in favour of the poorer classes was that dealing with the pawnshops. During the depression caused by the war, many workers, who were mostly artisans and craftsmen, had been forced to pawn the tools of their trades, thus losing the possibility of ever again being employed. Many others had been forced to pawn the bare necessities of decent existence. The rent decree had assured them a roof; the Commune had on the same day forbidden the further sale of pledges. The Labour Commission, staffed exclusively by Internationalists, had been asked to prepare a report, which was read to the Commune on April 25. Outstanding loans amounted to some 38 million francs. A number of people, hearing that it was proposed to release articles gratis, had pawned their property in order to make an easy profit. It was suggested, therefore, that withdrawals should be limited to 50, or even 20, francs to check this abuse. Even so, there were at least 1,800,000 articles to be dealt with.

The discussion turned on the question of pawning as an institution in general, and lasted some time. Finally, the Commune adopted a proposal by Jourde, on May 6, authorising the free withdrawal of articles pledged before April 25, 1871 (the date of the first debate), up to and including a value of 20 francs; the decree applied to clothing, furniture, linen, bedding, books (there was a heated debate as to whether books could be classed as tools and necessaries of life, the workmen in the Commune denying this fiercely) and tools. The pawnshops were to be indemnified. As Avrial said, the institution of the pawnshop must eventually disappear altogether, but in the meantime the brave men fighting for the Commune must be given some satisfaction. There were only two distributions, on May 12 and May 20.

Most of the Commune's truly socialistic legislation was carried out by the Commission for Labour and Exchange, staffed exclusively by members of the International, with one of its best militants, Léo Franckel, as delegate.

Franckel was one of the leaders of the German section in Paris, and a frequent correspondent with Marx himself. He several times wrote to Marx for suggestions: " I should be most happy if you would help me in one way or another with your advice," he wrote on April 25, " for I am practically solely responsible for all the reforms which I propose to introduce at the Ministry of Public Works." Another member of the Commission, Serrailler, was the official delegate from the General Council in London.

The old German militant, Victor Schily, who was a friend of Léo Franckel, actually invited Marx to come over and make use of the library at the Ministry of Agriculture, then in Franckel's occupation, to gather material for a study of French agricultural conditions, these official reports having hitherto been too expensive for Marx to procure. " But," he wrote, on April 29, " you must hurry up, for I am very much afraid that the Commune will not hold out much longer." Unfortunately, none of Marx's suggestions seem to have survived.

The Commune outlined the Commission's functions: " [It] is charged with the propagation of socialist doctrine. It must look for means of equalising work and wages. It must also concern itself with furthering French and Parisian industries . . . and with methods of developing international trade and attracting foreign industries to Paris, in order to make Paris a great producing centre." The Commission further outlined its own aims: " The study of all the reforms to be introduced into the public services of the Commune and into the relations of workers, both male and female, with their employers; the revision of the commercial code and tariffs; the revision of all direct and indirect taxation; the compilation of labour statistics."

The actual measures adopted by the Commission, partly under pressure of immediate circumstances, were quite different, but conceived in a similar spirit. These were: the abolition of fines in factories; the abolition of night work in bakeries; the occupation of factories abandoned by their owners and their reorganisation on a co-operative basis; the regulation of contracted wages.

The Commission tended to work beside the Commune rather than in it, although it took an active interest in all social discussions, such as the debates upon the rent question and the pawnshops. Franckel had even thought that the workers' interests would best be furthered by a Commission acting as intermediary between the Commune and the Federal Council of the International. The Commission itself did in some measure fulfil this function, since Serrailler kept up the connection with London, and, on April 6, a room in the Ministry of Public Works was put at the disposal of the Workers' Syndical Chambers.

The Syndicates welcomed this arrangement; and one of the most important, Camélinat's Mechanics and Metallurgists, appointed two delegates to go there " to suppress the exploitation of man by man, the latest form of slavery, and to organise labour by united associations with collective and non-transferable capital."

The Syndical movement was very active with the eager support of Franckel, who had realised, as he wrote to Marx on the morrow of his election, that " if we can bring about a radical alteration of social relationships, the revolution of March 18 will be the most fertile of all the revolutions in history."

As early as March 23, the stone-cutters had drawn up a form of workmen's insurance against accidents; and they

continued very active throughout the period. The tallow-
and stearin-founders met on April 27 to form a union and
co-operative. The butchers followed. The women workers
also wished to organise, and Franckel's friend, Elisabeth
Dmietrieva-Tomanovsky, a member of the Russian section
of the International in Switzerland, where she had supported Utin and Marx against Bakunin and Nechaev,
assembled them in her Women's Committee for the
Defence of Paris and the Care of the Wounded. About
3,000 women were organised, and held 24 public meetings
between April 11 and May 14. At a meeting at the Bourse
on May 10, Franckel asked her to appoint delegates from
each trade and set up unions and a federation. This
organisation was a great success, although, as Dmietrieva
wrote to Hermann Jung, at one time President of the
General Council of the International, she was very ill,
pessimistic, fatalist and " expected to die on the barricades
one of these days." Louise Michel gave her some assistance
in this work.

So far did this activity of the unions progress after the
torpor of the later years of the Second Empire that the
printers actually made a formal protest to the Commune,
on April 30, against the suppression of ten newspapers; not
on political grounds, but because of the resulting unemployment.

With the official encouragement given by Franckel to the
Syndicates, the International, which could gather 29 local
sections out of the 90-odd workers' organisations to an
extraordinary meeting on May 20, became very active,
not only centralising local social demands but also supervising its representatives in the Commune. A special commission, sitting at the Hôtel de Ville, passed on to the
Commune demands received at its own headquarters in the
Place de la Corderie, where it still shared offices with the
Federation of Syndical Chambers.

This trades union action, especially with its new tendency
towards political interest, was of the greatest importance,
since it represented a healthy awakening from the stagnation

into which it had fallen under the alternate paternalism and repression exercised by Napoléon III. The owners had not yet learnt how to corrupt and tame the unions, and the measures taken on their behalf by the Commune appeared shocking to Conservatives and to most *laissez-faire* Liberals.

Thus, when the Commune, on April 28, forbade the practice of levying fines for alleged carelessness in all factories, private and public, and ordered all fines imposed since March 18 be refunded, a fairly liberal paper such as the *Petit Journal* could head its report: " A Bounty to Idleness and Incapacity."

Another concession to the workers, now partially gained by trades union pressure, was brought in almost by accident: the State regulation of contracted wages. On May 4, the Commune had appointed Lévy and Evette, both members of the International, to look into the manufacture of uniforms for the National Guard. From their report, read by Franckel at the session of May 12, it appeared that the prices paid had caused a lowering of wages. Under the Government of National Defence, workers had received 6 francs per tunic, 3 francs 75 per pair of trousers; but the Commune, which had originally taken over this rate, had, since April 25, adopted a contract system, the work going to the lowest tender. Tunics were now being made for 4 francs, trousers for 2 francs 50: " one may say, then, that the Social Republic has done a thing which those besieging us refused to do: it has lowered wages." Franckel protested: " We must not forget that the revolution of March 18 was made exclusively by the working class. If we do nothing for this class, we who hold the principle of social equality, I see no reason for the Commune's existence." The report concluded that in future the workers' associations should be consulted and used. Vésinier and Jourde then proposed a decree which was adopted by the Commune: the Labour Commission was authorised to revise contracts made hitherto and to give preference to the workers' associations for future contracts on the basis of estimates, drawn up by the Intendance, the Syndical

Chambers and a delegate from the Labour Commission, fixing the minimum wage for day- or piece-work.

Franckel had proposed the eight-hour day; but in the most important of the Commune's State workshops, the Louvre arms-repair shops, the ten-hour day was adopted and approved by Avrial, of the International, then Director of Artillery. This shop was of course engaged in emergency work. It was organised on a democratic basis, partly because it was reckoned as belonging to the Federation of the National Guard. The director, the shop foreman and the bench foreman were appointed by the workers and could be dismissed by them if unsatisfactory. A factory council met every evening to discuss the next day's work. The director received a salary of 250 francs a month, the shop foreman 210, the bench foremen 70 centimes an hour— that is, about 165 francs a month. The workers' wages were fixed by the factory council, but " for the present, and in view of the state of war, it may not exceed 60 centimes an hour."

Franckel took his cue from such organisations and encouraged their initiative rather than impose measures upon them by decree. At the beginning of April, he had thought of organising communal workshops, but this would only be necessary when it was a matter of controlling the activities of the great financial oligarchies such as the railways.

The most striking example of Franckel's co-operation with the unions was the decree of April 16: " Whereas a number of workshops have been abandoned by their directors in order to escape their civic obligations and without taking into account the interests of the workers; whereas the result of this cowardly abandonment a number of works essential to communal life have been interrupted and the workers' livelihood threatened," the unions were to draw up a list of the abandoned shops and suggest practical means of setting them to work again " no longer for the deserters who had abandoned them, but by the co-operative association of the workers employed in them." There was, however, to be an arbitral jury to settle the indemnity to be paid to the owners on their return. The plan was, however, never carried out, as the investigatory commission was not properly constituted until May 18. The reactionary Press loudly denounced this decree as mere looting.

Franckel himself declared that the decree abolishing night-work in the bakeries was the only truly socialistic measure taken by the Commune. This is true in a sense which did not occur to him—the sense in which the Commune was *objectively* socialistic. The Bakers' had been the one union without the right to strike, and the State had been empowered to fix the price of bread : consequently the industry was in a measure a State enterprise. The Commune recognised this, and, as in the Louvre arms-shops, began their Socialist experiments in their own establishments. This concession to the Bakers' Union established in principle their right to collective bargaining.

The discussion of the question was taken at the session of April 28, when the Minority first began to crystallise against Miot's proposal of a Committee of Public Safety. They made it a class question. Vermorel pointed out that to give in to the master bakers, who, alarmed at the disorganisation threatened by the immediate application of this measure, had held protest meetings and had attempted to " lobby " the Commune through Jules Vallès, who was in favour of giving them two or three days' grace, would be " to abandon an interesting class of workers separated from society for the benefit of the aristocracy of the belly." Malon pointed out that it was perfectly practical : work could begin at five o'clock; and the bread baked in the provinces during the day, or even in some places once a week, was quite as good as Paris bread ; luxury breads were unnecessary.

Franckel had not then joined the Minority, and had been sufficiently carried away by the heat of the Miot discussion to oppose his fellow-Internationalist, Theisz. He defined his position in two big speeches : " Before passing a decree, you must know if it is urgent to make any reform in a trade ;

you must take your inspiration from the needs of the people, and then tell them, make them understand the benefit of the reform you are carrying out. . . . We are here not only to defend municipal questions but also to make social reforms. And in making these social reforms ought we first to consult the employers? No. Were the employers consulted in '92? And the nobility? Again no."

The workers had held counter-demonstrations against the employers' protests and threatened to smash their windows. The decree was published on April 29, together with that abolishing fines, but was not to come into force until May 3. After this, it was vigorously enforced; the Commune sanctioned the seizure of bread made in contravention of the regulation, and, on May 12, the police confiscated irregularly baked bread in 27 Montmartre bakeries. The workers were very grateful, and held a mass meeting on May 16 to thank the Commune.

Another Commission which worked on socialistic lines was that for Public Education, under Vaillant.

Vaillant himself was a fine scholar, with degrees from Heidelberg, Tübingen and Vienna, a correspondent with Ludwig Feuerbach, Karl Marx's old master, and a member of the International. He had been Proudhonist by conviction and militant by temperament under the Empire, but had evolved away from pure Proudhonism with many others of the International after the 1868 Brussels split. During the Prussian Siege, he had become intimate with the brilliant young Blanquist, Tridon, who confirmed the high opinion of Blanqui Vaillant had heard from Longuet some years before. When Tridon was driven into the Minority by his dislike of his fellow-Blanquists Eudes and Rigault, Vaillant refused to follow him, but, preserving a sane independence, would not countenance the split in the Commune. His views, however, only became really clarified after the fall of the Commune, when Longuet introduced him to Marx in London.

Vaillant's aim was to render education not only secular, as demanded by the anti-clerical Jacobins and Blanquists, but also free and compulsory as decided by the International Congresses at Lausanne (1867) and Brussels (1868). He used Franckel's method of appealing to technically qualified organisations for advice and their requirements, "inaugurating what I may call the syndicalist method." He organised meetings of parents and men and women teachers to study reforms in the methods and principles of elementary schooling. He appealed to "all persons who have studied the question of regular [" *intégral* "] and technical education," and founded a Committee for Reorganising Education. Unfortunately, there was no regular organisation of elementary teachers, as there had been in 1848, and Vaillant had to be content with what help he could get from the municipalities. He was, however, able to encourage vigorously Courbet's Artists' Federation.

With only 1,000 francs at his disposal and little outside help, Vaillant could do little constructive work. He was more or less confined to reorganising the school system, which had fallen into utter chaos during the Siege, and to expelling the priests, who, after repeated warnings, received, on May 18, notice to quit within forty-eight hours. But it was not easy to find trained personnel to replace them. There were, too, no proper statistics of schools and attendance. Thousands of children were running loose on the streets. In the VIIIth district, which, under Allix, paid particular attention to schools, there were still some 4,000 children of school age uncared for.

One technical school was opened in the building in the rue Lhomond formerly occupied by the Jesuits arrested by Rigault.

Some of the bourgeois schools remained open, although most of their pupils had emigrated with their families to Versailles. The Ecole Monge, the pupils of which had enlisted as Mobiles during the war, continued its courses for some time, the pupils keeping their rifles hidden in the pianos for use against the Commune. The Ecole de France kept up a few courses, Taine walking across the devastated country round the Porte de Versailles every morning. The Academy of Science held two meetings as if nothing were happening outside. Vaillant also tried to reorganise the School of Medicine, which had suspended its courses, by appealing to doctors, officers of health, extern professors and students to draw up a programme. He appointed a delegate to the Natural History Museum to work with the professors to restore the courses and help preserve the collections.

There was not a great deal of Socialism in all this. Further in the direction of favouring the workers and poorer classes were measures taken by some of Vaillant's nominees. Gastineau, Inspector of Communal Libraries, forbade the borrowing of books by privileged persons who " had not feared to cut out a library for themselves from the national libraries by borrowing works which they rarely return, thus depriving the workers of the most necessary and valuable books." The Director of Public Assistance provided for reading-rooms in hospitals, " where the convalescent, the wounded and the aged would find the democratic organs which defend the Republic and propagate the social institutions of the future," thus " annihilating the unhealthy influences of the writers and books collected in the official libraries and destined to degrade the soul and to depress all patriotic aspirations."

The more interesting educational programmes were those drawn up in various municipalities, generally with Vaillant's approval. The manifesto published by the members of the Commune representing the IInd district, the internationalists Pottier, Serrailler, Durand and Johannard, was typical: " Absolutely convinced of the urgent necessity of preparing a strong and healthy generation, able to use in the future the results of the Revolution, we desire to set up a true system of education : an education which in the field of science will limit itself to known and proven facts, springing pure and without alloy from the crucible of the human reason, and in the field of ethics to those eternal principles of justice and liberty which should mould the man and the citizen. . . . It is necessary that humanity should come to fulfil completely that precept, old as society and the basis of all true equality, ' He who does not work shall not eat.' "

The IIIrd district provided school materials free, laicised three schools and established an orphanage. The VIIIth founded an orphanage and an elementary school, drew up statistics and proposed the founding of a " novel " school. The XXth provided the school children with free clothing and food. Other districts simply expelled the clergy.

The Public Education Commission also fulfilled the functions of a Ministry of the Fine Arts. In this capacity, Vaillant strongly supported another syndical organisation —the Artistic Federation founded by Courbet and Pottier.

This Federation did nothing to define the relations between art and revolution, but confined itself to strictly practical matters. According to an elaborate report drawn up by Pottier, the basis of the Federation was to be the free expansion of art, removed from all governmental control and all privilege; equality of rights between the members; the independence and dignity of each artist placed under the safeguard of all by the creation of a committee elected by all the artists. It was distinctly stated that the Federation could never act as judge from the artistic point of view: " The Commission does not replace one school by another school, it is only so to speak the driving force of a mechanism capable of assuring the liberty of all." The Federation was open to all plastic artists qualified by repute, recommendation or possession of an exhibitor's card. No political tendency was required, but Courbet appealed to all artists to repay their debt to Paris by supporting a Parisian revolution, " the apostles of which are the workers, the Christ Proudhon."

The Federation's tasks were a little vague : to preserve the treasures of the past, to bring to light and set in action all the elements of the present, to regenerate the future by education; this amounted to the care of galleries and museums, the encouragement of contemporary art of all tendencies, the setting up of art classes in elementary and technical schools, with teachers appointed by competition. The Federation would act as arbiter in all suits relative to the arts. The Commune would entrust its public monuments, festivals, etc., to members of the Federation, while preserving the artistic neutrality of the State.

This meant, in practice, something rather important. It meant the abolition of an " official " style, of official bribery by the State by means of advertised approval of academic " safe " painters; even more, it meant the abolition of the official boycott of the advance-guard and the prosecution of advanced art for immorality. A first practical step was the abolition of the subsidy allowed to the Beaux-Arts School.

An indication of this tendency was given by the choice of the 47 members of the Committee elected on April 17. There were 16 painters, 10 sculptors, 5 architects, 6 engravers and 10 " representing decorative, improperly termed industrial, art." Most of them were elected without being consulted. The most eminent were: the painters Courbet, Corot, Daumier, Manet, Millet and Picchio; the sculptors Moulin and Dalou (who made the bust of *Marianne*, the French Republic); the architects Boileau fils and Delbrouck; the engraver André Gill; the decorative artist Pottier. Not one of these or of the rest was an " official " artist. On the other hand, Manet took little interest in the Commune except to sketch street scenes; and Daumier was satirising both sides with impartial bitterness in *Charivari*. The Federation was a great success, more than 400 artists being present at its first meeting on April 13.

The Federation did very little except reorganise the staff of the Louvre, suppress the sinecure of Architect to the Luxembourg, appoint curators and open its galleries to the public.

In 1880, when Under-Secretary Turquet created the Society of French Artists, he borrowed many ideas from Pottier, without, however, seeing their implications. The statutes of the National Society of Fine Arts drawn up in

1890 are remarkably similar to Pottier's handling of the Beaux-Arts School in 1871.

There was some attempt to federate the actors and musicians, but it was hindered by internal disputes. Curiously enough, the Federation's first secretary was Antonin Louis, who later composed the propaganda songs for the reactionary Boulangist and anti-Dreyfusard campaigns. The theatres were brought by Vaillant under the control of the Public Education Commission; and he suggested that State subsidies be abolished and replaced by co-operative associations of actors.

Vaillant, therefore, was doing as much as he could, with the limited means at his disposal, to carry on the syndical policy favoured by Franckel. It was many years before the Third Republic, although more liberal in educational than in industrial reforms, went so far as the Commune. The secularisation of the schools had been an article in the programme of even Jules Simon and Jules Favre; but it was ten years before the Republic proclaimed education free and compulsory; fifteen before it proclaimed it entirely secular; thirty-three before it prohibited the participation of lay clerics in State schools; and this prohibition has never been completely enforced. There has been no serious effort by the State to organise workers' technical schools.

Practically none of the Commune's very mildly socialistic measures have survived. Vested interests have prevented a democratic State from carrying out reforms which are now considered by all workers' organisations as showing the Commune's revolutionary weakness, not its excesses. It is a striking demonstration of the impossibility of introducing *subjective* Socialism without first bringing about the *objective* —that is to say, without " breaking up the State machinery."

# CONCLUSION

THE COMMUNE passed in flame and fury over the scene of European politics, and vanished. Save for a small outbreak in Algeria, the Paris rising had no imitators. Only the immediate following of Karl Marx in the International even perceived the vast historical importance of the fact that the Paris workers had " stormed the heavens," as Marx put it, and for two months imposed the dictatorship of the proletariat upon the cultural capital of the world.

The immediate effect abroad of the Commune was to sharpen class antagonisms, or, at the least, to act as a touchstone for class loyalties. Workers and Liberals united in deploring the atrocities committed by both sides; but, in justice to the British bourgeois Press, it must be recorded that the surprisingly fair reports of their Paris correspondents describing the brutalities and the nauseating triumph of the Versaillese did much to dampen any foreign enthusiasm for the restoration of order. The general attitude was represented by *The Times*, which published full accounts of the Versaillese jail horrors and thanked Heaven in its editorial columns that such things do not happen in England.

*Punch* naturally took the gentlemanly point of view. After punning on the " Assi-nine " Government and the " National [Black]-guards," it depicted a righteous and rather overwhelming Britannia addressing a shrinking Republican mechanic, while she points over his head to a scene of pillage: " Is *that* the sort of thing you want, you little idiot ? " Most Englishmen thought the Commune meant that the French, driven to desperation by the war, had quite simply gone mad. Earl Russell attributed the Commune to " shocking atheism."

The only organised middle-class body in England which did come out in favour of the Communards was the old Positivist Society, of which Dr. Richard Congreve, Dr. Bridges, Professor Beesly (chairman of the first meeting of the International in 1864) and Frederick Harrison were the most prominent members. Fox Bourne, who was a frequent visitor at Maitland Park and met Communard exiles with Marx there, defended the Commune in his *Examiner*. John Morley, in the *Fortnightly*, like Frederick Harrison and Whalley in the House of Commons, spoke up in favour of the social ideals which " had animated those misguided men." Beesly received from Marx thanks for his favourable articles in the *Beehive*, but also a warning that the remarkable little review was " the organ of the renegades sold out to Sam Morley," the Liberal Bristol M.P. Bradlaugh and the National Secular Society, faithful to Manchester economics, deprecated Red Republicanism despite personal sympathies for some of the Communard leaders.

The International, of course, claimed the Commune as its own. As Marx declared in his *Address* of May 30 : " It is but natural that members of our Association should stand in the foreground . . . wherever . . . the class struggle obtains any consistency." William Morris, Hyndman and Belfort Bax supported Marx ; and Bax boasted, apparently without any foundation, that he had converted the General Council to this view.

On the other hand, Marx perfectly correctly repudiated the common statement that the International had done anything to foster the Paris revolt. When Jules Favre, deliberately or not, confusing the International with Bakunin's Social-Democratic Alliance, expelled from the Association in 1868, sent a circular to the European Cabinets, on June 6, to invite them to destroy the International, Marx published a refutation in several London papers, including *The Times*, which drew upon that respectable organ a severe reprimand from Bob Lowe. Thiers, however, continued to let his tame propagandists foster the legend of a great " Red international conspiracy " ; and the London *Observer*, in close touch with Gladstone's Government, actually threatened Marx with prosecution. For some time, Marx was, as he wrote to Kugelmann, " the best calumniated and most menaced man of London " and " a reporters' curiosity into the bargain." No prosecution, however, was attempted.

Marx's *Address* stirred up trouble within the Association. Reformists like the Republican George Odger had no stomach for a glorification of French violence, and resigned. The International replied by expelling Tolain, who had remained at Versailles to attempt conciliation. It admitted Communards besides its own members: the names of Arnaud, Cournet, Johannard, Dupont, Longuet, Ranvier, Vaillant, Franckel, Le Moussu and Serrailler are appended to the first published edition of the *Address on the Civil War in France*.

The split was largely instrumental in breaking up the First International. The Bakuninist anarchists saw in the Commune " above all, the denial of the State," and therefore disapproved of Marx's interpretation. The Italian, Spanish, Swiss and Belgian sections followed Bakunin on his expulsion at the 1872 Hague Congress; and when the General Council decided, at Geneva in 1873, to move to New York, the French Blanquists walked out. The Association dissolved after the Philadelphia Congress of July 1876. The Second International was formed only in 1889.

There was no party or group surviving from the Commune which could carry on underground propaganda against the reaction. This fact, which had led to the undoing of the Commune, equally prevented its perpetuation in political or agitational form. As after 1848, it was a time for reflection, for the slow gathering of proletarian forces for the next stage in the struggle.

It was not until twenty years later that Guesde and Jaurès revived the working-class movement in France; and here, as elsewhere in Europe, it left the revolutionary line laid down for it in the 'sixties. That this was so was due in some measure to the Commune, although it was primarily so conditioned by the French capitalist recovery, for which most of the political credit is due to Thiers.

While the Communards rot in New Caledonia, starve in Camden Town, yawn in Zürich, whisper in the broken streets of Belleville, the scene changes to Versailles and the provincial platforms and the inner offices of the great banks.

The transition from Empire to Republic merely represented in political form the readjustment of economic forces which, released and promoted by the *coup d'état* of 1851, had obtained virtual control of the Empire by about 1864, and began to assume political power openly after 1868. The Bordeaux elections of 1871 had been fought on the issue of peace, not of constitutional or social reform. The Royalist success did not mean, and was not intended to mean, a serious attempt at Royalist restoration, but simply an affirmation of provincial Conservatism. Royalism had ceased to be the expression of any important economic interest or grouping; and it could only have been imposed by a *coup d'état* which would have lacked the mass-support that enabled Louis Napoléon to survive the first difficult years after his seizure of power.

The Royalists did not disappear without a struggle.

In its early days the Third Republic was haunted by a fear of reactionary counter-revolution which has left its mark on its present constitution. Politically, the threat failed for three reasons: the pure stupidity of the Royalists themselves, the opposition of large bodies of provincial opinion which had formerly tended towards Orleanism, and the supreme vanity-inspired strategy of Adolphe Thiers.

The Commune had given the bourgeois in the provinces time for reflection. The conduct of the Bordeaux Assembly had shown up Royalism in its true colours. Bad as the Commune had seemed, the rule of the Versailles " backwoodsmen " appeared far worse.

Thiers had rallied big business and the middle classes by proving that the Republic was strong enough to smash its " lunatic fringe " and to keep order; that it had the army as well as the police to defend it. He had proved, even more importantly, that his Republic had no intention whatever of altering the social relations which had made, supported and broken the Empire.

Gambetta, no less opportunist than Thiers, played into his enemy's hands by rallying the petty-bourgeoisie, that class incapable of making its own political decisions, to reformism and nationalism. He declared that " the heroic age is over "; he was prepared, even as early as July 1871, to co-operate in restoring Thiers's " moral order," endowed with " the necessary liberties " in order to prepare *La Révanche* against Prussia. The policy won the Republic 100 seats out of 111 at the by-elections of July 2, 1871, and laid the foundations of the overwhelming importance in French politics of the grocer, the *rentier*, the small peasant and all those elements which now adhere to the Radical Party.

Thiers had thus tricked his enemy into supporting him. He had done what he could to prevent the Republic from " opening a fair field to the working class for the struggle for its own interests, and, in any case, bringing matters to a crisis by which the nation would be fairly and irresistibly launched in the revolutionary career, or else the *status quo* before the Revolution restored as nearly as possible, and, thereby, a new revolution rendered unavoidable " (Engels). Democracy, as Thiers boasted, had indeed been " bled for a generation."

Gambetta and the Left were forced into a policy of pure opportunism. He raised the new formula of " National Union." " Let us," he said, " return to the fertile ideas of 1789, restore the corporation [" *faisceau*," the Italian " *fascio* "] destroyed by criminals: the union of bourgeois with worker, of worker with peasant." This appeal to the " new strata " achieved its final effect in Waldeck-Rousseau's National Unity Cabinet in 1899, when the Socialist Millerand took his seat beside the Versaillese killer, Marquis de Galliffet.

The Royalists aided Thiers by committing political suicide as neatly and ostentatiously as possible with the manifestos of the Comte de Chambord, couched in terms so fatal that there was a current suspicion that one of Thiers's *agents-provocateur* must have inspired them. They finally alienated the provincial towns, who transferred their loyalty to Conservative Republicanism.

Thiers knew well enough that the Assembly was clay in his hands after the defeat of the Commune. He manœuvred them—" 150 insurgents and 400 poltroons "—into voting their constituent power to save their own existence, and to do so by a vote of confidence in their detested leader. On August 31, 1871, after a day of stormy intrigue, the Assembly voted itself Constituent by 434 votes to 225 : and by 491 to 94 the Royalist body declared Adolphe Thiers first President of the Third Republic, but only for the duration of the Assembly. Thiers had founded the Republic in spite of the Republicans.

The Republic was not finally constituted as the Government of France until January 30, 1875, and then only by the accidental majority of one vote.

Thiers was not there to see it. The Assembly had thrown over its saviour one evening, May 24, 1873, and the old Marshal MacMahon, Royalist at heart, but more strongly attached to his own dictatorship, had been elected President for seven years.

The Septennate favoured all the Monarchist interests without restoring the Monarch. It suppressed opposition papers, introduced espionage in factory and home, revived clericalism, rejected every motion for an amnesty for the Communards. It encouraged the building of the Sacred Heart as an " expiation for the crimes of the Commune."

The amnesty proclaimed its fall, the swing from reaction to opportunism. The Communards were pardoned at last on July 10, 1880. Galliffet wrote to Gambetta that it had made a deplorable impression upon the army. The Republic had still to submit to this form of political blackmail.

Owing to these peculiar political conditions, the immediate effect of the Commune appeared rather in the superstructural region of thought and philosophy. Sensitive and representative thinkers were horrified. Taine, who had begun his vast *History of Contemporary France* (published 1875–94) amid the roar of the Commune's guns, abandoned his *esprit geometrique* for the refuge of the *esprit de finesse*. The horror was inexplicable, man simply a " lubricious gorilla."

Flaubert, who had declared the creed of the 'sixties as the " faith in science, the idea, the peaceful and sincere study of nature and reality," could not recover from the Commune's " Gothicity." He who had so objectively described, in *Education Sentimentale*, the collapse of society in 1848, relapsed into ferocious self-parody in *Bouvard et Pécuchet*, from which it was but a step to the madhouse.

Renan, who had won his chair at the Collège de France only in 1870 in the teeth of the Emperor's hostility, a victory which had seemed the promise of intellectual freedom at last, relapsed into sterile pyrrhonism. His example, the flight to the Ivory Tower of sensualism or mysticism, was followed by those of the younger democrats, such as Anatole France and Catulle Mendès, as did not, like Gautier, Sarcey, Daudet and Dumas fils, simply disgrace themselves by the cold brutality of what they wrote about the Commune.

Even some military men, such as de Cissey's valued aide-de-camp, Colonel Hepp, buried themselves in the work of reorganising the army, and walked solitary in the woods in their leisure. They could never again he brought to mention the Battle of Paris.

In the course of time, the " canonising " tendency, which Lenin noted in the case of Marx, has been brought by the French bourgeoisie to bear upon the Communards. Many Paris streets now bear their names, and some of them are situated in the most " respectable " districts. There are the rues Antoine-Arnaud (XVI), J.–B. Clément (XVIII), Gustave-Courbet (XVI), Bénoit-Malon (XX), Edouard-Vaillant (XX), Jules-Vallès (XI), Eugène-Varlin (X), the Boulevard Auguste-Blanqui (XIII).

In 1934 a tablet was placed in Père-Lachaise in honour of the National Guards of the 55th and 120th Battalions

killed at the surprise at Moulin-Saquet. It is beside the
great memorial to the Commune, to which great pil-
grimages of Paris workers march every Whit Sunday, the
*Mur des Fédérés*.

The bourgeois who hated, slandered and killed the
Communards are now " forgiving " them. The Nationalist
Léon Daudet has praised their " patriotism." The revolutionaries Clément, Courbet, Vaillant, Malon are con-
veniently forgotten in the balladist, painter, municipal
reformer, Deputy. The Academy celebrated Jules Vallès'
centenary in 1932.

On the other hand, tens of thousands of workers of all
parties gathered in September 1932 to bury Camélinat,
last surviving personal link between the First International,
the Commune and the Third International. In the same
month the Red Municipality of Saint-Denis " at last shot
Thiers down the drain," as a Radical paper expressed it,
by renaming the rue Thiers rue Degeyter, the composer of
the music for the " International," the words of which
were written by Eugène Pottier, member of the Commune.

The ultimate historical importance of the Commune is
to be found, not in French social or political relationships,
but in the domain of revolutionary theory.

The Commune was the first concrete example of a
workers' seizure of power. The Commune was compelled,
by force of circumstances, even more than by inclination,
to adopt many of the forms of the proletarian dictatorship.
At the same time, adverse circumstances, conflicting aims
and tendencies and the general incoherence of the event
made it fertile in examples of every revolutionary hypo-
thesis. Thus the Commune became a valuable touchstone
upon which the validity of every kind of revolutionary
theory could be tested.

The two main questions raised during the theoretic
struggles which occupied the years between 1889 and 1917
were : First, What was the real character of the State-form
which the Commune had set up, and how far did it differ
from the true Socialist workers' State ? Second, Should the

workers take the offensive immediately they are threatened, even though a revolutionary situation might not have fully developed, even though defeat be practically certain ? In a word, Was the Commune too violent or not violent enough ?

The course of this controversy, brought to a head by Lenin in his attack upon Plekhanov's " they should not have taken up arms " in 1905, lies outside the scope of this study. It is, however, worth repeating that Lenin based his *State and Revolution* (1917) directly upon Marx's interpretation of the Paris Commune; and that *State and Revolution* is the basis of the Marxist-Leninist theory which now exercises a direct or indirect influence upon an enormous proportion of the world's population. If any proof of a theory's validity lies in its concrete effect, the controversy based upon the practical experience of the Commune must be allowed a very important place indeed in world history.

The police or judicial interpretation must be, for practical purposes, the final one, since it is the expression of the opinion of the State Executive. " No, gentlemen," replied Dufaure, the merciless Minister for Justice, to some Liberals who pleaded that the Commune was merely a rash but not unpardonable outburst of patriotic municipal exasperation; " no, gentlemen, it was not a communalist, a municipal movement; it was in its ideals, its ideas and its actions the most radical revolution ever undertaken ! "

There have been revolutions yet more radical since that of March 18, 1871. The Commune was only the first stage; the Russian October was the second. They are intimately linked, historically and traditionally, in the minds of those workers of France who, in numbers yearly increasing, demand each Whit Sunday at the *Mur des Fédérés* " *Les Soviets partout !* "

THE END

# BIBLIOGRAPHY

The following bibliography lists only a few of the main sources of information on the Commune. The works give some idea of the scope of the subject. Except as curiosities, the majority of the publications which appeared soon after May 1871 may be neglected. Naturally, the event became a publisher's speculation, and most of the response was either merely sensational or merely controversial. While such productions give a good idea of the state of mind prevailing at the time, they are useless for practical purposes. In general, only such works are listed as base themselves on first-hand documentary evidence.

## DOCUMENTS

Manuscripts in various archives, more especially in those of the Ministry of War, of the Seine, the Archives Nationales, the Bibliothèque pour l'Histoire de la Ville de Paris, the Bibliothèque Nationale, all in Paris; of the Marx-Engels Institute in Moscow.

*Published :*

Bourgin & Henriot, *Les Procès-Verbaux de la Commune de 1871.* Paris 1924. Only one volume published. The rest are in MS. in the Bibliothèque de l'Institut pour l'Histoire de la Ville de Paris; there is also a photostatic copy at the Marx-Engels Institute.

*Les 31 Séances Officielles de la Commune.* Paris 1871. (Reprinted from J.O.C.—see below.)

*Journal Officiel* (of the Commune) (J.O.C.). Containing the sessions of the Commune in a truncated version and the official decrees. (Reprint in one volume, Paris 1879.)

*Les Murailles Politiques Françaises*, Vol. II. Paris 1871.

MAILLARD, FIRMIN, *Les Affiches de la Commune*. Paris 1871.

FOUGEROUSSE, A., *Actes et Proclamations du Comité Central*. Paris 1871.

CHASTEAU, P., *Recueil des Dépêches du 16 février au 27 mai 1871*. Paris 1871.

CHASTEAU, P., *Recueil des Traités, etc., rélatifs à la Paix avec l'Allemagne*. 5 vols. Paris 1879. Published by the Imprimerie Nationale.

AUDOIN, HENRI, *Documents Officiels publiés par le Ministère allemand des Affaires Etrangères*, Paris 1927.

*Journal Officiel* (de Versailles) (J.O.V.). Versailles 1871.

*Annales de l'Assemblée Nationale*. First 3 vols. Paris 1871.

*Enquête sur le 18 mars*. 3 vols. (Reports, Evidence, Documents). Paris 1872. Published by the Parliamentary Investigating Committee. Useful for the documents quoted in Vol. III, and for many curious statements.

APPERT, GENERAL, *Rapport d'ensemble sur les Opérations de la Justice Militaire*. Paris 1875.

*Procès des Insurgés de la Commune*. Published by Ed. Mauger & Cie. Paris 1871.

*La Gazette des Tribunaux*. August 1871–73.

There are a great many small pamphlets reproducing parts of the above collections. Those by AMELINE, DELPIT, D'HEYLLI are the most important. Attention should also be drawn to the enquiry held by the *Revue Blanche* in 1900.

## NEWSPAPERS

*For the Commune:*

For an annotated list see MAILLARD, FIRMIN, *Les Journaux pendant le Siège et sous la Commune*. Paris 1871.

The more important Communard papers include: *Cri du Peuple, Vengeur, Père Duchêne, Commune, Montagne, Mot d'Ordre*, etc.

*For Versailles :*

The large Press, especially *Figaro*, *Gaulois*, *Débats*, etc.

*English Papers :*

The most interesting with reference to the Commune are *The Times*, *Daily News*, *Telegraph*, *Pall Mall Gazette*, *Reynolds's*, *Fortnightly*, *Examiner*, *Illustrated London News*, *Punch*.

*American :*

See especially *New York Tribune*, *New York Herald*, *Boston Radical*, *Scribner's*, *Fraser's*.

*Papers published by Communard exiles :*

London: *Qui Vive* (Vermesch), *Vermesch-Journal* (ditto), *18 Mars* (Bergeret), *Fédération* (Vésinier).

New York: *Bulletin de la Commune*.

New Orleans: *La Commune*.

Neuchâtel: *Le Socialisme Progressif* (Malon).

Geneva: *La Lanterne* (Rochefort), *Reveil International* (Guesde), *La Commune* (Lefrançais), *La Revue Socialiste* (ditto), *Le Caprice* (Vuillaume & Slom), *Révolution Sociale* (Claris).

## HISTORIES AND MEMOIRS

(a) *By Communards or sympathisers (contemporary) :*

LISSAGARAY, *Histoire de la Commune de 1871*. Brussels 1876. English translation by Eleanor Marx Aveling. London 1886 and 1898. German translations 1878, 1891, 1894, 1932. New and corrected French edition by Amédée Dunois. Paris 1929. The classic history of the Commune by an eyewitness journalist (*L'Action* and the *Tribun du Peuple*, in which Lepelletier (q.v.) collaborated).

An excellent list of other Communard publications is appended to the 1929 edition of Lissagaray. The most important of these are:

ALLEMANE, JEAN, *Mémoires d'un Communard*. Paris. n.d.

ARNOULD, ANTOINE, *Histoire Populaire et Parlementaire de la Commune de Paris*. 3 vols. Brussels 1878.

BERGERET, JULES, *Le 18 mars*. London and Brussels 1871. (Written by Alavoine and Leverdays.)

BESLAY, CHARLES, *Mes Souvenirs*. Paris and Neuchâtel 1873.

BESLAY, CHARLES, *La Vérité sur la Commune*. Geneva and Neuchâtel 1877. 2nd revised and completed edition, Brussels 1878.

CLUSERET, GUSTAVE, *Mémoires*. 3 vols. Paris 1877–8.

DA COSTA, CHARLES, *Les Blanquistes*. Paris 1912.

DA COSTA, GASTON, *La Commune Vécue*. 3 vols. Paris 1903–5.

FLOURENS, GUSTAVE, *Paris Livré*. Paris 1871.

JOURDE, FRANÇOIS, *Souvenirs d'un Membre de la Commune*. Brussels 1877.

LEFRANÇAIS, GUSTAVE, *Etude sur le Mouvement Communaliste à Paris en 1871*. Neuchâtel 1871.

LEFRANÇAIS, GUSTAVE, *Souvenirs d'un Révolutionnaire*. Brussels 1902.

LULLIER, CHARLES, *Mes Cachots*. Paris 1881.

MALON, BÉNOÎT, *La Troisième Défaite du Proletariat Français*. Neuchâtel 1871.

MICHEL, LOUISE, *La Commune*. Paris 1898.

ROCHEFORT, HENRI, *Les Aventures de ma Vie*. Paris 1895–6.

ROSSEL, LOUIS NATHANIEL, *Papiers Posthumes*. Paris 1871.

VALLÈS, JULES, *L'Insurgé* (Jacques Vingtras). Paris 1886.

VÉSINIER, PIERRE, *Comment a péri la Commune*. Paris 1892.

The following are also of importance, as written by eye-witnesses:

GUESDE, JULES, *Çà et là*. Paris 1914.

LAVROV, PIERRE, *Parizhskaia Kommuna*. Paris 1878. 4th ed. Moscow 1925. Best account of effect of Commune upon contemporary Socialist movement. At present available only in Russian.

For further Russian works see MASON (below).

VUILLAUME, MAXIME, *Mes Cahiers Rouges au Temps de la Commune*. 10 vols. Paris 1908–14. A careful compilation of eye-witnesses' reports, which corrects many of the errors in earlier works.

(b) *Republican:*

FIAUX, LOUIS, *Histoire de la Guerre Civile de 1871*. Paris 1879. Very sound contemporary study. Fiaux, although himself a Republican Liberal, got much of his material from Callet, a friend of Malon.

LANJALLEY AND CORRIEZ, *Histoire de la Révolution du 18 mars*. Brussels 1871. With a very careful and useful documentation.

LEPELLETIER, EDMOND, *Histoire de la Commune de 1871*. 4 vols. Paris 1911–13. A useful and fairly well-documented work.

MARGUERITTE, PAUL AND VICTOR, *La Commune*. Paris, n.d. (1904). A novel; but based upon admirable documentation, so that it has almost the value of a formal history.

PELLETAN, CAMILLE, *La Commune et le Comité Central*. Paris 1879.

PELLETAN, CAMILLE, *La Semaine de Mai*. Paris 1880.

PESSARD, HECTOR, *Mes Petits Papiers*. Paris 1887.

The following are also worth consulting:

GONCOURT, BROTHERS, *Journal*. Vol. IV. (1870–71).

HALÉVY, LUDOVIC. *Notes et Souvenirs, 1871–2*. Paris 1888.

HUGO, VICTOR. *Choses Vues*. Paris 1887.

HUGO, VICTOR, *L'Année Terrible*. Paris 1872.

(c) *Versaillese:*

CLARÉTIE, JULES, *Histoire de la Révolution de 1870–71*. 5 vols. Paris 1874–6. New edition. 1 vol. Paris 1877.

DU CAMP, MAXIME, *Les Convulsions de Paris*. 4 vols. Paris 1878.

The most important contemporary reactionary histories. Excellent documentation put to the most unscrupulous uses. See on Du Camp, Lissagaray (ed. 1929), pp. 462–66. Clarétie's book is more of a journalistic speculation, Du Camp's a political manœuvre against the granting of an amnesty for the Communards. Both must be used with extreme caution.

There was a great quantity of lesser anti-Communard literature produced between 1871 and 1879 for speculative or political purposes, the majority of which may be neglected entirely. A few memoirs and studies contain some useful information or a revelation of the contemporary political atmosphere; among these may be consulted the following:

DAUDET, ALPHONSE, *Souvenirs d'un Homme de Lettres*. Paris, n.d.

FALLOUX, MARQUIS DE. *Mémoires d'un Royaliste*. Vol. II. Paris 1888.

FAVRE, JULES, *Histoire du Gouvernement de la Défense Nationale*, 3 vols. Paris 1871.

MACMAHON, MARSHAL, *L'Armée de Versailles*. Paris 1871.

MENDÈS, CATULLE, *Les 73 Journées de la Commune*. Paris 1871.

SESMAISONS, GENERAL DE, *Les Troupes de la Commune*. Paris 1904.

SIMON, JULES, *Le Gouvernement de M. Thiers*. 2 vols. Paris 1878.

THIERS, ADOLPHE, *Notes et Souvenirs*. Paris 1901.

THIERS, ADOLPHE, *Histoire de la Révolution du 4 Septembre*. Paris 1882.

VINOY, GENERAL, *L'Armistice et la Commune*. Paris 1872.

(d) *Later Histories:*

BOURGIN, GEORGES, *Histoire de la Commune*. Paris n.d. 1925.

BOURGIN GEORGES, *Les Premières Journées de la Commune*. Paris 1928.

BOURGIN, GEORGES, " La Commune de Paris et le Comité Central." In *Revue Historique*, 1925. 150–2. Admirable, compressed and well-documented studies, valuable as introductions and summaries.

DUBREUILH, LOUIS, *Histoire de la Commune*. Paris 1908. Volume XI of Jaurès's *Histoire Socialiste*. Sound and useful, with a socialistic tendency.

LARONZE, GEORGES, *Histoire de la Commune de 1871*, Paris 1928. The latest and most important modern work. Has had access to much previously unpublished material. Treats the Commune mostly from the juridical point of view. In spite of copious and important documentation, perhaps a little confused in arrangement of narrative.

MASON, EDWARD S., *The Paris Commune*. New York 1930. Inaccurate as to facts, but extremely useful, despite a somewhat perverse attitude, for the study of the Commune in what he calls " Socialist mythology," using Russian sources and also the Blanqui MSS. in the Bibliothèque Nationale.

LUQUET, P., *La Commune de Paris*. Paris 1926.

TALÈS, *La Commune de Paris*. Paris 1924.

Two small communist studies. The *Talès* has an introduction by Trotzky.

DESCAVES, LUCIEN, *La Colonne*. Paris 1901.

DESCAVES, LUCIEN, *Philémon, Vieux de la Vieille*. Paris 1913. These works are novels, but based upon a thorough documentation. *Philémon* is the classic work upon the Communard exiles, partly from information supplied by Hippolyte Varlin, Eugène's brother.

Three recent " graphic " histories of some merit are:

CASSOU, JEAN, *Les Massacres de Paris*. Paris 1936.

DEFFOUX, LEON, *Pipe-en-Bois, Témoin de la Commune*. Paris 1932.

DOMINIQUE, PIERRE, *La Commune*. Paris 1930.

(e) *Foreign Works:*

Especially interesting are the contemporary memoirs:

BINGHAM, D. A., *Recollections of Paris.* Vol. II. London 1896.

VANDAM, ALBERT, *An Englishman in Paris.* Vol. II. London 1892.

WASHBURNE, E. B., *Recollections of a Minister to France, 1869-77.* London 1887.

VIZETELLY, ERNEST, *My Adventures in the Commune.* London 1914.

.    .    .    .    .    .    .    .    .

There are very few serious histories in foreign languages (other than Russian) besides those already quoted. The following have contemporary interest, although lack historical value:

BAX, BELFORT (with Victor Dave and William Morris), *A Short Account of the Paris Commune.* London 1886.

HOZIER, H. M., *The Franco-Prussian War* (appended to). Vol. II. London 1872.

MARCH, THOMAS, *History of the Commune.* London 1896.

See also:

POSTGATE, RAYMOND W., *Revolution, 1789-1806.* London 1920.

POSTGATE, RAYMOND W., *Out of the Past.* London 1922.

Contain sections on the Commune; the former with translations of contemporary documents.

ANON (Ruth Oesterreicher), *1871.* Berlin 1931.

A somewhat similar work, with an excellent iconography.

As an example of contemporary literature in defence of the Commune:

ANON, *The Paris Rebels Vindicated from the Aspersions of a Money-Shackled Press: the Truth at last, told in vigorous English.* New York 1871.

See also Fox-Bourne's articles in the *Examiner*, Morley's in the *Fortnightly*, Professor Beesly's in *The Beehive*.

# STUDIES OF PARTICULAR CONNECTED SUBJECTS

(a) *Of Individual Communards:*

CLÈRE, JULES, *Les Hommes de la Commune*. Paris 1871.

DELION, P. (P. Bourde), *Les Membres de la Commune.* Paris 1871.

D'HEYLLI, GEORGES, *Le Livre Rouge de la Commune*. Paris 1871.

DUPONT, LÈONCE, *La Commune et ses Hommes devant la Justice*, Paris 1871.

LABORDE, DR. J. V., *Les Hommes et les Actes de l'Insurrection de Paris devant la Psychologie Morbide*. Paris 1872.

These are all violently hostile studies, interesting rather for the light they throw upon the state of mind of their authors and public than for historical truth.

DOMMANGET, MAURICE, *Blanqui*. Paris 1924.

DOMMANGET, MAURICE, *Eugène Varlin*. Paris 1926.

FAILLET, E., *Biographie de Varlin*. Paris 1885.

GEFFROY, G., *L'Enfermé* (Blanqui). Paris 1897.

PROLÈS, CHARLES, *Les Hommes de la Révolution*. Paris 1898.

WOLOWSKI, BRONISLAW, *Dombrowski et Versailles*. Geneva, London and Lemberg 1871.

ZÉVAÈS, ALEXANDRE, *Auguste Blanqui*. Paris 1920.

Later and sympathetic studies, with some historical value.

See also the articles in Larousse, especially upon Ferré.

MARKET, JEAN, *Clemenceau*. Paris 1930 (contains valuable material on March 18 by Clemenceau himself).

(b) *Studies of Special Subjects:*

Interesting, if not always absolutely reliable, information is to be found in the following:

DALSÈME, A. J., *Histoire des Conspirations sous la Commune.* Paris 1872.

RAFINA, GESNER, *Une Mission Sécrète pendant la Commune.* Paris 1871.

VEYSSET, MME FORSANS, *Une Episode de la Commune.* Brussels 1873.

These three deal with conspiracies against the Commune. See also the work of WOLOWSKI, quoted above.

ALMÉRAS, HENRI D', *La Vie Parisienne pendant le Siège et sous la Commune.* Paris n.d.

MAILLARD, FIRMIN, *Histoire des Journaux pendant . . . la Commune.* Paris 1871.

MAILLARD, FIRMIN, *Les Affiches sous la Commune.* Paris 1871.

MAILLARD, FIRMIN, *Les Publications de la Rue sous la Commune.* Paris 1871.

MOLINARI, GUSTAVE, *Les Clubs Rouges de Paris pendant le Siège.* Paris 1871.

DOMMANGET, MAURICE, *L'Instruction publique sous la Commune.* Paris 1928.

## ILLUSTRATIONS

Besides the illustrated papers, the most important of which are *L'Illustration, Illustrierte Zeitung, Illustrated London News,* etc., there were a vast number of small illustrated publications, mostly satirical, treating the Commune. See specially *Charivari* (DAUMIER and CHAM), *Eclipse* (ANDRÉ GILL and ALFRED LE PETIT), *Caricature* (PILOTELL), etc.

Also, in collected publications:

BERTALL, *The Communists of 1871.* London 1874.

DORÉ, GUSTAVE, *Versailles et Paris en 1871.* Paris 1907.

Collections of photographs and drawings:

*L'Autographe*. Published by Villemessant & Bourdin. Paris 1871.

CLARÉTIE, JULES, *Almanach Illustré de l'Histoire de la Révolution de 1870–71*. Paris 1872.

DAYOT, ARMAND, *Paris pendant le Siège et sous la Commune*. Paris n.d. (1901).

*Les Monuments de Paris*. Paris 1871.

*Les Monuments de Paris après l'Œuvre de la Commune*. Paris 1871.

PETIT, P., *Guide-Recueil de Paris Brûlé*. Paris n.d. 1871.

## THEORETICAL WORKS ON THE COMMUNE

For these " interpretations " see MASON, above, especially for those in Russian. The most representative are:

(a) *Marxist:*

MARX, KARL, *The Civil War in France*. London 1871. Many editions, the most important being that in German with a long preface by Friederich Engels, 1891.

LENIN, V. I., *State and Revolution*. Petrograd 1917. English translation, London 1933. Contains a thorough theoretic commentary on Marx's work (above).

See also:

LENIN, V. I., *The Paris Commune*. London 1933. A collection of Lenin's articles and speeches dealing with the Commune.

(b) *Anarchist:*

BAKUNIN, MIKHAIL, *Œuvres*, Vol. IV.

KROPOTKIN, PRINCE PETER, *The Commune of Paris*. London 1891. It is of interest that Kropotkin is said to have tapped out this little work on the walls of his cell in the Peter-Paul Fortress in two years.

For recent controversy see:

KAUTSKY, CARL, *Terrorism and Communism*. English translation. London 1920.

TROTZKY, LEO, *Terrorism i Kommunism*. Petrograd 1920. English translation, *The Defence of Terrorism*. London 1921.

# WORKS ON SUBSIDIARY AND ALLIED SUBJECTS

*On Thiers:*

Those containing chiefly documentary or eye-witnesses' material have been listed from among the very large number of works dealing with Thiers, and only in so far as they treat particularly of the Commune period:

BOUNIOLS, GASTON, *Thiers au Pouvoir*. Paris 1921.

DREYFUS, ROBERT, *M. Thiers contre . . . la Commune*. Paris 1928.

HALÉVY, DANIEL, *Le Courrier de M. Thiers*. Paris 1921.

REMUSAT, PAUL DE, *Adolphe Thiers*. Paris 1889.

See also the large official biography by the librarian of the Bib. Thiers.

MALO, HENRI, *Thiers*. Paris 1932.

*On the International:*

*Les Séances Officielles de l'Internationale*. Paris 1871.

GUILLAUME, JAMES, *L'Internationale*. Paris 1905–10. 4 vols. Anarchist.

JAECKH, GUSTAV, *Die Internationale*. Leipsig 1904. Marxist.

POSTGATE, RAYMOND W., *The Workers' International*. London 1920. Socialist, with an excellent bibliography.

STEKLOV, YU. M., *History of the First International*. English translation. London 1928. A general history with Marxist tendency.

TESTUT, O., *L'Internationale*. Paris 1871.

TESTUT, O., *L'Internationale et le Jacobinisme au Ban de l'Europe*. 2 vols. Paris 1872. By an anti-International lawyer, but containing vast stores of original documentary material.

VILLETARD, *Histoire de l'Internationale*. Paris 1872. A general, hostile, but quite interesting work.

See also:

WEILL, GEORGES, *Histoire du Mouvement social en France 1852–1902*. Paris 1904. 3rd Edition, revised and completed. Paris 1924. A general synthesis, of the greatest importance for the antecedents and effects of the Commune.

# SUPPLEMENTARY
# BIBLIOGRAPHICAL
# NOTES (1965)

ACCESS TO THE ARCHIVES of the French Ministry of War, which before 1940 had been available only to the Senator who wrote under the name GEORGES LARONZE (see entry on p. 427 above) has now opened up a whole range of new source material. Although these archives have shed little new light on the actual events of the Commune of 1871, they are a main source of information about the participants themselves and those who influenced them.

Further information has come from the provincial archives (for example, ANTOINE OLIVESI, *La Commune de Marseille et ses origines*, Paris, 1950), from studies of particular aspects of the Commune (M. DOMMANGET, *L'Enseignement, L'Enfance, et la Culture sous la Commune*, Paris, 1964) and of the Communard exiles (MARC VUILLEUMIER in *Le Mouvement Social*, No. 38, Jan.-Mar. 1962), and from a reassessment of the factors under the Second Empire which gave to the Commune the form it took (notably, E. DZELUBUSKAYA, *The Fall of the Second Empire and the Birth of the Third Republic in France*, Moscow, 1959).

An extensive bibliography of works on the Commune published in many countries between 1940 and 1960 appeared in Nos. 37 and 38 of *Le Mouvement Social*, the quarterly of the Institut Français d'Histoire Sociale, Paris.

A detailed list of publications by Communards themselves is given in CHARLES RIHS, *La Commune de Paris: Sa structure et ses doctrines (1871)*, Geneva, 1955.

A further list of sources is provided in the most ample of recent studies: JEAN BRUHAT, JEAN DAUTRY, and EMILE TERSEN, *La Commune de 1871*, Paris, 1960.

Recent work on the Paris Commune of 1871 has

tended to fall into the following categories: research on individual Communards; a partly sociological approach, somewhat similar to that initiated by Lefebvre, Soboul, and Rudé for the French Revolution; further discussion of the Commune's place in the general history of the working-class revolution, and, in that connection, a closer analysis of the ideas of Karl Marx and the Communards themselves.

An interesting book of the first type, published too recently for inclusion in the bibliographies cited above, is EDITH THOMAS, *Les Pétroleuses*, Paris, 1965, which deals with the women of the Commune.

The most recent Marxist-sociological study is HENRI LEFEBVRE's *La Proclamation de la Commune*, published in March 1965, in Gallimard's series "Thirty Days Which Made France," to coincide with the ninety-fourth anniversary of the Commune. This work, which may not be wholly acceptable to some historians, suggests that some of the earlier works dismissed as biased and not founded on sufficient research may contain valuable elements for other approaches, especially the sociological rather than the purely historical or political. From this standpoint, it would be well to review the remarkable work, done in several countries, on French nineteenth century social movements as a whole, from L. CHEVALIER's famous *Classes laborieuses, classes dangéreuses* onwards.

The historian becomes increasingly aware how much is owed to the steady work of GEORGES BOURGIN.

The Commune's place in the international revolutionary movement and the classic works on it by Marx and Lenin have stimulated some important work, especially in Poland and the USSR, of which P. M. KERJANTSEV's *History of the Paris Commune* (in Russian), Moscow, 1959, is probably the most interesting. Leon Trotsky's introduction (in French) to C. TALÈS, *La Commune de 1871*, Paris, 1921, is receiving some attention, although it adds little to our understanding of events, being written in a sort of "past hypothetical."

The Commune has not been neglected in fiction, poetry, and drama: for instance, BERTOLT BRECHT's last play, *Die Tage der Commune*.

To English-speaking readers the most puzzling feature of the bibliography in *Le Mouvement Social* may well be the absence of modern full-length studies from the United States and Britain, despite the great increase in French and revolutionary studies since 1937 and the wealth of new material and new insights available. The Paris Commune of 1871 has, of course, been referred to at some length (but not always with great accuracy of detail) in many recent American and English works on modern French history, on Bakunin, on the First International, and on the Anarchists, among others. However, a full study, making use of the new material, still awaits publication (March, 1965).

NOTE ON THE ORIGINAL BIBLIOGRAPHY

The author's judgments on various works listed in his bibliography may seem somewhat arbitrary in the light of later studies. The fact is, however, that no strictly impartial work on the Paris Commune yet exists. This, in itself, would seem an historical phenomenon worth examining.

# INDEX